Praise for Dmitry Bykov

"Blending a novel of ideas with a fairy-tale and satire with lyricism, Bykov in *Living Souls* gives a picture of Russia in the near future and—as so many others before him—tries to understand the eternal contradictions of his country." —*Independent*

"A dreamscape, a panoramic survey of the obsessions and illusions that protect Russian society's sleep." —*Times Literary Supplement*

"Bykov stirs countless scholarly and pseudo-scholarly retellings of stories about race, religion, culture and geography, many of them toxic, into a comical fictional potion . . . Bykov has reminded a nation that among its most precious resources are the Russian language and its literature." —*New York Review of Books*

Also by Dmitry Bykov
in English Translation

Living Souls

VZ

Volodymyr Zelenskyy and the Making of a Nation

By Dmitry Bykov

Translated by John Freedman

OPEN LETTER
LITERARY TRANSLATIONS FROM THE UNIVERSITY OF ROCHESTER

Originally published in Russian as *VZ: Портрет на фоне нации* by Freedom Letters, 2023

Copyright © Dmitry Bykov, 2023

Translation copyright © John Freedman, 2025

First edition

Library of Congress Control Number: 2024060758

ISBN (pb): 978-1-960385-39-0 | ISBN (ebook): 978-1-960385-40-6

Cover design by Matt Avery

Published by Open Letter Books at the University of Rochester

Morey Hall 303, Rochester NY 14627

www.openletterbooks.org

Printed in the United States of America

I ask you not to shout because the whole world is watching us.
Volodymyr Zelenskyy, April 24, 2019

Dad jokes a lot. But when he gets serious it becomes difficult to believe that he ever joked.
Oleksandra Zelenska, "Make the Comedian Laugh" children's program, 2016

Who doesn't know how welcome guests are in Ukraine!
But then all kinds of challenges await the guest!—dumplings with garlic or honey, pies with cabbage or liver . . . And, then, topping all that off, a bottle sealed with homemade wax will rise above the plates and bowls.

Yevgeny Popovkin, *The Rubanyuk Family*

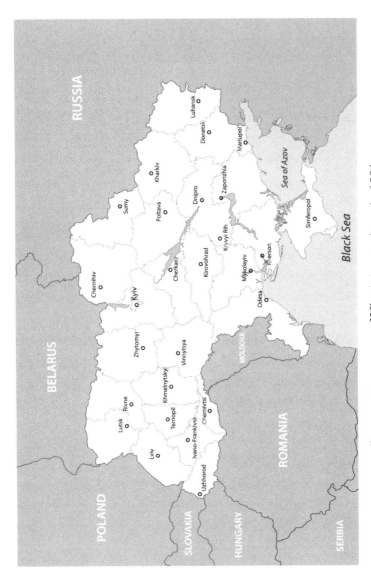

Representative map of Ukrainian territory in 1991

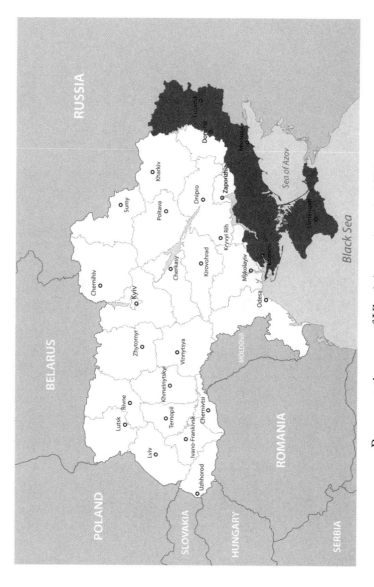

Representative map of Ukrainian territory in 2024

TABLE OF CONTENTS

A NOTE FROM THE TRANSLATOR

As Ukraine and Russia are at war, so too are their languages and everything they involve. Dmitry Bykov, who is Russian, declares at one point herein: "The question of the state language(s) of Ukraine is an ideal pretense to lead any discussion away from the resolution of pressing problems. An endless argument begins, eventually reaching fisticuffs."

This includes the way the two languages are represented in English through transliteration.

I think nothing explains the situation quite so precisely as another work I translated recently, "Call Things by their Names" by the Ukrainian playwright Tetiana Kytsenko.

"By the way, about names," Kytsenko writes, "I've noticed one interesting nuance. It's not so recognizable in everyday life, because I speak both Ukrainian and Russian. But when corresponding in English, I have noticed feeling irritation when foreign colleagues address me not as Tetiana, but rather by using the Russian version. My dear friends, Tatiana is something else entirely. The difference of one letter is enough to contain an entire worldview."[1]

In translating a book like *VZ: Volodymyr Zelenskyy and the Making of a Nation* the opportunities to "irritate" and mangle "entire worldviews," to

1 Published in *A Dictionary of Emotions in a Time of War: 20 Short Works by Ukrainian Playwrights*, ed. John Freedman (Laertes Press, 2023): 72.

borrow Kytsenko's words, are myriad. Bykov, who wrote his book in Russian, did not have the problem that we do. Again, as suggested by Kytsenko, confusion arises only when a text like this is rendered in English.

The English-speaking world is accustomed to perceiving Ukrainian names and places through the prism of transliteration systems that we generally use for Russian. This has often been a lazy choice, if not downright wrong. Okay, sure, there are good reasons why we know the great Ukrainian writer Mykola Hohol as Nikolai Gogol. He wrote in Russian from the start of his career, and moved to Russia in 1828. But that was 200 years and a couple of empires ago. In fact, we can no longer ignore this issue at a time when Russia has waged a full-scale war against its neighbor for over 1,000 days (to say nothing of the ten-plus years that have passed since Russia occupied large swaths of territory in Ukraine's east and south in 2014).

Accordingly, I made the decision to allow both languages to stand forth, and stand side-by-side, in their own systems of transliteration. Mind you, there are many such systems, and I chose what I perceived to be a line of least resistance. For Ukrainian I used the system presented to the United Nations by the Cabinet of Ministers of Ukraine in 2010 under the title of "Romanization System in Ukraine." For Russian I used a system that I helped create for *The Moscow Times* in 1991; it, in turn, was drawn from the system used by Victor Terras in his *Handbook of Russian Literature*, first published in 1985.

All rules must be broken, however, and in our case we deviate from the Ukrainian system immediately in favor of what we consider the optimal rendition of the name of our main hero Volodymyr Zelenskyy. Rather than the "Zelenskiy" form that our system would dictate, we opted for "Zelenskyy," which may be easier on some eyes, and has gained some traction. Many major international news organizations, frankly, have taken the lazy, not to say incorrect, approach of employing the age-old Russian system to render the name as "Zelensky." The New York Times does it, as do CNN, the BBC, The Times of London and some others. Meanwhile, NBC, the Associated Press, GOV.uk, the Voice of America, the official website of the President of Ukraine, and many other popular sources opt for "Zelenskyy." This deviation in the narrative that follows applies only to Zelenskyy;

all other names and places with a similar ending (i.e., General Oleksandr Syrskyi) remain within our chosen transliteration system.

Do note that the name "Volodymyr Zelenskyy" will occasionally appear in a few different forms throughout the book. When Bykov quotes Vladimir Putin referring to the Ukrainian president, the spelling is rendered as Russian would have it—Vladimir Zelensky. There is no circumstance, aside from mockery, under which the Russian president would refer to his Ukrainian counterpart using the Ukrainian forms of Volodymyr or Zelenskyy. Along those lines, this book contains a quote of a Russian journalist allowing his sarcasm to drip through by referring to the Ukrainian president with the Polish rendering of Waldemar while Zelenskyy was on a state visit to Poland. I allow that, and the disrespect it represents, to stand.

At first blush the mash-up of the Ukrainian and Russian systems may appear to be jarring, but there is solid reasoning behind every choice, not the least of which is the fact that we have done this forever in the transliteration of Russian texts involving other Slavic languages. When translating a letter by Alexander Pushkin to the great Polish poet Adam Mickiewicz, we would never write "Mitskevich." Or, in translating a Russian news report about the Czech writer and president Vaclav Havel, we would never write "Vatslav Gavel." So should it be with Ukrainian. And so it is in this book.

We spell the Ukrainian capital city as "Kyiv," unless it is a quote from an official Russian source, in which case it is "Kiev." The southern Ukrainian city is "Odesa," unless we are referring to the Russian-made film *Odessa*. Names such as Borys, Oleksandr, and Serhii are the norm in Ukrainian. I render the name of the Kyiv-based, Russian-speaking poet Alexander Kabanov with Russian transliteration precisely because he identifies as a Russian-language writer. I transliterate the names of characters in Zelenskyy's popular *Servant of the People* TV series using the Russian system because, although it was filmed in Ukraine, it was performed in Russian. And I render the director of *Servant of the People* as Oleksii Kiriushchenko because, as Bykov writes, "he continued to consider himself a Ukrainian," even though he worked for many years and gained a professional reputation in Moscow.

One final thought on transliteration. I explained the force of history and habit in explaining why we spell the name of the writer Nikolai Gogol as we do. But I rather suspect that, when we begin work on the second edition of this book in ten or fifteen years, the world will have caught up with us and it will be high time to render that name as Mykola Hohol.

Briefly on other topics:

Whenever possible I present the texts of interviews as they were originally published in English in the *New York Times*, *Washington Post*, or other English-language sources, such as the Jewish online magazine *Tablet*. The many speeches of Volodymyr Zelenskyy are quoted from the official website of the President of Ukraine (https://www.president.gov.ua/en/news/speeches). I generally treated the English translations on this site as official documents, meaning my rule of thumb was to quote what the site provided. On occasion, however, I did edit these texts in small ways for clarity or stylistic reasons.

All quotations of Russian-language journalism, poetry, and prose–aside from quotes of Vladimir Nabokov–are offered in my English renderings.

John Freedman
2025

AUTHOR'S NOTE

Before describing someone else's biography, you must at least briefly touch on your own. That is, you must explain why anyone should listen to what you have to say.

Throughout my literary life in Russia I have published approximately ninety books, among them several biographies, mainly of writers. But that is not why you must read what I have to say.

At present I am one of three writers in Russia who are included among the lists of hostile foreign agents and as a member of the fifth column. In other words, to use the current terminology, I am an enemy of the Russian people; in Ukraine my name is included on the Peacemaker website which lists enemies of Ukraine. I was blacklisted in Russia (meaning a complete ban on journalistic and pedagogical work) for speaking out against the government, and against the war, while in Ukraine I was singled out for calling Odesa a city of great Russian culture, and for calling nationalists fools.

As a hero of an old book once said, if they throw rocks at you from both sides of the road you are, most likely, on the right path.

This book will almost surely be met with friendly hostility in Russia, and friendly suspicion in Ukraine. In Russia, they will name the fantastic sums for which I agreed to write it, while in Ukraine there will definitely be those who will say it was the Kremlin that paid me these sums—for writing a bad book about Zelenskyy. All this is entirely *de rigueur*, and it would be much sadder for me if the book were not noticed at all. I put a great deal of effort into it, and I expressed in it many thoughts that are important to me. After all, Zelenskyy rehabilitated not just the creative intelligentsia—he defended the meaning of our entire life, everything that humanity, in principle, considers important. Putin reset it; Zelenskyy defended it. I wanted to understand how he did that, and how we all can be worthy of this era, which, regardless of the outcome of the war, will be known as the Zelenskyy era.

It seems to me that most books today are written as if by obligation. A writer worries and procrastinates for the longest time, then finally forces himself to sit down at his desk, struggles painfully with his own problems and complexes, abundantly spilling his own blood over clumsily heavy phrases in hopes that the reader will recognize in them some of his or her own childhood traumas, and on that basis will understand the text on at least the simplest of levels: Is it really like this for everyone? Back in the age of Enlightenment—long compromised by subsequent history—someone instilled in us the notion that reading is more prestigious than doing something, for example, slalom skiing or engaging in sex.

This book was written for entirely different reasons. The author sincerely wants to grapple with the primary mystery of the twenty-first century. Over its first two decades plus, this century has offered us nothing more entertaining than Zelenskyy. Not COVID, nor the mass insanity of Russian citizens, nor the subversion of the Big Bang theory by recent observations (apparently the most distant galaxies are not flying off anywhere after all!) are capable of standing alongside the riddle of Volodymyr Zelenskyy.

Everything we know about Zelenskyy, including the gossip, preferences, and quotes, could be retold in an hour's time, and, to do that, you need not travel to Ukraine to meet with his colleagues and contemporaries. Paradoxically, he was precisely where he needed to be, but this is not only about him, it is also about the unique place that he occupies. The situation reminds us of some of the greatest twists and turns of history, the consequences of which are not fully evident even to distant descendants.

The actor and producer of a not-so-intellectual stand-up comedy show successfully led a nation opposing a fascist nuclear power. A fascist armed with nuclear weapons, the worst nightmare of the inhabitants of the twentieth century, who thought no beast was more frightening than Hitler, has been broken right before our eyes by a European country that is fifteen times Russia's inferior, geographically speaking, and four times inferior in its population. Over the first two years of a full-scale war, this country, whose annual budget ranked fifty-eighth in the world (Russia was fifteenth), backed with technical assistance from the United States and Europe, resisted the aggression of its neighbor, which still possesses the largest territory in the world. This country whose army is nineteenth in the world in terms of size (Russia's is fifth) has buried the myth of the invincibility and heroism of the Russian soldier right before our eyes. A jester defeats the devil, a comedian defeats the KGB officer, the actor (even if he is a buffoon, even if he is a circus clown) defeats the villain. Right in plain sight, Yevgeny Schwartz's fairy tale about a dragon, read and watched by all of Russia, despite all the Soviet prohibitions, is now in the process of coming true. A great empire is collapsing, trying to trap in its zone of influence its unloved stepdaughter, with whom it has cohabited for 450 years, since the time of the Pereiaslav Rada when Hetman Bohdan Khmelnytskyi led Ukraine into an alliance with the Russians.

There are actually two mysteries here: how Zelenskyy won the presidential race in the wake of the most serious political crisis in Ukrainian history, and how he stood his ground at the head of a nation that entered the most serious war in its history. How did David defeat Goliath once again? And how did this David, who composed psalms in the format of feuilletons, manage to remind the whole world of the inviolability of the great biblical truths—he, who just yesterday was amusing Russian leaders at corporate parties, or portraying a phallus playing the piano on his own show?

This is one of those divine miracles, about which legends are later composed. And although the miracle was forged by the people of Ukraine with their examples of heroism and self-sacrifice, the miracle bears Zelenskyy's expressive Jewish face, Zelenskyy's quick brown eyes, Zelenskyy's familiar, husky voice. Whatever his fate, he was in the first half of the '20s an instrument of that Absolute One, in whose existence the world, corrupted by its inability to distinguish between good and evil, and by the myth of ubiquitous corruption, hardly believes in anymore.

Could a writer have a more weighty topic? It is rather like a dinosaur emerging from the forest, and addressing you in a human voice.

And I would add: think as you will, but don't pass this book by.

Dmitry Bykov,
Ithaca, August 2023

PART ONE

COMEDY

I. RISE AND SHINE

On February 24, 2022, the Ukrainian writer, journalist, and adman Valerii Primost was preparing to celebrate his fifty-fifth birthday. In fact, you can find in almost any group of people in Kyiv someone whose birthday falls on February 24. Either the majority of Kyivans were, in fact, born on this day, or they consider it the day of a new life beginning.

The night before, Primost and his then-girlfriend got quite drunk, went to bed late, and woke up at 9 A.M. from the vibrations of a mobile telephone. A friend from across the city asked how intensively they were being bombed. Primost did not hear any bombing.

"It's war," the caller told him.

"So, it really did begin," he said, and woke up his girlfriend.

"Did Zelenskyy skip town?" she asked.

"He's not going anywhere now," Primost said confidently. "The whole world is watching him. No actor would ever leave the stage when ten billion people are watching."

This phrase was a universal explanation of what was happening. And it was the second instance of Primost anticipating almost entirely on his own what awaited Zelenskyy. In early 2014, while working as an editor at the 1+1 TV channel, he glanced through a draft script of the *Servant of the People* series and went to his immediate supervisor, the CEO of the 1+1 Media group, Oleksandr Tkachenko, who later became the Minister of Culture of Ukraine (and was forced to resign in 2023, a story to which we will return).

"Sasha," Primost said, using the diminutive form of his name (Ukrainians treat figures of authority with minimal respect, and anyway these men were of the same age). "This is a ready-made presidential platform."

Tkachenko laughed, but he shouldn't have. In 2014, Volodymyr Zelenskyy, the star of the *Servant of the People* TV series, was already planning to take part in the presidential campaign, undaunted even by an application fee of one hundred thousand dollars. But he subsequently changed his mind, apparently realizing that there would be no good scripts for a president of Ukraine between the years of 2014 to 2018.

Four years later, he won the presidential election by an unprecedented margin—73.22 percent of the vote versus the 24.45 percent received by the incumbent president Petro Poroshenko—and during his first presidential term, he transformed the sitcom of our common lives into a fundamentally new genre. That is what we are going to discuss here.

II. ALL POWER TO THE POETS

In 1917, Nikolai Gumilyov, who was sent to contact the Allies by Russia's Provisional Government and waited out the October revolution in Europe, met with G. K. Chesterton. Both made highly positive impressions on each other, but each thought the other to be a hopeless eccentric. "Russians are endowed with all gifts except common sense," Chesterton recalled. "When he went out the door, it would have seemed just as natural for him to go out the window." Gumilyov told Chesterton how, as a child, he had tried to stop the rain with words (this notion, reflected in Gumilyov's poem "Memory," subsequently reappeared in Chesterton's story "The Shadow of the Shark"), and he also suggested that poets should rule the world. Firstly, they always agree among themselves, and, secondly, they know how to select the most eloquent phrase from a million possibilities, so somehow they will manage to handle a state. "He offered

Italy to D'Annunzio, France to France, England to me. At this moment, a bomb raid began. What could be more poetic than to die in a mansion in Mayfair during a bomb raid while a Russian madman offers you the crown of England?"

From that time on, the romantic idea of handing power to humanitarians or members of the creative intelligentsia ceased to be taken seriously. Gumilyov's own political activity ended with his execution supposedly for participating in an anti-Soviet conspiracy (which never existed); Gabriele D'Annunzio surrendered the republic to Fiume and returned to literature; Yukio Mishima committed hara-kiri after a failed coup; in Russia the novelist and political activist Eduard Limonov served time in prison, his party was banned, and he himself died a political outcast. Actors such as Ronald Reagan and Arnold Schwarzenegger were rather luckier, but this seems the proper time to tell an anecdote about this topic that involves Anton Chekhov's wife, Olga Knipper-Chekhova:

"I'm so afraid of death! They say all actresses go to hell . . ."
"Oh, don't worry, sweetheart, you're not much of an actress . . ."

Creative personalities have a reputation for being frivolous people who understand nothing about economics and sociology, who are unable to negotiate, and most importantly, who think unrealistically. But Ukraine, with Zelenskyy at the fore, rehabilitated the reputation of artists and humanitarians: it proved that relying on shrewd calculations in extreme circumstances is only harmful. I don't know how things are in prosperous countries, but in situations where there can be no retreat, nations are saved by those who are guided by idealism. Moreover, the narcissism, and even coquetry, inherent in actors and writers most often do not allow them to exhibit cowardice. A snob dies beautifully precisely because he cares about his appearance. An actor is accustomed to being watched by millions, and does not want to compromise himself before them. This is a big deal for a state on the verge of destruction. It is an ancient virtue that makes you remember the dying aphorisms of the Spartans and Romans.

On February 26, 2022, when Volodymyr Zelenskyy responded to a proposal from the United States to leave Kyiv by stating, "I need ammunition, not a taxi," the free world was able to welcome an undisputed leader, and Europe—its most prominent politician. Moreover, he redirected the political narrative into a cultural, perhaps, even, religious, sphere. Ukrainian politics, which had been teetering back and forth between tragedy and farce for the longest time (periodically fully entering one or the other), passed into the category of the mystery play. Hennadii Korban, the de facto boss of the city of Dnipro, a playwright by education and a graduate of the Literary Institute in Moscow, received me in his office at the end of June 2022. To my question about whether he sensed that Ukraine was making a transition from the world of politics to the world of literature, he answered quite decidedly: "Cinema, in fact. A TV series even. But one of high-quality."

Had a career politician been in Zelenskyy's place, he could have resorted to his powers of prudent calculation. But Zelenskyy was not relying on his calculative powers in February 2022—it is possible that someone will eventually accuse him precisely of doing that, but only after the war ends. Shrewdness was not a saving grace at that moment. Zelenskyy rejected all options for personal safety, and Ukraine transformed what was happening into a grandiose artistic phenomenon, a spectacle of the global spirit. Like the hero of Rossellini's famous movie, *General della Rovere*, the actor played a hero, and believed he was a hero. After all, in the contemporary world, where post-truth prevails, only actors believe what they say. Otherwise, they will not be convincing.

A peculiarity of this war is that it eliminated nuances: not every war so clearly reveals the workings of off-screen historical forces. The moment when Russia fired the first missiles at Ukrainian territory, hybridity—the term used today to designate an undeclared war—lost its value. There arose an irrefutable certainty, which Thomas Mann termed as extremely beneficial: the forces of good were finally able to unite against obvious and unalloyed evil. Zelenskyy set a new standard of behavior. From that time on, he was increasingly called the Ukrainian Churchill or the TV comedian Churchill. But Churchill, strictly speaking, was not an insider politician either. A brave military journalist, a (not too bad) amateur artist, a (not too bad) amateur mason, a good writer, a Nobel Prize-winning speaker, a poseur, and a wit, he always thought about how he looked and what would be said about him. He always considered theatrical effects, and was remembered for his catchy aphorisms. To call him an insider politician would be to diminish his titanic personality immensely. Zelenskyy accentuated a big trend in world politics: in fact, political and economic decisions are increasingly made behind the scenes, and the fates of nations now depend not on the people themselves, but on elite professionals, "effective managers" as we say. The narrative, the national character, the idea that a nation has about itself, is created by people who know how to do that. For example, Zelenskyy's economic and political policies are systematically criticized by all so-called professionals. But only one professional quality is crucial—the actor's ability to inspire the hall so that people become better for a few seconds.

Zelenskyy commands that quality in the highest degree.

"One day in 2013," Irina Pobedonostseva, a long-time employee of Zelenskyy's press service, said, "we played an exceptionally difficult hall. It was all politicians. First skit, second—they all sat there like bumps on logs. Zelenskyy called everyone together backstage and said, 'Don't panic. I'll go out there and rock them.' And by the end of his sketch, they were smiling and even interrupting him with applause. He has no peer in his ability to conquer a hall."

Today's Ukraine is a tough audience with many different spectators who agree on little. But when an actor pushes himself to the limit, putting everything on the line, there is no crowd more grateful. Our theme here is the transformation of world politics into a Shakespearean drama where the fool pronounces his verdict on the king. We don't yet know the end of this drama. Our book ends at the climax. Things are easier for the reader—you know more than I do.

But we are living at the finest moment of our lives—an era when absolute values have come back into our lives. Whatever happens next, we will be grateful for this not only to a great actor, but to his audience, who performed this mystery play together with him and gave meaning to the existence of this huge Shakespearean theatrical space that bears the familiar name of "the globe."

III. MEASUREMENTS

Volodymyr Zelenskyy stands at 5 feet, 4 1/2 inches. He weighs 137 pounds. His eyes are hazel.

He wears a size 42 shirt (that's a medium in the United States). He wears a European-sized 42 shoe (size 9 in the U.S.).

His favorite color is green.

His favorite drink is a dry red wine.

He has ridden a motorcycle since the age of twelve, has driven a car since eighteen.

The information differs in regard to his favorite dish. Most likely, for the hipper among us, the middle and upper-middle class, there is a version in which he prefers a good, medium-rare steak. But for the poorer voter, the version making the rounds is that Zelenskyy likes to fry up some tomatoes, peppers, and eggplant—any vegetables at hand—and pour an egg over it all. Basically, he doesn't care what he eats. While working—this is repeated by everyone who saw him on the set—he never thinks about food at all.

Zelenskyy never made the impression of being a great man. Neither in personal communication, nor during speeches, film roles, at his inauguration, or even during speeches to the political elite of other nations and their parliaments. There are people whose imposing nature is not characterized by their height, complexion, or the severity of their features: they just walk in, and it is as if a wind has blown in from another dimension. Zelenskyy is mobile, and energetic. He is quick to react, has a memory that is rare even for an actor, and possesses what is usually called a positive aura. He puts people at ease—but does not encourage familiarity. It is obvious—I don't know how he does it—that you will never pat him on the shoulder. Maybe it's his quick, appraising gaze, or maybe it's his manner of instantly switching to a cold, businesslike manner. But for all of this—you might easily sympathize with him, or you might suspect him of all kinds of sins—there is nothing irrational, supernatural, or strange about him. The only oddity in his biography is the role he came to play; but even this role never made him consider himself a superman. I wouldn't call him modest, and, anyway, I don't really understand what that means: Churchill agreed that Attlee, who succeeded him as prime minister, was a modest man, and added: "he has plenty to be modest about." Zelenskyy is a good actor, a talented manager, and a brave politician, but he is not a god, nor a tsar, nor, by appearance, a hero.

He listens to you attentively, but does not feign empathy. He does not solicit you, nor does he try to pretend that your every word is vital to him. He behaves like a man who has precious little time. Most of all he inspires his interlocutor with one feeling, but it is a decisive one: you sense for a short moment that you are doing something important. Speaking in the language of the KVN comedy project, you are playing on the same team. You get the feeling—especially if you are vain—of participating in some kind of conspiracy with him. It's not that he constantly winks, as if hinting "now, you and I understand," nor that he flatters you, making it clear that you are his equal if you are in amenable communication with him. Just that you both are on the same side. Maybe that is precisely how he managed to inspire his nation, thus winning the election first, then the war.

IV. COPPERFIELD KIND OF CRAP

Readers are accustomed to skipping over the beginning of a biography. Parents, childhood, and all that David Copperfield "kind of crap," as Salinger's hero put it, are of interest only to historians. But Zelenskyy's childhood took place in unusual times and unusual places. Many aspects of his life were determined in that period.

Zelenskyy was born at two o'clock in the afternoon on January 25, 1978, in Kryvyi Rih, a Ukrainian city founded two hundred years before his birth, and located in the Dnipropetrovsk region of Ukraine. However, it received the status of a city only in 1860. The population at the time of the future president's birth was 820,000 people, mostly Russian speakers. At least 7 percent of the population was Jewish (in reality, probably more, because people in the USSR preferred not to admit they were Jews). The city was proud of its reputation as the longest city in Europe at 66 kilometers, or 41 miles. Some patriotic publications take metropolitan sprawl into account and they give it a length of 126 kilometers, or 78 miles, which makes it third in the world after Mexico City and Sochi. "Rih" in the local dialect is a rocky peninsula, and the city got its name from an extended, nearly 3.5 mile-long, peninsula between the Saksagan and Inhulets rivers. (The local legend that the settlement is named after the lame Cossack named Rih who founded it is unconfirmed: no such Cossack was found in the population censuses.) Kryvyi Rih, literally, "crooked horn," is most famous for its iron ore mines, and mining and processing plants. Before the beginning of Russia's so-called "special military operation," Zelenskyy's parents, Oleksandr Semionovich and Rimma Vladimirovna, lived in a four-room apartment in Kryvyi Rih on Zemliachka Street (named after Rosalia Zemliachka, real name Zalkind, best known for her murderous activities in Crimea in 1920). After war broke out, they were urgently moved to Rishpon in Israel. The Russian media have repeatedly mentioned that relatives of the Ukrainian oligarch Kolomoiskyi and the Russian Prokhorov live in the same neighborhood; however, they never produced any photographic evidence.

Zelenskyy's father was born December 23, 1947, later becoming a mining engineer and surveyor. He became the Head of the Department of Computer Science and Computer Engineering of the Kryvyi Rih Economic Institute in 1995. His mother was born September 16, 1950, also in Kryvyi Rih. She worked as an engineer for forty years and is now retired. Zelenskyy's father is shorter than his wife, and somewhat resembles the Russian comic author and actor Mikhail Zhvanetsky in complexion and manners. He spent most of his time at work, while his wife took on the upbringing of their son. Zelenskyy's facial expressions, however, his character, and his occasional sarcastic wit come from his father, a professor (he invariably makes fun of this title). His parents were married a year before the birth of their son. They intended to celebrate their forty-fifth anniversary in 2022, but the war intruded. Throughout their son's professional acting career, they gave very few interviews—some say because of personal modesty, others emphasize that they weren't approached because they live quietly and did not influence Zelenskyy's life in any way. One more or less lengthy conversation with both of them was published by the Kazakh journalist Zhanna Nurlanova in *Tengri News* in June 2019. It is known from this interview that the status of Zelenskyy's parents did not change after his election victory, that he frequently brought them to Kyiv, that they had no plans to move, that they are extremely upset by the dirt opponents sling at him, especially the accusations of drug addiction ("He never even smoked"). When asked if their son's lack of political experience frightens them, his father answered quite specifically: "Experience in stealing? Who needs experience like that?" Of all the luxuries offered by their son, the father admitted only that he had acquired new teeth. Zelenskyy Sr. spoke openly about the smoldering war with Ukraine at that time: "I don't like it when my son calls Russia an aggressor, but that's probably necessary."

From 1979 to 1983, Zelenskyy and his parents lived in Mongolia, where his father built the Erdenet Mining and Processing Plant, the pride of the Mongolian People's Republic. (Later the son and mother returned to Ukraine, while the father remained to work in Mongolia: his mother's health suffered because of the steppe climate with its endless temperature changes.) As he has repeatedly admitted in interviews, the only word from the Mongolian language that the current president of Ukraine remembers is "bahuy," or "there is none"—and not because of the similarity with a Russian obscenity, but because there really was almost nothing there. (In fact, "there is nothing" translates as "baihgui"; so as we see, he remembers everything correctly.) "There were two shops, the upper one and the lower one. I was often sent to both, and both of them were almost always empty."

The father said that his son as a child was deeply interested in weight-lifting, and so he entered him in a sports club, although he considers dancing to be Volodymyr's main success. "That's how the KVN comedy show started." (In general, everyone who has known Zelenskyy since his youth notes his excellent physical condition: Irina Pobedonostseva said that for the "Ze Cubes" sports program, whose purpose was to promote a healthy lifestyle, the leader of the Block production team worked diligently in the gym and, in a month's time, easily firmed up his abs, that is, his "cubes.")

V. JUMP TO PUNCH

Zelenskyy spoke regularly and cheerfully about his Kryvyi Rih childhood in stand–up routines, such as in a sketch called "Evening Kyiv": "Being strong in Kryvyi Rih in the '90s was like having a car. It wasn't a luxury, it was a means of transportation. But with my height, it was difficult not to hit opponents below the belt. So, I had to jump to punch."

Zelenskyy's childhood and adolescence came during the roaring '80s and criminal '90s, when the main entertainment among Kryvyi Rih youths was wall-to-wall fights. The city is divided into numbered blocks—in memory of which his Block 95 production company got its name—and it was downright dangerous to cross over into someone else's block. Participants of youth gangs were called "runners" (an article about this Kryvyi Rih subculture by the Strana.ua portal seemed to offend Zelenskyy's father). At some point during any disco somebody would inevitably start shooting: young men were searched before the dances, so weapons were smuggled in by girls under their skirts. Zelenskyy did not participate in the gangs. His block 95 was considered "dormant," and corresponded to the reputation of a professor's son. He studied well, and played the piano.

"They asked me not to join in the fist fights.

"'Vovan, why not just hold our coats?'

"Guys, it's summer! What coats?!

"'We wore our coats on purpose to give you something to hold.'"

He graduated from School No. 95 in 1995, and that is where he met most of his comrades in the future *Block 95* comedy team, including Olena Kiiashko, his future wife. He earned four Bs in his final grades—in physical education (despite all his athleticism), Russian, Ukrainian, and chemistry.

All his teachers . . . but what do you expect teachers to remember about a president? He was persistent . . . capable . . . grasped things quickly . . . actively participated in school amateur performances . . . and played the supporting role of Scrambled Eggs in the school play of Nikolai Gogol's *The Marriage*, although everyone remembered his performance. His voice began to drop early. By the seventh grade he was singing in a hoarse bass, and he made that his trademark. He participated in dances, weightlifting, he sang in a school group run by music teacher Tetiana Soloviova. In the tenth grade, he won a grant to study for free in Israel, but did not want to leave his family. He was popular with his classmates. But this is no wonder: according to another graduate, Serhii Zhukov, by the time of graduation there were only four boys left in the class (most dropped out after the ninth grade) and more than twenty girls.

Zelenskyy's math teacher Yelena Bogachyova sought me out: she wanted to help me write my book by sharing her memories. She arrived to teach the tenth graders in the fall of 1995 as an intern, and was only five years older than these graduating students. "I prepared very carefully for the first day of school: floor-length pants, white top, black bottoms. Their homeroom class teacher shut me down unceremoniously: No pants! I cried all the way home. Well, I thought: I'll give you a skirt! And I put on a skirt with a cut-away up to here!"

Class 10 B took very kindly to the intern.

"I noticed Zelenskyy immediately, because he fairly shone with interest in people! He asked me about everything. And you know, it was obviously not easy for a person with his appearance and surname in our city, because our city is not an easy one. It's not for nothing that we have these mines everywhere—it feels like evil is rising up from underground. There's a lot of mutual irritation. And he . . . maybe also because his class was so good . . . he wasn't shy about being Jewish! He didn't hide it at all. I knew many people who changed their last name, identifying as Ukrainian or Russian in their passports. But he—maybe because the whole city knew and loved his father—took it all in stride.

"We had independent work for the first lesson of the day. He got a C for that. He wasn't very good at math at all. He would come up, very charming, and say, 'Yelena Nikolaevna! Don't give me a C! Father is angry.' I was principled, and I gave him his C. I felt terrible about that. I thought he'd be mad at me. But he gave me a beautiful bouquet for Teacher's Day!

"Once we were talking about something after school, and he asked what I was going to do when I finished my studies. I said that I doubted I would work in a school. I didn't really like it. So he and a friend of his said, why not go to agricultural school with us! We have two big universities in the city—agricultural and mining. And I applied for agricultural school. It's now called the Kryvyi Rih University of Economics, and was a branch of the university in Kyiv.

"Did you vote for him in the 2019 election?"

"Of course."

"I imagine all of Kryvyi Rih voted for him."

"Oh, no of course not. Many were against him because they were jealous. I told you, ours is a difficult city. But if you've been able to . . ."

"Survive?"

"Make your mark. If you've made your mark in Kryvyi Rih, you won't be broken later."

Following his father's advice, Zelenskyy applied to the Faculty of Law of the University of Economics, since he wasn't interested in the hard sciences. There, despite his busy schedule of performing as an actor, he graduated with the highest honors, receiving a "red diploma."

For the most part, his school years played a much greater role in his life—partly because post-Soviet higher education had deteriorated more significantly than school education. Universities have turned into a kind of respite from adulthood. Zelenskyy created his first KVN comedy team with his classmates, regularly attended alumni meetings, and celebrated the twentieth anniversary of graduation with a shared photo. His father worked at the Department of Cybernetics at the University of Economics, whose help Zelenskyy did not need when applying. With his photographic memory, he passed the entrance exams without problem. He never worked a day as a lawyer. His most outstanding success in his student days, according to Ivan Kopaigora, head of the Department of Law, was probably his participation in a business game imitating the election of the president of Ukraine. Of the three candidates who reached the final, Zelenskyy was the most convincing of them all, so it happened that he first tried on the role of Ukrainian President back in 1997. According to the words of the same teacher, Zelenskyy "peppered his diploma defense with jokes," and charmed everyone. (Zelenskyy appointed his teacher's daughter, Irina Kopaigora, to the post of Commissioner of the State Antimonopoly Committee in 2019, for which he received his share of criticism from the Ukrainian media.) The head of the Luhansk, and later the Transcarpathian administration, Petro Poroshenko's ally Hennadii Moskal doubted that Zelenskyy really defended his diploma, and demanded that he provide a thesis. The institute fulfilled this request.

While studying at the institute, Zelenskyy created a miniature theater called Street Urchin, where he was noticed by members of the Zaporizhzhia—Kryvyi Rih—Transit KVN team. They asked him first to stage dance numbers, then to perform with them. In 1997, Zelenskyy and a group of friends separated from Transit and created their own team named after his hometown neighborhood—*Block 95*. This brand was destined to become one of the most popular in Ukraine.

VI. KVN.

There was no legal way in the USSR to build a career outside the Communist Party and the Komsomol, the Communist Youth League (exceptions were scientists associated with the defense industry). But there were two mysterious social institutions, thanks to which a talented artist or intellectual could claim, and even achieve, a certain status thanks solely to their abilities, as is customary in humane societies. These institutions, which have never been properly researched by academia, were known by their abbreviations: KVN (Club of the Cheerful and Resourceful) and ChGK (What?

Where? When?). In jest KVN is said to be a decoding of a Soviet maker of televisions, which, in folklore, was deciphered as "Bought—turned on—doesn't work" (in fact, it is an acronym of its creators' names, Soviet engineers Konigson-Varshavsky-Nikolaevsky). The KVN program was founded by journalist Sergei Muratov, doctor and director Albert Axelrod, and television engineer Mikhail Yakovlev. The show traditionally ran live and presented student teams pitting their wit against one another. The ability to improvise was an indispensable condition for victory. The program ran on Soviet Central Television from 1961 to 1972, was taken off air at the height of the so-called "period of stagnation," and then revived in 1987. But for all its fifteen years of absence, clubs of cheerful and resourceful individuals existed in Soviet universities, competed against one another, and performed at concerts.

Standing at the origins of the second incarnation of the intellectual club was a man whose biography would be worthy of an international bestseller: Vladimir Voroshilov (1930–2001), theater artist, and student of Alexander Rodchenko, who was a famed Soviet designer, and Vladimir Mayakovsky's visual co-author. In the case of Voroshilov, the connection between stage and social engineering was especially obvious: having been forced by circumstances to spend his entire life working in Soviet television—and he did it rather listlessly—he was undoubtedly born for grand-scale social transformations. Perhaps his bilious and irritable manner of conducting the *What? Where? When?* program, which became his trademark, was associated with the constant sense that his talents were going terribly underused, and his annoyance about this forced a lowering of the bar. Curiously, the brightest stars of KVN—Volodymyr Zelenskyy, Semion Slepakov, Alexei Kortnev—have embraced liberal views, while ChGK generated mainly strident reactionaries, imperialists, and Putinists, such as Anatoly Wasserman, Nurali Latypov, and Maxim Potashev. The most notable exception (apart from the ever-silent Alexander Druz) is Ilya Novikov, a lawyer who in 2015 defended the Ukrainian war hero and politician Nadezhda Savchenko against charges in Russia, and eventually emigrated to Ukraine. His hometown club disavowed him. It may be that the smart ones in Russia understand best with whom power lies, while the funny ones know how to act, ignoring this circumstance.

KVN was an excellent social springboard. First of all, it was a business school, because ever since the beginning of the '90s, the concert performances of the most popular teams promoted by television gathered top audiences on national tours. One of the creators of KVN, reanimatologist Albert Axelrod, when asked what his profession and his hobby have in common, once replied: "Revival in an auditorium." The business side of this entertainment show was something of a revival of the Soviet economy: many major Soviet, and later Russian, showmen and television personalities emerged from the ranks of KVN. The most famous of them was the charismatic captain of the Baku Medical Institute team, Yuli Gusman (now a famous film director, director of mass spectacles, creator of the first teleconferences, and permanent head of the Nika Film Academy, who lives most of the year in the United States). Also graduating from the ranks of KVN were TV presenters Mikhail Marfin and Mikhail Borisov, musicians and showmen Alexei Kortnev and Valdis Pelsh, politicians Vladimir Semago and Mikhail Lesin (who took his first steps in business as the organizer of KVN tours), and the teams bearing the titles of Odessa Gentlemen, Ural Dumplings, and Diesel. They created their own shows, including a number on television, although the concert tours brought in no less money. Russian television's most popular comedy program was Comedy Club, born from the team that created a program called "New Armenians." We can say with full confidence that were it not for a comic show exhibiting elements of political satire (such as have consistently failed on Russian television), Ukraine would have had a different president in 2019.

Zelenskyy's own television career did not look sensational at first. He originally appeared on Channel One as one of the final eight in the 1997 competition as a member of the Zaporizhzhia—Kryvyi Rih—Transit team. It was Ukraine's top national team, and it eventually won the 1997 final. Its captain was Mikhail Gulikov. Zelenskyy did not distinguish himself in any way. I only remember his comment about Crimea—as if he were giving voice to a thought in Boris Yeltsin's head: "And so he gave up Crimea! He has a dacha with a swimming pool and a yacht there" (which was seen as a paraphrase of a replica from Leonid Gaidai's legendary comedy *It Can't Be*: "We have a private apartment with a separate bath"). In fairness, we note that none of the other stars from *Block 95* shone brightly on the Ukrainian national team. But to tell the whole truth, the overall level of humor in the 1997 season was depressing. This applies also to the finale, where Zelenskyy worked well in several musical numbers (for example, employing a mind-reading device), but the improvisations and social wit fell flat. Perhaps ORT, as Russia's First Channel was called at that time, was reflecting a general degradation of all things Russian. Social satire makes no sense when it influences nothing. In fact, the 1996 elections clearly showed that Russia had no choice. It was either Yeltsin, who was in complete decline, or the Communists with a frankly repressive program and utter lack of prospects. Throughout the entire competition program, in which the Ukrainian national team was opposed by the "New Armenians" under the leadership of the famous stand-up comedian Garik Martirosyan, one more-or-less successful joke was made: "Armenians are a close-knit group. One Armenian gets a good job, and, by the next day, five Armenians are already working there! Russian solidarity is good, too: a Russian gets a job, and lo and behold, by the next day five Armenians are working there!"

It is hard to watch this finale now: certain hints of interethnic discord (in particular, the cancellation of all Soviet holidays in Ukraine) are still quite peaceful, and anecdotal in nature. Moscow is still the common capital for the entire former USSR. All former Soviet nations are equally eager to make jokes about Jews—although the humor usually hits below the belt: after an Armenian is circumcised in Moscow, he reports to his mother, paraphrasing the words of the Soviet hit "Victory Day"—"Hi, Mom, I'm not all back." Today, such a joke could never be aired—and not because of a politically correct dictatorship, but because it would be seen as a mockery of the Great Victory, with two capital letters, in World War II. In short, it becomes clear why Zelenskyy and his team eventually chose Ukraine as their main concert venue: political satire there was still, firstly, effective, and secondly, practically uncensored.

Zelenskyy parted with KVN and its permanent leader, Alexander Maslyakov, quite amiably, making an astute choice in doing so. In 2003, he received an offer to work for the club in Moscow, for which he would have to leave Ukraine. A career in the big city would have seemed quite promising at that time, but Zelenskyy refused to leave the team, placing his bet on Ukraine. In this fork in his life's path, many later saw an analogy with Napoleon, who had asked to join the Russian army in 1788, but did not agree to a reduction in rank, which was mandatory for a foreign officer. Zelenskyy was asked to abandon his team of friends, and he didn't agree either. He did, however, play Bonaparte in the 2012 Russian film comedy *Napoleon vs. Rzhevsky*.

Zelenskyy never said a bad word about Maslyakov, and in his first big interview after the presidential election—which he gave to the uber-popular journalist Dmitry Gordon—he said that the breakup was conflict-free. Maslyakov was asked by *Komsomolskaya Pravda* in 2021 to comment on Zelenskyy's words about the possibility of a full-scale war with Russia. Maslyakov then replied:

"I already forgot that we had such a player. He's no longer a player, but a doll . . . what's it called . . . I forget . . ."

"A marionette?" obsequiously suggests reporter Gamov.

"I don't know. But he's no independent player. They don't play like that in KVN."

"Will you hire him for KVN when he ceases to be president?"

"No, of course!"

Alas, most Russian stars who shone in the '60s and '70s did not enjoy an especially dignified old age. Incidentally, in 2019, answering a question from REN TV about his thoughts on Zelenskyy's election, Maslyakov again said that he hardly remembered him, but that he had organizational skills.

"Are you proud?" the journalist asked.

"So far no one from KVN has become a president. But no, I'm proud and not proud" (*O, the gift of prophecy of an old veteran of the television trenches!—D. B.*). "But it's interesting."

Two years later, Maslyakov was no longer interested. By then he had understood something about this tough nut who left his club so easily. An important constant emerges here in Zelenskyy's life. In general, writing a biography involves a kind of reconnaissance: you must highlight a recurring situation, a leitmotif, that indicates either the hero's main problem (if the repetition is obsessive), or his main character trait. In Zelenskyy's life, primarily as an actor, this meant parting with the director, that is, the controlling head who was useful to a certain point, but then exceeded his authority. Zelenskyy's psychological profile is that of an actor who takes charge of his own destiny. As such, he had to part with mentors and senior colleagues, and, most often, this parting was peaceful. Thus he broke with Maslyakov who wanted to separate him from his team; thus he later broke with the oligarch Ihor Kolomoiskyi, who stood at the origins of his success; and with Oleksandr Rodnianskyi, the producer of the "1+1" channel. (Alas, the break with Kolomoiskyi was more painful, but by that time they had not communicated for a long time.) Thus did he delete (without reprisals, of course) Andrii Bohdan, the head of his office, who claimed Pygmalion-like functions in regard to Zelenskyy-the-politician. In his work—and in his whole life—Zelenskyy embodies the type of actor who, first, becomes a director, then a theater manager, and then a commander of the audience.

Vladimir Putin, his main opponent and, in a sense, a symmetrical figure to him, also has a curious constant: the elimination of his bene-factors. Thus did his former boss and Mayor of St. Petersburg Anatoly Sobchak die mysteriously; thus did the oligarch-turned-politician Boris Berezovsky commit suicide under strange circumstances; thus did Boris Yeltsin drop off the radar, remaining utterly silent for eight years. Inaudibly and mysteriously, all the architects of Putin's victory abandoned the political scene, one of whom, Anatoly Chubais, was lucky even to escape from the Russian ship of state, albeit at the cost of contracting a strange disease (Guillain–Barre autoimmune syndrome) in August 2022. Putin sincerely grieved, it seems, only for his first coach, the judoka Anatoly Rakhlin. Rakhlin was also lucky: he died at the age of seventy-five, still in high esteem. Then it was as if the last obstacle in the Russian president's mind fell away—the next year, in February 2014, his annexation of Crimea began the war with Ukraine.

VII. WIFE

Everyone I talked to about Zelenskyy's family, ranging from colleagues in *Block 95*, to press secretaries and presidential aides, agreed that if Zelenskyy is a well-designed automobile, his wife is the vehicle's gearbox.

Volodymyr Zelenskyy and Olena Kiiashko were married in Dnipro (then Dnipropetrovsk) on September 6, 2003. They are the same age. She was born February 6 in the same year of 1978. They met at school (studying in parallel classes, she in group "A," he in group "B"), but at that time their relationship did not blossom into a school infatuation. However, a romance lasting eight years ignited while she studied at the Kryvyi Rih University of Civil Engineering.

Hardly anyone from the Block team will admit today what is true in their story and what is PR, but the legend is built cinematically. Zelenskyy had not seen his future wife since his school years. A year later he met her on the street holding a videotape of *Basic Instinct* in her hands. He asked if he could borrow it and at the same time asked for her phone number—to return the cassette, naturally. Whatever movie was really on that tape, *Basic Instinct* is perfectly scripted. And if it's actually true, it's even more fun. Oleksandr Pikalov, a participant in the Block and a friend of Zelenskyy's, clarifies the situation in *Medusa*, a film that tells the story of Zelenskyy's election. In fact, Zelenskyy was too shy to approach Olena himself, and Pikalov, being older and "more popular with younger schoolgirls," in his own words, borrowed the tape from her, and later sent Zelenskyy to return it. "And he stayed there."

Olena Kiiashko had a classmate for a boyfriend, but Zelenskyy intruded. The reason it took so long from their happy meeting to marriage vows is explained in official interviews by the fact that Zelenskyy wanted children, but his busy career prevented it. Finally, allegedly following an evening out to see some romantic comedy, they decided to get married. Their daughter

Oleksandra was born on July 15, 2004. Their son Kyrylo was born in Kyiv on January 21, 2013.

Like her husband, Olena Zelenska never worked in the field of her specialty (her father, Vladimir Timofeevich, then the head of Monolitbud, a construction company, and now an associate professor of the Department of Building Structures and Edifices at the Kyiv Institute of Railway Transport, sent her to study construction engineering). She became one of the scriptwriters of *Block 95* and was quite successful. Much of her current activity demonstrates her dramatic talent. In any case, she professionally arranges her interviews—rare and spread out over time—although interviewers swear that her participation in editing and shot selection is minimal. She gave three especially notable interviews in 2022: *Die Zeit* (March), *Vogue* (April), and *Time* (July). The most revealing of her interviews was with *Die Zeit* in February 2023.

Before the war, Zelenskyy's wife appeared next to him in public relatively rarely. They both tried not to abuse with sugary stories from the life of a happy family. On the contrary, many of Zelenskyy's sketches revolved around disputes, disagreements, and misunderstandings. This was not merely a play on the classic theme of family feuds, but, above all, a desire to emphasize domestic equality. In Zelenskyy's family mythology, at least of the pre-war period, cooperation, confrontation, "and the fateful merger, and fateful duel" of two equally strong and stubborn personalities were important. "Why do I often continue to argue with my wife in my performances? Because here, at least, I will be heard out to the end." And this, it seems, was only part joke.

The notion of a submissive wife was never relevant in Ukraine. The patriarchal family is rather ridiculed there. Ever since Gogol, Ukrainian authors have loved to portray proud, independent, sometimes self-satisfied women, sometimes femmes fatales. Olena Kiiashko was an unofficial, but full-fledged participant in *Block 95*, the co-author and editor of many sketches. Their children have mentioned in their rare appearances in the press that Mom is stricter than Dad. As the first lady, Olena Zelenska has worked a great deal on the problem of school meals—this topic is beneficial for her image, but it is also a truly unexplored topic in Ukraine. Her second favorite area of activity (and the term strongly associated with it) is "barrier-free space." A barrier-free environment is the new name for an "equal opportunities society." This term became fashionable at the end of the 2010s. Barrier-free space is understood as an environmental design— whether urban, educational, or commercial—that de-accentuates any forms of inequality: gender, age, or physical. It is a space where disabled people are comfortable, where children are at ease, where the problems of elders are taken into account, and it is a popular European topic of recent times. To the extent that Zelenskyy (especially in wartime) can be an irritant in the European context for violating the requirements of political correctness, can appear more demanding than grateful, and does not shy away from speaking his mind, his wife continues to demonstrate loyalty to the latest European trends, paying attention to detail and noble restraint.

On August 23, 2021, the First Kyiv Summit of First Ladies and Gentlemen took place in Kyiv. Zelenska made no effort to avoid a face–to-face meeting of the wives and husbands of the top officials from a dozen friendly states. Eleven participants joined the event, not bad for the first post-COVID year. The stated theme was "Soft Power in the New Reality," and ten first ladies were present—from Latvia, Lithuania, Serbia, Israel, Germany, Türkiye, Croatia, Costa Rica, Brazil, and the European Council, plus the daughter of the President of Lebanon, and Olena Zelenska herself. The second summit was held on July 23, 2023, in the St. Sofia cathedral in Kyiv in the format of a teleconference—twenty-two countries participated, including Poland, Belgium, the United States, and the United Kingdom. The first ladies of Lithuania and Latvia attended in person, Richard Gere and Mila Kunis participated via video link. The post-war reconstruction of Ukraine and the speedy release of prisoners were among the topics discussed. Zelenskyy spoke to the participants as first gentleman. "Ukraine has never enjoyed such support in its entire history!" he said, and there is no arguing with that. "The heart of the world beats in Ukraine," Zelenska wrote in a column following the summit. She held a marathon to raise funds for ambulances for Ukraine, and, as an auctioneer, she looked very professional, collecting $5.4 million.

Everyone who has heard Olena Zelenska's public speeches surely recognizes that "soft power" is a phrase that expresses her essence perfectly. Very rarely did she reveal that for the first three months of the war she lived separately from her husband, although she did not leave Ukraine. Later she returned to the capital. The children completely lost their familiar environment (Zelenskyy's son Kyrylo admitted that he only plays with dogs and bodyguards). The First Lady curtailed all public activity and gave her first big interviews with photo shoots only in June (the March conversation with *Die Zeit* was still done remotely).

As befits the wife of a trickster—Solveig in *Peer Gynt*, Nele Ulenspiegel, Guljan Khoja Nasreddin—Olena Zelenska is in no hurry to appear in the same frame with her husband and does not give him public advice. She has turned down numerous journalists who wanted to write biographies about her, and has refused to participate in the creation of a script about their romance. "I don't see myself as anyone's movie heroine . . . unless, perhaps, it's Tarantino!" She called participation in writing scripts for *Block 95* her favorite activity, but she has no plans to return to this hobby. "Everything has changed irreversibly," she says over and over again. "Nothing will be the same. Although the Block team was and remains our second family."

Among fashion designers, she especially respects Ukrainians—Artiom Klimchuk, Katia Silchenko (the COAT brand), and Yulia Bohdan (brand SIX). She likes pantsuits, and if she chooses dresses, they are from Lilia Litkovska. Her favorite color is light blue. She gets her earrings and pendants from Valeria Guzema. The shoes are from Jimmy Choo, although, by her own admission, she prefers sneakers. What kind? Well, for example, eco-sneakers from the French Veja brand. Very advanced shoes. Meghan Markle wears Vejas, and here is its advertising description:

> Veja shoes are made of rubber, environmentally friendly cotton, as well as material that is obtained from recycled plastic bottles. Leather for sneakers is processed by vegetable tanning with acacia extract, that is without chromium and other heavy metals. The shoes are made in Brazil and come in boxes made of recycled cardboard.

It was precisely at these words that I realized with overwhelming clarity what nonsense all this is, and how much all these conversations, even in mere gossip columns, cannot be applied to Zelenska. This seems the proper moment to consider words that Zelenska addressed to the British in an interview with BBC's Laura Kensberg: "While you count the money, we count the corpses." More precisely, this is how it was translated in Russia. A more correct translation would be: We count catastrophes and tragedies. This is quite a good interview, very incisive: "I am offended by talk that I was the wife of an actor, and suddenly I turned out to be the wife of the leader of the nation in wartime. He didn't turn into anyone. He's always been like that. He could never have done otherwise!"

The most candid interview with Zelenska over this entire period—defiantly direct, with no thought whatsoever about her image since she likes to shoot without makeup—is the aforementioned conversation with *Die Zeit*, which was conducted by two journalists—Catherine Gilbert and Amelie Schneider. It was published on February 15, 2023, and is called "I Don't Want to be a Victim." Its first exchange is excellent:

> **How are you doing?**
> I'm alive.

It is every bit as good as it continues:

> **What is your sensation of yourself?**
> A hamster in a wheel. I'm functioning. I do not have a second of peace, and if a second does arise, I am too exhausted to hear myself think.
> The war changed everything. It once seemed to me that the most difficult thing would be to follow protocol and be in constant view of everyone because I so love my independence. All fears like that seem so funny today. The war changed everything. In the first months of the war, we did not see each other at all. But the most difficult thing is not physical separation. There are many separations now. We have lunch together at least once a week, but I can't say that I feel better

after those meetings or conversations. He has changed so much. We used to laugh so much. Now I'm happy when I can make him smile.

What is the biggest change?

I lost my lightness. The constant pressure. All over the country we are organizing therapy for children who have lost a relative. But I'm not much better off myself.

Are you receiving psychological help?

I'm in therapy and I see no point in hiding it. For example, my eyesight is deteriorating. It's crazy. I've never had any problems with my eyes for forty-five years. But it's because we're constantly looking at phones. And we've lived in the dark for a year. Either the electricity is cut off, or we are in a basement. Sometimes it seems to me that Russians are waiting for people to get tired of running to bomb shelters or basements to hide. Then they will strike suddenly and kill larger numbers . . . as they recently did in Dnipro.

Do you have a strong hatred for the Russians?

We definitely don't have Stockholm syndrome, where the victim sympathizes with the tormentors. We do not see or feel a mass movement against the war in Russia. We don't see anyone sympathizing with the children dying in Ukraine. Instead, after each missile strike, we read numerous comments on social networks like, "May they all finally die there." We did not attack, we were attacked, and we are being destroyed. Is that a satisfactory answer?

Do you sleep well?

Sleeping is very difficult. You know what I've noticed? It has become difficult not only to expend energy, to smile, and command attention. It has become difficult for me to empathize.

You wrote scripts for your husband's company. Do you write now?

I can't anymore. I used to like coming up with funny things. I had a very ironic attitude to life. That's all gone. Although I don't want to be at the center of a tragic, dramatic story. I don't want to be pitied. I don't want to be a victim. *(And here she makes a very astute remark about Tarantino: that his films always have deeply tragic content, with traditional morality and an easy, rather cynical way of presentation.*

But in Django Unchained, *a deep seriousness occasionally breaks through which has now long been reflected in Zelenskyy's eyes.—D. B.)*

How about your children?

They're not children anymore. They watch the news, they understand what is going on. As do all children in Ukraine, they have to try to keep living on. But they sense that their lives have been paused.

Have you become accustomed to the horror? Is that even possible?

No.

You did a photoshoot with Annie Liebowitz that was criticized in Ukraine . . .

I couldn't say no. Working with Annie Liebowitz was too big an honor for me.

You were criticized for your aggressive posture and fierce gaze.

I see no reason why the wife of the President of Ukraine should not have a fierce gaze in 2023. I have no need to hide. The war may have taken much from me, but not everything.

In the narrative that Zelenskyy consciously or unconsciously builds, his wife plays an exceptional role, far more serious than Solveig, who only loves and waits. Zelenska is active and engaged, she conducts meetings and, please pardon my use of such an officious term, hosts humanitarian events every day. But on top of this role, hatred and shock, as well as the shock of hatred, reveal themselves as a secret dark layer under everything she says and does: No, she was not prepared for this.

She really does not believe all this is possible in the twenty-first century. Furthermore, she is from a Russian-speaking region and a Russian-speaking family, and when there is a dispute about the fate of the Russian language in Ukraine, the dispute involves her too. She and the entire circle of her hometown friends will now forever more feel guilt. From here on out—it is hard to doubt this now—she will have to wean herself from the Russian language.

No image maker could have anticipated all of this: Zelenskyy's wife always looked strong, ironic, confident, independent, in many ways equal to her husband, even superior in her smooth sense of strength. She did not seek publicity, but never avoided it either. She imperiously ignored discussions of her image and tastes. She asserted the values of mutual understanding across borders. And then people saw her literally frozen, and deathly tired—she continues to allow herself to be what she is: a shocked, exhausted woman. She doesn't understand what's happening, she can't wrap her head around it. But she is not at a loss—she knows how to hate. The soft, cautious, moderate Zelenska responds to aggression with icy, unforgiving hostility before the entire world, and at the bottom of this hostility there is confusion. In her every word we hear the roar of a world collapsed, her own personal world, not just the interwar world order. (Her horror is also a recognition that we now realize: There is no post-war world anymore. There is only an interwar world. Will there be a generation that will not have to be convinced of this?) The horror of the situation is that Zelenska wants and knows how to look good. Generally speaking, few sights in the world are more heartbreaking than that of a person whose every reason for being has collapsed entirely, but who continues trying to look good at the same time. And succeeds. Truly, these words could be the motto of Zelenska, and of Ukraine: "You can't take everything away."

She admitted she has a dream: to get in the car all alone, leave the city, turn the music on full blast and just watch the scenery pass. Her three favorite tracks are "There You Go" by Kristina Solovei, "No Promises, No Apologies" by Viktor Pavlik, and "Someone Like You" by Okean Elzy. Like the legendary Russian film hero Stirlitz, who sits on the spring earth and strokes the soil as Marika Rekk sings "Seventeen Moments of Spring." It sits deep in all of us. I admit, much more can happen to Olena Zelenska, as is true of all of us. After all, she did not call herself target number two for nothing. Anyway, any one of us just might go out of our minds. But a good ending for a film about this war, and maybe even for a blockbuster titled *Zelenskyy*, seems to me precisely to be this passage about a beautiful woman in a beautiful car traversing a beautiful landscape from this deafening song called "Hold On," which I also find attractive:

You will yell at me right in my house.

For how can you wound me and break my heart?

Don't you hear how captivity frightens me?

Nothing compares to your embrace.

Even a bird struggles to spread its wings

When a poor girl is ruined by love.

Take me firmly by the hand.

Kill me hard and softly.

Go ahead, torment me with your hands.

Heal yourself with my lips.

Normal people who have not lived through bombing raids for a long time will howl in unison: "Wow, how incredibly kitschy! What about our modernist utopia?!"

Wow, indeed! Peace on earth, goodwill to men! We earned these three minutes and twenty-seven seconds of superkitsch!

VIII. *BLOCK 95*

I would like to warn the reader, especially the Western one, not to make an inevitable mistake (yes, inevitable, but at least we tried). Having become immersed in the genesis of Zelenskyy, his political success, and his military courage, a reader will start watching the best episodes of *Block 95*, its sketches, its holiday specials, and serial episodes, and will inevitably be disappointed.

> "Bring in another five hundred euros!" a doctor says to a secretary (referring to the next visitor).
>
> "After having sex with my wife, I have problems with my vision: I don't see the point."
>
> "I can't feed everyone in our family, someone will have to be fired. You're the wife and the boss, you choose: It's your mom or my dog."

"How can you compare my mom and your Bobik?!"

"At least Bobik didn't vote for Yanukovych!"

Yes, people! *Block 95*'s popularity is not the best way to characterize it. Even by carefully selecting scenes with Zelenskyy's participation (sometimes played alone, sometimes as a supporting actor), they amaze thanks to the crudity of the humor, the frank bad taste, the playing down to the spectator's baser instincts, as well as stooping to old jokes speculating on ethnic (horrors! even Jewish!) subject matter. And yes, Zelenskyy sometimes employs a cliched local accent. And it's true, it's not always funny. The level of most of the jokes parallels that about which the Russian satirical poet Sasha Chyorny once said: "Before Averchenko, mothers-in-law reigned in our humor." The level of *Block 95* does not rise to that of *Satyricon* at all. And if it weren't for the political relevance of some really pointed jokes, if it weren't for the laudable absence of hypocritical taboos, which is a sign of true freedom in the spirit of *Charlie Hebdo*, *Block 95* would be an ordinary stand-up show of low taste that is typical of low-grade television. It's not Monty Python, oh no. Nothing like that.

But who among the creators of Monty Python even remotely influenced British politics? Which of their films and TV series, including the brilliant ones like *The Meaning of Life According to Monty Python*, brought serious political dividends to its participants? Even if Terry Gilliam (who, by the way, was honored at the Odesa Film Festival in 2021 and confused Ukraine with Russia in his response speech) remained a cult director for a narrow stratum of connoisseurs, what can we say about the rest of its group members? True, tickets for a reunited Pythons concert in 2014 sold out in 43 1/2 seconds, but this is not an indicator of their true impact on the masses. Speaking more broadly, Russian elite culture has been in fine shape, but Russia has never been able to resist, in any way, its own totalitarianism throughout its entire history. Not everything is bad in Russia (at least until the war and the final takeover of fascism) with its arthouse cinema and postmodern literature (whereas the grassroots, television level of culture is pure and unalloyed trash). But in Russia, no actor would ever reach the post of president, or even a ministerial chair (the short-lived exception being Minister of Culture Nikolai Gubenko during the collapse of the USSR). In Russia there is a negligibly small stratum capable of resisting vulgarity, but categorically unable to object when it is deprived of all the rights of the state, and put to the pillory. The qualitative vulgarity of *Block 95* probably belongs to the middle layer of culture, the absence of which Russia has always suffered. The middle class is no standard of good taste, but it is an entity that, having reached sufficient numbers, is the only serious barrier to totalitarianism and ochlocracy, which, as it turned out, do quite well on Russian soil.

If we seriously study the output of the Block team, it is worth considering it from this point of view: a professional, well-executed vulgarity that was able to promote to national prominence neither reactionaries, nor Stalinists, nor security officers, but humorists who did not fear to say rude things about the authorities out loud. In general, when humanity has time for cultural studies again after this war ends, a book about the costs of good taste might be very useful.

IX. THE 1+1 CHANNEL. RODNIANSKYI. *BLOCK 95* ON TV

The first person to bet on Zelenskyy was Oleksandr Rodnianskyi, a well-known Ukrainian, later Russian, later German producer, creator, and head of the 1+1 channel, known colloquially as "Pluses."

Immediately following Zelenskyy's election as president, Rodnianskyi gave an interview to the Russian edition of the Meduza news portal that had been forced into emigration in Europe. Ilia Zhegulev, a specialist in Ukrainian affairs, posed the questions. The interview contains much valuable information and insightful assessments.

> They (the Block) were always a team—Zelenskyy was not separate from the others. There were the Shefirs and Zelenskyy, he never existed apart from them. He was the undoubted leader on stage—the

most artistic, lively, and witty—but in life they were a trio. The She-firs are older, and one of them, Serhii, is rather more communicative than Borys. As such, as a rule, he took over the business part of the conversations. Although Volodia Zelenskyy also participated. They decided to organize a big show at the October Palace. Since we real-ly loved them, after asking around and making sure they had enough content for an entire hour-and-a-half program, I decided to take a chance on them. In principle, the main advantage of the Shefirs and Zelenskyy was that they wrote very well.

I was not a television person, nor was the entire team that I did 1+1 with. You must understand that 1+1 was a unique channel. I created it from scratch, basically avoiding people who had worked in television before. They were either film people like myself who came from docu-mentaries, or just journalists. There were a lot of young people. When we created the 1+1 channel, we wanted to make it a part of social and cultural life. Since I didn't have any money, we received investments from an American company called Central European Media Enter-prises right from the very beginning. It invested in independent tele-vision companies, primarily in Eastern Europe. But due to the colossal success of 1+1 from the first year of its existence, I had the absolute right to make decisions. That was not codified on paper, but it was absolute. Of course, if something failed, that would give them an argu-ment to try to grab more influence inside the TV company. Partner-ship with the Americans taught us a lot. After that, I will never again repeat the experience of being dependent in such matters.

An active struggle for control of the media ensued, which led to a tragic period for them in 2004 when, for 140 days during the presidential campaign, it was impossible to show just one of the two leading candidates on the air. As a result, Ukrainian television on the whole looked bad, humiliated and disgusting. I confess to you hon-estly, I never sympathized with Viktor Yushchenko, because to me he seemed a hundred times more unprepared for power than Zelenskyy does now. He seemed to me weak, uneducated, and very out of date. He talked all the time about history, about the Battle of Konotop, about the Ukrainian language, about culture, the village, and so on.

He did not talk about the modern nation, the economy, the future, high-tech, young people, technical universities, or anything else that a huge number of living people wanted to hear. I didn't like him. I always said, "Give him the opportunity to prove himself on screen." But they never did.

What happened after the first TV broadcast of *Block 95*?

I remember trying to persuade them to do it more often. I wanted to do it every day. Well, "every day" is an exaggeration, but at least every month. That didn't happen. They said they were in a position to do it four times a year.

Did you begin communicating with them more closely then?

On the contrary. I remained a shareholder of 1+1, and chairman of the board of directors of the channel. But after moving to Moscow to manage STS Media, I basically did no operational work for the channel. Somewhere around 2005 or 2006, they were bought out by a competitor, the Inter channel, which was owned by a major entrepreneur and later a politician, a member of the government, Valerii Khoroshkovskyi. The return of *Block 95* to 1+1 was a result of their business relations with the entrepreneur Ihor Kolomoiskyi, who became the owner of 1+1 in 2009.

So the team first began a relationship with Kolomoiskyi, then moved to his channel?

Yes. As far as I understand, Kolomoiskyi bought a part of *Block 95*, a minority share of some kind, and they returned to the channel, receiving the same airtime that they were guaranteed on Inter, or maybe even more. They de facto controlled and still control prime time on 1+1 even today. The channel's success and audience share largely depended on them. It goes without saying that the role they played for 1+1 has always been colossal.

But the most important thing is that they were transformed into a regular political theater in Ukraine because all the local elite and connoisseurs of edgy humor flocked to their show at the October Palace. This was not just stand-up comedy, not just KVN with its rather conservative, timid jokes that rarely had any relationship to reality. They were always edgy. This was real political satire, much more barbed than in Russia, and they allowed themselves to make jokes about everyone.

Those who say they could imagine Zelenskyy's foray into politics are prevaricating. Who could have imagined it? Yes, at some stage Ukrainian politics turned into a puppet show where nothing was surprising. I knew that Zelenskyy would attract significant numbers in the elections. The electorate was tired of politicians, because they had already made everyone sick, and so there would be a natural reaction of rejection—there would be a collective candidate "Against Everyone." The surprise was that Zelenskyy began pulling down numbers that led him to victory in the first round. It doesn't seem to me, for example, that Vakarchuk (rock musician, leader of the Okean Elzy group) could achieve this, because Vakarchuk's intonation is lyrical pathos, which is what Poroshenko used in part. This is the Ukrainian pathos—we are a humiliated and insulted nation, colonized in the past, now, rising from its knees, regaining the right to life, history, independence, our own language, our own church, our own faith, our own army, borders, and so on. Zelenskyy took a different tone—his political satire, his lightness, his dancing, his wit, his joviality are all very characteristic of Ukraine. This is part, if you like, of the genetic cultural code of Ukrainians—constant jokes, irony, unwillingness to clash in direct discussions, or put up rigid defenses. Ukraine has always been distinguished by the ability to treat things, even serious things, with wit and irony. Zelenskyy, of course, is the embodiment of this spirit. He emerged as a supranational character, one who was not damaged by the line in his passport that identified him as Jewish, the one that had such tragic consequences in Soviet times. No one has ever cared that he is not an ethnic Ukrainian. He confirmed everyone's attitude to him as a person capable of holding an independent opinion. In Ukraine, where everyone knows who, to whom, how many times, and for what amounts anyone has sold himself—I'm talking about the press, the media, and many public figures—Zelenskyy's independent behavior on stage for many years had the ready look of a principled position. He abruptly detached himself from Kolomoiskyi, with whom he had been tightly connected from the very beginning. As much as it surprised Zelenskyy's opponents, discrepancies clearly emerged between the two. In my opinion, he is not the puppet of the public perception. I am convinced that Zelenskyy is an independent individual. After all is said and done, he's a self-made man. This is someone who grew up in the most depressed city in Ukraine. You know, there was Lenin Street—ninety kilometers long, dotted with factory after factory after factory. He lived there in one of those neighborhoods, all his friends are from there. This is a unique experience. Then there were the notorious '90s in Ukraine with the failing factories, and people out of jobs. He experienced all of this, he took shape as an individual, and came to know himself. He found a team he could work with, he trusted them, and stayed with them as he entered life. This does not mean he is dependent on them, it is a partnership. I have no doubt that, of course, they will play the classic Ukrainian political game of suicide chess—but having succumbed to that, they will end up on top.

As President, Zelenskyy is in no one's pocket. That's just not possible. Presidents are not pocket-sized anyway—it's obvious that the position itself does not allow this. People you were familiar with yesterday, and who clapped you on the shoulder, will turn into extremely polite and well-mannered individuals, addressing you deferentially in formal terms, addressing you in interrogative intonations, waiting for approval of the words they have spoken. And only, maybe, the closest ones will retain a special relationship with you, but that won't happen in public. Everything else will be exactly as I have stated it.

This, of course, would provoke the same psychological changes in a person that power always provokes in anyone. This group claimed that their primary task—note this well—was to change the tone of power. For example, they said they would not take up position in the building on Bankova Street, that is, in the classic building of the Central Committee of the Communist Party of Ukraine, where the headquarters of Ukrainian presidents have always been located since the country gained independence. No, they said, we will find a way to set up office outside the city. First, because there are constant traffic jams in the city center, and second, they planned to reduce the number of people working in the administration.

Is Zelenskyy capable of changing life in the country as well as the system of power?

It seems to me that, despite the 73% that voted for him, few people believe that. He'll definitely be able to change the tone of politics. To those young people tired of the hopelessness of power, the corruption, and the system, he can say that life is changing. You know, this is, after all, the first government in the post-Soviet territory—apart from the Baltic states—that has nothing to do with the Soviet past. These young people are forty years old, a huge number of people in the country have grown up the same as they have. They want to hear about their future life, that's important to them.

A professional question. How do you rate [Zelenskyy's TV] series _Servant of the People_? In terms of its impact on the population, and the quality of the series itself?

The idea itself is marvelous, and it's perfect for a sitcom. It is no coincidence that Oleksii Kiriushchenko, who directed the most successful Russian sitcom _My Fair Nanny_, was its director. We did this series in Moscow when I still owned 1+1. _My Fair Nanny_ was a huge success in Ukraine as well. We worked with a large number of people who now work in the Block team.

Obviously, _Servant of the People_ is an exaggerated reaction to the state of affairs in Ukraine. A satirical metaphor. That's one. Two, the quality of the series at some point ceased to be important. It didn't matter whether you liked it or not. It became a public phenomenon. It presents the notion of a simple man insulted by the authorities and the injustice of life in the country, who suddenly and unexpectedly becomes president, and tries successfully or unsuccessfully to restore order. The idea, as it turned out, was incredibly relevant.

There was an attempt in Russia to make a similar series. In 2015, on Rain-TV, Roman Volobuyev released a pilot of a series called _Tomorrow_, about how a certain team of liberals, having won fair elections, suddenly enters the Kremlin and finds itself in the circumstances of holding power. What is it like, in other words, to lead the country? But they kept it serious. Serious people thinking seriously, good-looking, contemporary people basically. And it was dreary because they admired themselves.

Nothing was as primitive as Poroshenko claimed, who at the final debate in the stadium even said that Zelenskyy was not his character, the TV-president Vasily Goloborodko. In fact, no one was mistaking him for Goloborodko. Everyone knew perfectly well that it was time to conduct the same experiment in the country that had been carried out on the screen. But only in earnest. With a completely new person coming to power. Maybe there's something he doesn't know, maybe he knows nothing, but those who do know are exhausted. This is the attitude that the film captured.

As the Russian literary theoretician Mikhail Bakhtin would have it, Ukrainian culture is a culture of laughter, festive and ceremonial in nature. It makes fun of its own power, and makes fun of itself. It is a self-mocking culture. To speak seriously and with pathos while addressing the people, means arousing their suspicions. Only irony, only an understanding of how the world is unfairly arranged, only ridiculing power. Then you can submit to it. The hetman, before anyone would obey his orders, thus putting the lives of ordinary soldiers at risk, would be ridiculed in a circle, doused with mud, and literally with feces. He would be utterly humiliated before the people would give them the opportunity to lead them. It is part of the genetic code.

But when Zelenskyy, figuratively speaking, was doused with feces, he did not react stoically, as a hetman would, but rather aggressively. It was a hard experience for him.

Yes, indeed! We are speaking at the very beginning of his presidential life. He has terrible days, months, and years ahead of him. (*A prophet, and a shaman!*—D. B.) To be honest, you can't envy him, and I am convinced that the hostility for him has not yet even begun.

All kinds of things will happen, and he will face a monstrous lack of understanding, humiliation maybe, probably even insults. All this is coming. He's not Reagan in any way. He has no clarity on a huge range of important issues affecting the life of the country. There is just a monstrous disagreement with how things were. It is a clearly expressed, articulated, and wittily debated disagreement.

Did you congratulate Zelenskyy on his victory?

No, I didn't, I'm not that close to him, and I'm not trying in any way to ... (*Rodnianskyi's son, also Oleksandr—[Rodnianskyi himself is called Liosha by his friends]—was an economic consultant to Zelenskyy's team, but he had long been an adult and his own independent person. He is now a member of the supervisory board of Oshchadbank.—D. B.*) I just made a decision in the interests of the 1+1 channel, understanding the talent and potential of Zelenskyy, his colleagues, and partners. Let's be honest: I did nothing for this very pleasant, charming person who evokes such affection in everyone. No one would have failed to single him out. Curiously, by the way, there were two leading teams in the Ukrainian KVN that remain in my memory. One was the Block, the other was Piatigorsk, whose leader was Semion Slepakov.

Did you watch the debate between Zelenskyy and Poroshenko? You once organized debates yourself. As a producer, what do you think of using a stadium?

I very much like the idea of debates on its own. I have always supported them. But at a stadium? That was Zelenskyy's idea. And it was the right move, because it emphasized his direct appeal not to the elite, but to those who gathered at stadiums. And later he prepared some wonderful home-prepared surprises.

That is, if you had voted, you would, of course, have voted for Poroshenko, not for Zelenskyy?

How do I put it? I know both of them. Poroshenko is a longtime friend. And I was sure he would be successful when he first ran for president. He disappointed me. I wouldn't have voted for him a second time.

Rodnianskyi is a unique and talented person. I worked with him myself in 2010, when, while rebranding Channel Five in Russia, he launched my *Oil Painting* talk show (shortly after which, the Moscow opposition marches began, and I was entirely deprived of access to television). From my communication with Rodnianskyi, I learned a few things about that Russian stratum of artists and producers, who, to a certain extent, believed they could coexist and even cooperate with the authorities, even though they had no illusions about the subsequent evolution of Russia's power structure, and even the final form it would assume.

Rodnianskyi is a wonderful example of how Zelenskyy sets people right, even if they are more experienced and set in their ways. For a long time, nearly fifteen years, Rodnianskyi made peace with Putin's government, although from the very beginning, albeit in a roundabout way, he tried to speak out about what was happening. Having produced with great difficulty (barely breaking even) Fyodor Bondarchuk's *Inhabited Island*, based on the Strugatsky brothers novel with a script by the husband-and-wife team of Maryna and Serhii Diachenko, the top Ukrainian science-fiction writers, he included a prophetic reference to the former Soviet provinces that are now plotting against Russia. After the Bondarchuk project, he worked with Russian director Andrei Zvyagintsev, and together they spoke out more and more radically. For twenty years he supported Russian cinema with his Kinotavr festival. He spoke out against the annexation of Crimea, although in reserved tones. He was the one who, although the mission failed, brought the oligarch Roman Abramovich into the negotiations between Russia and Ukraine in March 2022; Russian Defense Minister Sergei Shoigu sent a letter to the Ministry of Culture with a request to exclude Rodnianskyi "from the public agenda." On October 21, 2022, Rodnianskyi was declared a foreign agent. On May 17, 2023, he was arrested in absentia "for spreading fake information about the Russian army." He announced the closure of all his Russian projects, and now lives in the United States where he runs the AR Content development company.

Undoubtedly, the main reason for the persecution of Rodnianskyi was that he was involved in Zelenskyy's career and welcomed his election enthusiastically, and not because he once produced an insufficiently patriotic movie. Today in Russia, everyone who stood at the origins of Zelenskyy's career walks beneath the sword of Damocles—that's why the old fox Alexander Maslyakov preferred to distance himself from him, constantly repeating that he had not seen him for ages, and that they had never communicated in earnest. Friendship with Zelenskyy, support for Zelenskyy is the most toxic asset in today's Russia. I suspect that the comedian Maxim Galkin was also declared a foreign agent primarily because he hosted New Year's shows with Zelenskyy in 2013 and, horror of horrors, in 2014.

Rodnianskyi is impeccably accurate in defining Zelenskyy's métier as "political theater." The fact that the leader of the Block immediately banked on politics, rather than on "flowers of innocent humor," which is how virtually every Russian humorist earns their living, is just more proof of his impeccable instincts. The politicization of Ukrainian humor (and the Ukrainian worldview in general) is due precisely to the fact that one of the main occupations of Ukrainian society in the last thirty years has been the desacralization of power. Zelenskyy unmistakably realized that he had no future in Russia, and preferred to take his risks in Ukraine.

Zelenskyy's and Rodnianskyi's paths, as we see, intertwined three times. First, Rodnianskyi took on Zelenskyy's show for his channel, and in 2022 he helped him find intermediaries (in particular, Abramovich) for negotiations. But in between these two moments, there was another intersection of paths. In 2012 at Rodnianskyi's Kinotavr Festival, the most representative and prestigious of all Russian film festivals, always significantly out ahead of Moscow, the main prize was awarded almost unanimously to a film produced by the Block. The jury there was filled with heavyweights—Vladimir Khotinenko presided over a jury of Alexei Fedorchenko, Vera Glagoleva, Nikolai Khomeriki, Alexander Kott, and Bakur Bakuradze, and the competition was not bad—*To Live*, *Kokoko*, and *Stories* . . . But Pavel Ruminov won with his film *I Will Be There*.

This film had a rather rocky fate, almost no distribution and extremely conflicting reviews. The subtitle of "based on real events" looked ambiguous in this case, because the story told in serialization differs from that of the film version. It takes place in Moscow. A young single mother named Inna suddenly learns she has aggressive brain cancer and, at best, has a few months left to live. She is played by Masha Shalaeva, the actress's best role. Her son, who is six, is played by the fabulously charming, nervous, and agile Roma Zenchuk. The extraordinarily close relationship of the single mother and her son is conceived beautifully and subtly observed. He is a dreamer who composes fairy tales, and engages his mother in humorous games that he invents himself, something about dinosaurs and robots, but with eccentric plots that mark him as a bookish child. He invents plots all the time, and always suspects the worst—something that will play out later. But she now learns she is doomed, has no relatives, and her ex-husband is a drunk who constantly borrows money from her (she works in a café). In short, she begins to look for foster parents for her son—something similar to what Lyudmila Petrushevskaya writes in her story "Our Circle," but believe it or not, it is more frightening here because the boy is even younger. The company that seeks adoptive parents for him is creepy, harsh, and bureaucratic, and insists that Inna make a video about her son to show it to potential adopters. What follows is a whole series of potential adoptive parents, Russian and foreign—all of them utterly empty inside. They speak empty words. When she begins to imagine her homebound dreamer of a child, who is so ferociously attached to her, going to live with these utter strangers, the picture becomes not just gloomy, but grotesque, with a desperate intonation, for we see right through this whole, falsely-stable, utterly fake Russia where a single humanely spoken word is worth its weight in gold. There is one utterly excruciating scene where the boy begins to suspect he is being prepared for something terrible, but he cannot formulate what it is. Since he watches TV all the time, a yellow-journalism version of outcomes begins to form in his brain. He asks his mother point-blank: are you planning to sell my organs?

You can roughly imagine her state of mind, and everything is shot in a documentary style, as was popular then, in the style of Dogma 95, with extremely natural intonations. She starts giggling madly: "What are you talking about, what organs, where did you get that idea?" "Well," he says, "I don't know. Maybe I make you angry. For example, I never wash the dishes"—and he naturally begins to wash the dishes. Thus he drives her to tears, while Ruminov is the one who does it to us. But Ruminov, although he's self-taught (or maybe precisely because of this), never overdoes it. He has an innate tact that keeps him from making excessively showy acting decisions. "Well," says Inna, "if you don't want me to, I won't sell your organs." And since she improvises fairy tales for him all the time and easily joins in his games, she takes out her mobile phone and makes a call: "Hello, is this organ trafficking? No, I've changed my mind. I'm not selling him for spare parts. I need them myself. Yes, yes, he even washed all the dishes."

Then the plot takes a turn. She finds a seemingly decent, childless couple (played very well by Ivan Volkov and Maria Semkina), and they diligently and meticulously display what is, in fact, an utterly lifeless parental love. In the film, the heroine enters the hospital but is discharged in a hopeless condition, and a silly, funny migrant worker from hospice, a well-meaning nurse who understands nothing, comes to her aid. In the series Inna unexpectedly recovers and asks the new parents to return her child. But it's too late, he's officially adopted, and the new mother goes after the old one like a tigress. The serialized version, less successfully made and more drawn out, has a rather artificial happy ending, so that it's not quite clear what the whole story has been about unless it was just intended as effective melodrama. The film version, however, despite being overwrought—or perhaps thanks to that—possesses a monstrous feeling of complete impasse, where, indeed, nothing can be done. Here she sits alone at home, this Inna, who is already forgetting words and cannot finish a single sentence. The nurse feeds her and leaves, and she sits and watches the DVD about her son endlessly. He tells his fairy tales, plays, and laughs. Most critics criticized the film precisely on the grounds that it was so direct and obvious. But life is also terribly direct, that's just how it is. And, despite God's mercy, utterly hopeless situations do happen. This film about the subtle horror and unbearable pain of a lonely mother and a bookish child turns out to be a film about how the tank of life runs over the weakest and the loneliest, and how it's impossible to escape this tank. I know of what I speak, I am the son of a single mother. All my life my biggest fears were for her. It's quite possible that had I had been at Kinotavr in 2012, I too would have ridiculed these blatant moves along with my colleagues, although that is unlikely. But now that we have all been thrown out of the ruts of our usual lives, and the icy wind of omnipresent disorder blows through us regardless of whether we feel good or bad in our foreign climes, I am much more susceptible to this film's tale. I understand much better what it is about. Sentimentality can be mocked by people who are well protected. Zelenskyy somehow knew from the very beginning what life was about, and therefore he presented at Kinotavr precisely this version, the producer's version, editing out the slightest hint of a happy ending.

He liked the story so much that for his own directorial debut, the 2018 film of *I, You, He, She*, he engaged a similar plot: a husband learns he is terminally ill and begins putting his wife in good hands. That all goes through many changes before it turns out to be a sad comedy about divorce, about a month's probation, and about the stupidities that smart and, apparently, melancholy people seem to be capable of committing. Zelenskyy's eyes reveal unbearable ennui all the time, as if he understands perfectly, clearly foresees, and despises everything that awaits him in the coming five years. For anyone who has ever watched and listened to the work of the Block, it is obvious that all these jokes are always underpinned by ennui, an understanding of the risk and horror lurking on all sides. That's the only way decent satire can turn out. The great Abkhazian writer Fazil Iskander said that humor is the trace left by one who has looked into the abyss and is now crawling away from it. That's not the Zelenskyy we knew, we wanted to imagine him a comedian. Yet for some reason he invested in the creation of this film, and he apparently shares its understanding of things. This is another explanation why he did not escape: there is, basically, nowhere to run.

To my question about what Zelenskyy is really like, Rodnianskyi once answered: No nonsense.

X. THE TSYTSKO BROTHERS

The independent life of the Block team after it left KVN began in December 2003 with a series of five holiday shows under the general title of "5 O!" (it was an Olympic year, and this title referred to the rings representing the Summer Olympics in Athens). The shows were:

- An anniversary show called "O! Five—Ninety Five."
- "Martitsa the 8th" (in honor of International Women's Day on March 8).
- The presentation of the Golden Pumpkin prize (an award given by the Block for "Boundless Achievements in the Field of Show Business").
- The Mysterious Peninsula concert in Yalta.
- A New Year's show.

"Martitsa" was a parody playing on the name for the month of March and the popular cult film at that time of *The Matrix*. It contained two, count 'em, good jokes. One of them was:

> "I am the chosen one!"
> Timokha (*in a lecturing tone*): "Around here the chosen one is the President."

The rest of the jokes were on the level of a resort concert in the Crimea in the 1990s: "C. C. Catch and C. C. Capwell are two different C-cup sizes!" That will only get a smile from someone who now remembers that C. C. Catch was the Dutch-born German pop star Caroline Müller, and C. C. Capwell was a character from *Santa Barbara*.

On the whole, all of the *Block 95* shows in the first years of Zelenskyy's career were musical spectacles perfectly filmed but not at all witty. Zelenskyy was the genuine engine of action, the most lively and fearless, a clear leader, yet no one today would ever have seen the current Zelenskyy in him.

More thought and caustic witticisms go into any one of his speeches today than into any of the early *Block 95* shows.

The main players of *Block 95* were (ladies go first):

Olena Kravets (until 2002—Maliashenko), the only woman among the group's actors. Born January 1, 1977, in Kryvyi Rih. After graduation from the Economics Department of the Kryvyi Rih Institute of Agriculture, she became director of the Kryvyi Rih branch of McDonald's. She performed in KVN, and in 2000, she became the director of *Block 95*. In 2002, she married Serhii Kravets, the executive producer of *Block 95* (they have three children—a daughter and opposite sex twins). She is the godmother of Olena Zelenska. Her husband is the godfather of Sasha Zelenska, the president's daughter.

Yevhen Koshevoi, also known as Baldy. Born April 7, 1983, in the Kharkiv region. The youngest of the *Block 95* stars. From 2000 to 2005, he performed in Va-Bank, the KVN team from Luhansk. He was invited to join *Block 95* in 2005, and after that became the studio's leading actor, the co-host of the popular *Ukraine, Stand Up!* program, and a member of the jury of the *Make a Comedian Laugh* show. He played Mukhin, Minister of Foreign Affairs, in *Servant of the People*.

Oleksandr Pikalov. Born in Kryvyi Rih January 30, 1976. Known for being a "stilyaga," or hipster, in his school years, he studied for ten years at the institute (Kryvyi Rih Technical University), but never worked in his chosen field. He headed up STVM (Student Theater of Variety Miniatures), which is where he started up the whole business of the Block. He hosts the *Evening Block* talk show, *Evening Kyiv*, *Made in Ukraine*, and others, of which there are about a dozen. He portrayed Yanukovych more than any of the others. He donated three automobiles to the Ukrainian Armed Forces, took the oath, and joined the National Guard of Ukraine on April 6, 2022. In tandem with Koshevoi, he puts out news releases under the title of "Bayraktar News."

Yurii Krapov. The oldest of the *Block 95* actors (born September 13, 1973, in Kryvyi Rih). Mining engineer. Member of *Block 95* since 2003. He portrayed a dozen Ukrainian politicians in *Evening Block*, most often Petro Poroshenko.

Stepan Kazanin. Real name Serhii. Born December 19, 1974. Graduated from the Luhansk Institute of Culture. Portrayed Putin in *Evening Block*. Mika Fatalov (Tasunian). Born in Baku in 1981. Graduated from the Luhansk Institute of Culture. Played the head of the Ukrainian Security Forces (also as Mika Tasunian) in *Servant of the People*. Instead of the ubiquitous caricature of the pompous Caucasian—the imperial narrative, as they would say today in Ukraine—he played Goloborodko's chivalrous, honest, ardent, uncompromising colleague with a soft spot for traditional shish-kebab, which he prepares on camera at every opportunity.

The Shefir brothers. The brains of the Block group, the founders, authors, and organizers, who later followed Zelenskyy into the leadership of the country. Serhii Shefir was born May 25, 1964; his older brother Borys was born June 14, 1960. Both graduated from the Kryvyi Rih Mining Institute, both were primarily engaged in writing scripts for KVN, writing for a total of a dozen teams, and selected gags for *Evening Block*.

"What are the Shefirs like?" I asked Oleksii Kiriushchenko, who worked with them on *Servant of the People*.

"Serhii always doubts everything. Boria is a true Russian fableist akin to the legendary Ivan Krylov, both in build and in temperament. When he and Zelenskyy would be selecting gags, everything happened very quickly, and everyone was on fire. When he couldn't be present during the writing of scripts, everything went forward in a much more matter-of-fact way. The Shefirs—with and without Vova [Zelenskyy]—were different Shefirs. But their work with Vova was occasionally humorous."

As we see, the Block comprised a unique acting collective which produced itself, wrote its own material, and ran numerous television programs on its own. Soon enough, there was no competition left in Ukraine.

It's odd now to go back through their best numbers—it was a completely different Ukraine then, one that treated Russia with humor, routinely ridiculed its political squabbles, and never shied from broad-stroked folk humor ("A stream of piss will reach the fountain from the balcony," how charming). But what is most interesting is to look at the faces in the hall. When you look at photos of Soviet citizens on the eve of World War II, their joy seems artificial, their demeanor is determined and austere. You can understand it, they had been living amid full-fledged terror for a long time. Even in moments of merry-making there is a kind of hysterical anguish, while, when trying to portray human feelings, actors tend to break into wild grotesque. In Ukraine, however—even in the darkest days, during and after Maidan, after the annexation of Crimea—you encounter normal, lively faces, sincere laughter, and a sense of goodwill and kinship. For all the suddenness of the German attack in the summer of 1941, people then were much better prepared for war. Not in the sense that they fought better. In fact, he fights best who believes he is fighting for a just cause, not he who is intimidated. No, it was just a healthy country. And if creeping fear gradually embraced everyone in Russia after 2011 with the dispersal of rallies, and never did let go again, happy people in Ukraine were not yet affected by mutual ill-will, and eagerly attended *Block 95* concerts. They knew there was a war going on, but it was not yet omnipresent, and many, it seems, did not really notice it. They paid a price for this too—is it really true that only Muscovites refuse to notice war and pretend that the good old life is still in force? In Ukraine, too, many did not believe it, did not acknowledge it, did not accept its reality. That made the February shock all the greater.

It's true, the humor of *Block 95* was not especially sophisticated. But it differed at the outset from Russian humor in that it courageously trampled on everyone's calluses and spared no one, as is evident in this reference to presidential candidate Petro Poroshenko:

> "Somehow everyone has an equal number of ballots. Let's count the damaged ones too! Look there's a write-in here for Asshole."
> "That vote is for me!"
> "Why do you think it's for you, Pyotr Alekseevich?!"
> "That's what I've been my entire political life!"

Most of all, Zelenskyy took criticism—and continues to—for the *Block 95* skit titled "The Tsytsko Brothers," in which the future president of Ukraine portrays playing the piano with his penis as part of an ensemble of fellow students. This skit was performed September 24, 2016, in Jūrmala, Latvia, at the Jurmaleto concert. Its inclusion in the Russian *News of the Week* program on January 23, 2022—exactly one month before the war—was, of course, a fake: *Block 95* had backed it with Bizet's "Habanera," not the Ukrainian national anthem that was clumsily edited in by Russian propagandists. Moreover, as early as January 11, 2021, the Ukrainian media (i.e., Strana.ua) not only focused attention on this concert number, but also on the fact that it was not a *Block 95* creation. It turns out that it was drawn from the repertoire of the American Freakling Brothers duo, even with the same musical accompaniment. The essence of the number is that the performers approach the piano, pull down their pants, raise their hands—"Look! No hands!"—and imitate playing the piano with their penises. The number had enormous success among less demanding audiences, and the *Block 95* team shaded it with its own inimitable hues, embellishing the pianist's usual bows before the keyboard with a rich glissando and the coarse wagging of hips.

It is noteworthy that the indignation of Ukrainian audiences came about not because of the profane humor—there is no real profanity; and why not laugh at sophisticated music lovers or various contests of exquisite ugliness?—but because it was an imitation, a plagiarism. They instantly remembered that *Block 95* had already borrowed, to put it mildly, the "English Lesson" number from the humorous Ukrainian *Diesel* show.

What can I say? There is no great wit in this piano number, but it is funny, whatever you may think. And it becomes especially funny if you imagine that this number is performed by the owner of the *Block 95* brand, the leading TV producer of Ukraine, later its President, who has subsequently received ovations from the U.S. Congress and the British Parliament. For a second, imagine Putin playing his favorite song "Where the Motherland Begins" on the piano—with his penis, yes, his penis! He did play the song, several times even. Someone taught him to do it, most likely Denis Matsuev, the number one pianist among Putin supporters and non-supporters, and it was funny too. But Putin himself imparted no ironic meaning to it. It was a demonstration of unique abilities, without a shadow of humor. Rather like his hockey prowess, when he scores up to ten goals per game. Now, imagine that someone who plays piano with this body part is elected president of Russia. It is unthinkable. It is beyond the realm of possibility. And that is why—yes, this is the very root of the problem!—Russia is on the attack, and Ukraine is defending itself. Russia stands at the head of all the cannibalistic forces of the world, while Ukraine stands at the head of free humanity. Oddly enough, this is determined by a key difference: can the president play the piano with his penis or not? and the point here, as you understand, is not about size. Size doesn't matter when it comes to love or greatness.

XI. KOLOMOISKYI

Once again we encounter coincidences that parallel all the work that's been done on this book, and that inspire the notion of its necessity, not just its expedience. As I was editing this chapter, news agencies were reporting the arrest of Ihor Kolomoiskyi. Strana.ua writes: "The Shevchenko Court in Kyiv remanded businessman Ihor Kolomoiskyi into custody with the option of bail in the amount of 509 million Ukrainian hryvnia. The due date is in sixty days, October 31. Today the Ukrainian Security Forces served Kolomoiskyi a notice of suspicion on two articles: fraud and legalization of property obtained by criminal means. According to the investigation, during the years of 2013-2020 Kolomoiskyi legalized more than half a billion hryvnia by withdrawing them abroad, while using the infrastructure of controlled banking institutions."

Kolomoiskyi did not post bail. Although I doubt that 509 million Ukrainian hryvnia, or $14 million, was a critical figure for him—according to Ukrainian *Forbes*, as of 2023, he was worth a billion, or, at least, $800 million plus. But he did not agree with the court's decision and chose to make a valiant gesture, putting his opponents in a very difficult position.

Alexei Venediktov, the head of Russia's now-disbanded Ekho Moskvy radio station, opined that Pinocchio had arrested Karabas Barabas. I don't think that's fair. This Pinocchio emerged from wood and made himself into a person on his own. There was no Karabas Barabas at his theater, its functions were carried out collectively, by the actors themselves. Rather, in Alexei Tolstoy's novel *The Golden Key, or the Adventures of Buratino*, this is Pinocchio's fate from the moment he takes over the Lightning Theater in the finale of the fairy tale. (Why "Lightning"? Tolstoy saw it as a strange hint or epiphany. Did he really have in mind the Nazi symbol, the "grabende blitz"? But the lightning-strike symbol is more like the Russian Z—the chief symbol of Vladimir Putin's current special military operation.) All the tales about an animated doll—the Faustian plot about the homunculus— end with the fact that it becomes human and acquires free will, as in Carlo Collodi's story about Pinocchio, or Yevgeny Veltistov's *The Adventures of Electronics* series. Sometimes a homunculus settles scores with its creator, as in the story of Frankenstein, but this is not true of Papa Carlo, and, anyway, there was no Carlo in the events involving Kolomoiskyi and Zelenskyy. If Pinocchio sent someone to prison in this story, then it was Basilio the cat, whom Kolomoiskyi even resembles, at least as the cat was performed by the beloved Soviet actor Rolan Bykov. But the cat has nothing to do with the creation of Pinocchio. Perhaps he duped him, which is a pity because he's a sympathetic character. It's just that Alexei Tolstoy never described the Bolshoi Theater attacking the Lightning Theater because it did not want to have a competitor. There is, of course, no place for sentiment in such circumstances, especially if Broadway intervenes for the Lightning Theater.

I find Kolomoiskyi to be quite attractive—because he has the cheerful cynicism of Isaac Babel's beloved hero Benia Krik, because he gave his most famous interview to the Russian journalist Yulia Latynina while ravenously devouring cheap fried chicken from KFC, and because an un- doubted artistic vein runs through him. I know perfectly well at the same time—after all, I spent a lot of time in Dnipro, it's my favorite city in all of Ukraine—that he has a sketchy reputation, that he has overseen raider seizures, that he was declared an enemy among the press for firing his journalists, and that he is a typical oligarch with a turbulent post-Soviet past. But I am either nostalgic for the 1990s, which struck me as disgusting at the time, or I think these pirates who broke the Soviet empire are more attractive than the Chekists who replaced them. Of course, there is little difference between thieves and bloodsuckers, but there is an insurmountable barrier between bloodsuckers in the private and government spheres. Putin himself called him a con man which, these days, is an impeccable recommendation: "A unique con man. He even cheated our oligarch Abramovich two or three years ago; as they say in our enlightened circles of the intelligentsia, he 'set him up.'" Well, if you set Abramovich up—this is, as they say in enlightened circles of the intelligentsia, a whore getting kicked out of the whorehouse for prostitution. However, Putin's remark was, in all likelihood, a response to Kolomoiskyi's words, spoken at his first press conference as the governor of Dnipro:

> I do not understand how Ukrainians and Russians can fight, given—I'll say it undiplomatically—the schizophrenia of the other opponent. His messianism to restore the Russian Empire of 1913 or the USSR of 1991 may bring the world to disaster. We already had one big schizophrenic, now we have a small one. He is utterly incompetent, and completely crazy.

The big schizophrenic was Yanukovych, about whom Kolomoiskyi spoke with rather more sympathy: "We saw what happened to Yanukovych: how his unwillingness to part with small things led to the loss of everything. Today he is a prisoner of war in a hostile country. He can engage in provocations, even to the point of publishing orders there, and he can be brought to Crimea, to Sevastopol, as a puppet, and he might even declare that he is the current president." As we see, Kolomoiskyi assessed Putin's plans quite clearly, only it was Viktor Medvedchuk who was the intended puppet for Kyiv in 2022. But overall, Kolomoiskyi understood everything perfectly, and it is no wonder that Putin smacked him down, as they say in our circles (while also greatly distorting the story of Abramovich's deal with Kolomoiskyi: he merely sold his Sukhaya Balka mine to Abramovich's Evraz group, then sent his people to cut the access roads to it so that Abramovich could not export ore; he did that because he wanted to control the activities of Evraz). As for oligarchic showdowns, Latynina knows them through and through. I love it that in Putin's mind, a person who set Abramovich up is a super-con man, in a league by himself. The oligarchs themselves quarrel quickly and reconcile easily, which we saw in the example of Boris Berezovsky's relationship with Vladimir Gusinsky in the romantic ages of Russian business.

I would not want to be Kolomoiskyi's enemy, even less his friend, and I certainly can't imagine being his subordinate. But the romantics of the get-rich-quick era were somehow more humane than the politicians, who behaved no better, but were far more boring. And if Kolomoiskyi really did promote Zelenskyy, it means he holds a share in Ukraine's greatest triumph. Zelenskyy's connection to Ihor Kolomoiskyi, a Ukrainian oligarch of Jewish origin, is the subject of endless speculation in Ukraine and abroad. The range of opinions is colossal: from "Zelenskyy was and remains a puppet of Kolomoiskyi" to "Zelenskyy hates Kolomoiskyi." There is even a version that they hardly know each other.

Ihor Kolomoiskyi was born February 13, 1963, in Dnipropetrovsk. His parents were engineers, and the first education of the future oligarch, who now occupies eighth place in the ranking of the richest people in Ukraine, was also engineering (Dnipropetrovsk Metallurgical Institute). He is the founder and one of the principal owners of Privatbank, the largest private bank in Ukraine, the owner of the 1+1 media holding, and, moreover, a Jewish activist, a successful entrepreneur, owner of a dozen factories, two airlines, and several dozen offshore companies. A commonplace was the assumption (disputed by Kolomoiskyi himself and, of course, Zelenskyy) that the *Servant of the People* project was conceived by the oligarch to bring his puppet into power. The wild success of the series and Zelenskyy's transition into politics, unexpected for everyone in the Block team, could not have been calculated in principle—and Kolomoiskyi, of course, could not have foreseen that the captain of the KVN team, even if it was the most popular satirical show in the country, would replace the staid Petro Poroshenko. Kolomoiskyi could have relied on more serious creatures from among radical, but still thoroughly insider politicians. These included Dmytro Yarosh, the leader of the Right Sector; Oleh Liashko, leader of the Radical Party and deputy of the Rada; and the nationalist Oleh Tiagnibok, chairman of the Freedom Party. Kolomoiskyi quarreled with everyone, but first he sponsored everyone. This was his primary argument when he was accused of supporting nationalists: How could I, a Jew, an activist of the Jewish community, support nationalists?! If I support them, they are not nationalists! Kolomoiskyi (together with Hennadii Korban) was one of the first organizers of armed resistance in Ukraine after Russia initiated hostilities in Donbas. According to Forbes, Kolomoiskyi recruited and maintained 3,000 fighters from the so-called *dobrobats* (volunteer battalions), spending up to $10 million a month on food and weapons for them. Alexander Borodai, the Russian-backed Premier of the Donetsk People's Republic in the years 2014–2017, has claimed that Kolomoiskyi's troops were the best equipped, armed, and motivated.

Kolomoiskyi and Poroshenko had reasonably good relations, which ended in a stormy break. Kolomoiskyi was appointed head of the Dnipro administration, but did not share UkrTransNafta with the state, where he held 42 percent of the shares. Meanwhile, the chairman of the Board of UkrTransNafta was suspended by the updated board of directors, locked himself up in the office and was prepared to shoot anyone who tried to come for him. It reached the point that Kolomoiskyi and his deputy Hennadii Korban came to his rescue with machine gunners. We will speak separately about Korban as a smart and colorful person. (He told an anecdote about Kolomoiskyi in an interview: Kolomoiskyi walks down the street and finds a wallet. Picks it up. Counts the money. "Mmm-yes . . . something is missing!") Poroshenko gave Kolomoiskyi a reprimand. Kolomoiskyi had blocked $50 million of the assets of Poroshenko and his family in Privatbank, which he later explained as a technical failure. There was a rumor that two battalions of National Guardsmen were sent to Dnipro, where Kolomoiskyi intended to convene a people's assembly. This was not confirmed, and the matter ended with Kolomoiskyi's resignation and his declaration of resignation from politics.

As we can see, Kolomoiskyi had reasons to seek revenge on Poroshenko, but he chose nationalist deputies with populist potential for this revenge, and not actors by any means. Rumors that Kolomoiskyi financed Zelenskyy's election campaign were spread especially by Poroshenko's supporters. In the main, it was the former president who tried hardest to tarnish Zelenskyy with ties to the Ukrainian oligarchy, and in a sense, his campaign truly was funded by Kolomoiskyi, since the three seasons of the *Servant of the People* series—the main element of this campaign—were filmed on Kolomoiskyi's money, and at his studio. But it was Kolomoiskyi who owed more than $4 million to the Block. If anything ties Kolomoiskyi to Zelenskyy, the director of *Servant of the People* told me, it is debts.

In an interview with Radio Liberty on April 19, 2019, Kolomoiskyi said:

> I have been tip-o-the-cap familiar with Zelenskyy since 2009. We got to know each other better in 2011 when his contract with Inter was coming to an end, and we were interested in him switching to the Pluses (1+1). He wanted to negotiate not only with channel management, but also with one of the controlling shareholders so he would know that the terms of the contract would be fulfilled. He has worked for us since July 2011, and we have communicated regularly. I sometimes wished him happy birthday—I visited him once, he visited me twice. It was a normal relationship between people who have common interests in terms of a contract, which, by the way, ends in 2022. So who will be our frontman? No one has canceled the contract. The fact that he is going to be president was a surprise to everyone. Inklings about it appeared in 2017; he announced his candidacy in 2018. But looking at things in reverse order, I suspect he was already thinking about it when they started making their film. It was entirely his independent decision. If he wants to ask me something, I'll give him advice, but only if necessary. Basically, I'm ready

to hold my silence for five years. I will neither be a shadow leader of the country, nor a gray cardinal. There are difficulties when assuming power. What's the honeymoon period—a hundred days? He'll fit into a hundred days.

When asked about the fact that several guards previously seen with Kolomoiskyi were filmed with Zelenskyy, he replied that they used the same security company, and since Kolomoiskyi himself had not been in Ukraine for a long time, the best guards from the same firm were attached to Zelenskyy. "I want him to become president. I don't hide it. I want it. But this is what most of the country's populace wants" (this statement looked quite natural against the background of the conflict with Poroshenko).

He spoke about the early results of Zelenskyy's presidency in various interviews, stating that not everything suited him, but in general things had become much better. It was probably impossible to meet all expectations. In an interview with *Ukrainska Pravda*, he stated that all the oligarchs supported Zelenskyy (not with their money, but with their secret wishes), adding that, back in 2016, he had heard from Rinat Akhmetov, Ukraine's richest individual:

> Zelenskyy will be president. *(Zelenskyy himself had not yet made such a decision.—D. B.)* Zelenskyy and I celebrated the end of the fiscal year. It was March 2017. We had a few drinks and called [Sviatoslav] Vakarchuk: "Do you support Zelenskyy?" It surprised him, he had not been thinking about it. [Dmytro] Firtash never publicly supported Zelenskyy, nor did [Viktor] Pinchuk, but they all supported him. There was nothing like the oligarchs agreeing among themselves to support him. But the general opinion was for him.

In 2019, Kolomoiskyi described Zelenskyy himself not just positively, but enthusiastically: "He has a biting sense of humor . . . It's hard to keep up with him. I think only one person could compete with him—and that would be [Russian showman Ivan] Urgant. I'd love to watch them trade barbs. The word 'comedian' sounds insulting. But he's an artist, a great artist . . . He's a cynic in business matters. You don't want to go out on a limb with him . . ." (I suspect this is the only kind of compliment Kolomoiskyi is capable of making. Zelenskyy always fought for the interests of the Block but no one has called him a cynic in my memory.)

I can fully imagine that Kolomoiskyi sought to bring his own man into power, but I do not think Zelenskyy would have been this individual. I also admit that Kolomoiskyi's communication with Zelenskyy could have been quite altruistic: he just wanted to make the best TV channel in Ukraine with the best content. That is, in addition to having resources or leverage, he was also interested in achieving power over minds. That has no meaning today in Russia, but in Ukraine in the 2010s it meant a lot. After all, people don't only have vulgar desires to dominate, or passions to subjugate—sometimes they are interested in doing something great, or being remembered for doing something impressive. By the way, among the Russian oligarchs, for example, Vladimir Gusinsky, whom Kolomoiskyi most resembles with his media empire and his work in Jewish philanthropy, also had such intentions, which is why Gusinsky was pushed out of Russia. Under Putin, only primitive individuals with cruel and boring desires survive in Russia.

Here I must make a confession, which, of course, is terrible from a professional point of view. After all, I am painting a portrait of Zelenskyy, tempered by a picture of the background of his era, but I cannot, and should not, allow myself to skip over certain topics. On the other hand, I know from my teaching experience that when you talk about being bored, the class is bored, too. So, here it is: I find it unbearably tedious and pointless to dig into Ukrainian pre-war politics.

Don't talk to me about arrogance, imperialism, and my misunderstanding of Ukrainian specifics: the Russian specifics were so unbearably boring, they almost didn't exist. Ukrainian showdowns, bribes, and threats, the periodic fights in parliament—all this was a completely legitimate form of political life, although even then it was a boring task to figure out who gave a bribe to whom, or who was threatened with murder. Zelenskyy was elected because he promised to take a leap out of this paradigm. He leapt out, revealing to one and all a fundamentally new, outsider type of politician.

But he, too, was sucked into the swamp, and he instigated internal squabbles. He went as far as beginning criminal prosecution of his predecessor, Petro Poroshenko, and had no choice but to put Viktor Medvedchuk in prison because Medvedchuk was a direct agent of Russian influence who, moreover, had made an attempt to escape. Later he turned out to be useful as exchange bait when Medvedchuk and fifty-five Russian soldiers were exchanged for 215 Ukrainian soldiers, including 124 officers, 108 people from the Azov Steel Factory, and three foreign citizens who had been sentenced to death in the Russian-backed Donetsk People's Republic for mercenary activities. Zelenskyy created a new paradigm of Ukrainian politics and a new type of leader, but he was overtaken by the shadows of yesterday, from which there is no escape. The war, of course, presents a great opportunity to leap into the future, but the past also still offers its opportunities, and a radical renewal of Ukrainian politics has not yet taken place.

One thing is certain: Oligarchs will no longer play their former role in it, and this is perhaps the only true news in the internal affairs of Ukraine. Why it happened this way is a separate matter. It is partly due to Zelenskyy, and partly to the changeover of political generations, but after all, the victors of the initial accumulation of wealth usually change drastically during the second generation before, ultimately, leaving the scene. In Ukraine, they managed to make their exit relatively peacefully—war began, and nobody cared about them anymore. The question is who will replace them? Members of the security forces, as in Russia, or new people, as it may turn out in Ukraine? In any case, there are no guarantees. In this context, Kolomoiskyi's arrest looks quite incongruous. It is not in Zelenskyy's ethos to make arrests, especially since Kolomoiskyi had not been heard from in some time. I know so far only one version of his arrest (I give no credence to Stanislav Belkovsky's exotic guess that Roman Abramovich promoted his man Rustem Umerov to the post of Minister of Defense of Ukraine. First, Umerov is not Abramovich's man, they are only related by the poisoned atmosphere surrounding the March 2022 negotiations. Moreover, Ukraine's Minister of Defense Oleksii Reznikov had long been criticized, although the outcome of the war in the case of Ukraine is decided by the Ukrainian Armed

Forces and generals on the ground, not by the Minister of Defense, whose job is merely to honestly distribute Western aid. I say this noting that I have always liked Reznikov personally, although my opinion is my private matter.) One version is as follows: the U.S. allegedly demands something be done about the oligarchs, and since Kolomoiskyi has been banned from entering the United States, Anthony Blinken accuses him of corruption and attempting to undermine American democracy. Generally speaking, Kolomoiskyi is a thorn in the Americans' side. So the U.S. tries to impose two unpopular decisions on Zelenskyy in order to position themselves advantageously before their own elections: first, to hold a presidential election, which is directly prohibited by the Ukrainian constitution in wartime, and secondly, to arrest figures of the shadow economy, above all, the oligarchs who, as we recall, were Ukraine's saviors in 2014.

That's the story going around, I'm just the messenger here. We all passionately want American assistance to Ukraine to be ideological and selfless. But apparently, Zelenskyy, as three political commentators have written to me independently and without collusion, was forced into choosing between a rock and a hard place.

Now wouldn't that be a trick if independent Ukraine were able not only to defeat Russia, but to slip out from under American control? I don't like people being sent to prison. Look what that drove Russia to.

COMMENTARY FROM DNIPRO: *I showed what is written above to some of my good friends, with whom I do not always agree at all. I have more of these friends in Dnipro than anywhere else in the world, more even than in Odesa, and certainly more than in Moscow. Here is the commentary of one of Dnipro's best writers.—D. B.*

Regarding Kolomoiskyi. IMHO, of course, he is precisely Karabas Barabas. He has always been a puppeteer, and the owner of a circus. He dealt harshly with rebellious puppets.

Ukraine in 2014 was fortunate that its interests coincided with Kolomoiskyi's. Had they not matched, bad things could have happened.

Is Ihor a patriot? I think so. Is there shrewdness in this? Undoubtedly.

Was President Zelenskyy his project? Partly yes. Ihor loves escapades like this. He is an actor at heart, a wonderful storyteller who loves to bring unusual situations into being simply out of his love for art. At the same time, he's always thinking about the benefits, calculating everything ten moves ahead.

They say he is an excellent chess player, and this is a special way of thinking.

Undoubtedly he foresaw all the opportunities that Zelenskyy's election would provide him, and contributed to this outcome in every possible way. But was he the architect of Zelenskyy's victory? I think not. Zelenskyy forged his success on his own. Kolomoiskyi-Benia [Krik] moved to take advantage of this success. He wasn't the only one trying to do that. All the oligarchs wanted a ride on this horse. Everyone was rebuffed. But then his past, his fearsome influence, his odiousness, his remoteness from current political projects all worked against him. As well as his reputation as a good player, currently in a defenseless state.

He has no partner who can take his side. He has no place to escape to because the investigation in the U.S. cut off his ability to travel. His methods of solving business conflicts were always taken without regard to morality, the law or the preservation of relationships. He trampled on every callus that was within a reachable distance.

He was troublesome for Poroshenko and Putin, and he remained troublesome for Zelenskyy. He is troublesome for everyone.

And he deserves the reputation. He's a scoundrel, boorish, charming, arrogant, cruel, and occasionally sentimental.

He is a relic of the 1990s, who has not been changed by any subsequent upgrades.

XII. MAIDAN

February 2014 was a turning point in Ukrainian history: the second Maidan ten years after the first, Yanukovych's escape, and the peaceful revolution (the victims of which, however, were civilians, dubbed the "heavenly hundred." To be precise, 106 people died, most of them on February 20). In Ukraine itself, disputes still rage about who shot at civilians: opponents of Maidan claim that the provocations came from the rebels (who, naturally, were sponsored by the West). There is a version about Russian snipers participating in the shooting of protesters.

> **RUSSIAN EDITOR'S NOTE**: I am absolutely sure that this is true . . . It's just that I knew a woman who was a military doctor who participated in all of Russia's dirty military tricks (and continues to participate in them now). She lived in the same complex with us on Bolshaya Pushkarskaya St. in Moscow. She disappeared during Maidan. Then reappeared. We had a serious argument. She yelled that I failed to see the Bandera beasts, and how they hammered our boys who had fought in Chechnya. I quickly calmed down and asked: "Excuse me, but what were our boys with combat and, presumably, sniper experience, doing in Kyiv? . . ."
>
> "Well, they . . ." my acquaintance began to answer automatically, then shut up. "You don't need to know that," she said, then turned around and quickly left.

The agreement with Yanukovych to abandon the storming of Maidan was broken, the opposition went on the offensive, and Russia began exaggerating the version that a peaceful resolution of the situation was unprofitable primarily to the West. (Vladimir Putin has repeated this regularly for eight years, claiming that the West first of all deceived Russia, because on the eve of February 20, he allegedly gave guarantees for a compromise, and for new presidential elections.) The case is not closed beyond question, although in

October 2015, the then Prosecutor General of Ukraine Vladyslav Kutsenko declared his unequivocal confidence in an investigation establishing the guilt of former President Yanukovych, who ordered the use of military weapons.

But the problem of the "Kyiv snipers," about which an entire book could be written, does not fall within the scope of our current consideration. We are interested in the position of Zelenskyy and the Block during the stormy days of Maidan, and after the annexation of Crimea, undertaken by Russia on February 27 to March 1, 2014, according to a long-standing plan of the General Staff.

One of the paradoxes of Zelenskyy's position is that the military clash with Russia fell at the feet of a politician who is hardly the most radical in Ukraine. On the contrary, he came to power on a wave of fatigue caused by the sluggish war of the years 2014 to 2021. He always emphasized his loyalty to the east of Ukraine, to Donetsk, to the Russian language. He traveled to Russia and performed there almost more often than any other Ukrainian performer. He starred in Russian films. He preferred to speak Russian among family and friends. *Block 95* traditionally mocked Ukrainian nationalism and the forced transfer of state business into the Ukrainian language. Even in the days of Maidan, when Ukrainian society was extremely united, he assumed a compromise position. In December 2013, at a relatively peaceful New Year celebration, when *Block 95* ran its traditional holiday show, Zelenskyy made an introductory speech: "It's amazing: four thousand people in the center of Kyiv—and there is no Berkut!" ("Berkut," or "Golden Eagle," is the Ukrainian equivalent of Russia's OMON riot police. The audience laughed amiably, there was still a month and a half left before the confrontation became an armed uprising.) Zelenskyy's best joke about Maidan caused a friendly shout of approval: "Many now ask: will this Maidan be the same as the one in 2004? I will answer in genuine Ukrainian: 'Tak mae byt'" ("It just might be"). The Ukrainian phrase of "it just might be" reverberates as a pun with a Russian word for "fuck," and may be translated into English roughly as: "You ask, will it be tough? Yes, it will be puff" (although that is much softer). He then spoke words that came back to bite him more than once:

"As always, everything is done via one specific passage, an amazing place! All roads lead to it, all money is kept there, and hands grow out of it too! How proud we are to possess this passage too!" Russians gloated because, de facto, he called Ukraine an asshole (to do anything via a certain "passage" is a Russian idiom denoting the most absurd and time-consuming manner of action). But for *Block 95*, and for Ukrainian humor in general, this was no big deal—it was Putin who insisted on nauseating seriousness in talking about the motherland, never realizing that this is a trait of idiots. Russian folklore puts it this way: "So serious, important, businesslike, as if he wants to fart from his head."

On March 1, during the broadcast of the Television News Service, Zelenskyy addressed Yanukovych personally, in Russian (although the presenter spoke in Ukrainian):

> I will speak harshly, setting all jokes aside. Mr. Yanukovych! I know you personally, we have met many times. You are a strong man. You more than once have appealed to my reason and said that *Block 95* must not make such harsh jokes. I paid no attention. But, you never closed *Block 95* down. You were wise then, and strong. Today you must remember that you are strong, and step aside. You are no longer a part of history. Everyone in the West, and the East, and in my Kryvyi Rih, agrees on this. Don't allow separatism to become a possibility. Second. I want to appeal to the current administration. I may say many unflattering things about them, but I will not do it on air, on a respected channel. If people in eastern Ukraine and Crimea want to speak Russian, leave them alone. That is their right. Language never makes people quarrel, it binds them. I have Jewish blood. I speak Russian. But I am a citizen of Ukraine, and I love this country. Third. You said everyone in our government is from Donetsk. But the government presently includes everyone but people from Donetsk. And yet you said that the government would consider the interests of the entire nation, including Donetsk. I also want to address Mr. Putin. Dear Vladimir Vladimirovich, I ask you not to allow the undertaking of any military action. We truly are brotherly

peoples. I know that millions of wonderful people live in Russia. We have the same blood. If you want, if you need it, I am ready to beg you, to get down on my knees, but do not bring Ukraine to its knees. And I want to appeal to Ukrainians. Friends. We are a great people. You are a great people. We all love each other madly. No Europe, no Russia—think only of yourselves. If God does not help us, may reason help us. We love each other madly. I love you (the last words being spoken in Ukrainian).

How many times Zelenskyy was reminded of these words that he was ready to kneel before Putin—if only Putin would not bring Ukraine to its knees! I think today he himself would repudiate these words, but we must not forget that all this was spoken in the euphoria of victory, when Ukrainian society truly seemed to be united—at least in its passionate unwillingness to live as it had before. Back then it still seemed that everything could be negotiated. And, of course, neither Zelenskyy nor anyone else in Ukraine had any idea that the medals "For the Return of Crimea" were ratified in Russia not on March 21, 2014, as the official order of the Minister of Defense stated, but a month earlier.

On April 12, 2014, Zelenskyy delivered one of his most famous monologues in the *Evening Block*:

You know, not long ago those of us in *Block 95* watched Putin's speech in the Hall of Columns in Moscow. Everything there lacked pathos, unlike with Pshonka. Everything was more modest. *(Viktor Pshonka was the Prosecutor General of Ukraine under Yanukovych, who fled to Russia; he was under U.S. sanctions for corruption. Following his escape, Maidan activists entered his residence and discovered things that made Yanukovych's golden loaf of bread a trifle. Note how Zelenskyy manages to touch on all the items on the current agenda.—D. B.)* One of his phrases was utterly unforgettable: "Kyiv," he said, "is the mother of all Russian cities."

And you do your mother! . . . of all Russian cities!

That's why I have a question for Russians now: Kids, you are our children. (Ovation in the hall.) Why DO you say such nasty things about your mother in the news, huh? Your own mother? You say she can't live without you kids, that she'll take to walking the streets without you? I'll tell you what: she'd be happy to go out for unfettered walks! Only without you.

What is this? Normal children want to live without their mother. But no! You want to stay in our apartment. You even pinched a room from us recently. With a sea view. But your mom is independent, okay? Maybe she even found a boyfriend for herself. A European. Rich. And you want her to be with you and him, too. Your mom's not like that. She's not a party girl. She's loyal. She'll go with whoever has the most money. (Ovation.) Your mom is smart. Quit harassing your mom. You too, little Russian daughter. When she lived with Putin—your mother didn't say a word. Although she should have spanked your butt. Then she married Dima [Dmitry Medvedev], but kept living with Putin. Your Mom was mum. Is that clear? And then look what you pull, for God's sake. But Mother loves you with all her heart. She gives you milk and candy. But you stick your nose in the air. Your mother wants nothing from you, though. Just warmth. Gas. Cheap gas. She doesn't need expensive stuff, Mom isn't picky. Then, most importantly: "Mom herself is to blame,'" says her daughter. "Mom herself is to blame for signing a contract like that." Just one question, though—who signs contracts with their mother? It's your mother!

And then . . . you got so big. More land than anybody else. This great big place. But you had no place to put your ships except at Mom's ports. Right? And, incidentally, the mother of all these goods never once lost a thing for over twenty years. It's true. Well, for the first two years a few things may have disappeared, but after that—never again. What kind of kids are these? You're better off not giving birth to them at all. And so you want to tell them, from the bottom of your heart, as a mother to her children:

"Stop fucking with your mom."

But still, you know, I want to end on a positive note . . . Love . . . All of us here at *Block 95* believe that the time will come when Mom, and her kids, everyone, they'll grow up, get smarter, sit down honestly at the same table and we'll all drink tea together . . . On the summer terrace. On Mother's summer terrace.

When fighting began in June 2014 in Slaviansk, and the Russian reconnaissance officer Igor Girkin-Strelkov, a part-time historian-reenactor and a hack writer, headed there with his squad, Zelenskyy donated a million hryvnia for the needs of the armed forces, and began giving regular concerts at the front. Performing for the soldiers of the Ukrainian ATO (the war in the Donbas in Ukraine was called an anti-terrorist operation), he said: "Men! I bow low before you for protecting us from all kinds of riffraff. You're beautiful. You're the bravest people in our country." And he told the journalists covering his concert that his generation at one time had feared the army, had hidden from it, but he would willingly give his son to an army like this.

Zelenskyy uttered a curious prophecy in August 2014 in a *Block 95* parody program called "Pure News": "The Speaker of the Rada, Oleksandr Turchynov, promised that in five years Ukraine would join the EU and NATO. We advise the EU and NATO countries to strengthen their currency and social sphere, because in five years they will have much more serious problems."

Truly, both Zelenskyy and Turchynov had premonitions of the future.

XIII. *SERVANT OF THE PEOPLE*

It would be no exaggeration to say that it was the television series *Servant of the People* (2015–2018, three seasons, fifty-one episodes) that brought Zelenskyy to power.

In 2015, the Block group wanted to create its own comedy series. The Shefir brothers concluded that it should be a story about a people's president.

As mentioned previously, the strength of *Block 95*—with its mediocre taste and high percentage of rude jokes—has always been its excellent sense of what the biggest problems are. In Russia, the main advantage of comedy shows has always been the ability to bypass the most pressing issues. In Ukraine it was to touch upon them. In Ukraine in 2014 the main problem was the existence of a power vacuum. No one was willing to assume unprecedented responsibility, to show the country a new path, and at the same time brave the growing confrontation with Russia. In fact, the war was well underway, although both sides avoided calling it a war. It was in the conditions of this vacuum that power ended up in the hands of Petro Poroshenko—a man who was not afraid to expose himself to universal criticism. He was, perhaps, the optimal figure for this transitional period. But in order to move forward, a new national type of politician was needed. Who could represent this renewed Ukrainian nation, who was ready to stand at the head of the country? A comedy series took on this very serious issue, becoming popular and influential beyond anything anyone could have predicted at that time.

At first the Shefir brothers—the main ideologists of the Block team—undertook to find a director. They believed the best candidate to be Oleksii Kiriushchenko, who had gained fame as the director of the *My Fair Nanny* sitcom in Russia.

It was impossible to walk around Kyiv with Kiriushchenko: every second person wanted to have a photo taken with him, while all the rest wanted-ed autographs (sometimes asking for one from me, too). Before becoming a director he had graduated from the Shchukin Institute of the Vakhtangov Theater in Moscow, where he met Sergei Makovetsky, another popular Russian actor of Ukrainian heritage, born in Kyiv. Kiriushchenko still subconsciously imitates his intonation, and both look somewhat alike. He worked quite a bit in film, mainly in secondary comic roles. He finally got the chance to try himself out as a director in 2004, something he had been striving for since he left the theater institute in Dnipropetrovsk without graduating. Working for the Amedia Studio, he directed the Russian remake of the American *Nanny* sitcom.

My Fair Nanny brought Russian (and Ukrainian) fame to Anastasia Zavorotniuk, a graduate of the Moscow Art Theater studio school, about whom no one knew anything at that time. She got the part because of her sparkly appearance, and marvelous ability to imitate the Ukrainian accent. Kiriushchenko recalled that Zavorotniuk had never starred in comedies before—and that is precisely what he focused on. Never once playing for laughs, she looked extremely natural in her role, and millions of viewers fell in love with her version of a *Gastarbeiter* nanny. Kiriushchenko had been friends with members of the Block since 2011, when he played in the fifth and sixth seasons of *The Matchmakers* TV series. He participated in the production of a dozen Russian TV series, including the very-successful *Voronin*. He had a well-known peculiarity: he actively participated in the adaptation of scripts, sometimes rewriting them entirely. In fact, he invented most of the plot twists of *My Fair Nanny* himself, and he constantly improvised on the set of *The Matchmakers*.

At first, the Shefirs' offer did not interest Kiriushchenko precisely because it was so banal. "I immediately did a search for the words "a simple man becomes president," and pulled up seven pages of films and TV series on this very plot." But that precisely was the challenge—to find a purely Ukrainian twist to the situation. Although Kiriushchenko had lived and worked in Moscow for twenty years, he continued to consider himself a Ukrainian, and during the filming of the series he received a residence permit in Ukraine, since he spent most of his time there. The filming of the first season ran from June to October 2015 in an atmosphere of cheerful madness. The script was rewritten, or even improvised right on the set, and the producer was Zelenskyy himself. No one in the Block had any doubts about the main role—the role was written specifically for Zelenskyy, who magnificently possessed the features of a small man and an authoritarian leader. I asked one specific question of almost everyone who stood at the origins of *Servant of the People,* and of many of the program's original viewers: Did anyone have a feeling then, in 2015, that they were joining together to begin sculpting the future president of Ukraine? Everyone, the director included, answered amicably: "Yeah, right!" Most likely, if someone had posed the task of grooming a future President Zelenskyy right from the beginning (in Russia, for example, that's exactly what would have been done), nothing would have come of it, either artistically or politically. But the Block had a different task—to bring the so-called common man to the screen while emphasizing how awkward he was. If you think about it, the main character—a history teacher named Vasily Petrovich Goloborodko—was the ideal choice. His was middle class, a thoroughly common man with common parents. According to the psychological type, he was a cultured individual, whom, however, could easily be pushed out of his comfort zone, making him susceptible to scandals and exploits.

I suspect that the Shefirs' idea was most influenced not by foreign projects about a simple man in the presidential office, but by the Russian film *The Geographer Drank Up the Globe* (directed by Alexander Veledinsky based on Alexei Ivanov's novel). Veledinsky, one of the scriptwriters of the cult TV series, *Brigade*, managed to offer the public the almost perfect image of a modern hero: a drinking, unsuccessful, but principled and charming lumpen intellectual, who, having long been unemployed, must settle for becoming a schoolteacher of geography. In *Servant of the People*, Goloborodko's relationship with his students, as well as the main types of students in his class, almost perfectly copy the school line of *Geographer*. As the teacher named Sluzhkin, whom Ivanov called the new Prince Myshkin, the famous Russian actor Konstantin Khabensky offered a wonderful combination of intellectual nervousness and lumpen irascibility. Zelenskyy had to expand his acting range significantly for his character: *Servant of the People* is not a sitcom, but a tragic farce, and in some episodes Zelenskyy works no worse than Khabensky. It would be fitting to dream about what kind of cult film might have emerged from *Geographer* if it had touched on the serious political issues of the time, but the plot about a teacher had its own effect: Khabensky was soon named the head of the Moscow Art Theater, Russia's main theater, its artistic showcase. And, with proper promotion, he might reach . . . but no, he couldn't, of course. An actor, who is also half-Jewish, could not have been elected for anything in post-Putin Russia. It would require a long period of schooling in freedom and social experimentation for an actor who had played a school teacher to be perceived in Russia as a national hero who eventually reaches the height of power.

Despite the speedy pace of production, *Servant of the People* was well-made, on a par with a good full-length movie (based on the series' second season, a two-hour cinema release was made for the Ukrainian market). The series was filmed on a RED camera, providing up to 120 frames per second. This makes it possible to achieve truly cinematic image quality in digital format. The series cost 15 million hryvnia (that is, about $700,000 — you can't even shoot a mini-series in the States for this amount). Its premiere took place on November 16, 2015, and *Servant of the People* became the highest-rated series of the year, ahead of sports broadcasts in terms of share (the rating of each episode was about 10, the share was 25). The target audience of the series was eighteen to fifty-four year olds, but it overcame these limits, becoming a favorite among the elderly and teenagers alike.

To an outsider's eye—and the series was picked up in over twenty countries, including the entire post-Soviet space—it was far from a masterpiece. However, it draws you in immediately, and you want to see President Goloborodko again and again: Zelenskyy is endlessly charming. Secondly, the popularity of the product was largely explained by its relevance. (I would be lying if I explained my interest in Zelenskyy's figure solely by lofty literary considerations: I also want to speak out about a problem that concerns everyone, a desire that is quite natural for a writer.) The main thing in *Servant of the People* is not the jokes, sometimes quite barbed, and sometimes predictable and banal. The main thing is the urgency of the problem, the ability to touch on the most pressing issues, from the problem of language to ineradicable corruption; *Servant of the People* is a kind of communique from the viewer's subconscious. Everything that frightens, worries, or shames one is spoken aloud here, so that the series becomes an act of collective therapy. But in addition to this direct addressing of topics, a unique intonation in *Servant* made it a huge breakthrough in—and I do not fear overstating this—Ukrainian art as a whole. The creators of the series do not separate themselves from either the heroes or the audience. They don't merely ridicule specific politicians or Ukrainian politics with its corruption, shameless PR, and provincial show-offs. It is a situation of firm and even proud knowledge of the best and worst about oneself; it provides a feeling of a collective social experiment in which the entire nation takes part. This experiment—the departure of a part of the former Soviet Union on an independent and risky voyage—is executed with many mistakes and stupidities, and yet we regret nothing. We are all in the same boat, and our sense of self-respect does not allow us to harbor any illusions about ourselves. We allow ourselves to say out loud whatever we want. We work for our audience, not for foreign public opinion. The slogan of the series could be taken from Goloborodko's half-drunken speech: "Citizens! We're all going to be screwed now." It's very funny, but the main thing is it's true.

A skilled advertising campaign should be added to the accolades for the talented work of the screenwriters, actors, and director who constantly played on the genre of the American political thriller (or sitcom). Elections for the Upper Rada, the Ukrainian parliament, were held on October 24, 2015, and an advertisement for "people's President Goloborodko" appeared simultaneously on the streets. Postcards with mocking slogans were distributed in Kyiv: "I will lustrate right up to my immediate predecessors"; "We'll tell the officials about officials taking benefits"; and most importantly, "May teachers live like presidents, and may the president live like a teacher." Thus, the virtual candidate Goloborodko (whose name, according to Zelenskyy, was taken from an old Kryvyi Rih friend of the Block) first announced his presidential ambitions, and the series began coming to life during the very first season. But there was a huge difference between 2015 and 2017 (the year of the premiere of the second season): throughout these two years, Ukrainian President Poroshenko had managed to disappoint many of his former supporters. This is natural for a country whose government changes regularly. *Servant of the People* was a parody in 2015, but by 2017 it was the campaign program of a future president. The slogan about "the story of a future president" was no longer perceived as silly. Many began to take it seriously: Why not? It was quite in the spirit of the new Ukrainian statehood, within the tastes of a country where everything happening was happening for the first time. By 2019, when Kiriushchenko unleashed the utterly untethered third season, pulling out all the stops, Zelenskyy was already the most obvious presidential candidate. The third season guaranteed him victory—Poroshenko was starring in nothing, while Kiriushchenko himself, starring in the caricatured role of the previous president Sergei Pavlovich, was unmistakably Poroshenko-like.

The plot is elementary: the school history teacher Goloborodko speaks the bitter truth to a colleague about the situation in Ukraine in the aftermath of the Maidan revolution, which disappointed many of its supporters, for money was still scarce, corruption did not decrease, and the smartest people remained the poorest. This conversation was overheard and captured on a mobile phone by one of Goloborodko's students. The viral video brings him unprecedented popularity on the internet, and, in the next presidential election, unexpectedly and with no preparation, the foul-mouthed teacher, the proverbial salt of the earth, wins. The gray-haired head of the administration (Stanislav Boklan) comes to him and asks him to take office: he won the presidential election in a landslide.

Goloborodko is divorced and now lives with his parents and sister. He is a good son, but his parents sincerely believe they now have a chance to live in luxury. In the best traditions of the post-Soviet bourgeoisie, they hire a designer and begin turning their suburban three-room apartment into a warehouse of sundry luxuries. Goloborodko reins in his father with difficulty and returns everything to the status quo.

The success of *Servant of the People* is to a great extent ensured by the fact that virtually everything is an object of its irony: its satire attacks everything from the Ukrainian national character to Ukrainian corruption. The satire of *Block 95* never had forbidden topics, and this was the key to its über-popularity. Intonations of the grotesque and emotionality dominated in *Servant of the People*, but there was never a whiff of that self-satisfaction that permeated Russia's cultural products.

XIV. THE ACTOR

Evaluating Zelenskyy as an actor is no trivial task, for he is not really an actor in the classical sense. He is a character, a stand-up comedian. He usually plays himself, even when pretending for fun to be Napoleon (as in *Napoleon vs. Rzhevsky* in 2012). His work in *I, You, He, She* (2018)—the best and most lyrical of his roles, despite the fact that the film is full of frank, rather self–parodic nonsense—is a self-portrait. This is his fundamental character, features of which he imparted to the character of Novoseltsev in a remake of the legendary Soviet movie *Office Romance*. It is his most interesting acting achievement. Previous actors who engaged in political careers—say, Ronald Reagan, and Arnold Schwarzenegger—sharply separated the political game from life. And, anyway, it cannot be said that Reagan created a fundamentally new type of character in cinema. Zelenskyy is another matter: Ukrainians chose his hero, the mask that he exploited in television shows created by the Block (producing and performing more than twenty of them), and in feature films. This is no easy mask to don, nothing like this has ever happened before.

The easiest and stupidest thing to say would be that Zelenskyy plays a traditional "little man," but Goloborodko is not a little man in any way. He is, rather, a hero who is not yet aware of his power, and Zelenskyy inspired his nation with precisely that identity during the election campaign: "We ourselves don't yet realize our capabilities. They are dormant in us. But at some critical moment we will—boom!" The main plot of *Servant* is a story about how a person of emphatically unheroic appearance and profession, once assuming the highest position in the land, demonstrates the best human qualities, and above all dedication, determination, and strength.

And that, basically, is how it turned out. Zelenskyy has always played a common man, into whose lap great historical opportunity falls. Things are not so simple in *Rzhevsky*, either, for all his roles have an unexpected quality: He does not portray Napoleon, but a comedian who happens to play Napoleon. I think Ukraine saw itself in Zelenskyy—a nation that had a chance to achieve greatness. The people showed that first during

Maidan, then again in the unprecedented elections of 2019 when they made the unpredictable choice, and finally—during the war. Zelenskyy plays a common man, a modest professional in whom slumbers a budding hero, a comedian in whom a tragedian abides. Ukraine rightly saw itself reflected in this hero.

Everything about Zelenskyy's acting technique is in good order. He is a strong pro, a versatile performer, and a good screenwriter (who, by the way, created what was most likely the most successful TV series of the century's first decade—*The Matchmakers*). He has viewers eating out of his hand, easily establishing contact with even the most difficult audience. But even all these qualities would not be enough to account for his across-the-board success in television, drama, and film. His theme as an actor—the way he steps out of a role, his evolution from farce into tragedy—coincided with tendencies at play in the society around him, and this always gives an artist the opportunity to raise everything up another notch to heroism. In a sense, the whole of Ukraine seconded Zelenskyy's path, the path of General della Rovere, who played a hero and believed he was a hero.

Look: a nation that is sometimes arrogantly, sometimes approvingly joked about, which tells highly irreverent jokes about itself, which created the capital of European humor—Odesa with its great literature and unfading myth—creates a new genre of European politics, namely the Maidan, in 2004. In 2014 it raises this genre to perfection. Maidan is a phenomenon not only and not so much political as it is theatrical—it is very much theater. A "concert" runs continuously on Maidan Square in central Kyiv, and the speeches there are indistinguishable from sketches. The stage is never empty for a second. During the 2004 version of Maidan people could be beaten up. By the time of Maidan-2014 they could be killed (as more than a hundred were, the so-called "heavenly hundred" that Putin, with his craving for conspiracy, declared "sacral victims," and an American provocation).

Putin believes the whole Maidan concept was a staging of American special forces, although its most interesting feature was that it directed itself. Maidan was a revolution in the genre of a show, or, if you like, a show where the shooting was for real, as is the way that the country's image was changed for real too. *Block 95* was also a new genre, a stand-up comedy show that directly influenced the fate of Ukraine (note that most Ukrainian talk shows, primarily Savik Shuster's *Freedom of Speech*, also claimed to decide the fate of the authorities in live broadcasts). Ukrainian politics is a complex combination of a continuous show of cruel, occasionally blasphemous parody, risk-taking, and heroism. The weakness of officialdom, the pop nature of the state narrative (especially as performed by Yanukovych, and partly as stylized by Poroshenko) leads to the broad triumph of populist political activity, the politics of the people. And just as corruption is a folk model of the economy, so too were Ukrainian political shows culminating in Maidan, a folk model of grand politics, a revolution in the form of a round–the-clock concert, a rock festival on Kreshchatyk Street.

I have often said that Yury Lyubimov, at Moscow's Taganka Theater in 1971, isolated the main theme of *Hamlet*, and Vladimir Vysotsky played it more accurately than anyone else has: that is, a strong man in a weak position, a genius, an aristocrat and a thinker, driven into the unusual, humiliating space of palace intrigues, gossip, and secret villainy. Under Hamlet the elder, known to us mainly in the guise of a ghost, the Danish court lived according to the laws of the blockbuster, it was a heroic genre promoting military virtues. Under Claudius, the court became a place of conspiracies, lies, and debauchery, and in this space the prince, a philosopher and a warrior, is completely lost. He becomes entangled in sticky nets, like a spider's web, and is forced to act in an unusual genre for him: He was born to fight and rule, but must kill and pretend to be crazy. The basis of Shakespeare's theatricality (and this is the leitmotif of all his plays) is the image of a man in an unusual role: the bon vivant and frivolous Romeo falls in love seriously; the honest, straightforward military commander Othello becomes the victim of a petty intriguer; the witty Hamlet portrays a madman; a beggar king wanders around a desert; the honest warrior Macbeth becomes a tyrant and usurper. All of Shakespeare is about how we resist roles that are imposed upon us. Zelenskyy's case is similar, but essentially the opposite of *Hamlet*. This is a game of promotion: the comedian turns out to be Napoleon, a tragic role is imposed upon him. And Ukraine rightly recognizes itself in this mirrored image: This European province finds itself playing a lead role, not only in Europe, but in the world. This nation that had long positioned itself as a collection of merry, thieving fellows like Homa Brutus in Nikolai Gogol's mystical short story "Vyi," discovers that it possesses chivalrous features and takes on the guise outlined by Gogol: a synthesis of Cossack freemen and members of the Kyiv-Mohyla Academy.

Zelenskyy, from his first stand-up gigs, has always played a man with an inner drama, initially driven by fate into small and comedic roles, but always ready to stand tall. He was cast as both D'Artagnan (2005) and Napoleon for a reason: his heroic essence, pardon the allusion, was as a protuberance all could see. Maybe it came through in his unexpectedly hoarse, rugged voice, maybe in his manner of speaking harsh, angry, caustic words in the middle of a corporate concert. All of his stand-up monologues are those of an anecdotal character suddenly speaking in a sober and tragic manner. Zelenskyy outgrew KVN because KVN tried to be anything but satire; it cornered itself in the framework of a student skit, even when played out on a sinking Titanic. The theme of Zelenskyy's acting is the transformation of an anecdote into a tragedy, of a stand-up routine into a sermon. He did not even have to change his approach during the election campaign because Ukrainian politics already functioned as an entertainment.

Oddly enough, Zelenskyy had a direct analogue in Russia, who, had he possessed the basic human qualities, could have taken a similar path and become a spiritual leader. I am, naturally, not speaking about Mikhail Yevdokimov, who was a good governor and humorist in Barnaul. He never pretended to be anything more. I am speaking about Yevgeny Grishkovets, a stand-up performer with claims to being a dramatic actor who was also a playwright, a performer of his own solo shows, which were wonderful monologues in a club format, but instantly broke down into sugary kitsch as soon as they began claiming to be more. Grishkovets was remarkably accurate in his details and conditions, and if he had possessed a world-view, that is, if he had dared to say a few serious and important things to the spectator's face, he could have had a completely different audience. But Grishkovets broke into pathos at the first opportunity, and, furthermore, he was the classic Russian character of an "underground man." That is, while portraying modesty and unpretentiousness, he sincerely considered him-self a great playwright and artist all in one. On top of everything else, he had the weakness of speaking ill of his colleagues, for example, about the Quartet And theater group, which excluded him from working in a team. Zelenskyy without the Block, without the ideal working atmosphere within it, and without a brain trust of screenwriters, would at best be just one more among many other author-performers. Zelenskyy had something that is practically non-existent in Russia (or only occasionally occurs under the external influence of totalitarian oppression): the sense of an ensemble, an orchestra, camaraderie.

As a group, Quartet And had decent chances. They grew up and studied together in Odesa, and, incidentally, never feared extremely harsh politi-cal jokes in their *Election Day* performance. But they deliberately refrained from serious political statements, and, even after the outbreak of the war, never said anything specific, calling only on both sides not to shoot at ci-vilians. I have a soft spot for Quartet And, and I understand their difficul-ties. But I sincerely do not understand how in this situation they could not return home to Odesa. Maria Galina, the first-rate poet and novelist, and her husband, the poet and translator Arkady Shtypel abandoned all their matters in Moscow and left immediately. Quartet clearly was not eager to imitate the Block—realizing, probably, that in Russia the actor will always remain a "clown." But this, I'm afraid, is barking up the wrong tree: it is why actors will remain clowns, because they won't dare to become anything more. One digs a tunnel like this from both ends.

I can't help but mention Semion Slepakov, now classified as a foreign agent by the Russian government, and a resident of Israel. Slepakov truly had something to lose, he was one of the main stars of the popular Comedy Club show. Up to a certain point, the careers of Zelenskyy and Slepakov developed in parallel; they even filmed their most important TV series at the same time. Zelenskyy produced and created *Servant of the People*—Slepakov worked on *House Arrest*, which was equally relevant for Russia. In it, Pavel Derevyanko played the role of a mayor who was becoming increasingly popular. The difference between Russia and Ukraine is especially obvious here: Derevyanko did not and could not become a national hero, let alone president. The situation of house arrest itself is radically different from the situation of elections. That's why Slepakov, for all the popularity of his songs, felt completely dependent on the authorities—and in January 2021 he spoke out quite harshly about protest rallies in Moscow. Let us quote his own words, although it is no pleasant task to remind a beloved author of his failures:

> Your righteous and heart-rending howl
> Is unpleasant to me as a poet,
> But, on reflection, I'll answer your
> Aggression by making the sign of my sexual organ.
> Still, something else interests me—
> Your point is infinitely liberal,
> And you look with such high morality
> At life in Russia tomorrow:
> The shackles will fall and the people will sigh
> Feeling freedom, breathing free . . .
> The dictator will be brought to justice,
> And life will take a new turn . . .
> But I see a different scenario:
> What will come rule my country,
> If the people's anger should flare up?
> Only scum of a more reckless kind.
> But this is merely my opinion—
> It claims not to be truth.

The result of this compromise became clear quite soon: Slepakov has not written a single hit since. He himself ended up abroad immediately after the outbreak of the war, and would appear not to have said a single word in support of Putin. However, he did recently tell the popular Russian video blogger Yury Dud that he is more inclined to like Putin than to dislike him. This, precisely, is the answer to the question about the prospects for the Russian creative intelligentsia.

As for Zelenskyy, from the very beginning he and his team worked at turning anecdotes into absurdities, stand-up monologues into theater, theater into revolution, and comedians into tragedians. I currently teach a course titled "How Gogol Invented Ukraine" at an American university. In other words, we explore how the most important Ukrainian novelist constructed a national myth. Nikolai Gogol is credited with the honor of creating the first "little man" in Russian literature, not counting Alexander Pushkin's briefly sketched Samson Vyrin. But literature is not interested in the little man, it does not sympathize with him. It wants great passions, not snotty, condescending tenderness. Gogol's story is about how Akaky Akakievich becomes a two-meter-tall ghost, ripping fur coats off of officials' backs; Gogol's fate reveals a narrator of down-home tales from the village of Dikanka who emerges as a European Homer. The exceeding of one's own limitations, not geographical, of course, but personal and creative, is a central theme of Ukrainian culture, from Lesia Ukrainka's dramatic poem "The Stone Master" to Maryna and Serhii Diachenko's novel *Vita Nostra*. A Ukrainian enters European culture telling the jokes of a provincial relative, holding a bottle of vodka and a chunk of bacon fat, and suddenly discovers that he or she is the only person in the room who possesses a personal myth, while everyone else in attendance has long since buried their myths, and generally lives in the material world. This is why Anton Chekhov, already being the leading novelist and playwright of the European Art Nouveau, the direct heir and superior of Maeterlinck and Maupassant, shyly stated in his letters: "I am a lazy Ukrainian peasant."

The butt of all jokes, the Ukrainian *khokhol*, or peasant bumpkin, suffered condescending attitudes only for a time. The nation leaped out of one genre into another and reconfigured itself. This transition of genres, pulling one's own self out of the swamp of provincial comedy by the hair, became Zelenskyy's primary internal theme, and it resonated with the development of the Ukrainian character.

The fundamental mistake made by Putin and his cronies in the Ozero dacha cooperative was that they geared up for a battle with lowly Ukrainian peasants and buffoons—but these people had already become full-fledged Ukrainians with a Joker at their lead.

P.S. *The editor of this book's Russian-language version, one of my most beloved literary critics, whose name, for obvious reasons, I cannot state, wrote in the margins of this paragraph.—D. B.* I am in a quandary. Maybe it's because I really love Quartet And (one of the few films I know by heart is *Election Day*). Maybe it's because two of the Quartet members were born in Odesa (Leonid Barats and Rostislav Chait), but Kamil Larin is from Volgograd, while Alexander Demidov is from Sverdlovsk. Yes . . . It's worth beginning with this: it is not entirely clear why an Odesan IN THIS SITUATION must be in Odesa? What changes fundamentally? Ilya Novikov is not from Kyiv. Ildar Dadin is not from Ternopil. Sebastian Hafner was not English. To emphasize ORIGINS is not the point. If I was in the U.S. and the Ukrainians were to attack Moscow, I would not return to Moscow. I would say, as Thomas Mann said about the Anglo-American bombing of Germany: "It serves the Germans right. They deserve it." I'll say the same thing here, if it gets too hot. Now another thing. I understand . . . I understand—Hafner said in his last interview: "Internal emigration is nonsense. Every intellectual who did not emigrate worked for Nazi Germany. He didn't paint, shoot, or draw anything Nazi? Yes, but he created the scenery of a normal, ordinary life, for which Goebbels was so grateful to him . . ." BUT . . . the same Hafner in the same interview remarks: "EVERYONE could not emigrate, and with what, and with whom would Germany have remained if all the non-Nazis or anti-Nazis had left?" Now, regarding Quartet And. Unlike the Russian writers Maria Galina, Yulia Belomlinskaya, and Arkady Shtypel, they are satirists or humorists, entertainers. They need an audience not just for success, but because they speak the language of the audience and they feed off the language of their audience. If they went to any other country, they would have to change their profession. Humor, especially stand-up comedy, is very national. Nobody reproached Werner Fink (the famous cabaret player) for staying in Germany.

For my part, I believe that changing a profession is not always the worst form of payment for saving one's face. But I also understand that this opinion is not universal, and Quartet And always evokes in me the best of feelings. What are we to do if the key to the interrelationship of the creative intelligentsia in Russia and in Ukraine precisely mirrors the relationship of Quartet And and the Block, as does everything else in this war?

XV. THE NARRATOR KING

Nassim Taleb (the author of *The Black Swan*) earned money and fame with a simple, yet precise notion, from which all his subsequent books followed. The future is always a) absolutely logical when viewed in hindsight, and b) equally unpredictable.

Zelenskyy's election as president of Ukraine by a landslide would have seemed incredible just a year earlier, although in retrospect it was absolutely logical, and reflected two closely related trends that the world has not yet comprehended or even really noticed. But the main result of what is happening now in Ukraine is precisely the result of these two trends rising to history's surface.

First: the world is tired of systemic politicians, bureaucrats, the deep state, hereditary career diplomats, and professional economists. They can exist somewhere in the depths, as befits a deep state, carrying out their activities, some of which may even save lives, but it's the specialists who should know about them, not the voting citizens. Second: the head of state becomes a showman, actor, and writer—one who creates narratives. A nation is not interested in following real politics, or to put it more precisely, politics descend to the regional level, where the citizens themselves decide on the elimination of a monument or the construction of a bridge. Meanwhile, the so-called big politics is now formed by those whose professional duty is composing plots.

As paradoxical as it may be, Donald Trump's 2016 victory in the United States was dictated by the same two factors. He was not only not a systemic politician, he was anti-systemic. He was not merely a freak, but was a professional showman whose only truly successful activity was running a TV show. Trump and Zelenskyy demonstrate, of course, a different level of showmanship—Zelenskyy is a much more gifted actor. But I do not advise overestimating his education. Furthermore, Trump's ability to learn is not bad, only his conceit is greater. This is, first of all, age-related, and secondly—it is typically American.

Here we must introduce the concept of the narrator king, since this is a new type of leader present not only in Ukraine.

RUSSIAN EDITOR'S NOTE IN THE MARGINS: Actually, the "narrator king" (as you describe him) is a constitutional king. A king who represents. And you know: the first narrative king was . . . Wilhelm II. He was, basically, a narrator. Tirpitz built the fleet, Ludendorff ran the war, and Rathenau oversaw the economy. As for Wilhelm, he handed out memes. When he repealed the exceptional law against the Social Democrats, he said publicly, "I want to be the king of the poor" (it sounds ambiguous, but everyone understood the emperor correctly). War began and again there was a meme: "I presently do not know parties, I know only Germans!" You have touched on a very fruitful topic.

As always, the United States was first with Trump, but the first Trump turned out to be a failure (although we shall see who laughs last when the new U.S. President is inaugurated in January 2025). We will call the narrator king a ruler who, leaving professionals to deal with economics, industry, and military affairs, is himself engaged in what gives society its Plot of Existence.

This key concept was introduced not by a political scientist, but by a writer. "The plot of existence is more important than any economic laws, or rather, economic laws themselves can work only when a person has a plot of existence. If depositors stop believing in the plot of the bank's existence, the bank bursts. If the citizens of a country do not sense the state's plot of existence, it will fall apart. Give me a plot! Give me a plot!"

This is from a 1997 story by Fazil Iskander. And when I asked the author about this plot—thank God I had such an opportunity—he replied: "My dear man! Had I sensed even a shadow of a plot for Russia, I would be doing nothing else right now." But there was no such plot, and when it appeared, it was the plot of a caveman's revenge, of war. One must possess a minimal literary ability in order to invent a plot.

Undoubtedly, the narrator king rules. Although he rules not by gross material things, but by the moods and hopes of his subjects. He puts them in the space of an artistic text, a series, a television show, and does not tend to such boring things as economics. The narrator is fundamentally different from the ideologist. The ideologist creates a system of control and demands—the narrator motivates citizens with the aid of what is IN-TERESTING, not useful or moral. Yakov Golosovker, the philosopher, mythologist, and author of a profound work on the phenomenon of what is interesting, postulates that the interesting lies a) outside of ethics, and b) outside of aesthetics. We label as aesthetic, i.e., beautiful, rather boring things like Proust or Shelley (there is no disputing taste; Golosovker gives some examples, you can pick others). Everything that is right and proper is ethical, but that is of little interest. Robert Sheckley confessed to me in an interview (I also talked to Sheckley!) that he would certainly go see a public execution. Is it good? No. But it's interesting!

Ideology always depends on ethics and often on aesthetics. The narrator has nothing to do with either. He makes sure the population is entertained and engaged. This is the main task of the authorities in the postmodern era: modernity tries to put everything under the control of reason. Postmodernity, on the contrary, distracts from it. In postmodernism, the main thing is that a person never gets bored. And here is another important consideration expressed by Konstantin Ernst, the CEO of Russian TV's Channel One, once again in conversation with the interesting author of these interesting lines: In modernism one wrote in words or colors, in postmodernism one writes in crowds. In modernism, art took to the streets; in postmodernism, it directly took on the organization of life, politics, and everyday life. Virtual reality replaced the tangible. Mankind has moved into the TV set. The main projects of writers of the postmodern era are the creation of narratives for readers. Zelenskyy achieved everything he wanted with his series, and then he wanted to take on the nation. I suspect this was not so much love of power, as it was a normal expansion of production.

It is another question that, by electing Zelenskyy, Ukrainians demonstrated a downright prescient intuition: any systemic politician in his place would soberly assess the prospects, estimate the chances of survival, and take advantage of the opportunities offered by the West. There is no doubt that if Zelenskyy had fled, it would not only have put an end to his political career, it would also, to a huge degree of probability, have undermined the Ukrainians' faith in victory. An actor cares most about how he looks. Running away would have looked bad.

Moreover, an actor is the only one who truly believes the words he speaks. Without this faith, the actor's performance will be unconvincing. It seems that this is the meaning the prophet puts in the words, "I revealed myself to those who did not ask for me." A professional actor possesses more opportunities to believe than a theologian. Similarly, the chances of an actor reaching the top in any particular profession are higher than those of a true professional. Peter Ustinov said in an interview with the very same author of these lines: "I don't know Russian words well, but I imitate the

Russian intonation so well that I give the impression of a Russian aristocrat, no matter what nonsense I may utter." Zelenskyy's facial expressions, his intonations, his T-shirt all told Ukrainians more than any of his speeches. And the nation believed it had acquired a heroic president, while Europe called him "Churchill in a T-shirt."

This is not the case of Ronald Reagan (who, when he was elected president, had not made a film in thirty years), and even less like the Arnold Schwarzenegger variant, who never claimed to have great acting talent. This is a fundamentally new emphasis in world politics: as everything in the world has diversified in recent years, so politics has increasingly divided into substantive and narrative aspects. The content is handled by the military (in whose affairs Zelenskyy does not interfere) and economists (Zelenskyy actually did not have an economic program, as discussed below). The president becomes a character who is interesting to watch, someone you want to look at, someone who can provide the voter a fascinating narrative. As such, the two main figures in Ukraine were the commander-in-chief of the Armed Forces Vitalii Zaluzhnyi, and the head of the presidential administration Andrii Yermak, while the two faces of Ukrainian politics were the professional actor and showman Zelenskyy, and the professional PR man Oleksii Arestovych (he has many other professions, but this one turned out to be the most trendy; it was not by chance that a spa salon was named after him, a place where they professionally relieve stress. He was not offended at all. On the contrary, he was flattered).

I am convinced that world politics will follow this path precisely: talented artists or fascinating storytellers will become presidents, and managers will implement policy. The nation should care not about pragmatic matters, nor about "arguing over taxes," as Pushkin put it, but rather about making life interesting. Zelenskyy is an indication of the brilliant prospects of the creative intelligentsia in the field of politics: the most successful leaders of the twenty-first century will be recruited from this setting.

XVI. ZELENSKYY AS A UKRANIAN

Now let's answer a fundamental question: can Zelenskyy be called the nation's leader?

The question has baffled most of my Ukrainian interlocutors, and this indicates that it hits a nerve. For Zelenskyy is a new type of leader: not one who leads the nation somewhere, but one who embodies its main features.

This does not mean that a leader in the sense of "one who leads" has finally become an anachronism, no. That will not happen soon. But Ukraine is not a country that can be led anywhere. Perhaps, in some sense, this is a minus. It is difficult to unite it in peacetime, and it is difficult for it to achieve consensus even on basic values. In general, Russia has provided it a unique opportunity to unite in hatred. No matter what the latest history textbook tells us, Ukraine was never anti-Russian, even after the Maidan of 2014. But it has become totally anti-Russian thanks to Vladimir Putin, who always achieves the opposite of what he strives for, no matter what he undertakes. He wanted to see Russia as the most influential force in the world—and he turned it into a rogue state; he wanted to defeat Chechnya—and subjugated Russia to it; he wanted to make Ukraine totally dependent—but made it more independent of everything Russian than Stepan Bandera—no lover of the northern neighbor—could ever have dreamed.

Ukraine, as we have known it since 1991, is proud of its non-authoritarianism, its town-hall-like Maidans, its networked way of governance (corruption is one of the forms of this popular self-government). Zelenskyy is not leading the country to victory—he corresponds to its desire not to submit, he serves as an expression and symbol of this desire. The peculiarity of the narrator king is not in his formulating a strategy and pointing out paths of progress. His main role is to serve for the whole world as the embodiment of the qualities that the nation most values today. The question of what these features are in the case of Zelenskyy allows us to answer the question of what Ukraine is in general: Zelenskyy, in a very timely fashion, created the image of the modern Ukrainian for the whole world, and he has not compromised that in any way yet. And since Ukraine today is the spiritual leader of the Slavs, these features are very important for world history.

There are many, and each individual can emphasize their own. But I would prefer to focus on five.

1. Arestovych has said that Zelenskyy's main quality is obstinacy. And this trait, which arises in many Ukrainian anecdotes, is truly part of his makeup. Zelenskyy is extremely proud and has always been exceptionally successful. As such it is easier for him to disappear than to retreat, it is easier for him to die than to lose. This vanity is not so much an actor's trait as it is something becoming of a producer. The actor is expected to have a flexible psyche, but Zelenskyy has been rather harsh and rigid in recent years. He has the fanatical tenacity of a provincial conquering the capital, and the pride of the leader of a country that is accustomed to assuming secondary roles in geopolitical affairs. Today, the world talks about Ukraine more than about America and China, because ultimately Ukraine holds the key to whether the world survives or perishes. Some do not admit this, but, honestly, it doesn't take great intelligence to see that.

2. Self-irony. For all the pathos that is inevitable in the present existential situation, Ukraine is perfectly capable of seeing itself from afar, of being aware of its shortcomings and vices. No one mocked its national complexes and self-delusions more persistently than *Block 95*, no one exposed Ukrainian folly more vividly than Zelenskyy. Obliged constantly to reinforce everyone's belief in victory, he never gets on a high horse. Even now he is still ready to mock himself and his surroundings, although the situation is clearly not conducive to humor. His sense of humor has turned black, and his cheerfulness has departed him. But, still, rather than seeing the tragedy of the war, Zelenskyy sees its absurdity as well. This is probably a key source of his mental health.

3. Artistry. Ukraine possesses a rich folkloric heritage. Nothing is done in Ukraine without a song, which, once again, has become the butt of countless jokes. The hero in this folkloric world is almost always a performer, a jokester, a storyteller. In Russia one usually sings criminal chansons or songs from popular Soviet films at holiday gatherings. In Ukraine folk songs ranging from the lyrical to the salacious remain a living element of any feast. The Ukrainian character presupposes an artistic reinterpretation of any situation, and this is due partly to another national trait—*ponty*, which we may render as *buffoonery*. I do not know how to translate this into foreign languages, there is no such word anywhere else. Self-presentation? But that is not so expressive. Bombast? This is true, but it's too negative. I think maybe it is a kind of aestheticization of life, which *a priori* assumes narcissism as a characteristic. But with such self-irony, "force is more expensive than money," and victory is certainly more important than life.

4. Independence. The love for exercising free will is the most stable trait in self-characterizations of Ukrainians. Zelenskyy does not tolerate being controlled. He is increasingly becoming his own director, his own producer, and his own image adviser (although not in matters of economics or military issues, which is important). Highly self-critical since he was a child, Zelenskyy has never been particularly tolerant of third-party criticism. And in light of the Soviet tradition of self-abuse and self-oppression, I tend to appreciate that. Mayakovsky formulated it wonderfully in a letter to a woman he loved: "I can do anything with pleasure if it's of my own free will, even if I burn my hand, but under compulsion, even if it's carrying some kind of purchase, the smallest chain of beads makes me feel sick." Ukraine can do whatever it pleases with itself, it can endure hunger and mortal danger on its own whim. But the slightest discomfort suffered at someone else's will seriously offends any Ukrainian, especially now, when first the Maidan, then Crimea and Donbas, and then the full-scale war escalated this sense of independence to intolerance. And

intolerance, to tell the truth, is much better than tolerance of anything and everything.

5. Quick wits. Ukrainians are improvisational. They don't like the slow-witted, and, themselves, are quick to act—you can't say about them that they take a long time to harness the horse, but drive fast. I suspect that slow-mindedness is somehow connected with prudence and stinginess—traits that are especially often attributed to Ukrainians. "What are you eating, good sir?"—"Bacon fat." "Oh, no you won't!"—"And why is that?" "Because I'll give you none." I have observed in my experience that Ukrainians part with money almost too easily, it's an understanding they have of money's irrational nature: money comes not to those who are economical and thrifty, but to those who love it. Again, the folklore is especially frank here: "Money is not the main thing: profit is." "Pennilessness precedes profit, wealth precedes death." "Cling to a penny, lose two." You can also find examples of the opposite—that God loves faith, and money loves to be counted—but the prevailing attitude toward property is flippant, and almost disdainful, again because putting up a good show is more valued. And you can understand the attitude of Ukrainians living a life in debt, for example, their notorious ingratitude when it comes to Western financial and weapons aid: "If you don't want to be associated with someone, lend them money." Zelenskyy has tried all his life never to borrow. Arestovych says that the leitmotif of what the Ukrainian philosopher Andrii Baumeister was writing in the early period of the full-scale invasion has been repeated by many Ukrainian bloggers: dependence on Europe is shameful, it must be overcome as soon as possible. Although, hand on heart, how could Ukraine, whose economy has been catastrophically undermined by the war, maintain independence? Here you can only choose what your dependence will be—to borrow ammunition, or to flee to European territory. Zelenskyy here made the perfect choice.

It goes without saying that Zelenskyy has his wits about him. He confides in no one. You can hear that from his friends (who accept this trait of his), his colleagues in the studio, and from politicians. I would go even further: He is more likely to be frank in his public speaking—which is acting, of course—than in a one-on-one conversation. Perhaps there is a special kind of spiritual chastity in this aversion to confessions, something natural in an actor: His life is already too public and therefore he demands that his inner world be left untouched. Zelenskyy can be outspoken in his televised speeches, he does not always hold back his emotions when speaking to the nation. But in one-on-one interviews, and even more so in friendly communication, he says precisely as much as he wants to say, and does not tolerate mental lack of discipline at all. Everyone knows he does not tolerate screaming: Screaming causes him pure physical pain. The director of *Servant of the People*, Kiriushchenko, recalls once breaking down on set in a tense moment, threatening to strike an actor for arriving late on the set. Zelenskyy literally hung over him, demanding that he calm down.

No, he doesn't like people waving their arms about. It is said that the war has changed him. And that is just another bit of proof that war can only improve a president's rating, although one suspects Zelenskyy would willingly give his life if only the war and this rating would not be part of his biography.

As is well known, the Yandex portal is not merely Russian, but has long been in Putin's back pocket, which is quite obvious from the triumphant newsfeed it offers. Google is American, and as such courts the possibility of being banned in Russia. The first thing Yandex tells you is that Ukrainians are traitors, greedy, and nationalists by nature, while Google will tell you that independence, irony, and entrepreneurship dominate the Ukrainian character.

Strictly speaking, Zelenskyy is an ethnic Jew whose Jewish roots can be traced back five generations, but we are not talking about ethnic identity now. The President of Ukraine is, in a sense, the face of the nation, and in this sense it is most symbolic that Zelenskyy is not Ukrainian. Let's venture to say that today Ukrainians are the world's team, in about the same sense that the Spaniards were in 1936–1938 during the first armed struggle with fascism. Everyone who opposes the new incarnation of fascism put forth by Russia is fighting on the side of Ukraine—on the front lines, in diplomacy, in ideology—to the point that the ethnic Englishman Boris Johnson becomes an honorary citizen of Odesa, and soldiers from all over Europe go to Ukraine as volunteers (not to mention the international journalistic teams covering Ukraine's life and struggles in all their details). In this sense, Ukrainians are an emerging nation, which, so far, willingly includes everyone prepared to prove their friendliness and usefulness to Ukraine. Today this country is under attack, and tomorrow it will be an ideal place to invest money, an economy that will be restored literally by the whole world. I dare to hope that this social and psychological rehabilitation that will restore Ukrainian enterprises will be provided for Russians too.

XVII. THE PERIODIC TABLE

Before speaking about Zelenskyy as a non-systemic, or outsider, politician, we must understand what defines a systemic politician, that is, outline the approximate typology of Ukrainian politicians in the 2010s. At present there are six such categories. Zelenskyy comprises a seventh on his own (although this column of the table is gradually being filled in).

The first, now-disappearing type of Ukrainian politician is a mastodon who made a career during Soviet times, and who tries to apply his acquired skills in the post-Soviet era. This individual is over sixty, was most likely connected at some point with the defense or special services, sometimes with commercial production. These are Leonid Kuchma (the second president of Ukraine, CEO of Yuzhmash), Mykola Azarov (Finance Minister under Kuchma, Prime Minister under Yanukovych, geologist, director of the Ukrainian Geological Institute), and Borys Tarasiuk (Soviet diplomat, later Minister of Foreign Affairs of Ukraine).

The second type is an oligarch, who, as a rule, was formed in the Soviet era, but who took advantage of post-Soviet opportunities to acquire capital. As Viktor Pelevin, Russia's most popular post-Soviet writer, put it, in post-Soviet conditions the initial accumulation is also final, that is, due to the extreme brevity of the period of reforms and turmoil, due to the ephemerality of the window of opportunity, which closes after two years or so, everyone is left with what they managed to grab at first. Ukrainian oligarchs have extremely interesting interrelationships, but think nothing negative about that: they often compete, fight, even attack each other, but due to their shared Komsomol past and professional solidarity, common among pirates or soldiers of fortune, these "men of Flint," as the Russian writer Valery Alekseev termed them in his popular science-fiction of the same name, respect and support each other in a peculiar way. Ukrainian oligarchs can compete in elections as much as they like, but during periods of "de-oligarchization" they all find themselves in the same boat. All of them supported Zelenskyy (morally rather than financially) and had high hopes for him, although objectively speaking, they all turned out to be his opponents in 2022. Few have realized this yet, and some may try to displace him in the future, although time is working against them. All their biographies are similar, while their manners are different, although these differences are purely cosmetic. This group includes: Yuliia Tymoshenko (one of the most successful businesswomen of Ukraine, Prime Minister under Yushchenko, leader of the Batkivshchyna party), Ihor Kolomoiskyi (Komsomol activist, later corporate magnate), Hennadii Korban (broker, investor), Serhii Tihipko (Komsomol activist, banker, later Deputy Prime Minister and Minister of Economy), Petro Poroshenko (founder of Roshen, Ukraine's top confectionery enterprise, and fifth president of Ukraine).

The third type is a political leader, a party leader, a professional politician. This type was formed in the aughts, but quickly compromised itself. Viktor Yushchenko belonged to this type, although he did not possess leadership qualities, and, after the victory of the first Maidan (2004) quickly squandered his popularity.

The fourth type is a nationalist. It goes without saying that Ukrainian nationalism gained a second wind with the outbreak of the war, but it had consistently showed low results in the pre-war elections. It is difficult to say what this is due to, whether it is an instinctive fear of national radicals, a fear based on Soviet internationalist mantras, or the fact that nationalists build too much on a negative agenda, that is, on prohibitions, refusals, demolition of monuments, renaming streets, and other breaks with Soviet identity. Any nationalism is good in the war against the Russians, but it is basically provincial and rather harmful for contacts with Europe or America. The undoubted merit of the nationalists is their participation in combat during the Maidan of 2014, their high self–organization, their merits in defense (suffice it to recall the Azov battalion, consisting precisely of ideological nationalists who engendered dozens of heroes). But building Ukraine as a nationalist state is not so much an unattractive idea, as it is an unworkable one; everyone in Ukraine firmly understands this. A nationalist-leaning politician might gather a crowd at a rally, but would have a hard time convening a large parliamentary faction, let alone the presidency.

The fifth group consists of regional leaders; if one has hopes of occupying top levels of power (not necessarily presidential, it might also be ministerial), one inevitably must pass through the stage of regional leadership. Presidential power in Ukraine is not absolute, but rather nominal in peacetime. And this is not because the role of parliament is so great (it is just more entertaining—both for parliamentarians and for voters). Ukraine is a country of real self-government, a country of mayors who are given very broad powers. This position is dangerous—as I write these lines, the mayor of Odesa, Hennadii Trukhanov, has been arrested on suspicion of bribery, and the city military commissar also took bribes for deferrals from conscription. They gloat loudly about this in Russia. The mayor of Kyiv, Vitalii Klitschko, is known for his opposition to Zelenskyy, but this does not affect his status in any way. Most Ukrainian mayors are local business executives with experience in city councils. Their average age is forty-five (the average age in the Cabinet is thirty-nine).

The sixth category comprises the members of the military. Their true consolidation is yet to come, but one thing is already clear: Zaluzhnyi may have lost the post of commander-in-chief of the Armed Forces of Ukraine, but he did not merely head off to London as an ambassador. His political influence has long been comparable to Zelenskyy's popularity. Syrskyi's authority is also high, but he is not nearly as charismatic. The next generation of top-tier Ukrainian politicians will most likely be recruited from the military. The question is what will be stronger in them, ambition or loyalty. It is clear that for the military, loyalty to the current government is part of a set of professional virtues. Let's hazard to say that an ideally elected candidate (like Russian General Alexander Lebed once was, although he never justified the hopes placed on him), will be a charming and successful military man who quarreled with his superiors, and emerged as an alternative to them. Stalin understood this danger perfectly, which is why he preferred to push Marshall Georgy Zhukov into disgrace. (Zhukov was a dubious alternative to Stalin, but in popular opinion that's precisely what he was, and he never ruled out such an option in his secret dreams; subsequently, he began interfering with Khrushchev, whom he actually saved during the attempted Stalinist coup of 1957.) For the time being, the Ukrainian military does not mess with politics, they have other concerns. But the chances of Valerii Zaluzhnyi becoming more politically involved, if he sours on his military career, may be high.

Is a non-systemic politician possible after Zelenskyy? Will his example be perceived as negative or as attractive? There is no answer to this question yet, but on an intuitive level I would not bet on the return of adherents to the "system." During the war they revealed themselves to be confused, not ready for new challenges. The maximum they are capable of is to supply the army with bulletproof vests, like Poroshenko. The oligarchs behaved quite meekly, realizing that wartime is no time for rebellions. The chances of potential candidates from the military are growing, but the powers-that-be see this and, for the time being, will control the most popular potential saviors among them. It is impossible to predict the appearance of a new trickster (and what field he might currently be occupied in), since a trickster is a trickster for a good reason. Volunteers? Why not? Davyd Arakhamiia has risen from this environment. One thing is clear: the president(s) of Ukraine will appear from unexpected places in the next twenty years. This is the only definitely positive experience that Ukrainians are left with from the 2019 elections.

It is impossible not to notice that writers are the primary reserve of Ukrainian politics, the primary squadron of the creative intelligentsia from which leaders are recruited. This is natural—they are traditionally associated with ideology; only rarely could Ukrainian or Soviet authors stay out of politics. Journalists and bloggers claiming political influence now form a promising reserve of power. The role of the media in Ukraine is generally high, as it was in pre-Putin Russia. The problem is that the flip side of their influence is a lazy antipathy on the part of the electorate: according to Pelevin, again, the media are good to "observe and hate." So far, there is not a single large-scale media figure on the horizon that can compete with any candidate from a place of power in the parliamentary, much less the presidential elections. (Dmytro Komarov? It would depend on the post he might eye: his two-hour film *The Year* containing an unprecedented frank interview with Zelenskyy was seen by everyone in Ukraine.)

But before the Zelenskyy phenomenon emerged and took hold, Ukrainian (and separatist) powers were stormed by a squadron of writers. Few people paid attention to these writers entering positions of power, yet Zelenskyy's success was partly prepared by this wave: fatigue from systemic politicians led to the fact that in 2014 the war was waged (and ideologically justified) primarily by journalists and science-fiction writers. This phenomenon is worthy of note precisely because they, in fact, paved the way for an actor to become the national leader.

The Russian-Ukrainian war had long been predicted, described in detail, planned, and subsequently carried out by writers: Igor Girkin-Strelkov, Fyodor Berezin, Andrii Valentynov, as well as Arsen Avakov, the co-chairman of Kharkiv's Star Bridge festival of fiction. Girkin-Strelkov's novel *The Detective of Heldiborn Castle* was noticed by few due to artistic weaknesses, but he is a writer who should not be forgotten when considering his power of political analysis.

Fyodor Berezin is a rocket brigade officer born in 1960 in Donetsk. He retired in 1991 with the rank of captain. Subsequently, he was the plenipotentiary representative of Igor Strelkov, the Minister of Defense of the Donetsk Republic. He is a regular participant of the Star Bridge Fiction

Festival, the patron of which is Kharkiv mayor Arsen Avakov. He made forays into entrepreneurship—not particularly successfully, and is the author of two dozen novels in the genre of combat fiction, of which two cycles are most popular—*War 2030* and *War 2010: The Ukrainian Front*. The events of the latter unfold mainly on the territory of the Donetsk and Luhansk regions. The plot revolves around NATO troops invading Ukraine, which has become a testing ground for a large-scale war between Russia and the West. He describes a peaceful population, enthusiastically supporting the army; Russia being forced to enter the conflict as peacemakers; and the massacre of traitors. The first novel of the cycle ends with precisely just such a massacre, depicted with a certain element of delight.

Arsen Avakov (Minister of Internal Affairs under Poroshenko) has a direct relationship to fiction: he is the co-chairman of Star Bridge, a true fan of combat, historical, and "alternative" fiction, who solemnly opens and closes the festival. Avakov took pride in the largest congress of science-fiction writers being held in Kharkiv, but he hardly imagined that their dreams (or nightmares) about the Ukrainian war would come true so soon, and that he himself would be on the opposite side of the barricades. Still, it was Avakov who first noticed the trend. Back in 2009, he published a critical review on the *Ukrainska Pravda* website, "Do Russians Want War?" wherein he described the books *Battlefield Ukraine: The Broken Trident* (by Georgy Savitsky, a Donetsk science-fiction writer, author of a dozen novels about future wars on the territory of Ukraine), *Russian-Ukrainian Wars* (by Alexander Sever, obviously a pseudonym, inclined to futurology and conspiracy), and the aforementioned *Ukrainian Front* by Fyodor Berezin. "I know Fyodor personally!" Avakov wrote. "He received awards at our Star Bridge science-fiction festival in Kharkiv. How could you let yourself be dragged into this???" Avakov asked, question marks his. Avakov correctly noticed the vector, but did not understand the reason.

One need not mention the Russian writer Zakhar Prilepin, who was given a battalion under his personal leadership mainly for PR purposes, although that did not stop him from speaking endlessly about his own participation—exceptionally ruthless—in the fighting. Prilepin combined the leadership of his battalion with active trips to book launches, meetings with readers, and dabbling in politics, but diligently positioned himself as a combat commander, which at first caused smiles in Donetsk, and later disdain. Prilepin once promised to participate in Russia's presidential elections and I believe it was this, not Ukrainian revenge, that brought about an assassination attempt that killed his driver, and left Prilepin himself in six months of convalescence. It would appear that he drew all the proper conclusions and he no longer talks about a future in politics. For all his monstrosity, Prilepin was so comical that it was always difficult to take his political prospects seriously. Still, anything is possible in Russia. And if writers could not hope to achieve power (except for minor positions in separatist republics), they did make their debut in 2014 as ideologists and field commanders. Zelenskyy is far from the first cultural figure who grew tired of confining himself to the world of art. There are two reasons for this. The first is the general fatigue from corrupt and manipulative politicians. The second is the transition of politics (and even war) into a post-industrial PR phase, when the interpretation and PR-positioning of war becomes more important than the fighting itself. Hence poets as military commanders, prose writers as advisers to separatist leaders, and journalists (or psychologists) as military analysts. Ukraine was the first to demonstrate a global trend—the expansion of narrative artists, storytellers, and science-fiction writers into military politics, and I think the expansion into the field of economics is not far off.

The seventh type of politicians is the master of discourse; Zelenskyy is the first to succeed, but he clearly won't be last.

XVIII. WHY?

We rarely raise the question of why politics is needed precisely because of its apparent infantile naïveté. Nevertheless, the answer is not so predictable: Politics—along with sports and culture—distract a person from death and give him the illusion of his own influence on the world. In fact, according to

Slavoj Zizek's just remark, politics is nothing more than the button on the elevator panel that supposedly accelerates the closing of automatic doors. In fact, it most often does not affect the behavior of the elevator door in any way, but gives passengers the illusion of participating in their own destiny. The role of personality in history varies in different social systems, but it cannot affect the vector of history—except for the pace and number of victims.

However, the motivation for people entering politics varies in different societies. In the West, politics, with all its proclaimed idealism, is primarily one of the most profitable types of business, the surest means of enrichment. In Russia and China, politics is a way to achieve power, a demonstration of dominance (in Russia, this is laced with a fair quantity of sadism, since long ago sadomasochism in general became a favorite form of national entertainment). The goal of power in Russia is precisely to enjoy power as such, and to humiliate others. The people do not appreciate any concern for their well-being, but they accept any scope of atrocities as a sign of greatness, and are ready to participate (passively) in this greatness as much as possible.

In Eastern Europe and especially in Ukraine, which is one of the youngest European democracies, politics is a form of gambling. Money is not the end in itself here—there are many ways to earn it without risk, corruption permeates all institutions, and, anyway, it is not so much corruption as it is a sign of a corporate state based on mutual assistance. Introducing civilizational norms (as the United States is now trying to do with Ukraine, so that of the $40 billion of humanitarian and military aid only half will be stolen) is time-consuming, and, most importantly, lacking in perspective. The amount of money in the criminalized Ukrainian economy is determined not by proximity to power (because positions of power are quite vulnerable and the next Maidan can always cast them aside), but solely by sleight of hand. Power is a way to realize one's ambitions, a test of strength, participation in an exciting and dangerous competition. The case of Poroshenko, who increased his fortune somewhat during his presidency, is, more likely, an exception here, for there is no telling whether or not he might have increased it much more significantly outside of power.

Zelenskyy did not come to power for the sake of money, and even more so not for the sake of dominance. He was quite firmly established in his own profession. But the question of his true goals remains open. I suspect that, after his resounding victory with 73 percent of the vote, Zelenskyy asked himself for the first time why did he ever get involved in all this? I think the same question was asked by those who voted for him: Wonderful, we won, but to what end?

It was much easier for those who voted to answer this question. The main slogan of political life in Ukraine was explained to me back during the 2004 Maidan by a film critic: "Let things be worse, just let them be different." Novelty—and the ability to renew—is in itself more valuable than the quality of life, because it is life's chief quality. Even though Leonid Kuchma's chapter on the differences in national characters occupies almost fifty pages in his 2003 book *Ukraine Is not Russia*, he paid almost no attention to what I believe is the defining difference between the Russian preference for stability, on the principle of "just so long as things don't get worse," and the Ukrainian thirst for change. Kuchma formulated it this way: "According to my observations, Russians are rather less optimistic than Ukrainians. If something bad or merely undesirable happens, the Russian will most likely think: 'I knew it!' The Ukrainian will conclude, 'It could be worse!' Nevertheless, Russians mostly adhere to their own healthy saying (they invented it, they didn't borrow it from anyone): 'Eyes fear, hands do,' and in the end they often bring their plans to fruition."

Here one will inevitably remember Chekhov: "It's not a matter of pessimism or of optimism, but of the fact that ninety-nine out of a hundred people have no brains." Stability is dear to those who are afraid of the future. That is, they feel their weakness and uncertainty in the face of any change. Joseph Heller's *Something Happened* says it even more directly: "You can't change circumstances and never will." This weakness, that is the certainty that nothing will get better, really does exist in Russia. The independent Ukrainian state can afford, after thirty years of incessant experiment, another risk—"Let's elect an actor and see what happens."

As for Zelenskyy's motivation, everything is more complicated, because, in my opinion, it has changed over time. At first, like Trump, he acted at random, according to the principle in the joke about the rooster and the chicken: "If I don't catch up, at least I'll get warm." He had an excellent opportunity to get warmed up—neither the Trump show nor *Block 95* could have obtained such an advertising campaign for any amount of money. Gradually, when the chance of victory began to seem likely—a total surprise for both voters and Zelenskyy, as well as for the oligarchs allegedly backing him—a formulation appeared that even Trump would have signed on to, and Zelenskyy personally made it public in his inaugural speech. "My election shows that citizens are tired of experienced systemic politicians who have created a country of opportunities. Opportunities for kickbacks and payoffs. We will build a different land of opportunity."

Trump, his entourage, and his supporters constantly talked about fatigue from systemic, professional, hereditary politicians. Zelenskyy won, as almost always happens in Ukraine, not because of his program, but because of fatigue from all the previous options. In these situations, Russia chooses a military or security officer who puts a stop to all political life, and single-handedly, with a swift, decisive blow from an axle jack, drives the country to the brink of disaster. Ukraine chooses according to the principle of "what has never been before" (this is how the title of Boris Savinkov's novel about Russian terror should be interpreted. It is not for nothing that Savinkov, like his double Savenko, was born in Kharkiv).

Zelenskyy decided to participate in an unprecedented experiment—and he won. Perhaps for himself (he never said it publicly) he really did decide to become the voice of the people, that is, to embody the best features of the Ukrainian character: democracy, adventurism, and sarcastic humor.

In at least one respect it is useful to bring a street creature into world politics: you quickly learn what the folks on the street are living by, and what they are capable of. The election of Zelenskyy (as well as Trump) is the most interesting sociological event that has taken place in the world over the past twenty years. Curiously, most sociologists could not accurately predict it. Roughly speaking, the professionals screwed up here too.

But another motive turned out to be decisive. Get the whole of Ukraine into your audience, and after February 24—the whole world! It sounds cynical. But all the noble deeds ever done had exceptionally cynical motives: just as no one (in their right mind) commits a base act out of a desire to commit a base act, but solely out of good intentions, so a great heroic feat is not performed out of a longing for something heroic. The road to hell is paved with good intentions, the road to heaven is cynical and selfish. Sometimes you can't help thinking: maybe if Russian revolutionaries were driven not by love for good, but by a thirst for enrichment and personal love of power, maybe the people would have lived a little better under their rule.

Or as Andrei Voznesensky told me in his last interview: "Yes, many poets of my generation behaved decently only because millions of people were watching them. But it is better to behave well out of vanity than to behave like a scoundrel in silence out of modesty."

XIX. A FEW MORE MEASUREMENTS

As a presidential candidate Volodymyr Zelenskyy declared:

- Two royalties from *Block 95*—1,048,000 hryvnia and 3,306,832 hryvnia (totaling 4.35 million hryvnia, or just over $160,000),
- A 235,000 hryvnia ($8,650) royalty from Kinostolitsa,
- A house in the Kyiv suburb of Ivankovichi (353.5 square meters) and a plot of land (12,000 square meters) in the village of Maetok (30 kilometers from Kyiv). The house was bought in 2008 for $118,610, plus land for $91,200,
- An apartment in Kyiv (131.9 sq. m.) and two parking spaces,
- An apartment in Kyiv (269.7 sq. m.) registered to Aldorante Ltd. in Cyprus, in the so-called "Monster House" at 9a Hrushevskyi Street,
- A quarter share of an apartment in Kyiv (254.5 sq. m.), of which 50% belongs to Borys Shefir, and the other 25%—to his brother, assistant to the president, Serhii Shefir,

- Half share of an apartment of 198.6 sq. m (the other half belongs to Serhii Shefir).

Property of Olena Zelenska:

- Apartment in Crimea (129.8 sq. m.) with a parking space,
- Non–residential premises (337.8 sq. m.)—a 50-50 share with the Shefir brothers,
- An apartment in Kyiv (284 sq. m.).

Zelenskyy's foreign real estate: an apartment in the UK with an area of 91.9 sq. m., a rental and sublet,

- A residential building in Italy of 413 sq. m. (through the company San Tommaso S.R.L.).
- "Unfinished construction"—five rooms in a hotel in Georgia.
- According to the declaration, Zelenskyy had $112,000 and €6,300 in cash at the time of taking office. His holdings in OTP Bank were 4,062,000 hryvnia, and $6,776.
- A personal account with Privatbank, a legal entity registered abroad, $399,772. The same legal entity, but different account held $25,303.
- Olena Zelenska held 96,329 hryvnia and $3,776 in OTP Bank, and $5,706 in Privatbank.

Not bad, basically. Not a billionaire, but not a starving man either, and he explained everything quite clearly. For comparison, Vladimir Putin declares an apartment in Moscow with an area of 230 square meters and a Niva car with an M-21 trailer from year to year. His income for 2021 amounted to 10,202,616 rubles (approximately, $140,800), and according to the election commission, he had $179,600 in his account. A beggar compared to Zelenskyy. Unofficially, his possessions in real estate alone—including the famous "palace in Gelendzhik"—is estimated at $6.1 billion. No one has accurate data, including, I think, Russia's boss himself, who is not bound to be worried by such trifles.

On April 19, 2019, the Olympic sports complex chosen by Zelenskyy as a platform for debates, was packed to the rafters. The debate began at seven in the evening. The regulations were approved in advance: each candidate had five minutes for an introductory speech, followed by questions and answers. Zelenskyy was the first to speak by drawing lots (they tossed a coin). Both spoke in Russian. Zelenskyy began his speech with a joke ("I feel a little like Vakarchuk"—Sviatoslav Vakarchuk had gathered a full sports complex for an Okean Elzy concert the year before). He called himself a simple guy from Kryvyi Rih, admitted that he himself had voted for Pyotr Poroshenko five years ago, but was cruelly disappointed in him: he even reproached the incumbent president for a split personality. "Peter the Great" bravely fought against Putin, "Peter the Second" sent greetings to him through his godfather Viktor Medvedchuk and opened branches of his Roshen chocolates company in Russia. Other reproaches were standard: the war had not been stopped, suffering large-scale defeats (specifically mentioning Debaltseve), and the oligarchy still ran rampant.

Poroshenko was much more aggressive: "Mr. Volodymyr has been running from debates and the Ukrainian people" (this did not correspond to reality in any way—Zelenskyy insisted on certain conditions, no more). "They say he started studying to be a young warrior. He should have done that four years ago, but instead evaded mobilization at that time." (This reproach against Zelenskyy was the most common, and the Ministry of Defense made a special declaration on April 13 that he failed to appear for his summons four times. Speaking about 2014, we touched earlier on the true background to this scandal about Zelenskyy's draft summons and hypothetical non-appearance.) Poroshenko concluded with a flat insult, crossing a line that distinguishes a risky joke from rudeness: "You say you don't want to be a pig in a poke. Now, you're just a poke."

The audience greeted these words with a roar of approval: the fight from the very beginning turned out to be gladiatorial.

Zelenskyy fired back his first question: how did Ukraine become the poorest country under the richest president? And who has been punished for Debaltseve?

Poroshenko evaded a direct answer, repeating his basic theses: I rebuilt the army while you were running from it; I fought while you took money from Russia for movies; I saved the country while you exposed her as a prostitute, and apologized to Ramzan Kadyrov. Poroshenko's retaliatory volley missed its mark: "You said you were still learning, but would you entrust your plane to a student pilot, or your operation to a student surgeon? People aren't taught to be president." Poroshenko is also an international lawyer by education.

"I'm a public person, I hide from no one. Why couldn't they find me to hand me the summons?" Zelenskyy replied. He stressed that he had never been to Russia since the beginning of the war, that he had never spoken with Putin (while Poroshenko had done so repeatedly, including through Medvedchuk). "But why does your entourage still have both hands?" (Poroshenko had promised that people stealing from the army would have their hands cut off.)

In general, the debates made a strange impression—precisely because they demonstrated two different genres. Zelenskyy demonstrated peacefulness and even compassion, Poroshenko—aggression; Zelenskyy said what sounded good, Poroshenko—what kindled the most unequivocal and not always best feelings among the audience. Poroshenko wanted to win, Zelenskyy showed that his opponent's time was up. As a result, there was no dialogue and, apparently, one was never planned. What did take place was the manifestation of two different strategies. Everything about Zelenskyy's strategy was clear—he won precisely as a showman. Poroshenko's strategy was a losing one precisely because he fought back against his opponent's calm, irony, and advertised kindness. It wasn't so much like a wave hitting a rock as it was a fist punching foam rubber. Zelenskyy did not respond to direct insults and looked almost like Christ before Pilate. At the time of the debate, this was probably the ideal role. Sadly, nothing new of substance was spoken, but this only confirmed the trend: politics had finally moved from the category of meaningful polemics to the genre of a stadium show, during which it was almost indecent to talk about state problems—rather like mourning at a wedding.

XX. PRESIDENT (2019–2021)

1.

When conducting conversations with Zelenskyy's team and entourage, I had a simple criterion for separating those who are truly loyal from those who are purely opportunistic, potentially ready to turn away from him at the first opportune moment. In any team, in any elite group, there are those who praise the leader inventively and intelligently, but at the first sign of risk they will betray him. This is part of the very nature of government and its servants, who are especially sensitive to the current state of affairs. When asked if Zelenskyy had changed much since becoming president, some answered:

"Oh, come on! He was already one of the most influential producers around, he had experience with power. He has remained exactly the same—resolute when necessary, but sensitive . . . in general, one of us . . . and have you noticed how democratic he is?"

Others answered laconically: Yes, he has become different. Some even said, "completely different."

So: you can trust the second group, because they are objective. They see things as inevitable—even in a provincial school, a teacher becoming a principal is doomed to change. The president of the country is radically different even from a winning presidential candidate. The president—no matter whether it's in an authoritarian or democratic country, even where his position is purely nominal—buckles under the huge symbolic load, not to mention real responsibility. And in Ukraine, with all the influence of parliament and the experience of civil society, the president truly does wield significant power. It was literally during the inauguration that Zelenskyy began to change subtly: a completely different person emerged to shake hands with voters. It was no longer his character Goloborodko.

One can argue with oneself that Zelenskyy began feeling like a real president after the start of the war, when the burden of historical responsibility fell on him with all its weight. This would be partly true, but short-sighted. Even after rehearsing his presidential campaign in the TV series, repeatedly, moreover—a typical actor's skill—after imagining his debut in a position of power, he believed in victory only after being sworn in. He was never again one of the boys after that: he might be able to *play* it, but he'd never feel it. This was especially evident at the 2021 New Year celebration, when he visited the *Block 95* show—for the first time as president and not as captain of this entertainment team. He was as distanced from them as—well, I don't know—as an ex-husband at the coming-of-age party of his son, whose parents have long been divorced. This father comes to the party (sometimes, the former spouses may even have new companions), he congratulates his son, saying something like "Congratulations, old chum." The line separating them is terrible, and the more carefully it is masked, the more noticeable it is. Why did I use this specific comparison? Because, unfortunately, I know of what I speak.

After the election, Zelenskyy was irreversibly different. Many rightly noted that the lessons of playing Napoleon had not been lost on him.

2.

The first two years of Zelenskyy's presidency will go down in history as the pre-war period. From a political point of view, these were unsuccessful years that led to a precipitous drop in his rating (he won 79 percent of those voting in the second round, but had a 37 percent approval rate in December 2021). From a conceptual point of view, these are exemplary figures, because Zelenskyy marked a new type of politician and was coping with this task well.

Modernity requires entrusting everything to professionals, while placing in the roles of public politicians those who are good at distracting the public from the main problems. This modus operandi was described by George Bernard Shaw when he called democracy "a big balloon, filled with gas or hot air, and sent up so that you shall be kept looking up at the sky whilst other people are picking your pockets." These golden words, unlike most common Internet quotes, are not fake, but are drawn from the author's preface to the political farce *The Apple Cart* (1930). And they continue: "When the balloon comes down to earth every five years or so you are invited to get into the basket if you can throw out one of the people who are sitting tightly in it; but as you can afford neither the time nor the money, and there are forty millions of you and hardly room for six hundred in the basket, the balloon goes up again with much the same lot in it and leaves you where you were before."

RUSSIAN EDITOR'S NOTE: Is it worth noting that it is precisely in this preface that Shaw expresses his admiration for a politician like Mussolini?

As regards Zelenskyy, Shaw's observation turned out to be fallacious, since, in this case, most of the passengers were pushed out of the balloon, and a large part of the parliament (about 43 percent) went to supporters of Zelenskyy from the hastily created Servant of the People party.

Zelenskyy's inauguration on May 20, 2019, was stylistically, substantively, and demonstratively the antithesis of Putin's 2018 inauguration. Putin drove to the Kremlin through an empty Moscow, said nothing really meaningful, and never came out to meet his constituents. Zelenskyy invited all his supporters to the Rada, the Ukrainian parliament, where the inauguration took place, and went out to them immediately after the ceremony to shake hands for ten minutes, separated from the crowd only by a low partition decorated in the colors of the flag.

Zelenskyy's speech naturally differed significantly from his character Goloborodko's speech in the finale of the first season of *Servant of the People*. Moreover, he did not replicate the scene of Goloborodko famously leaping at the presidential podium and clicking his heels, although some incidents did raise eyebrows. When speaking about Donbas, Zelenskyy switched into Russian, prompting Oleh Liashko, the leader of the Radical Party known for his extreme views and an initiative to ban 500 Russian cultural figures from entering Ukraine for supporting the annexation of Crimea, to shout that the people of Donbas understand Ukrainian. Zelenskyy replied seriously: "Thank you, Mr. Liashko! Thank you for continuing to divide people."

In general, the main thrust of his speech was precisely unification, the erasure of borders, and solidarity despite differences: "Today I address Ukrainians all over the world. There are 65 million of us! Yes, don't be surprised, there are 65 million of us—those who were born on Ukrainian lands. In North and South America, Australia, Asia, Africa—I appeal to all Ukrainians on the planet: we need you! I will be happy to grant Ukrainian citizenship to all those who are prepared to build a strong and successful Ukraine. Come home to Ukraine, don't just come visit. We are waiting for you. We don't need souvenirs from abroad, bring us your knowledge, your experience and your intellectual capabilities. All this will allow us to begin a new era. Skeptics will say this is science-fiction, that it is impossible, but perhaps this is our national idea—to unite and do the impossible. Against all odds. Remember the Icelandic national team at the European Soccer Championships, when a dentist, a director, a biologist, a student, and a custodian fought and defended the honor of their country. And they did that, even though no one believed in it. This is our path, too. We must become Icelanders in soccer, Israelis in defending our land, Japanese in technology, Swiss in the ability to live with each other regardless of all differences."

He then recommended adopting a law to abolish parliamentary immunity during the first two months of the sitting of the new Rada, and declared that his priorities would be to return all annexed territories (including Crimea), and to lead the fight against corruption. Instead of a portrait of the head of state, he suggested people hang portraits of their children in their offices, so they could always look them in the eye and think not about upcoming elections, but about the future. This surely was the most effective rhetorical move in his entire speech; it brought about a storm of applause.

Let's note as an aside that, today, it is especially interesting to look back at the faces and figures of the military brass as they greeted Zelenskyy according to ceremonial protocol. Almost all of them have the stately faces and corpulent bodies of Soviet generals. Their average age was from forty-five to fifty. Three years later, all of these positions (not only as a result of the war, but as a result of the gradual turnover in the previous year) were occupied by fit young wolves with combat experience, their faces showing irony and determination. Let's say Zelenskyy had nothing to do with this, let's say the war, and, by extension, Putin, did it. What is important is the result.

On May 21, 2019, Zelenskyy dissolved the Upper Rada, the upper chamber of parliament, justifying his action by the low level of public trust in it (4 percent was the figure repeated in most polls). The Constitutional Court of Ukraine confirmed the legality of this decree. New parliamentary elections were scheduled for July 21. The Servant of the People Party received the right to form a government independently. Zelenskyy needed the dissolution of the Rada—the previous parliament twice refused to dismiss Foreign Minister Pavel Klimkin, who, bypassing the president and without coordination with him, refused an offer of negotiations from the Russians (the topic was the release of Russian sailors detained in November 2018 in the Kerch Strait). Zelenskyy had emphasized his readiness for dialogue from the very beginning—Klimkin defiantly disrupted that potential dialogue. It was clear that any of the new president's proposals would be met with direct sabotage in the former Rada.

A few words now on Zelenskyy's attitude to his predecessor where the narrator king also referenced classical drama. In Zelenskyy's trickster-like *Hamlet* drama (he fulfills the dream of every actor—to play Hamlet, and does a relatively good job), Poroshenko plays the entirely respectable role of Claudius. Any political intrigue—there's nothing new about Zelenskyy in this—is built according to the Hamlet scenario, especially if it involves a young leader who is popular with most of the population. It is not entirely clear who the father's ghost is here who—as Alexander Pushkin puts it in *Boris Godunov*—adopted him. In this case I would advise you take a closer look at Leonid Kuchma, who, in relation to Zelenskyy, behaves exactly like the political father addressing his son over the heads of his successors. He was never able to cultivate relationships with Yushchenko or Yanukovych, but with Zelenskyy he did. It was Kuchma who was entrusted as a political heavyweight to conduct negotiations in Minsk in 2016. He warned Zelenskyy against harboring illusions in negotiations with Putin, warning that he was the most difficult negotiator he had ever met, and he asked journalists not to ask the new president risky questions about Putin (such as "is he a murderer?"—after Biden's famous claim): "There are things that can only be said to your face." Kuchma repeatedly criticized the actions of

Poroshenko's team, reproaching him for not fulfilling promises, while, on the contrary, he declared his trust in Zelenskyy. In August 2022, answering questions from the BBC, Kuchma spoke unequivocally: "No one can do everything right. But, given the unprecedented extreme and critical nature of the situation, the Ukrainian authorities are doing much more and much better than anyone could have imagined or expected from them before the Russian invasion. Especially if, at first, as far as I know, Putin only saw them as a bunch of amateurs. This was another fatal miscalculation of the Kremlin. And I, in turn, am sincerely glad that in the spring of 2019 I believed in the great potential and honest intentions of Volodymyr Zelenskyy—and supported him."

Why does Kuchma act here as "the father's ghost" who lends Zelenskyy legitimacy on behalf of the past? It's simple: Kuchma was, in fact, the first president of independent Ukraine. Leonid Kravchuk remained in office only thirty-two months and was not so much the first president of the new Ukraine as the last Soviet leader, a signatory of the Belovezha Accords that brought an end to the Soviet Union. Hopes for a democratic, free, happy Ukraine were connected with Kuchma, he was the only one who served two terms, and, although his departure was marred by the scandal involving the journalist and filmmaker Georgy Gongadze, whom he allegedly ordered to be murdered (it later turned out that the actors were overzealous), many people retained confidence in him under both Yushchenko and Yanukovych. Compared to them, Kuchma was perceived as a people's leader. The same hopes were attached to him as to Zelenskyy, although he was not a new type of politician, but rather a classic Soviet manager.

As for Poroshenko, he was the perfect Claudius, combining pragmatism, cunning, and loyalty to his clan. Zelenskyy had to deal with the consequences of Poroshenko's policies, including the Minsk agreements, a negative attitude to which he never hid. Poroshenko accepted the country at a critical moment, he had to create an army from scratch—the very one that subsequently rebuffed the aggressor—and hastily negotiate the status of Donbas. We will not enter into a polemic about Poroshenko's activities here, especially since they provide no material for aesthetic and mythological interpretations. He was never for a minute a narrator king or an artist in power in any way; although Claudius's ambivalence is very clearly manifested in him. He is a big, cunning businessman who sought to implement his familiar business strategies in his position of power. That is, to make everyone happy, himself most of all. But Kuchma had said it was impossible to play games of the "win-win" type. A Claudius figure had no business being here—Poroshenko came up with a rating below thirty for the 2019 elections.

But Hamlet had to rethink his strategy. Imagine that precisely at the moment of him exacting vengeance for his father—a plot detail that, fortunately, Zelenskyy did not have to perform—Denmark is attacked not by Fortinbras, but by something a hundred times worse. I suspect Hamlet would have no time left for reflection, and all monologues would have to be delivered in the format of television addresses to the nation. He would be required to possess a perfect combination of deep tragedy, grotesque parody, and folk drama. Boris Pasternak's characterization of Hamlet was perfectly applicable to the drama going down in Ukraine in 2022: "Lack of will was unknown in Shakespeare's time. It didn't interest them. Hamlet's appearance, described by Shakespeare in such detail, is clear and does not fit the idea of faint of heart. According to Shakespeare, Hamlet is a royal-blooded prince who never for a minute forgets his right to the throne. He is a darling of the old court and a self-confident prodigy due to his great talent. In the totality of traits that the author endowed him with, there is no place for weakness, his character excludes it."

And that's just how it all turned out.

3.

There is a certain difficulty in describing the first two years of Zelenskyy's presidency from the high ground of knowing what we know about the following two. When we talk about a president whose rating had fallen to 25 percent before the start of the war, we must not forget the 90 percent that he scored in March 2022 and did not lose after that. But let's try to make that reversal seem even more striking.

Judging by the results of the first half of Zelenskyy's presidential term, which is cut precisely in two by the war, all participants in the experiment—Zelenskyy and Ukrainian society—were disappointed.

Society expected rapid change—as radical as the change in the image of authority. That didn't happen. Zelenskyy could rightly have counted on a more motivated and cohesive nation, but that nation remained the same—corrupt and scandalous, provincial and ambitious, waiting for everything to happen by itself. One miracle had happened—a non-systemic candidate had won the presidency; another miracle, cruel and terrible, happened two years later, which is not to say that Zelenskyy or society brought it about. It was the war that made him, that is, the forces that controlled the main participants in the drama.

Let's consider Zelenskyy's activities as president in those areas associated with the biggest expectations.

First of all, let's recall that the second year of Zelenskyy's presidency coincided with the pandemic, in other words, extremely unfavorable conditions. Next let's point out that in October 2020, he himself was ill with COVID at the same time as Andrii Yermak, later the head of the presidential office, and then an adviser, who recuperated with the President at the Feofania hospital. (A rumor immediately spread that Zelenskyy's stay there costs millions of hryvnia, he denied these rumors on Instagram, stressing that he was being treated the same as a common patient.) He spent two weeks in self-isolation and, fortunately, recovered easily. Merkel called him at the hospital to wish him a speedy recovery—Zelenskyy used the occasion to ask her for help with Pfizer vaccines for Ukraine. Deliveries were not long in coming. Recall that Pfizer was unavailable in Russia—the author of these lines had to be vaccinated in Odesa. However, I have no complaints about the Russian "Satellite" vaccine—I was one of the first to get this vaccination in Moscow and I never got sick.

The President's office, from the first day of the coronavirus threat, has imported more than 700,000 respirators, and more than 120,000 protective suits. Sixty thousand protective glasses for doctors in designated hospitals where patients with coronavirus are brought. Seven million pairs of gloves; 20,000 thermometers; 250,000 PCR tests; 550,000 express tests; 200,000 extraction reagents. This weekend we are bringing in 350,000 respirators; 105,000 protective suits; 800,000 reagents for RNA extraction; and raw materials for the production of Ukrainian-made tests. In general, we have about five planes a week coming in. —*Zelenskyy on Savik Shuster's* Freedom of Speech *talk show.*

In the same interview he asked people to refrain from visiting churches en masse for Easter (and he himself did not pose for photos in church).

In an interview for the *Globe and Mail* (Toronto) during the pandemic, with his usual faith in collective intelligence, Zelenskyy proposed revising the debt system in the global economy, warning of a deep economic crisis if that were not done. According to Vitalii Klitschko's statement, quarantine had caused Kyiv losses amounting to a billion hryvnia, and in the whole country—more than 20 billion. The European Union allocated 190 million euros to Ukraine (according to government estimates, three times more was needed to fight the pandemic). Zelenskyy directly appealed to the oligarchs with a request that they chip in. He immediately ordered the purchase of all vaccines (except Russian ones): vaccination in Ukraine was extremely fast and disciplined, and there were fewer victims of the pandemic than the average in Eastern Europe: about 110,000. Of the adult population, 44.9 percent of the adult population underwent a full course of vaccination (this was especially active during the second wave). In February 2022, the Ministry of Health of Ukraine stopped issuing bulletins, the pandemic had been replaced entirely by war.

The Democratic Initiatives Foundation conducted a survey, and the actions of the authorities during the pandemic were given a rating of 2.5 on a five–point scale. They received 2.6 for communication with the population. However, Zelenskyy's charisma at that time was still such that 46 percent of respondents positively assessed his activities (about the same as those who were vaccinated).

The reduction of expenses for the maintenance of the state apparatus were reduced by only 10 percent, and there was no radical reform of the Ukrainian state administration. The main thing Zelenskyy did was that the president's office replaced the administration. The difference is that the presidential administration claimed great political influence, while the office works mainly for Zelenskyy himself, providing him with information and coordinating his schedule. Of course, the president did not ride a bicycle to work, that was the sarcastic opening sequence of a satirical TV series; but another promise was fulfilled: no big caravans, no personal driver. Zelenskyy traveled around Ukraine (at least he did before the war) in his personal Range Rover Vogue Autobiography, offered commentary several times from a Tesla Model X, and, if Zelenskyy was accompanied by a motorcade, it consisted of two cars—a Volkswagen Transporter T6 and a Toyota Sequoia. No luxury, but also no demonstrative austerity: after all, Goloborodko was a history teacher at the start of his career, and VZ was one of the most successful producers in Ukraine. What has come about is the complete repudiation of road closures; another reason to compare with Putin, but if only that were the main difference!

LANGUAGE. An interesting thing took place with the Russian language in Ukraine—and this is still another story about Zelenskyy's so-called actor's intuition.

The question of the state language(s) of Ukraine is an ideal pretense to lead any discussion away from the resolution of pressing problems. An endless argument begins, eventually reaching fisticuffs. Throughout the years of 2005-2019, Zelenskyy in Block productions and in politics often mocked excessive attention to the language issue. During Poroshenko's presidency Zelenskyy repeatedly encouraged letting people speak the language that is most convenient for them, stressing that Russian-speaking Ukrainians had never been discriminated against. Nevertheless, Poroshenko signed a law on April 24, 2019, according to which all office work, all teaching, and all journalism of Ukraine must be carried out in the state language, which was proclaimed to be Ukrainian. Zelenskyy has never tried to repeal or challenge this law, which, for all intents and purposes, was the last large-scale initiative of his predecessor, although he noted in social media that more than two thousand amendments were proposed in the Upper Rada alone.

At the same time, he willingly would switch into Russian when addressing Russians or meeting with Russian journalists. (That happened twice.) *Block 95* continued to be released in Russian. But the law on language remained unchanged—perhaps because in 2014 it still made sense to proclaim Russian the second state language. This would have deprived many opponents of Maidan of their main argument. But by 2019 most of the Ukrainian population no longer had any intention of speaking "the language of the enemy," as the best book of poems by the Russian-speaking Kyiv poet Alexander Kabanov was titled.

It so happened that Russia decided the language question for Ukraine, as Russia had wished. True, the result of the decision turned out to be nothing like what Putin and his cronies had dreamed of. All of Ukraine, including the recent ideologues of bilingualism, abandoned Russian entirely. On July 13, 2023, the Kyiv City Council posted on its website a ban against using Russian publicly in the capital—that is, against speaking Russian and selling Russian-language books (the ban on the import of books from Russia and Belarus was declared in an order that Zelenskyy signed on June 22). Everything about this ban on the import of books from the Russian Federation was complicated. The European Union believed that it contradicted the constitution, and its text was sent to the Venice Commission of the European Union for consideration, but either it was approved, or Ukraine did not wait for approvals. The Rada adopted the law, and the president signed it. Russian books could not be sold; Russian-language concerts could not be held; and Russian music could not be listened to in Kyiv—and I have no doubt that this is just the beginning. Three years ago, no one would have believed this, but, to be honest, after listening to Russian talk shows and reading the press, I also would not have believed that such a thing on paper and on screen was possible in principle.

At first, people wrote about Zelenskyy, if not sympathetically, then at least with interest. They laughed at his acting profession—of course, we have been mocking actor-presidents since the Reagan era. Obviously an actor can only enact someone else's texts! A president obviously can be from the special forces, or a county official, or, even, at worst a cook as Vladimir Lenin famously said, but a representative from the creative profession will ruin everything—precisely because he professionally requires freedom! However, as the war drew closer, the tone of writings and conversations about Zelenskyy—not only on the web, where lawlessness reigns by tradition, but also in the print press—became downright indecent. Someday, truly, we will remember this, and we will not believe it ourselves.

Ukraine's president (for now) Waldemar Zelensky arrived in Warsaw on a planned visit, emphasizing by his appearance that he had just swept in from the front, and was in no joking mood. His military khaki pants, military boots, military sweater (although this time it seemed to be black, rather than an ordinary jacket or T-shirt—he probably sent it to the laundry) and his unwashed head only emphasized the masculinity and asceticism of Ukraine's current leader, who lacked only a blood-soaked bandage on his head, and a Mauser in a wooden holster on his hip to top off the image. Against the background of this courageous little shrimp, Polish President Andrzej Duda looked like a spruced-up staff civilian who, in the presence of such a visitor, could only follow him with his eyes and bark out clearly: "Yes, sir! I will, sir! What else, sir?" However, for some reason Zelensky, and not the staff civilian, wiped his hands on his pants before shaking hands (he must have perspired suddenly). But he did it in a completely boyish way, like a street urchin from the neighboring yard.

Both presidents were accompanied by their spouses, but what is there to say about the ladies: Olena Zelenska, unlike her husband, demonstrated that she had not come here from the trenches: she wore a stylish coat with matching high-heeled shoes, and loose hair. There was nothing to say about Duda's wife. She, as an unabashed traitor, greeted the Zelenskys in pure Russian: "Dobry den'!" Rather like taking a sickle to a piano Zelensky plays upon! This picture is unredeemed even by her clothes that showed a hint of the colors of the Ukrainian flag.

This was from Russia's *Komsomolskaya Pravda*, dated April 5, 2023, but you could take any day, and any author, not just the reporter Alexander Grishin: he stands out especially, but the others aren't much better.

It goes without saying that I am no fan of government interference in the work of the press. But in any self-respecting state, a journalist from the most popular daily newspaper (650,000 copies) who wrote like this about the president of any unfriendly neighboring state—the largest in Europe—would be summoned by his superiors and called down on the carpet in such a way that the echo would be heard in all other federal publications. It would be assumed that the journalist would be fired for unprofessionalism, followed by his immediate superior and, probably, the editor-in-chief.

But that's the only way they write about Zelenskyy in Russia. Analysis is offered in the tone of street punks, which is especially pitiful because the authors are trying to be witty but can't pull it off. This cannot be compared to the sarcastic irony of such late Soviet-styled political observers as Genrikh Borovik or Farid Seiful-Mulyukov. The then Soviet diplomatic corps, and the loyal Communist Party detachment of political observers, were busy strenuously drowning out their own native sour aromas with exquisite perfume. They all wanted to look like peacemakers, and to be more European than the Europeans themselves. In Russia during the Ukrainian war, the style of street bullies prevailed, as if to declare we can afford ourselves this pleasure. They peered into all the international organizations, unbuttoned their pants and, shaking their business, took to proving it.

This style is called "Achtotakova" (so-what-of-it?) among professionals. Against this backdrop, Ukraine need not exert much effort to look like a living reproach to them, but this is the late-period Putin method: a period that has seen all restrictions lifted.

Whatever one may say, the complete ban on printed products of a state that has not only dropped lower than the baseboard, but has trampled itself in mud, is purely a hygienic measure, not a political one. The language problem in Ukraine has been solved through the end of the twenties. After that we will see what happens.

Many will say that language is not to blame, and they might even remember Bulat Okudzhava:

> Words and sub-phrases merge into one,
> But Warsaw and Moscow aren't to blame . . .
> It is not language that's guilty, but the vile spirit of a serf—
> be it from Warsaw or Moscow—lurking in a poisoned brain.
> When the fire of enmity is ruthless and worse,
> when a knife trembles in the hand, and an eye pains
> to look through a sight, why is language,
> great and mighty,
> the storehouse of love past and future, to blame?

But language long ago ceased to be a depository of love, and it is to blame—it was taken hostage, and it's too late for postmortems. German is to blame, it merged with the barking of German shepherds, who also were seemingly entirely innocent. There's nothing to be done about it: Russian after 2014 has become the language of lies and hatred, and we will be cleansing it for a long time. And as a response to the closure of the Ukrainian library in Moscow and the complete ban on the study of Ukrainian language and literature, it was high time for Ukraine to limit the use of Russian at home. I knew this library, I constantly drove past it to work at City FM radio, where at first (after participating in the Moscow protest rallies of 2012) I was fired, and then (for covering these rallies) the management was fired, and then the entire radio station was shut down, along with those who remained working under the new management. It is unclear who has done more to oppose the Russian language, that is, among those who speak it—the Russian government or the Ukrainian? But the Ukrainian government, unlike the Russian, has the right to do what it is doing. Nothing will happen to the language. And I swear, if it comes down to a launch of this book in Ukraine, I will conduct it in Ukrainian. My vocabulary is big enough for that, and they will somehow forgive me for my accent.

GOVERNMENT ADMINISTRATION. The first prime minister under Zelenskyy was Arsenii Honcharuk, a thirty-five-year-old lawyer who was considered the most liberal in terms of his economic views (before that he had been an adviser to the Minister of Ecology, later—an adviser to the Deputy Prime Minister as the Minister of Economy). Honcharuk was called a protege of Andrii Bohdan, under whom he spent a month as first deputy before he was confirmed for the post of prime minister. He worked in this capacity for seven months, after which he resigned.

The immediate reason for his resignation was the so-called "Honcharuk recordings" scandal (the publication of recordings of private conversations is a frequent thing in Ukrainian politics, starting with the famous recordings of Mykola Melnichenko, during which Leonid Kuchma indirectly sanctioned the murder of opposition journalist Georgy Gongadze. Ukrainian politicians do not worry about propriety in personal conversation, which can be considered another sign of inner freedom if you wish). In conversations with ministers, Honcharuk called himself a neophyte on the economy, but if only he had limited himself to himself! "Zelenskyy has a very primitive, simple understanding of economic processes. You just need to explain it to him in a human way: 'Vova, the fact that the rate is lower now means that potato salad at the next New Year's table will not be more expensive than this year.'" (Salad "olivier," roughly a kind of potato salad, is a frequent topic of jokes in the New Years' segments of *Block 95*.) Maksym Buzhanskyi and Oleksandr Dubinskyi, deputies from the Servant of the People party, initiated the matter of Honcharuk's resignation in the Rada. Davyd Arakhamiia, the leader of the faction, said that Honcharuk always communicates with the president respectfully and that they share an excellent relationship. Honcharuk firmly stated that the leaking of the tapes was a provocation of the oligarchy, whose members were unhappy with the systematic battle against corruption. Behind the publication of the leaks they saw primarily the hand of Ihor Kolomoiskyi, who was offended by the seizure of Privatbank. Kolomoiskyi, naturally, called it nonsense, although he spoke very negatively about Honcharuk's team.

The next government formed after Honcharuk's resignation began working on March 4, 2020. It was headed by Denys Shmyhal, a forty-seven-year-old economist (educated as an engineer), who at that time was the chairman of the Ivano-Frankivsk administration. The first drama he had to face when taking office was the COVID epidemic, which brought down the world economy; Shmyhal was considered a temporary figure and not particularly influential. However, he remained in power for two years, and COVID is usually blamed for the Ukrainian economy tumbling by 4 percent in 2020-2021. Budget revenues increased slightly under Shmyhal, and the deficit jumped almost three times (217 billion vs. 71 billion under Honcharuk). The reason Shmyhal was able to retain his post for so long is usually put down to his lack of independence, he is blamed for the low pace of European integration, and the growth of tariffs. His most controversial measure is called the "hard lockdown" that he enforced in March 2020. Shmyhal declared during a report in parliament that the lockdown had allowed Ukraine to avoid the Italian scenario. Indeed, the mortality rate during the epidemic in Ukraine was one of the lowest in Europe—1.9 percent. At the same time, his government is regularly accused of making low (and sloppy) payments to doctors, and of delays in the import of vaccines. Shmyhal is credited with compensation payments paid out to businesses during the lockdown (there was nothing like this in Russia), but doing this meant a multiple increase in the state debt. In short, weighty objections were attached to any compliment, and the lack of new personnel changes in government in 2022 was explained only by the fact that war is not the best time for them.

According to the results of the first two years of Zelenskyy's presidency, this is the only area where he received minimal criticism, since he did not interfere with the work of the professionals. In the very first days of Zelenskyy's presidency, his representative in the Upper Rada, Ruslan Stefanchuk, told the Left Bank portal: "The presidential administration must cease to act as a parallel government, and limit itself to three functions—an administrative office, an analytical center that develops new ideas and programs, and a place that exerts control over the President's decisions."

Zelenskyy's first Minister of the Economy ("economic development, trade and agriculture") was Timofii Mylovanov, who was forty-five years old, the honorary president of the Higher School of Economics of Ukraine, and an associate professor at the University of Pittsburgh in the United States. He held office until March 4, 2020, when he was replaced by a peer, Ihor Petrashko, who also held the job for less than a year. Oleksii Liubchenko, who was also appointed first deputy prime minister, took office on May 18, 2021. The title was now shorter (Minister of Economic Development). Liubchenko was fifty years old and held a PhD in Economics. He remained in office only until November, after which he was replaced by Yuliia Svyrydenko, thirty-seven, who was previously first deputy minister. She remains in the position to this day. In the history of Russia, such a rapid change of leaders is called "ministerial leapfrog" and does not suggest a sign of success. For Ukraine, however, which was plunging from a pandemic crisis into a military crisis, such operational management was quite normal.

However, in a relatively objective article (impartiality was still possible at this point) by Vladimir Chernegi, a leading researcher at the Institute of Scientific Information on Social Sciences at the Russian Academy of Sciences, Zelenskyy's achievements were evaluated modestly—but with a certain benevolence:

> Reality turned out to be much more complicated than V. Zelensky, who was engaging in politics for the first time, apparently assumed it would be. There is no doubt that he sincerely wanted to change the situation in Ukraine for the better. (*In 2022, it was the opposite that was not doubted, but in the course of a single year Zelenskyy had turned into Russia's number one enemy.—D. B.*) But he inherited a very difficult legacy, formed during the years of independence, and aggravated by the rule of P. Poroshenko. After the collapse of the USSR, Ukraine's economy slipped significantly lower than Russia's, and in the years 2000–2007 it did not enjoy the growth that our country had. As a result, if in 1990 the GDP per capita in the Ukrainian SSR was slightly higher than in the RSFSR, by 2014 it was almost

three times lower than Russia's. In 2018 the World Bank considered Ukraine the poorest country in Europe. True, in terms of purchasing power parity, Moldova "overtook" it in this regard, but this could hardly be a consolation for Ukrainians.

Even under P. Poroshenko, Ukraine found itself in debt dependence on the IMF, the World Bank, and other international financial institutions, most of them controlled by the United States. V. Zelensky and the Ukrainian government had to prove for a long time to its main creditor, the IMF, that they were carrying out market reforms according to prescribed patterns in order to receive in May 2020 consent to a new advance of 5 billion dollars over the next 18 months. For its part, the EU has also allocated a soft loan of 1.2 billion euros, stretched over 12 months, with the condition that Ukraine continues cooperation with the IMF. Zelensky, following the latter's demands, pushed through a law in Ukraine's Upper Rada authorizing the purchase and sale of land, which caused a very mixed reaction in Ukrainian society. Finally, although loans from the IMF, the International Bank and the EU are provided at a low interest rate (1.2–1.4 percent per annum), they still must be paid. In 2020 Ukraine had to pay \$5.45 billion on its debt obligations, of which 1.35 billion is owed the IMF alone. In other words, the country is in a vicious circle, which it cannot break yet.

Zelenskyy, however, never declared himself a strong economist. The biggest achievement of the Ukrainian economy in the first two years of his presidency was the lifting of the moratorium on the sale of land. The sale of agricultural land began in Ukraine on July 1, 2021. In 2020, the Ukrainian economy was falling due to the pandemic, in 2021 it showed a slight increase, and in 2022 it fell by a quarter due to the war. But the payment of salaries in Ukraine was not delayed, pensions were paid, and there was no shortage of food. Of course, this is largely due to European aid—but it also displays a wonderful adaptability to any crises.

In general, the situation has changed little since Zelenskyy delivered a lecture on the Ukrainian economy in *Block 95*: "We have achieved the highest economic level: we are beggars. This is a reliable practice—tested by the Romany. The scheme is as follows: you give us your money—we do not return it to you."

However, John Kennedy once told Walter Cronkite, when asked what was the biggest surprise for him in the first months of his presidency: "Everything turned out to be just as bad as I said it was during the election campaign."

CORRUPTION. Zelenskyy was asked about this at every pre-war press conference—I myself witnessed how, in August 2021, answering questions from German, Ukrainian, and Russian journalists (I was the Russian), he spoke with great irritation about Ukrainian corruption being mythologized. A myth and cliche had been made of it, where, in fact, it was no worse than anywhere in Europe, etc. Speaking at Stanford University on September 3, Zelenskyy answered students' questions, including those about corruption: "Digitalization is one of the priority reforms in Ukraine, it is moving forward very successfully, potently and quickly. The outcome of this reform is a victory over any medium, petty corruption in the state. Digitalization of all public services, digitalization of the government, the Office of the President, and the Upper Rada. A paperless program has now been launched . . . We want more online voting. We are developing a cashless program with the Minister, which will be a real breakthrough."

Opinions differ about the breakthrough in the fight against corruption under Zelenskyy. He himself repeatedly called this issue a priority. The opposition, however, like any Ukrainian opposition, accused him and his entourage of corruption. New recordings regularly surfaced with Andrii Yermak discussing appointments to positions and the corresponding rates. Zelenskyy himself was accused of flying on vacation to Oman at the expense of the host party. Prosecutor General Iryna Venediktova was systematically scolded for not fulfilling her own demands to the state—no large-scale successes within the framework of de-oligarchization had occurred. Even if they had happened, Zelenskyy would have been accused of rewarding people who had promoted him to power. The president's rating held steady in 2020 mainly on the remnants of pride in the unprecedented risk that Ukraine took upon itself by choosing a fundamentally non-systemic politician. In 2021, the rating fell because Zelenskyy made perhaps his most offensive and most understandable mistake: he underestimated the seriousness and cruelty of Vladimir Putin's intentions. This mistake, however, was made by the whole world (except for Oleksii Arestovych, who became famous for this). Zelenskyy did not believe until the last that Putin would start a war. Allowing himself increasingly harsh statements against the Russian government, Zelenskyy clearly hoped he could manage the situation.

And incidentally, one more thing, although this idea is unlikely to earn the support of readers, especially these days. Everyone talks about "corruption, corruption," but it really does seem to be invincible. Even on July 12, 2023, when NATO offered Ukraine a one-stage path into the bloc with maximum favorability, the battle against corruption was named *de rigueur* as one of the two conditions for entry (the first, predictably, was the end of the war). This is the time to recall the great phrase from Mikhail Uspensky's novel *The Paradise Machine*: "Why say 'corruption' when the word 'tradition' exists?" I wish to say a word in defense of corruption—who will regret it except for me? Let's call a spade a spade: anyone who served in the Soviet Army remembers that regulations were worse than hazing. Regulations can screw a soldier over so badly that any kind of hazing would seem humane. The law of thieves is more humane than the law of camp authorities, although this has nothing to do with the romantic concept of honor, as Russian chronicler of the Soviet labor camps Varlam Shalamov showed. Corruption is one of those horizontal ties that oppose the state vertical. If you do not want to live under the yoke of the state mafia, you will have to tolerate a self-organized, democratic mafia, so to speak.

Ukrainian society is corporate in nature, it knows how to negotiate, it is capable of excellent self-organization, which Maidan proved. But wherever there is self-organization, there is also an informal negotiated economy. The fact that corruption in Ukraine turned out to be invincible was just more proof that Ukraine is invincible as a whole. And if someone wants to object that everything is fine with corruption in totalitarian Russia, I will answer very honestly: maybe corruption is the only living thing that remains in Russia's dead society? I don't remember the author of the formula that, without corruption Mexico would be a completely fascist state; it must belong to a Mexican. We ought to suggest a slogan for Russia's reconstruction period: "Corruption is the last refuge of humanity!" It's a shame that Ukraine won't pick up on that. Ukraine will join NATO, but no one will invite Russia anywhere. Noble crooks like Ostap Bender, a lovable rogue from popular satirical novels by Ilf and Petrov, were the only decent people in the great year of transition. The human in general more often survives in its negative manifestations, because the positive ones die first in times of troubles. They say only cockroaches will survive a nuclear war—like Mayakovsky posited that, under communism, only the bedbugs survived: everyone else is already an android.

OPERATION AVENUE. The biggest scandal of the pre-war period of Zelenskyy's presidency was Wagnergate, or Operation Avenue—the failed arrest of thirty-three members of the mercenary Wagner group who were fighting in Donbas.

By the fall of 2019, the Main Intelligence Directorate of the Ministry of Defense of Ukraine possessed data about more than a thousand Russian mercenaries. Most of them were lounging around doing nothing in 2019. It was decided to create a fake mercenary military company and recruit former mercenaries in order, allegedly, to protect oil fields in Syria. These individuals would be transported out of Russian territory—and would be arrested. The initial plan was to lure them to Hungary, ostensibly to training camps, which really did exist on Hungarian territory, and from there they would be transported to Ukraine. An internet domain, office-rosneft.org, was created in September. It was intended ostensibly to recruit guards from oil fields being developed by Rosneft in the Middle East. Unemployed mercenaries readily fell for it. They were promised a salary of 225,000 rubles a month. But the approach was flawed: too many people wanted to enlist, including ordinary unemployed Russians who had no combat experience, especially from Donbas. The next approach was more successful: now the applicants were required to have combat experience. Artyom Milyaev was one of the first to enlist using the call sign "Shaman"—it was reliably known that he had fought in Donbas and had commanded a unit there. He was promised 2,000 rubles for each recruit. By the summer of 2020, the militants had sent to the Ukrainian intelligence service (which produced the stationary of a non-existent private military company with the proper stamps and seals) more than 200 questionnaires containing detailed descriptions of their exploits on the territory of Donbas. They themselves, voluntarily and in detail, divulged all their data, including their measurements, photographs of their military awards (including those issued by the Kremlin) and detailed descriptions of war crimes that were hitherto considered unproven. In its grace and simplicity, Operation Avenue superseded by far all previous achievements of Ukrainian intelligence. Analysts of the Bellingcat group engaged in international cyber investigations were given access to these confessionary questionnaires, listened to recordings of telephone conversations between recruiters and candidates, and could not contain their delight (the investigation was published in November 2020).

Amazing things surfaced. First of all, there was evidence of the Russian army's direct leadership of the so-called Donetsk rebels; what propaganda in Russia presented as an uprising of supporters of the "Russian world" turned out to be a banal special operation, the participants of which were trained at the Military Academy of the Russian General Staff. The mercenaries were eager to fight, but the State Intelligence Agency (GUR) had still not worked out all the details of the operation. There were occasional comic moments—to justify the delay, they had to "kill" one curator, and appoint another. Zelenskyy was made privy to the course of the operation only on June 15, while the operation was scheduled to take place on July 26. According to the plan, the plane transporting mercenaries from Belarus to Istanbul was to enter the airspace of Ukraine for half an hour. One of the passengers was supposed to simulate a heart attack, but in this case it would have been easier for the pilots to return to Minsk; so then they began developing a variant with a bomb on board, information about which an employee of State Security was to transmit from Minsk. The operation was overseen directly by Borys Burba, director of GUR, the state security services.

The "first platoon" was formed (no one said there would be no second). It consisted of forty-seven of the most wanted militants who had participated in the fighting in eastern Ukraine, including the town of Debaltseve. However, they managed to purchase only thirty-four tickets to Istanbul. The candidates for the non-existent private military company were first taken to Minsk by bus, then had to be taken to the airport. They left Moscow on July 24. Burba and the deputy head of the Ukrainian Security Forces, Ruslan Baranetskyi, were supposed to report to the president on their state of readiness on July 23. But then the peculiarities began. Zelenskyy was busy, and the head of the presidential administration, Andrii Yermak, received them instead. He asked—or did he order?—that the operation be postponed for a week, since on July 23 Zelenskyy (at a joint press conference with the President of Switzerland) announced a truce reached in Donbas as a result of the efforts of the Normandy Format. Operation Avenue could allegedly disrupt this truce. The thinking appeared to be that if everything were to happen a week later, there would be no disruption.

Not only was this explanation impossibly artificial (a week in this situation would have solved nothing), it simply does not stand up to criticism, if only because the head of the presidential administration could not make such a decision. An operation of this scale is supervised directly by the President. And if it was Zelenskyy himself who made this decision, it remains utterly unclear why he made it, then withdrew it, and then, afterward, dismissed the head of military intelligence Burba (who, however, suffered no consequences, switched to teaching, and subsequently became a lawyer in Kyiv).

But the operation was postponed, the tickets were changed with great difficulty, and a group of mercenaries, divided into two detachments (they could not send everyone in one day), had to leave the Belorusochka boarding house near Minsk a week later. And then the inevitable idiocies intervened. They were of the kind that are present in any senile regime that is capable only of carrying out missions by force: The Belarusian special services came into play. No one, of course, had informed them of anything in order to avoid leaks. Anyway, who would trust the special services of Aleksandr Lukashenka, who was totally dependent on the Kremlin?

The fact was that Lukashenka was then facing reelection. The elections were fictitious, as always in the Belarus that had been entrusted to him. As they always had been during his twenty-six years in power, they were faked, causing outright ridicule not only abroad, but also inside the country. Plus, there were elections! This time there were even three competitors who were not puppets at all: Sviatlana Tsikhanouskaya, the wife of an arrested opposition leader; Viktor Babariko, a diplomat and the head of Belgazprombank; and Valery Tsepkalo, the creator of Belarus's Hi-Tech Park. Lukashenka was nervous. And then a message reaches him that in a boarding house near Minsk, a group of relatively young, well-built Russians had arrived in Belarus with an unclear purpose. They were conducting regular evening checks on the second floor—and refraining from drinking alcohol! It was so unlike the behavior of ordinary Russian tourists that the Belarusian KGB decided to arrest all the mercenaries. And so, in the early morning of July 29, Belarusian special forces soldiers arrived at the boarding house in a minibus, put all potential participants of the private military company face down, searched their rooms and belongings, then escorted them away under arrest. That day, all Belarus's news programs showed footage of the detention of Russian militants who allegedly had arrived in Minsk in collusion with the Belarusian opposition.

Nobody in Ukraine, except for the leaders of the operation, was aware of any of this. There was shock in Russia, since no one, of course, had sent militants to overthrow the Lukashenka regime. Lukashenka was so unnerved that he repeated the mantra of an attempted coup (soon he would have to talk about it around the clock because mass protests against the upcoming election had begun in Belarus). Dmitry Peskov, the press secretary of the Russian president (there is a joke about him that doctors can never give him the right diagnosis, because he cannot stop lying), disavowed the version of the coup, but did not offer any other. Ukraine sent a request to extradite the mercenaries, handing over documents to the Belarusian security forces about their participation in hostilities on Ukrainian territory. Although Lukashenka had been trying to maneuver between Ukraine and Russia for some time, he flatly refused to hand over mercenaries to Kyiv, and on

August 16 they were sent to Russia. The "Wagnergate" scandal broke out in Ukraine. On August 5, Zelenskyy dismissed Burba and appointed his deputy Kyrylo Budanov, at that time thirty-four years old, as head of GUR. Burba was indignant and demanded that everyone who knew anything about Operation Avenue be checked by a lie detector for leaks. No leaks were detected.

There are three main versions of this stunning failure—that is, the disruption of the potentially most successful operation of Ukrainian intelligence for the entire time of its existence. First: the betrayal of Yermak, who, according to unconfirmed information, is the son of a GRU officer, and is Russia's "mole" in the Ukrainian leadership. Since Yermak consistently causes enmity and envy, and the secret of his influence on Zelenskyy remains undisclosed, we cannot confirm or refute this version. Second: Zelenskyy's fear of Putin, who could have responded to this international scandal in any way he saw fit, including the beginning of military action. Zelenskyy obviously believed in the possibility of a truce with Russia in 2020 (and continued to in January 2022, even as he was receiving all the evidence of an imminent conflict from Western intelligence agencies). His promise to end the war was one of the main points of his election program. Zelenskyy himself publicly repeated several times in August 2020 that this was "not our operation," and that Ukraine was being dragged into it (without specifying by whom—Russia or America). It is clear that this outright lie did not stand up to any criticism, instead covering up more serious problems.

The third version is present in all attempts to explain many Ukrainian failures: Russian agents introduced back in the time of Yanukovych, or notoriously ubiquitous leaks. The level of folly in post-Soviet politics in the post-Soviet territories is always high, and if, in the preparatory stages of the operation, things went without a hitch thanks to the greed of the unscrupulous potential mercenaries, someone may have just blabbed in the final stage. Be that as it may, Zelenskyy's near grandiose success became the loudest scandal of his entire pre-war presidency—a scandal all the more insulting because, despite the Wagnerians' serious war crimes, the whole thing had an element of farce running through it. The *Servant of the People* confidently entered its fourth season.

FOREIGN POLICY. UKRAGATE. On the eve of the expiration of the previous president's powers, during the celebration of Europe Day in Kyiv, Petro Poroshenko uttered some farewell words to Zelenskyy in regard to foreign policy. He should continue moving toward the European Union, and create a broad global coalition to deter Russian aggression. Poroshenko urged Zelenskyy to establish membership in the European Union by 2023, and to sign a plan to join NATO. Zelenskyy did all this, and on June 23, 2022, during his term, at the height of the war with Russia, Ukraine was officially granted the status of a candidate for EU membership. But truth to tell, Ukraine already had more serious problems at that moment.

The development of relations with the United States was complicated by internal American scandals: Zelenskyy neither dissembled, nor flattered Donald Trump when he said he was learning from his achievements and, in part, following his path. Trump is also an artist of the conversational genre, although much less professional. He is a showman with claims to being a narrator king, who, however, provides his nation not so much a plot of existence, as reasons for continuous discord. The scandal surrounding Zelenskyy's conversation with Trump was called Ukragate, following the Watergate scandal naming convention.

This was the first (and so far the last) clash between Zelenskyy and another showman in a lofty state post.

There are two versions regarding Trump and his position on the Ukrainian issue. According to the first, the war would not have started at all under Trump; according to the second, Trump would not have helped Ukraine and would have taken an unambiguous pro-Putin position. That today's Trump criticizes Biden's position is nothing sensational, it is natural and does not express his personal view of the war in any way (especially since he has never taken a personal position on most political issues: he merely follows trends, populism, outrage, and other simple mechanisms slavishly). Most likely, Trump, as usual, would have acted in his own interests (which position he tried to impose on the whole country with commendable frankness). If Zelenskyy had fulfilled certain conditions, he would have supported him, if he had balked, he would have abandoned him. And if for Biden the support of the democratically elected Ukrainian president is no empty phrase, then Trump shares with Putin a total lack of any moral or legal guardrails.

(I remind you that this book has the goal of offering a full plate of information, but is, by no means, objective; I have seen many things in my life, but never objectivity.)

The plot is as follows: on July 25, 2019, two months after Zelenskyy's inauguration, Donald Trump, in a telephone conversation, asked him to facilitate an investigation into Hunter Biden, Joe Biden's son, who by that time was Trump's chief rival in the 2020 elections. The request was accompanied by a promise to step up assistance to Ukraine—primarily military— if Zelenskyy agreed. An anonymous U.S. intelligence officer, who found out about the content of the conversation, saw in it pressure on the President of Ukraine, and submitted a report to his superiors (that is, to the director of the national intelligence). He concealed this appeal from the Senate, although he was obliged to acquaint the legislature with it immediately. The information became known to the Speaker of the House of Representatives Nancy Pelosi, who announced the beginning of impeachment proceedings against Trump.

Hunter Biden worked with the Ukrainian company Burisma Holding. Trump's lawyer Rudy Giuliani has repeatedly stated that Zelenskyy is surrounded by Trump's enemies and people interfering in the American elections. The July 25 conversation was published by the Americans, and it is not a very good conversation—on the part of Zelenskyy, firstly. Trump says nothing illegal here, which was confirmed by the Senate's vote to find Trump innocent in his impeachment trial of February 2020; but Zelenskyy almost demonstrates servility. Of course, one can object that the published text is not a transcript, but rather a reconstruction, which, in reality, might make everything look different. But, alas, the text seems to be authentic. In the spirit of Zelenskyy—in the spirit of an actor who wants to please the public, he says exactly what is expected of him.

Furthermore, this is a conversation of fellow showmen, which Zelenskyy strongly emphasizes. Indeed, the second half of the 2010s was marked by the stunning victories of two TV stars in the United States and Ukraine. Both were shameful for the entire field of political science, yet marked the beginning of a new political style. Zelenskyy sincerely believes that his colleague Trump cannot be a "bad person" (both often use this phrase). But Trump is an experienced master recruiter, as is Putin, and he is also very good at being pleasant.

I will quote this conversation in part, although it is already well known. It reminds me of something. Oh, I know! It reminds me of some of the most caustic numbers of *Block 95*. And it develops very much in the genre of *Block 95*, as if Baldy (Yevhen Koshevoi) were speaking for Trump, and Zelenskyy for Zelenskyy, of course. Here is this reconstruction of the conversation, as it was published by the administration of the president under pressure from the curious public.[1]

Donald Trump: Congratulations on a great victory. We all watched from the United States and you did a terrific job. The way you came from behind, somebody who wasn't given much of a chance, and you ended up winning easily. It's a fantastic achievement. Congratulations.

Volodymyr Zelenskyy: You are absolutely right Mr. President. [...] I would like to confess to you that I had an opportunity to learn from you. We used quite a few of your skills and knowledge and were able to use it as an example for our elections and yes it is true that these were unique elections. We were in a unique situation that we were able to achieve a unique success. I'm able to tell you the following; the first time you called me to congratulate me when I won my presidential election, and the second time you are now calling me when my party won the parliamentary election. I think I should run more often so you can call me more often and we can talk over the phone more often.

---

1 https://s3.documentcloud.org/documents/6429027/White-House-Transcript-2019.pdf
 https://s3.documentcloud.org/documents/6550423/Trump-Zelensky-April-Call-Transcript.pdf

Donald Trump (laughter): That's a very good idea.

Volodymyr Zelenskyy: Well yes, to tell you the truth, we are trying to work hard because we wanted to drain the swamp here in our country. We brought in many many new people. Not the old politicians, not the typical politicians, because we want to have a new format and a new type of government . . . You are a great teacher for us and in that.

Donald Trump: Well it's very nice of you to say that. I will say that we do a lot for Ukraine. We spend a lot of effort and a lot of time. Much more than the European countries are doing and they should be helping you more than they are. Germany does almost nothing for you. All they do is talk and I think it's something that you should really ask them about. [. . .] Angela Merkel talks Ukraine, but she doesn't do anything. A lot of the European countries are the same way so I think it's something you want to look at but the United States has been very very good to Ukraine. I wouldn't say that it's reciprocal necessarily because things are happening that are not good *(In Ukraine's behavior.—D. B.)* but the United States has been very very good to Ukraine.

Volodymyr Zelenskyy: Yes you are absolutely right. Not only 100%, but actually 1000%. [. . .] I did talk to Angela Merkel and I did meet with her. I also met and talked with Macron. I told them that they are not doing quite as much as they need to be doing on the issues with the sanctions. They are not enforcing the sanctions. They are not working as much as they should work for Ukraine. [. . .] Logically, the European Union should be our biggest partner but technically the United States is a much bigger partner than the European Union and I'm very grateful to you for that because the United States is doing quite a lot for Ukraine. Much more than the European Union especially when we are talking about sanctions against the Russian Federation. I would also like to thank you for your great support in the area of defense. We are ready to continue to cooperate for the next steps—specifically we are almost ready to buy more Javelins [. . .].

Donald Trump: I would like you to do us a favor though because our country has been through a lot and Ukraine knows a lot about it. I would like you to find out what happened with this whole situation with Ukraine, they say Crowdstrike . . . I guess you have one of your wealthy people . . . The server, they say Ukraine has it. There are a lot of things that went on [. . .]. I think you're surrounding yourself with some of the same people. I would like to have the Attorney General call you or your people and I would like you to get to the bottom of it. As you saw yesterday, that whole nonsense ended with a very poor performance by a man named Robert Mueller. [. . .] They say a lot of it started with Ukraine. Whatever you can do, it's very important that you do it if that's possible.

Volodymyr Zelenskyy: Yes it is very important for me and everything that you just mentioned earlier. [. . .] We are open for any future cooperation. We are ready to open a new page on cooperation in relations between the United States and Ukraine. [. . .] I just recalled our ambassador from United States (*Valerii Chalyi; immediately upon taking office, Zelenskyy changed out twelve ambassadors.—D. B.*) and he will be replaced by a very competent and very experienced ambassador who will work hard on making sure that our two nations are getting closer. I would also like and hope to see him having your trust and your confidence and have personal relations with you so we can cooperate even more so. [. . .] One of my assistants spoke with Mr. Giuliani just recently and we are hoping very much that Mr. Giuliani will be able to travel to Ukraine and we will meet [. . .] I just wanted to assure you once again that you have nobody but friends around us. I will make sure that I surround myself with the best and most experienced people. I also wanted to tell you that we are friends. We are great friends and you Mr. President have friends in our country so we can continue our strategic partnership. I also plan to surround myself with great people and in addition to that investigation, I guarantee as the President of Ukraine that all the investigations will be done openly and candidly. That I can assure you.

This whole thing was purely a monologue from *Block 95*. I don't believe, I can't imagine, that he said any of this seriously. How good it is to be an actor, when you can always say you were just joking. Better yet to be two actors so you can always say you were both joking.

Donald Trump: Good because I heard you had a prosecutor who was very good and he was shut down and that's really unfair. A lot of people are talking about that, the way they shut your very good prosecutor down and you had some very bad people involved. Mr. Giuliani is a highly respected man. He was the mayor of New York City, a great mayor, and I would like him to call you. I will ask him to call you along with the Attorney General. Rudy very much knows what's happening and he is a very capable guy. If you could speak to him that would be great. The former ambassador from the United States, the woman was bad news and the people she was dealing with in the Ukraine were bad news so I just want to let you know that. (*This was Marie Yovanovitch, not at all a bad woman, she was just a Democrat and an opponent of Trump. Trump accused her of disloyalty, saying that she refused to issue visas to Ukrainians who were willing to bear witness about the conspiracy of Trump's opponents and the Ukrainian representatives.—D. B.*) The other thing, there's a lot of talk about Biden's son, that Biden stopped the prosecution and a lot of people want to find out about that so whatever you can do with the Attorney General would be great. Biden went around bragging that he stopped the prosecution so if you can look into it . . . It sounds horrible to me.

Volodymyr Zelenskyy: I wanted to tell you about the prosecutor. First of all I understand and I'm knowledgeable about the situation. Since we have won the absolute majority in our Parliament; the next prosecutor general will be 100% my person, my candidate, who will be approved by the parliament and will start as a new prosecutor in September. (*The previous prosecutor was Yurii Lutsenko, the next was Ruslan Riaboshapka, whom the Rada would fire just six months after he was confirmed on March 5, 2020. The reason for his firing was either that he was going to arrest Kolomoiskyi, or that he was unable to arrest Poro-*

shenko.—D. B.) He or she will look into the situation, specifically to the company that you mentioned in this issue. The issue of the investigation of the case is actually the issue of making sure to restore the honesty so we will take care of that and will work on the investigation of the case. On top of that, I would kindly ask you if you have any additional information that you can provide to us, it would be very helpful for the investigation to make sure that we administer justice in our country with regard to the Ambassador to the United States from Ukraine as far as I recall her name was Ivanovich. (*Yovanovitch, but who's checking?—D. B.*) It was great that you were the first one who told me that she was a bad ambassador because I agree with you 100%. Her attitude toward me was far from the best as she admired the previous President and she was on his side. She would not accept me as a new President well enough.

Donald Trump: Well, she's going to go through some things. I will have Mr. Giuliani give you a call and I am also going to have Attorney General Barr call and we will get to the bottom of it. I'm sure you will figure it out. I heard the prosecutor was treated very badly and he was a very fair prosecutor so good luck with everything. Your economy is going to get better and better I predict. You have a lot of assets. It's a great country. I have many Ukrainian friends, their [*sic*] incredible people.

Volodymyr Zelenskyy: I would like to tell you that I also have quite a few Ukrainian friends that live in the United· States. Actually last time I traveled to the United States, I stayed in New York near Central Park and I stayed at the Trump Tower. I will talk to them and I hope to see them again in the future. I also wanted to thank you for your invitation to visit the United States, specifically Washington DC. On the other hand, I also want to ensure you that we will be very serious about the case and will work on the investigation. As to the economy, there is much potential for our two countries and one of the issues that is very important for Ukraine is energy independence. I believe we can be very successful and cooperating on energy independence with United States. We are already working on cooperation. We are buying American oil but I am very hopeful for a future meeting. We will have more time and more opportunities to discuss these opportunities and get to know each other better. I would like to thank you very much for your support

Donald Trump: Good. Well, thank you very much and I appreciate that. I will tell Rudy and Attorney General Barr to call. Thank you. Whenever you would like to come to the White House, feel free to call. Give us a date and we'll work that out. I look forward to seeing you.

Volodymyr Zelenskyy: Thank you very much. I would be very happy to come and would be happy to meet with you personally and get to know you better. I am looking forward to our meeting and I also would like to invite you to visit Ukraine and come to the city of Kyiv which is a beautiful city. We have a beautiful country which would welcome you. On the other hand, I believe that on September 1 we will be in Poland and we can meet in Poland hopefully. After that, it might be a very good idea for you to travel to Ukraine. We can either take my plane and go to Ukraine or we can take your plane, which is probably much better than mine.

Donald Trump: Okay, we can work that out. I look forward to seeing you in Washington and maybe in Poland because I think we are going to be there at that time.

Volodymyr Zelenskyy: Thank you very much Mr. President.

Donald Trump: Congratulations on a fantastic job you've done. The whole world was watching. I'm not sure it was so much of an upset but congratulations.

Volodymyr Zelenskyy: Thank you Mr. President, bye-bye.

This is an ugly conversation on both sides—primarily for its selfishness; but on the other hand, what was Zelenskyy to do? He needs to enlist the support of the United States at any cost, and Trump seems to be a colleague asking for nothing more than help with an objective investigation of the Hunter Biden case. In exchange they promise financial assistance and a great economy. Even in the States, Trump was found innocent in the impeachment hearing which included this conversation as evidence. Besides,

Zelenskyy did not pass on any compromising material on Hunter Biden, which led to Trump's refusal to meet with him. Trump apparently thought Zelenskyy was a novice and a layman, while Zelenskyy, as mentioned above, is very, very sharp. Perhaps, with the same irrational instinct that guided Ukraine in choosing Zelenskyy, Zelenskyy himself guessed he would have to deal with Biden next, and Biden really did help him, albeit reluctantly, and not immediately.

Zelenskyy, however, hit it off immediately with Boris Johnson. They had one of their first conversations on February 24, and Johnson visited Kyiv three times after Russia's special military operation began. He was given a serious offer to become the mayor of Odesa after his premiership ended, and he jokingly agreed. He is similar to Zelenskyy in psychological type. He wasn't the least interested in oldsters like Trump and Biden, wars of *kompromat*, or a tug-of-war in the state of Florida. He wanted to open a new page in world politics. In fact, he did that, but at a catastrophically high price. But Johnson, more than Biden or even more so than Trump, was the new type of politician that Zelenskyy wanted to deal with.

What was so new about Johnson? Like Zelenskyy, he worked in the media. He had a total of thirty years of journalistic experience, of which the first ten were political journalism, after which he wrote a car column in *GQ*. Politically, he and Zelenskyy seemed to be at odds—Johnson had always been a Eurosceptic, and he was able to pull Britain out of the EU, while Zelenskyy is very eager to become part of the EU. The European bureaucracy does not frighten him, although it would not be an exaggeration to say that Zelenskyy, too, is a Eurosceptic, because the current Europe of tolerance and half-hearted solutions does not suit him at all. It can be said that both, each from their own position, were trying to wake Europe up, to restore its integrity, to teach it to resist (not on the basis of Russophobia, as many will hasten to say, but on the basis of modernity, which Russia has every intention of ending). They generally share similar styles, openness, extravagance, courage, and ostentatiousness. It was no coincidence that Johnson was initiated into the Cossacks in Chernihiv and recorded in the military annals under the name of Borys Chuprina

(Boris Chub, so to speak, although that's a nickname that would best suit Trump).

> He partied during COVID, on his birthday. He let COVID lockdowns go on too long. He let his girlfriend, now his wife, cut his hair. An expensive London barber cut his hair. The prime minister's official barber came to his house and cut his hair. He's sloppy in public. He's an aristocrat. He worked as a journalist. He drinks too much (see: journalist, aristocrat). He dyes his hair, though his sister Rachel insists that the entire Johnson family are natural blondes, which is a bit too much information, maybe. Someone has something else to say about his hair. His hair is the secret to his political success, as well as the secret flaw or Achilles' heel by which his political failure might have been foretold. The problem with Boris is that he's lazy. He was barely interested in being prime minister.

That is how the Jewish online magazine *Tablet* led into an interview with him in February 2023. The interview was conducted by David Samuels, the editor of *The Pill*, a very hip guy who does not bother with political correctness and is called the founder of neo-gonzo journalism. Here's how he writes about Johnson next:

> Only, on his way out of office, and actually a year before that, Boris Johnson did the most consequential thing that any British prime minister has done since botching the Suez Canal takeover, leaving India and Palestine, and winning the Second World War.
> Boris Johnson stood up for Ukraine, and against Putin, when Ukraine was alone in the world, on the front lines of democracy, which no one particularly cared to defend, except for the Ukrainians, whom the rest of the world had come to understand as patsies for the Russians, and as an ATM for corrupt American politicians who partied on their yachts, fucked their hookers, and stuffed their pockets with cash from their oil and gas companies, which were as much Putin's companies as theirs. Alone among the leaders of the West,

who had benefited from Ukrainian largesse, only Boris Johnson, the Muppet who thought he was Churchill, thought they would fight.

Vampire Washington, aged, wealthy and corrupt, was inclined to go along with whatever Vladimir Putin wanted, feeding him Crimea, and slices of Donbas, and warm water ports in Syria, and nuclear reactor contracts in Iran like canapes to a hungry crocodile. In turn, Putin believed that Western governments were staffed by hollow sissy men who would drop their pants and bend over for him. In fact, Putin believed, in their decadence and emptiness, they yearned for it, for a taste of the good old czarist lash.

As for the Ukrainians, Putin thought, when were they ever a nation? A weird mix of Nazified peasants and servile Jews, Stalin taught them who was boss. Putin, though perhaps only a modest tyrant by comparison, was a Russian leader, and Stalin's heir. There could be only one outcome to the fight, which would be over in a week, or two at the most. The triumphal parade of tanks through the heart of Kyiv would continue on for days. It would be the greatest sight since the Red Army entered Berlin, or Budapest, or Prague.

The Ukrainian people believed otherwise. As did President Volodymyr Zelenskyy, the heroic Jewish comedian, who played a president on TV, and then in real life, better than anyone had done since Ronald Reagan. Just as Boris played the role of British prime minister better than anyone since Margaret Thatcher, who was also famous for her hair.

What?! Now that's how you write! But who in politically-correct Europe, or even more so in Russia, could afford such a thing? In Ukraine, not everyone was ready for such directness and brilliance. But for Samuels it was no big deal. He was on the fringes, he could afford to do it. It was not for nothing that Johnson talked to him without the slightest self-censorship:

It's been a catastrophe. And the point, what I saw was how Putin is able to drop a 500-kilo bomb on an eight-story block of flats and just reduce it to nothing, with no conscience at all, no understanding of the laws of war or humanity. But he's doing it the whole time across all of occupied Ukraine and all the bits that he's attacking. And he's torturing, maiming, murdering innocent civilians the whole time. I'm so worried about Ukraine fatigue.

He gave a remarkable speech [in London], and he was very focused on planes. I was very struck by how much emphasis he put on the need for jets. It's absolutely true. They need a load of stuff to stop the Russian aggression, but also to retake the ground that Russia has occupied. That's the only way to finish this thing off. You have to get the land bridge.

But don't forget, there's always been a reluctance. So, right back at the beginning, a year ago, more than a year ago now, eighteen months ago. I remember when Ben Wallace, the UK defense secretary, and I were first considering whether or not to send shoulder-launched antitank weaponry, NLAWs. We had the system saying, "No, no, no, no, no. This would be an escalation. It'll provoke the Russians." We did it. It was invaluable, the NLAWs, the Javelins, which the U.S. sent, Donald Trump sent, actually, were invaluable in allowing the Ukrainians to protect themselves in that battle space that I saw around Kyiv. Then we had an argument about HIMARS. Then an argument about the Multiple Launch Rocket Systems.

Battle tanks, "They shouldn't have battle tanks."

Correct. And an argument about battle tanks. And every time we've come to these forks in the road, we've always taken the option of giving the Ukrainians what they need. But we've done it slowly. My argument would be, let's stop this titration of support. Let's stop these pipette drops of assistance. I'm not saying these are pipettes, we're giving huge amounts of assistance. By the way, I really congratulate and thank profoundly the United States of America. I think what America is doing is fantastic. I think once again, America is the arsenal of democracy and freedom.

But you must have heard the reluctance certainly on the Republican side of the aisle . . .

I thought that the overwhelming bulk of the Republicans I met [. . .] were actually keen to go faster even than Joe Biden is going.

There are some who take a very peculiar view of what is going on, and I really can't explain it. They somehow have come to identify, through a really weird piece of logic, Putin with conservatism or upholding conservative values and Ukraine as being woke. I mean, give me a break. How is it conservative to set about extinguishing democracy and freedom in an innocent European country? How's it conservative, by the way, to encourage the persecution of minority Christian groups, for instance, that don't subscribe to the Orthodox faith. There's nothing conservative about anything that Putin is doing. [But] the vast majority of the Republicans I met were really solid.

    ... Did you think that Putin was going to invade Ukraine?

Well, we had the evidence that he was going to.

Further on we learn something quite interesting. Johnson knew it, but didn't speak openly about it then. Zelenskyy knew it too. That was huge pressure on him.

This was April. I'll tell you why. It was because there was a sort of conversation building that there might be a deal. Do you remember all this stuff going on in Belarus, and there was . . .

    You've put up a brave fight for six weeks. That's wonderful. We all know you're going to lose eventually, let's end this.

[. . .] There was no deal you could do with Putin, even if you could persuade the Ukrainians to do a land for peace deal. Whatever you're going to give Putin, some of the stuff he'd conquered already in exchange. It'd be Mariupol, whatever, and then he retires from the rest. Even if you did that, which would be morally obnoxious, catastrophic, you couldn't rely on him to observe the agreement you'd reached. Because he's shown by his actions in 2014 and since 2014, that he's prepared to do it again and again and again. If Putin set out to prove himself wrong, he could not have done so in a more decisive and elegant way. It's over, that argument.

    How intense was that pressure [on Zelenskyy]?

I don't know. So I don't think that Zelenskyy came anywhere near to doing a bad deal for Ukraine. But I certainly think there was a lot of chatter in the West about it. And my purpose really, was to tell him that whatever, that he would have the U.K.'s unwavering support.

Ukraine has purchased its freedom, its nationhood, its place in Europe in blood. No one can deny that. That's what happened over the last year. They fought. They died. They held off this tyrant and this military machine. What do you think Europe and England and NATO owe Ukraine now? What do we have to do?

The Ukrainians are fighting for all of us. The Ukrainians are fighting for the Poles, for the Georgians, for the Moldovans, for the Balts. They're fighting for every country that could have its borders changed by force anywhere in the world. It's a massive sacrifice that they're making.

I think that they're also showing why Putin was wrong. They [. . .] deserve to be treated with immense, immense respect. Clearly, I think that their membership in the EU [. . .] should be accelerated by the EU members. [. . .] But certainly when it comes to NATO [. . .] if you'd asked me before the war, before Putin did his act of lunacy, is Ukraine going to join NATO anytime soon? I'd have said . . .

Well, Vladimir Putin asked you that question, right?

He did. I said, "No, not anytime soon." The reality was, to be frank, there was a strong enough caucus within NATO to block Ukraine that it wouldn't have happened till hell freezes over. But now, Putin has utterly destroyed, utterly destroyed the case against Ukrainian membership of NATO. Not having Ukraine in NATO meant the worst war in Europe in eighty years, colossal suffering, global economic disaster. The logic is to get clarity and stability and whatever . . . Moscow has forfeited all right to protest now. NATO is not a hostile alliance. NATO is a defensive alliance. And Putin, by his actions, has proved to the Swedes, to the Finns that NATO is essential for them and he certainly proved that it's essential for Ukraine.

All this already applies to Ukraine at war. But I introduce this fragment solely in order to show what a reliable friend Ukraine, and Zelenskyy personally, acquired in the person of Johnson. How right Zelenskyy was to bet on Johnson and believe him. This was the most valuable result of his foreign policy in the first years of his presidency, and on February 24, 2023, he had someone to call.

XXI. BATTLING THE OLIGARCHY

The initiative in the battle with Ukrainian oligarchs originated with the Council of Europe, which granted Ukraine the status of candidate for accession to the European Union. This formal requirement (as part of the fight against corruption, which Europe considered the country's main problem) was executed with the same formality, because the oligarchs were the government's main defense in the struggle against Russian influence and potential aggression. Their influence on politics continued to be media-driven: Zelenskyy and his team were not affiliated with any oligarchic group, and they were resistant to any lobbying. In future textbooks of political history, it will be written that the oligarchization of an economy is an inevitable stage in the development of any state transitioning from feudalism to capitalism—that is, if textbooks will retain the term "capitalism" at all.

Here is the problem: no civil society remains after totalitarianism—no institutions either. In the social construct, only business remains actively intact, and in troubled times it must grab as much as it can (something that it does quite well). Consequently, oligarchs take on the role of the primary social force—there is no one else to do it. Ukraine's truly active civil society, which needed political demonstrations less than the regular tweaking of self-governance, emerged not as a result of the second Maidan, but as a result of the war. So in pre-war times, anti-oligarchic measures were able to be purely a matter of statement—which is what happened.

Following a meeting of the National Security and Defense Council on June 4, 2021, Zelenskyy addressed the nation:

The most important issue of both this meeting and this week is the law on oligarchs.

First of all, I want to say: I didn't expect that there are so many experts on de-oligarchization in our country. If we knew, we would invite them to draft a bill. But, unfortunately, all of them for some reason have been concealing this knowledge for the previous thirty years. And none of the politicians, including those of the highest level, has ever raised the issue of oligarchs. Probably because talking a lot about yourself is impolite and immodest.

Secondly, I am grateful to all the critics of the law. Your remarks are valuable: you have been working with oligarchs for many years, either for oligarchs or under oligarchs, and therefore, you clearly understand all the shortcomings of the law, being, as they say, deep in the material.

And I would like to address separately the employers of all these independent experts and critics. As business sharks, you should have keen senses. Surprisingly, you do not feel that the country has changed and is starting a new story. Under the new rules. Not even so. Simply—by the rules.

You can accept them. Be a big, transparent business with the help of the state, not at the expense of the state. A business that pays taxes, not kickbacks. That finances charitable projects, not a group of deputies. That increases its capital not because it divides and takes away from the country.

Everyone who is ready to work only this way is welcome.

And those who do not want to live and work according to the new and fair rules of the game will be out of the game.

I will have one question for those who will try to rock the boat, persuade, break or reach an agreement with MPs on this law. This is a question about the status of oligarchs, which will be put to an all-Ukrainian referendum. This question will be the first. And for some, perhaps the last.

I also want to say that this bill is only the first step. This is the creation of a foundation for counteracting oligarchic influence.

You can't own deputies, ministers and any other officials. This bill is the first decision in all thirty years of independence that demonstrates our attitude to the oligarchic system. It claims: yes, there are oligarchs in Ukraine. Yes, they influence politics. And, yes—it will not happen again.

The full title of Zelenskyy's bill No. 5599 (which he proposed only after two years in office) is: "On the Prevention of Threats to National Security Related to Excessive Influence of Persons with Significant Economic or Political Weight in Public Life (Oligarchs)." An oligarch, according to Zelenskyy, is anyone with the verified possession of one million living wages (83 million dollars), who participates in political life, and has his own media. Persons falling under the criteria of the law are included in a special register and will be banned from financing political parties. Any civil servant or people's deputy who has contact with an oligarch is obliged to submit a declaration to the Security Council with a brief summary of the conversation, even if the conversation took place online.

The secretary of the Ukrainian Security Council, Oleksii Danilov, was quick to declare that inclusion in the register of oligarchs should not be perceived as a threat: "Nothing is being taken away from anyone," except that they are obliged to publish a full annual declaration of all their income. One sees an analogy with the register of foreign agents in Russia: they too are obliged to publish a declaration of income and the movement of their funds, while inclusion in the register threatens them only with a ban on teaching (just as oligarchs are banned from political activity). Obviously, these measures in both cases are purely declarative: all heirs of the USSR experience an unpleasant feeling of threat in their blood when they are included in a list (further, as a rule, they start listing you with small letters and in the plural). Feeling like an undesirable element was the main discomfort that the anti-oligarchic law threatened Ukrainian millionaires with.

Kyiv political analysts rightly called the law "a way to stigmatize opponents."

"Anyone in civilized business will do anything to avoid being included in this register," said then-Justice Minister Denys Maliuska. His phrase of "civilized" business meant business that was now frightened. Petro Poroshenko's European Solidarity party predictably said that an oligarch from Zelenskyy's point of view was someone he didn't like personally. Kolomoiskyi said he would gladly stitch the star of "oligarch" on his suit—and it was quite clear what star he meant; the foreign agent patch in Russia is also often called a "yellow star." Those who don it are despised, and those who do not are denounced.

The anti-oligarchy law was proposed in Ukraine at a difficult time for Zelenskyy. An opinion poll conducted by the Kyiv International Institute of Sociology (KMIS) showed that his nomination for a second term would be disapproved by more than half of Ukrainians. Nevertheless, on September 23, 2021, the Upper Rada passed the law in its second reading with the support of 279 deputies, 21 abstentions, and 54 votes against. At that time six months remained before the war would commence, and, during those six months, no register was ever compiled. The anti-oligarchic measures were never anything but a paper chase: everyone soon would be too preoccupied with other matters.

RATING. By the end of 2021, Zelenskyy was the leader in negative ratings among Ukrainian politicians, with his support limited to 25 percent. There were many reasons for this.

Zelenskyy was the first Ukrainian president to shut down three TV channels. On February 3, 2021, he discontinued the licenses of ZIK, NewsOne, and 112 Ukraine. They all belonged to Taras Kozak, a Rada deputy from the For Life opposition platform. This president who came to power thanks to television was expected to be highly favorable to the media. He betrayed these expectations in the most radical way, although his actions brought him the approval of the majority of voters. For all the democracy Ukraine has achieved, the public here sees decisive measures as one's understanding of one's power.

During the war (beginning in December 2022), Zelenskyy was badly damaged in the eyes of many observers, especially foreigners, by the measures he was compelled to take against the Ukrainian Orthodox Church of the Moscow Patriarchate. Anti-church measures are almost always bad PR, even where the church has no influence. In Zelenskyy's own words, "the National Security and Defense Council of Ukraine instructed the government to submit to the Upper Rada a bill to prevent religious organizations affiliated with Russia from operating within the country." The State Department for Ethno-politics and Freedom of Conscience was instructed to conduct a theological appraisal of the statute concerning the governance of the Ukrainian Orthodox Church, to search "for the presence of an ecclesiastical-canonical connection with the Moscow Patriarchate," and to take measures if necessary.

Referring to the president and "his band," Metropolitan Pavel, the abbot of the Kyiv-Pechersk Lavra, promised Zelenskyy: "Our tears will not fall on the earth, they will fall on your heads." Persecuting the church in the midst of war is not the best tactic. In Russia, of course, Zelenskyy was labeled with anti-Orthodox rhetoric, although his actions were directed specifically at the Russian Orthodox Church, and did not threaten Orthodoxy in any way. Anti-Semitic rhetoric—it couldn't have been otherwise—and anti-Bolshevik rhetoric also came in handy. Zelenskyy was described as a more radical enemy of Orthodoxy than even Lenin.

By peacetime standards, the only thing Zelenskyy fully succeeded in achieving was to establish a new type of government, but is it enough to be a Vasily Goloborodko when your country is going through a test of self-determination on every major historical issue? Zelenskyy's project was superb as an experiment, but, as shown in *Servant of the People*, that was not going to satisfy the populace, for they do not live and work in a TV series. It took a test that no one had dreamed of in 2019 for Zelenskyy to become a leader, and for the nation to unite. In truth, a war was already being waged, Crimea had been annexed, and Donbas was smoldering. But no one had thought about a full-scale invasion in the middle of Europe, or about the fact that the world itself would be drawn closer than ever to a nuclear catastrophe.

Due to a sharply declining rating and growing reactions to unfulfilled promises, by the end of 2021 Zelenskyy was looking worse and worse—both in the eyes of his supporters and in the literal sense. Of course, once fired, a former colleague will look at everything skeptically, but there is a special sobriety in the view of former colleagues, and their observations should not be neglected. In an interview with Dmitry Gordon, Andrii Bohdan, the first head of the president's office, who was fired in May 2020, said: "Power is eating Volodymyr Alexandrovich up. He has changed physiologically. The man was cheerful. He was light, humorous, handsome, sharp, and energetic. And you see? It simply hurts to look at him. I don't understand what he's saying. He doesn't know what he's saying. His face has gone gray. He's tired. He's always in some kind of depression or something. He's always nervous. He calls and threatens deputies."

It goes without saying that Zelenskyy's new associates, especially Mikhail Podoliak, reacted to Bohdan's assessments: "You were delicately asked to clear out—you took routine offense and started to be rude, to threaten and pontificate in the typical, routine way." But Bohdan did not back down. "When you take the road of the samurai," he said, "you must understand where you are going. If you have no goal, the best way, in principle, is to remain still. Right? Where are Volodymyr Zelenskyy and his team going? Where are they going? Nobody knows. Not even Volodymyr Zelenskyy. There is a set of boilerplate phrases: 'We support all that is good, and we're against everything bad.' But this is good in songs and speeches, not in public policy, no . . . I believe he is the strongest producer, scriptwriter, and actor in the entire CIS, the former USSR. He has absolutely no knowledge and no experience. He does not understand at all what is going on around him. Not only that, his weakness is that he limits himself to a small number of people and he listens only to them. He gets no second or third opinions. He only wants to hear good things."

All of this was said many times in 2021, and it was all forgotten, buried in the subconscious. A post-war glance back at the pre-war years of Zelenskyy's presidency is impossible primarily because now you can only speak approvingly or sympathetically about Ukraine (to a lesser extent about Zelenskyy)—in no way can you speak critically. Applying any other modality, you choose solidarity with the aggressor. It goes without saying that analysis, in this case, is impossible, just as it was impossible to criticize opponents of the tsarist regime during Stolypin's reactionary policies; as it was impossible to condemn Soviet marshals during Stalin's terror; as it was impossible to understand the prospects for the Prague Spring after Soviet tanks had crushed it.

Perhaps Russia exists in the world precisely to translate ethically ambiguous situations into extremely unambiguous ones by its exceedingly crude and strategically failed actions; to remove all moral ambivalence and establish rigid accents. It's a dubious role, but someone has to do it, and so the Bolsheviks are depicted as flawless; Stalin's marshals appear as paragons of military talent and courage; and the Prague Spring, with its more than dubious prospects, is presented as a genuine project to give socialism a human face. (Although that was always doomed to failure. There was never a single scenario by which the Prague reformers could have remained in power, even taking into account the utter inaction of the Warsaw Pact.)

In early 2022, the *Servant of the People* project—a courageous experiment to bring to power a representative of the creative intelligentsia, one whose image was created completely by a role in a TV serial—looked inopportune, if not an utter failure. But there was a hitch, a *zagogulina*, or squiggle, as Boris Yeltsin would have put it. I will try to describe it phenomenologically, that is, without evaluation, though that is virtually impossible. When you read reports about corruption or reputation scandals around Zelenskyy—and I do it compulsively, because for a book like this all such information is *sine qua non*, a perfunctory necessity—you feel the same as Lenin did when reading the minutes of the Constituent Assembly: it's all from another era. Zelenskyy made a valiant, albeit doomed, attempt to pull Ukrainian politics out of the provincial bog, out of the so-called territory of *ragulnost*, or provincial thuggery—but it faltered. It fell into its former state with the same kind of relief that a child feels when it continues to whimper long after it should have stopped. It all went nowhere—the issues of corruption; the low-key, glum tone of politicians' comments about each other, and journalists' comments about all authorities; the vulgar, petty criminal squabbles; the scandalous, hours-long and, in fact, pointless talk shows. Squabbles started up even within Zelenskyy's team. It took a war to radically change Ukraine, and the new president finally got his new society. Everything is hopeless, which is precisely why we are doomed to win. Zelenskyy may have disappointed the country and become disillusioned himself during the second year of his presidency, but that is precisely what gave rise to a common tone of stoic mockery that united Ukraine during the next two years of war. Everything is very bad, but there is no retreating; we are united in the fact that everyone has it bad, the oligarchs and the proletarians, the east and the west. Everything is bad, but we cling to our ability to laugh about it.

So Zelenskyy's failure to open a new historical stage in Ukraine once again was appropriate, and it led him to the stoicism with which he greeted the war: There was nothing left to lose. Naturally, there were a few idiots who insisted that the war played into Zelenskyy's hands, that it legitimized him and allowed him to keep his ratings up. Preserving one's rating at the cost of such tribulations and losses could please only an ogre—say, Putin, for example. In Zelenskyy, on the other hand, one clearly sees what it all has cost him. Paradoxically, the atmosphere of failure and disappointment of the first two years of his presidency prepared him for the terrible tension of the first months of the war. I realize that this thought is also sketchy, like Russian poet Olga Berholz's diary entry stating that, without the terror of the late thirties, the Soviet Union would not have been ready for war, and would not have been able to withstand it. Most likely, this notion was meant retroactively to justify the terrible experience of Bergholz herself. But it can be explained psychologically. The Zelenskyy who was accustomed to adulation and success would have been more vulnerable than the Zelenskyy who entered the war in a state of internal crisis. The war pulled both him and Ukrainian society to the level of solidarity that he had dreamed of achieving from the very beginning. He did not want to pay such a price. But the nation elected a man who was prepared for the unprecedented and who, in a sense, summons the unprecedented. It is a whole other matter that it did not take shape as expected. But this is the main feature of the future according to Nassim Taleb: a black swan comes along and sweeps away the past with the wave of a wing.

Had it not been for the war . . . Today we can't even imagine what we would have done without it. But what if we do imagine it? Then, in one way or another, Zelenskyy would have had to become an enlightened dictator (and there's a question for you: how enlightened?), or he would have had to surrender his presidency to nothing less than circus clownery. In peacetime, both options could have been possible, but Russia imparted meaning and drama to the situation: it flawlessly accepted the role of absolute evil, and the war became the proverbial eighteenth camel that solved the insoluble enigma.

It happened at the cost of enormous losses, the destruction of millions of lives in Russia, Ukraine, and the world. We dare to say that it happened at the cost of Russia's future, for there can be no future for an aggressor country with fascist ideology and a regime of executioners. Meanwhile, a genuine civil society and all the mechanisms of self-government have appeared in Ukraine.

XXII. DONBAS. NEGOTIATIONS—2019

The settlement of the conflict in the east of Ukraine was part of Zelenskyy's campaign platform. In April 2019, Zelenskyy warned that he would not negotiate with the separatists and would not accept the federalization of Ukraine (which caused criticism, including among Russian liberals, some of whom had proposed federalization back in 2014 as the optimal scenario). Zelenskyy repeatedly declared that he categorically opposed the distribution of Russian passports to the population of Donbas, and that he would seek peace on Ukraine's terms.

The first meeting between Putin and Zelenskyy (at the Normandy Format talks) took place on December 9, 2019. Truth be told, there is no reliable information about whether they had ever met before, but they might have. Putin periodically visited the tapings of KVN, and Zelenskyy occasionally performed in Moscow. Is it really so rare for two media personalities to cross paths?

As an aside, Zelenskyy has met and even talked to Dmitry Medvedev under very curious circumstances. On July 12, 2010, Viktor Yanukovych, who had finally been elected president of Ukraine, celebrated his sixtieth birthday in Crimea. (In fact, he had already begun to celebrate it in a close circle of friends near Kyiv, in Zalissia, where he danced like a madman. But he celebrated it on a higher level in the Crimea, at the so-called Gosdacha-3 in Malaya Sosnovka. This was Stalin's former dacha, later a vacation spot for Ukrainian leaders, and, since 2015, which is symbolic, a museum.) Invited guests included the presidents of the CIS countries (Serzh Sargsyan from Armenia, Heydar Aliyev from Azerbaijan, Aleksandr Lukashenka from Belarus, Nursultan Nazarbayev from Kazakhstan) and then-Russian President Dmitry Medvedev. The serving Minister of Culture of Ukraine agreed with Zelenskyy and the Block on a half-hour performance. The dinner (a main course of pheasant with *halushki* [potato dumplings], plus a variety of pastries that were ordered specially for Medvedev who was known to have a sweet tooth) preceded the evening's entertainment. When the members of *Block 95* came out on stage, it turned out that there were only two spectators in the hall—Yanukovych and Medvedev. Oleksandr Pikalov performed parodies of Yanukovych who laughed at what he saw. Zelenskyy himself told about what transpired next:

> We did our skits, and at the end I announced: "People's Artist, everyone's favorite, Taisiia Povalii will now perform! Give her a warm welcome!" But these two hotshots get up and leave! That is, Povalii comes out, plays her intro and begins to sing. And they just get up and go.

The two presidents had gone to the sauna to refresh themselves. The Minister of Culture ran into the dressing room to demand that the Block team continue its performance. The performers refused, and the Minister insisted. In short, they went back on stage, and saw that Medvedev and Yanukovych were now in their robes. They performed for another half hour, after which there was something of a chit-chat.

"Good jokes, edgy," praised Medvedev. "But don't do that when you come perform for us."

"By the way, did you know," Zelenskyy asked, "that our Block member Valera Zhidkov is a Russian citizen?"

(Zhidkov had lived in Ukraine since 2003, explaining that the jokes he made up about Vladimir Putin made his life in Russia incompatible with life.)

"Is that so?" Medvedev asked and looked at the performer carefully. "Well, it's good that you're here."

It's not difficult to understand what he meant. Obviously it was good for Zhidkov. Otherwise it would have been bad for him.

In his tweets, Dmitry Medvedev has repeatedly discussed the prospects of Zelenskyy's physical elimination, and called him "a figure in a dirty green T-shirt." He still seems to think of himself as a statesman, and that Zelenskyy is a lowly jester. He never realized that they exchanged roles long ago, and that he himself has long been a stand-up comedian, amusing both strangers and especially his own people. It would be interesting for them to get together with the same cast someday—I wouldn't exclude it happening in The Hague, with Zelenskyy as a witness for the prosecution, and Yanukovych and Medvedev again on a bench, but no longer wearing robes. As Dickens wrote in his most Gothic novel, "When shall these three meet again?" He never did write the scene of his heroes' final meeting, and today we can only imagine it. But something tells me it would have been something along these lines.

He did not meet Putin that day. The Russian president didn't come. Dmitry Peskov (not a very reliable source, but at least a source of some kind) claims that Putin and Zelenskyy never spoke before July 11, 2019. Their first phone conversation (an introductory one, according to the Kremlin's characterization) took place a month and a half after Zelenskyy took office as president of Ukraine. However, a history of their relationship was already in place by then. Putin did not congratulate Zelenskyy on his election victory—an unprecedented case. By comparison, he congratulated Yanukovych three times: twice in 2004 (when he was not elected and the first Maidan took place) and once in 2010. Putin was asked about the reasons for this move at the St. Petersburg Economic Forum on June 7, 2019, at a meeting moderated by Sofiko Shevardnadze.

Why didn't you congratulate Volodymyr Zelenskyy when he became president? (*Sarcastic applause in the hall—either for the bold question or for the president's boorishness.—D. B.*)

You know, he still continues a certain rhetoric. He calls us enemies, and aggressors. He'll have to make up his mind about what he wants to achieve, what he wants to do.

But you're the president of an enormous nation. He's well-liked, he came in with huge ratings. One little gesture can make all the difference, you know that. Why not just meet, no strings attached?

Have I said no? No one offered me anything . . . (Applause.)

But are you prepared to meet him?

(Laughs.) Listen to me. I don't know this man. Judging by what we know, he's a good specialist in the field he's been working in so far. He's a good actor. (Laughter, applause.) I'm being serious, but you're laughing. It's one thing to play someone, and another thing to be someone. (Applause.) To play someone, you need a talent for transformation. You have to change roles every ten minutes. Now you're a prince, and ten minutes later a beggar. You have to be convincing in both roles. That's true talent. But you need other qualities to handle state affairs. You need to see the big problems and how to solve them, to find the tools to solve these problems. You need to be able to collect capable people on your team, to believe in them, and give them the opportunity to think freely. You must be able to explain the motives for making these decisions to millions of people. Most importantly, you need the courage and character to take responsibility for the consequences of these decisions. (*Applause, though it is unclear what for: perhaps a hint that it is time for Mr. Putin to take responsibility for the consequences of his decisions? —D. B.*) I do not mean to say that Mr. Zelenskyy does not have these qualities. Maybe he lacks experience, but, as the common folk say, experience is acquired. Does he have all the other qualities I listed? I don't know. He hasn't revealed himself in any way yet. We don't see that. We see contradictory statements so far: one thing during the election campaign, another thing after the campaign. We'll live and learn. (*Applause, probably, for the fact that we will live.—D. B.*) I'm not saying that, without doing anything yet, he has already ruined everything with his statements. We'll wait and see.

At economic forums, Putin usually behaves in a relaxed and confident manner, enjoying the pose of the hospitable and powerful host, toward whom the entire world rushes in order to adjust their forecasts and hear his recommendations. These days, nobody goes to him, but back then that is precisely how they came to him. The devil always has excellent relations with those who are willing to plant a kiss beneath his tail. He'll deceive them at the very end, but otherwise he honors all contracts—as he does those with Gaddafi, Hussein, Ceausescu, and Putin. They all get a big kick out of it for the time being; the payback comes later. But, as they say in Russia, this is an acquired experience. One thing is clear here: a president must be able to prioritize clearly. Zelenskyy's priority should be contact with Russia, with Putin, and with everything that depends on them, not on someone else. But he never invited him "to meet with no strings attached."

And, by the way, the audience didn't laugh that much. It was Putin who wanted them to laugh. What a clown-president, ho-ho-ho-ho! We'll see who the clown is in this configuration, and who will have the last laugh. As they say in Russia, we'll take a look and see.

Few people now remember the Normandy Format. The war over-shadowed these attempts to negotiate and establish even the most meagre peace. The Merkel era, when the West was sincerely trying to tame Putin and negotiate with him on his terms, so long as he did not attack, is already several years gone. But there was such a format, and there were even hopes for it. Someday Normandy will not only be a symbol of the Allied landings, but also the embodiment of those Allies' last-ditch attempt to supplicate world evil. Here is a quick reminder of what that was about.

The Normandy Format is so called because the seventieth anniversary of the Allied landings was celebrated in Normandy on June 6, 2014. The president of France at the time was François Hollande—admittedly, not much to remember. He was the most unpopular president in the history of French elections and the only leader of the Fifth Republic who did not even try to run for a second term. It was Hollande who came up with the idea of inviting Putin and Poroshenko to the party at the same time, so that they could try to reach an agreement. The only thing they agreed on was that there would be regular meetings of foreign ministers, and consultations between the presidents on the margins of summits. Russia had been talking about the federalization of Ukraine and the special status of Donbas since 2014. On February 11, 2015, after long preparations, a seventeen-hour meeting was held in Minsk, organized by Aleksandr Lukashenka: he was the only one who actually benefited from it, because next to Putin he temporarily ceased to look like Europe's main monster, and even gained a reputation as a peacemaker. Russia stubbornly claimed it was mediating a civil war in Ukraine. This was Russia's beloved tactic: they are fighting there, and we are merely protecting the Russian-speaking population. The notion of *ikhtamnet*, "there's-no-one-there," became especially well-known, to the extent that Russian troops in Donbas were called *ikhtamnets* all over the world. Ukraine's position at that moment was catastrophic: the Debaltseve debacle had just taken place, and an agreement had to be reached under direct military pressure. The negotiations were held in the Minsk Palace of Independence, and the then-leaders of the self-proclaimed Donetsk People's Republic (Alexander Zakharchenko) and the Lugansk People's Republic (Igor Plotnitsky), participated in the negotiations with unclear status—each signed the agreements without specifying their positions. Zakharchenko was later assassinated in a bomb blast, while Plotnitsky was overthrown after an unsuccessful assassination attempt, and he fled to Russia where he has neither been seen nor heard since. He is mostly remembered for explaining the term "Euromaidan" as the seizure of power in Ukraine by Jews.

The Minsk agreements, which Poroshenko signed under extreme Russian pressure with the peacemaking acquiescence of Europe (Merkel and

Hollande were sincerely convinced it was possible and necessary to negotiate with Putin), were impossible to execute in principle. Putin has repeated many times since then that Europe and Ukraine deliberately deceived him, and that no one was going to honor those agreements. Above all, Russia itself had no intentions of doing so, for control of the border was never returned to Ukraine. From the very beginning Zelenskyy spoke of the need to revise or adapt the Minsk agreements. "The Normandy Format collective will not suffice for us, or for anyone else. The great powers of the world, including the States and Russia, will sit down and agree that there is a way to do it. But there must be three or four or five points involving the security of our country. Then we have a conversation." He called the agreements worthless for knowingly putting Ukraine in a losing position. On the eve of the full-scale Russian invasion, realizing there was nothing to lose, he spoke out bluntly: "I jumped on this train, which, frankly, was already roaring into the abyss. By 'train' I mean these agreements as a whole. Each clause is a carriage, and when you start to dismantle it, you realize that everything is arranged in such a way that if one side is unable to fulfill some stipulation, the other side freezes the conflict."

Of all of Poroshenko's legacy, let's be honest, it was the Minsk agreements that were the most problematic and, in a sense, shameful for Zelenskyy. He had to abandon Poroshenko's main principle of negotiating with Russia at any cost, while using the time in the interim to build a regular army. (Let's not make of Poroshenko a conciliatory pacifist. His rhetoric was by no means peaceful, and he realized from the very beginning that, first and foremost, peace in Donbas did not suit Putin.) Zelenskyy, to his credit, never criticized Poroshenko for his signing this, by definition, unworkable agreement under duress. I think the only people who even partially believed in its value were Hollande and Merkel, but even Merkel told Obama on the phone back in 2014 that Putin had lost touch with reality. Zelenskyy explained the Minsk agreements this way: "I did not see in the agreements a desire to preserve Ukraine's independence. I understand their (*The West's.—D.B.*) point of view. Primarily, they wanted in part to appease Russia's appetites at the expense of Ukraine. Delay is perfectly normal in diplomacy."

Well, they did procrastinate, and maybe they did gain something; Ukraine had at least six years to prepare for war (Poroshenko said eight in a BBC interview). Russia, though, had the same, although Ukraine used its time more efficiently.

Zelenskyy in general differed from Poroshenko mainly because he did not think it was necessary to adhere to the Minsk accords, he did not believe those endless negotiations arrived at a significant result. This does not mean he had no illusions about Putin from the very beginning. He did, but not so much about Putin, as about his own charm and the halo of success that surrounded him after his triumphant election. He thought he would be able to achieve an agreement with Putin; that there would be a mutual understanding between them, that Putin's sinister humor would somehow find common ground with the occasionally black humor of *Block 95*. God only knows what he was actually relying upon. I suspect charisma, most of all. That's a natural thing for an actor. But let's turn the page, for Zelenskyy's pre-election rhetoric emphasized the peaceful matter of language that he proposed to roll back, and negotiate anew. He harbored no great hopes, as he admitted later: "I focused on the issue of prisoner exchange, and I told the head of the presidential administration: Andrii (*Bohdan.—D.B.*), let's activate this, it's about people. And when we get an exchange according to the formula of 'all for all,' then we'll see what to do next."

So the first telephone conversation took place on July 11, 2019. Kyiv took the initiative. As was emphasized in the Russian media, Zelenskyy spoke in Russian ("that's how we humbled him!"). They discussed the release of Ukrainian sailors captured after the incident of November 25, 2018, when they entered the waters of the Kerch Strait, as well as the exchange of prisoners and the continuation of meetings according to the Normandy Format. The twenty-four Ukrainian sailors were repatriated to Ukraine on August 30, 2019. Also released was Ukrainian filmmaker Oleh Sentsov, who had been arrested on May 10, 2014, on charges of planning an act of sabotage in Crimea. He had been sentenced to twenty years' incarceration in a maximum-security prison, served time in Yakutia, and went on a hunger strike for six months, demanding the release of sixty-four Ukrainian prisoners, not just his own. Russia had consistently refused to release him, despite requests and protests from the world's artistic elite. At present he is fighting at the front. In an interview I did with him in the fall of 2019, he spoke of his personal gratitude to Zelenskyy, who managed to do what no one previously had. Many people remember the words of famed Russian filmmaker Alexander Sokurov, who said to Putin: "I ask, I beg you . . ." But Zelenskyy was able to strike a deal. Frankly, it was his last success in negotiations with Russia, although I think that is through no fault of his own. Soon thereafter two more large-scale prisoner exchanges took place—one known as "35 for 35" on September 7, and another known as "76 for 127" on December 29.

Even here, however, Zelenskyy came in for serious criticism, for he was compelled to return to Russia Vladimir Tsemakh, the gunner of the very BUK missile that shot down the Dutch Boeing on July 17, 2014. After two years of preparation, Tsemakh was abducted on June 27, 2019, in an operation planned by the Ukrainian security forces. He was detained in the Donetsk People's Republic and transported across the front line to Ukrainian-controlled territory, where he began to testify, but was returned on September 7, 2019, at Russia's insistence. His extradition was a condition for Oleh Sentsov's release. In Zelenskyy's view, Sentsov returning to Ukraine and hugging his children clearly outweighed the damage incurred from the release of a valuable witness who, undoubtedly, had much to say. The exchanges stalled in 2021. Zelenskyy claimed that Russia stopped them. Most likely, Russia expected to get what it wanted without further negotiations.

A meeting of the Normandy Format was scheduled for December 2019 and took place in Paris. A rather complicated schedule was devised. First, Putin met with Merkel—they had a long, relatively prosperous history of relations—while Zelenskyy met with Macron. Then they, as it were, switched partners (sounds awful, but how else do you formulate it?). Further on Putin and Zelenskyy met one-on-one, followed by a dinner attended by all four.

The Russian newspaper *Kommersant*'s report by Andrei Kolesnikov, Putin's chief court journalist who manages to maintain an ironic distance from all the government's maneuvering and the opposition's blunders, contains important details of the December 9 meeting. During Putin's speech at the final press conference, Zelenskyy's foot began twitching intensely under the table. That might have been okay. But then Putin spoke about a "permanent basis" of the special status for Donbas: "At these words, Vladimir Zelensky clenched his hand into a fist and bit his lip, pretending that he could, but did not want to laugh, and yet he still could not restrain himself.

"I was convinced he would begin making faces at any moment.

"Naturally, there had never been such childish behavior at such a forum."

It's very possible that Zelenskyy overestimated European influence and goodwill, or, perhaps he underestimated Putin's firm intention to push through the federalization of Ukraine. Or, maybe, he just thought it was funny. Whatever the case, Putin didn't forget it. As it is he sees humiliation everywhere, and here no effort was needed to make the insult more obvious. He expected Zelenskyy to be far more compliant. After all, the Ukrainian president was, indeed, exhausted by the war. He had not promised any compromises, but it seemed he had discussed Donbas, the language problem and respect for the populace of Eastern Ukraine with understanding. And then this insult:

"I would also like to outline the principles that I will never violate as President of Ukraine, principles that the people of Ukraine will never allow to be violated! We will not allow changes to the Constitution of Ukraine regarding the federalization of its structure! We will not accept any influence on the political development or political governance of Ukraine. Ukraine is an independent state that determines its own political path! The Ukrainian people do this! The very possibility of compromise in regard to resolving issues in the eastern territories is made impossible by the annexation of these territories! We repeat once again: Donbas, like Crimea, are Ukrainian territories!"

Many now believe that during that meeting Zelenskyy missed his only chance to find common ground with Putin. I don't think there ever was a chance. It is said that the writer Isaac Babel bitterly regretted failing to please Stalin during their first conversation; But could he have pleased him?

Summing up the meeting, Zelenskyy made a short speech in Ukrainian and emphasized that the agreement was lacking on the key points: Ukraine is a unitary state, there will be no federalization, and no special status for Donbas. "There can be no settlement on the issue of territories. We all know that, for every Ukrainian, both Donbas and Crimea are Ukraine." Crimea was not discussed at the Paris meeting, but Russia demanded political reforms provided for, as Putin said, in the Minsk agreements. "Primarily, we are talking about introducing amendments to the Constitution that will secure the special status of Donbas." The only thing that was clearly agreed upon was a ceasefire and the withdrawal of troops, but there were no agreements about holding elections in Ukraine (which would be recognized by the Organization for Security and Co-operation in Europe [OSCE]). Furthermore, nothing was said about the location of the next meeting scheduled for April 2020.

"You say Zelenskyy is an actor, and Putin is a bureaucrat. No, Putin is also an actor," philosopher and theologian Alexander Filanovsky told me in June 2022. "They both tried to ensnare each other, but curiously, both failed. They must be from different acting schools." Continuing this comparison, we might say that Zelenskyy belongs to the representational school of acting, and Putin to the presentational school, although if we are objective about it, this would be too seriously complimentary of Zelenskyy's acting technique. Both belong precisely to the school of representation that employs ready-made stereotypes. It's another matter that, right from the start, Zelenskyy banked on a humane approach, gentleness and flexibility, while Putin was emphatic in his disdainful rigidity (this word was earlier applied to Zelenskyy). Zelenskyy sought to negotiate, Putin—to manipulate. Zelenskyy hoped a conversation between equals was possible, and he retained that illusion until December 2019, maybe even later. Abandoning it turned out to be traumatic, but in December the world finally saw the real Zelenskyy.

This meeting turned out to be truly upsetting for Vladislav Surkov, who after this (and probably as a direct result) bade farewell to big-league politics. We must say a few words about Surkov here, if only because the territory of Donbas was his personal responsibility, and, one way or another, he failed to cope with what, let's be honest, was a hopeless cause. What's most interesting is that Surkov understood everything perfectly well. This is evidenced by a novella that he wrote, *Imitating Homer*, which contains cynical and exceedingly loathsome portraits of Russian patriotic writers and Donbas commanders. In all, Surkov was a demonic figure. (I say he was, although he is still alive, albeit now lacking all demonism. Individuals whose usefulness has been exhausted possess no demonism.) He has been called the most interesting politician of the Putin era, and this is fair if we place the logical emphasis not on the word "interesting," but on the word "most." It's just that the rest of them are flat-out rotten. Surkov's method was to manipulate gullible careerists, force them to sink lower and lower and, ultimately, to discard them. This is how the *Nashi*, or Ours, nationalist youth movement was created, led by Vasily Yakemenko, who now lives in Bavaria on a plot of land he shrewdly purchased in advance. But Surkov also conned his Kremlin bosses, whom he guaranteed that Zelenskyy would consent to federalization. Zelenskyy was a tougher nut to crack. Why did Surkov lose his position as assistant to the Russian president on February 18, 2020? In an interview with Alexei Chesnakov, his closest ally and de facto pupil, he himself said: "My resignation is purely a case of going AWOL. I will engage in politics in kitchens, in bars, and in strange treatises. I am a Putinist, a partly heretical kind. I wanted to leave back in 2013, when I realized that I had no place in the system, but I returned and chose Ukraine. Even then I had a presentiment that we would do battle with the West. Our relations with Ukraine were never simple, even when it was a part of Russia. I proved historically that you can control fraternal relations effectively by force." He then added: "At the summit in Paris everyone accepted Volodymyr Zelenskyy as president, he was no chump." Thank you for that, but as for his "purely going AWOL," that would seem to be a matter of his saving face in a lost cause. Arsen Avakov, at that time Ukraine's Minister of Internal Affairs, said in an interview with Dmitry Gordon that while ratifying the final communiqué, Surkov flung papers down on the table and shouted: "That's not what we agreed on!" Surkov commented that Avakov, although he was part of the Ukrainian delegation, was not cleared to participate in the negotiations, and furthermore, he admitted himself that he had drunk too much. But there is a certain logic in Surkov's dismissal if we assume that he assured the Kremlin authorities of Zelenskyy's absolute readiness to fold, while, in fact, Zelenskyy demonstrated unexpected persistence and skepticism regarding the Minsk agreements. Surkov himself subsequently said that "the context had changed," while commentators noted that the Kremlin shifted from attempts to reach an agreement to imposing unabashed forceful pressure. Perhaps he really did hope to avoid war, although it is also difficult to call him a friend of Ukraine and a supporter of negotiations. Most likely, he painted an overly encouraging picture for the Kremlin, and when Zelenskyy stubbornly stood firm, Surkov was no longer of any use.

Putin understood something about Zelenskyy as early as the first year of his presidency, and after one personal meeting. He realized that the new Ukrainian government had no reverence for the Minsk agreements, and that the coveted federalization, which would only have delayed the war, was not in anyone's plans. He also recognized that Zelenskyy was not afraid of him and even allowed himself to involuntarily grin in his presence. Zelenskyy was highly praised by his European colleagues during the Paris summit, while Putin has repeatedly made it clear that he doesn't care about this assessment. In all likelihood, the course for war was set precisely in that December, the first year of Zelenskyy's presidency.

Why did this war become inevitable? In fact, political scientists of various stripes had predicted it since the mid-'90s, when it became clear that Chechnya was not going to be an end in itself. War is a prime narcotic for a reinforced totalitarian regime. War rallies people around the state and makes it possible to put off change until victory or final defeat. Zelenskyy may have had a chance to avoid war had he agreed to the Kremlin's demands. But at that summit, he told reporters that if he were to be actively pressured to implement the Minsk agreements to the letter, a different president would be attending the next summit. Ukrainian society understood perfectly well that the federalization of Ukraine for Russia was not merely a way to shove the red-hot potato of Donbas down its neighbor's collar, but it was also the shortest path to infecting Ukraine at large with the same kind of infighting. To bring Ukraine to its knees, to force it to recognize the Russian presence in Donbas, to negotiate with hardcore separatists like Mikhail Tolstykh and Arsen Pavlov, known by their *noms de guerre* of Givi and Motorola—the goal was not so much geopolitical as it was psychological. The result would be that the young president would be the butt of endless jokes about his premature rise to power, while Putin would appear to be a savvy expert in world politics. But, as is well known, the first shall be last. Thanks to Alexander Grin's story, "Captain Duke," we know all about the "iron laughter of the decrepit past." But there is also such a thing as the laughter of the future, and Putin heard this laughter, albeit carefully hidden, late in the evening of December 9. The past does not forgive such things.

The meeting scheduled for four months later did not take place. The world was going through COVID, the first wave of turbulence that marked the beginning of the great crisis of the twenties. (For those who don't believe me, we can talk in ten years, assuming we survive, and if the collapse of the thirties doesn't completely flatten us.)

Now I must say something sad and, perhaps, blasphemous. The half-successes and outright failures of the first two years of Zelenskyy's presidency are due to the fact that a new type of politician, for whom consensus, mutual understanding, and a sense of team and unity of purpose are crucial, could be elected triumphantly in Ukraine, but could not possibly maintain his rating. He was faced with unpopular measures, and his former comrades and well-wishers were immediately disillusioned as soon as these unpopular measures affected them personally. Furthermore, he always had to enter into compromises—whether with the oligarchs, on whom too much depended, or with Russia, on whom a meagre (and ever more meagre) peace depended. He was unable to turn the new page that he had promised from the very beginning. Poroshenko's good qualities, which were almost immediately remembered nostalgically, were not accessible to a man who had proposed a new paradigm in Ukrainian politics, a new model for the nation, free from both Soviet relics and provincial arrogance. No matter how terrible it sounds, it took a catastrophe on a national scale for Zelenskyy to begin succeeding.

A close-knit community emerged, that very team of like-minded people he was accustomed to dealing with. From a modernist point of view, the necessary main qualities were in place: reaction time, good self-control, and high motivation. The opportunity arose to part with the most influential oligarchs, including some who were courageous individuals that had brought much benefit to Ukraine, but with whom a new type of president could not share power. Finally, the need to negotiate with Russia, to endure its blackmail and outright lies had vanished. War usually legitimizes dictators—we in Russia know that better than anyone—but it also gives a free hand to a new type of leader. War strengthened Stalin's power, but it also brought de Gaulle to power. World War II brought forward the servile prose writer Mikhail Bubennov, but it also gave us Vasily Grossman and Viktor Nekrasov. War does not solve a single problem. On the contrary, it drives them deeper into place. And we will not be able to help but notice that after the current war ends, all the deferred and unresolved issues will come crashing back down upon Ukraine, from its notorious corruption to its nationalism. War is a time of utmost national stress, and from the very beginning, Zelenskyy needed an atmosphere of radical novelty—not at this price, of course, but none other was offered him.

A participant or spectator of this drama can only be amazed at the black humor and paradoxical wisdom of the scriptwriter. The biggest paradox of Zelenskyy's biography is that this president who laid the groundwork for peace, who was elected to make peace because of the extreme fatigue from the smoldering war in Donbas, was not at all suitable for peace, was unable to achieve it, and, after two years of relatively peaceful work, disappointed even his most ardent supporters. And yet, this non-systemic, non-professional politician, unorthodox in all respects, was ideally suited for the conditions of war, for confronting a cruel, extremely cynical aggressor—something, it would seem, he himself thought he was unsuitable for. A nation's intuition, as it turned out, is an entirely material factor, a clear illustration of the words of Isaiah: "I revealed myself to those who did not ask for me."

Salvation thanks to the sole person who can bring salvation always comes unexpectedly, and regardless of how Zelenskyy ends his presidential term, he has already accomplished his mission. This will not be forgotten.

The results were precisely the opposite of what the Russian president intended. But the Lord uses people as instruments to accomplish His purposes, not their plans. The implementation of these goals on a global scale is what comprises the mystery play.

XXIII. COMPANIONS

Davyd Arakhamiia
Leader of the Servant of the People Faction in Ukrainian Parliament
Ukrainian politics in the years from 2019 to 2022 were essentially the fourth season of *Servant of the People*, and Zelenskyy subconsciously ensured that the main characters had real-life doubles. It was a unique situation—it usually happens the other way around. But the team in *Servant* was so well chosen, the roles were distributed so cinematically, and the personae were presented so harmoniously that most of them migrated easily from the screen to reality. Only one individual was added, and he was not created by an author. The Shefir brothers could not have created such a character, only our loose, borderline relationship to reality could have created him, but more about him later.

In the *Servant of the People* series there was a charming character from the Caucasus. He was not an actor, he was the managing director of *Block 95*, Mika Tasunian, who is known by his own name in the series. True, in actual fact, his last name is Fatalov—after his parents' divorce, he was given his mother's last name.

He was born in Baku in 1983. When the crisis began in Nagorny Karabakh, it first became unsafe for Armenians in Baku, and then later unbearable, and the family moved to Ukraine in 1988. Fatalov was very artistic from childhood, taking after his maternal grandfather, a well-known wedding musician, and graduated from the Luhansk Institute of Culture. Like almost everyone in the Block team, he performed in KVN. In Bulat Okudzhava's novel, *A Rendezvous with Bonaparte*, there is a character whose heels Napoleon invariably clings closely to. No matter what European country this character goes to, the Corsican immediately invades it. But he is finally shot in Moscow, which is where the Corsican stops. I had the occasion to tell Okudzhava that this was a brilliant idea—"This is your best idea!" I told him, and he replied that it wasn't invented at all. It was a true story that he read in the *Russian Antiquity* monthly publication.

"This kind of thing happens. I've seen it," he added seriously, perhaps referring to himself? Likewise, the interethnic wars following the collapse of the USSR seemed to be hot on the heels of the heroes of *Block 95*: Fatalov escaped to Luhansk, and war came to Luhansk. Fatalov went to Kyiv, and war came to Kyiv.

He is distinguished not only by his wicked wit and, so to speak, the agility of his psyche—he brilliantly inhabits joy, anger, and melancholy—but also by his organizational abilities, thereby confirming the famous Soviet joke that being a Jew is a calling, being a Russian is a diagnosis, and being a Caucasian is a profession. As you can see, all was well with humor on ethnic themes in the time of the empire when everyone was equal before the servile freedom of a joke.

In Zelenskyy's team, Davyd Arakhamiia embodies audacity, cunning, enterprise, and deep loyalty to friends, all as embodied in the Caucasian character. His role is partly PR—he is the leader of the Servant of the People parliamentary faction—but at the same time, as in *Block 95* and *Servant*, he is indisputably an intellectual. Arakhamiia was born in Sochi, then the family moved to Gagra, and then, after long journeys fleeing the Georgian-Abkhaz conflict, settled in Ukraine. Davyd graduated from school with a gold medal in Mykolaiv, entered the European University and by 2002 opened his own website development company. He truly came to the fore in 2014, when Ukraine had to mount a self-defense in a hybrid war. He was the main organizer of volunteer activities in Mykolaiv, and almost immediately thereafter, became the chairman of the council of volunteers in Ukraine's Ministry of Defense. Why Arakhamiia headed up the Servant of the People parliamentary party in September 2019 is difficult to answer rationally. Probably because, from the point of view of most Ukrainian political scientists, he was an ideal manager who knew how to find ways of communicating with everyone, and was distinguished by truly Caucasian concepts of honor. That is, despite all the efforts of his opponents to tease him (and there is a lot of unkind material about him), they never really dug anything up on him. "According to my information, for more than three months all kinds of different services have been trying to dig up something discrediting or compromising on me, but so far all they have 'found' are Photoshop fakes. I'd say that's a good result," Arakhamiia told Strana.ua when asked to comment on a scandal involving his purported American citizenship. Former people's deputy from the Radical Party Ihor Mosiichuk is the one who made the citizenship accusation. Mosiichuk is a shady character, as is, in my view, his entire party, which was founded by Oleh Liashko. It combines desperate Ukrainian patriotism with criticism of Ukraine's accession to NATO and the EU. Mosiichuk was once the deputy commander of "Azov," but was expelled when he quarreled with Dnipro mayor Borys Filatov. He periodically engaged in public fights, was deprived of his parliamentary immunity, arrested for bribery, then released. His case, like many Ukrainian cases against politicians, was dropped and hushed up. It was he who stated that Arakhamiia had a second citizenship, which is unacceptable under Ukrainian law. He immediately published a fake—a purported photo of the so-called passport which transposed Arakhamiia's first and last names—that was exposed for what it was. Arakhamiia, commenting on the ruse, remarked: "I would never in my life have worn such a vulgar sweater."

Arakhamiia worked in the United States for a while. There was an attempt to pin him with the label of "the FBI's mole in Ukraine," but, once again, there was no proof. He constantly asserts his belief in absolute transparency in business, and the priority of anti-corruption investigations. Apparently, for this reason, Zelenskyy approved him as a member of the supervisory board of the scandal-ridden Ukrainian Defense Industry (Ukroboronprom), and, in particular, of the investigations of corruption by Poroshenko's crony Oleh Hladkovskyi-Svinarchuk (we will return to this later). Incidentally, in the *Servant of the People* series the principled Caucasian Tasunian is put in charge of the Ukrainian Security Forces (SBU) and is the author of sensational revelations of embezzlement in road construction in Kyiv. This episode of the second season was definitely one of the funniest and most venomous. Arakhamiia is further related to Tasunian in his disregard for protocol: He claims that a parliamentarian looks best in shorts and carrying a laptop. In addition to his position in the party, Arakhamiia heads the commission for interaction with the American Senate, and in November 2022 he headed up the commission for monitoring the use of American military aid. He traveled to the U.S. with a report on monitoring this use, and, according to his own statement, enjoyed productive contacts with members of the Republican Party. This may be a questionable thought on my part, but if Arakhamiia's appointment to all these posts was lobbied directly by the United States (a version put forth, for example, by the unhinged and unabashedly pro-Russian "Antifascist" portal), the U.S. could not have made a better choice to control its expenditures. But once again, the reports about the Americans demanding that Zelenskyy appoint Arakhamiia were unconfirmed. The point seems to be that simply because the man lived in the United States, he must therefore have been a recruit.

Arakhamiia was a key figure in the February–March 2022 negotiations with Russia that achieved a certain rapprochement of positions. They, however, became irrelevant after the atrocities in Bucha. He supported Zelenskyy's statement that negotiations with Putin were unacceptable. As the war continued, he was one of the most restrained and confident commentators on what was occurring, never tiring of assuring readers and journalists of parliamentarians' unconditional loyalty to Zelenskyy in wartime. In his cell phone, the president is listed as ZeVova (representing not only "Zelenskyy Vova," but also "TheVova"), which reveals an attitude of respect more than unwarranted familiarity. The definite article, "The," hints at Zelenskyy's qualities, the same ones Arakhamiia often tells journalists about. And that, primarily, demonstrates the unambiguousness of his views, and his fidelity to the word.

Arakhamiia skillfully mixes doses of officiousness and humanity, and emotionality and rigidity. In short, he plays a flawless version of Mika

Tasunian. Sometimes his colleagues in the party faction have had to disavow his statements. In 2021, for example, he said that during an upcoming American visit Zelenskyy would be compelled to discuss military aid with Biden in heated tones. Commenting on that, deputy Yevheniia Kravchuk said, "Davyd is a hot-blooded guy." In fact, as far as we can tell, he is extremely calculating, by which I mean he knows how to appeal to the human side in politics, which is often something journalists discuss at length. It was he who said that Zelenskyy apparently had "chronic fatigue syndrome" (which was quite true, but both the friendly and hostile press then discussed this off-the-cuff remark for two weeks). Arakhamiia is a longtime friend and sympathizer of former Georgian president Mikheil Saakashvili, and has unwaveringly demanded the latter's release from prison. "I am Davyd Arakhamiia, chairman of the presidential party Servant of the People, and leader of the parliamentary majority, recording this video to express my support for the head of the National Reform Council, Mikheil Saakashvili. He is a citizen of Ukraine, a high-ranking official in Ukraine. We will defend every citizen of Ukraine regardless of what territory they are on. We demand he be released immediately. When in Georgia recently, I saw the tremendous achievements, and all the huge capital construction projects that Mikheil instigated. Mikheil is a true reformer, and is promoting many ideas of reform here in Ukraine too. Mikheil, Ukraine is with you. We need you. We wait for you at home!" Thus did Arakhamiia record an appeal in Saakashvili's defense on October 17, 2021. This is also an example of Caucasian chivalry, based not so much on national fraternity and solidarity, as on sympathy for an ideological ally.

Arakhamiia is not just a successful manager, but also the embodiment of the kind of Caucasian character that Zelenskyy wants to deal with. He is a man with his own uncompromising idea of honor. He is aristocratic, witty and temperamental. He is a Mika Tasunian, who was fortunate enough to work in the United States, and unlucky enough to work in a wartime parliament. Tasunian's main trait in the TV series is awareness. This was also emphasized by everyone, without exception, that I spoke to about Arakhamiia.

Fazil Iskander was once asked about the difference between an intelligent person and a wise one. Iskander answered in a way purely characteristic of a native of the Caucasus: A smart person understands how the world works; a wise person manages to live and act in spite of it. That is Arakhamiia right there.

The Mystery of Yermak

1.

Zelenskyy has no gray cardinal, which is hardly the most remarkable characteristic of his presidency. That is, various candidates are suggested for this role, the most frequently mentioned being the Head of the Office of the President of Ukraine, Andrii Yermak, about whom much is known, although none of this abundant information does anything to reveal the man's mysterious, invincible, and all-powerful nature. That aside, there is not a single character about whom it is reliably known to have the president's ear, whose influence is absolute. Zelenskyy has managed to build his policy and arrange his entourage in such a way that no assistant, advisor or administrator has a monopoly on access to the body. No one is a 100 percent reliable lobbyist. Zelenskyy makes decisions himself, or he delegates them to specialists. But if anyone in Ukraine was said to fill this role, it is Andrii Yermak. In the TV series, he had a very specific prototype (and, as we have said, only those who fit into the plot of *Servant of the People* have any chance of finding a place in Ukrainian politics). There is the TV figure of the Almighty Administrator Yurii Ivanovich Chuiko, played by Stanislav Boklan; Yermak resembles him a bit even in his mannerisms and facial expressions. His version of Chuiko is quite phenomenal.

No one can explain why Zelenskyy trusts Yermak and has not replaced him in the real-life fourth year of *The Servant*. The reasons put forth are:

> 1. Yermak is seven years older than Zelenskyy and 22 centimeters taller. Zelenskyy has a little brother complex about him, i.e. he trusts him, relies on him, and senses his reliability. Those to whom the factors of age and height do not seem important underestimate the role

of the Nietzschean phrase "human, all too human" in the behavior of people of power. (I think wistfully about the fact that I am writing about people who are much younger than I: Zelenskyy is eleven years younger than me, Yermak is four. Where did my life go? In countries more dynamic than Russia, people become ministers at thirty, and retire at fifty-five. In essence, my generation in Russia is still waiting for its turn to act. And there is no guarantee that it will ever happen.)

2. Yermak is an ideal organizer. He essentially lives at work (after the war began he put a sofa in his office, and moved in).

3. Yermak is Russia's mole in Zelenskyy's entourage, an informal contact for negotiations, as Medvedchuk used to be. The unreliability and absurdity of this version—especially after Zelenskyy demonstratively refused to have any contact with Russia—is obvious. And yet the opinion lives on, for conspiracy is invincible in principle. A huge percentage of Russians and a significant portion of Ukrainians (especially those living abroad, i.e., not living under falling bombs) are still convinced that Russia and Ukraine have a pact. This notion exists not because it is convincing, and not because any head of the presidential administration is ideally suited to the role of mole due to his influence and involvement in the secrets on Bankova Street, but because it is very scary to imagine how serious everything really is. That is, it is difficult to swallow the fact that Russia wants to raze Ukraine to the ground without any agreements whatsoever.

At the same time, Yermak—especially if we compare him to Russia's Anton Vaino, the Chief of Staff of the Presidential Executive Office—is a public figure who regularly talks to the press and gives commentary. How he ended up in this position, and why he still seems to be Zelenskyy's strongest administrator, remains a mystery. Rumors about his corruption or ties to Russia pop up regularly, but none of it sticks. Frankly speaking, of all Zelenskyy's entourage, he is not really the most mysterious, but somehow the least vulnerable. That is why it's interesting to understand his phenomenon, especially considering that I have no insider information. Neither do most of the augurs wondering about his plans.

Andrii Borysovich Yermak was born November 21, 1971 in Kyiv. His father graduated from Kyiv Polytechnic, an engineer, was engaged in radio electronics, later worked in the Committee for vocational education, and was sent to Afghanistan to construct a system of technical education there. He was the head of the personnel department of the Soviet trade mission in Afghanistan, which most likely had ties to the KGB. Hence countless speculations, but all lacking facts. Andrii Yermak graduated from Kyiv University (Department of International Relations, and Private International Law). He founded an international law firm, was engaged in intellectual property protection, and did battle against piracy in cinema. He was an assistant to Olympic freestyle wrestling champion Elbrus Tedeiev (a deputy of the Party of Regions). Tedeiev's cousin Dzhambolat Tedeiev is the head coach of the Russian freestyle wrestling team. Yermak has never hidden (in fact, he emphasized) his good relations with members of the Russian elite, in particular, his "constructive working relations" with Dmitry Kozak who supervised the People's Republics of Donetsk and Lugansk from Russia.

In 2019 he was appointed assistant to the president of Ukraine, and in February 2020 he replaced Andrii Bohdan as head of the office established to replace the presidential administration. The circumstances of Yermak's replacement of Bohdan are especially curious. Bohdan was called the most influential person in Zelenskyy's team (probably a matter of the post itself). He was never shy, but, in fact, quite bold, in emphasizing his own role in Zelenskyy's decision to run for president: "I said, Volodya, you have given people hope with your film!" In an interview with the journalist Gordon, Bohdan assessed Zelenskyy as follows: "He is very charismatic. He just attracts people. I myself have observed how great figures in world politics simply melted when talking to him. He evokes, you know, the feeling that he is—well, your son. Something you just can't be hostile toward. That is one of his very strong qualities. But you also must realize that he is a super professional actor. Super professional. He can turn on his charisma even with people he dislikes."

But at some point Bohdan began to irritate Zelenskyy, and he called him in for a frank conversation. "It's already written on the wall that you have fired me," Bohdan said, and Zelenskyy told him directly, "You are like an unloved woman. Everything you do evokes aggression in me." The conversation was a private one, but this phrase was quoted by many people: one wonders who made it public? It is unlikely that Bohdan did (he only confirmed to Gordon that it had been spoken). Generally speaking, it's not a phrase you would want to quote to others if you had heard it from a former friend who owes you much. The first time Bohdan sensed this hostility with all clarity was when the president had called in Arakhamiia who was conducting a brief, late afternoon meeting with Bohdan: "So what's he doing there?" he asked. Zelenskyy suspected Bohdan was scheming against him. But it was more likely that what irritated him was Bohdan's frequent and public whispering in his ear—whether it was a solution to a problem, or a way to formulate a phrase. Zelenskyy doesn't like to be controlled publicly and he doesn't try to hide that. Yermak, we will note as an aside, has never allowed himself any such thing.

Being fired was extremely painful for Bohdan. And, after two years of being exceptionally close to the nation's number one citizen, who would take a downfall like that easily? He sincerely believed that he, as his best friend and main director, had created Zelenskyy-the-president. He was the one who pushed Zelenskyy to compete for power. (Of course, self-indulgence is very naïve. Zelenskyy probably had this idea even before *Servant of the People*; he is not at all lacking in ambition.) It is quite natural that Zelenskyy would jettison former associates who considered themselves the forgers of his victory. There is no such leader who would not remove witnesses of, and participants in, his evolution. What is strange is not that Bohdan was removed, but that he was not ready for it.

But why Yermak as a replacement?

Bohdan said it was like Italian shoes: comfortable for the foot. Many answered my question the same way: Yermak says what Zelenskyy wants to hear. But for self-preservation that is not enough in the context of a global crisis. Yermak firmly knows his place and has never attempted to be a gray eminence.

Bohdan—while admitting that he had never seen any such document—spoke about Andrii Yermak's twelve (or thirteen, but politicians are usually superstitious) points, and about secret agreements that Yermak reached with the Russians (mainly in regard to the recognition of Crimea, changes to the Constitution, plus huge compensation for this). During a broadcast of Savik Shuster's *Freedom of Speech* program, Yermak decisively refuted what he called a conspiracy theory: "I can tell you with full responsibility that there are no secret agreements with the Russian Federation, and none can exist in principle."

He led a group of Ukrainian negotiators in the Normandy Format. He created the Center for Countering Disinformation. He is a member of the General Headquarters of the Supreme Commander-in-Chief. He participated as a producer in the creation of five feature films (the most successful being *The Rule of Combat*, the most interesting artistically being *Premonition*, a strange, disturbing drama by Viacheslav Kryshtofovich). He occupies second place in the ranking of Ukrainian politicians, and communicates with Zelenskyy more than any other colleague. But the influence of a politician in Ukraine is determined not by proximity to the president, but, in Yermak's own formulation, by the ability to provide him with expert information. He also played a decisive role in organizing the NATO summit in Vilnius, and his was the most persistent voice in convincing Ukrainians that the summit was a triumph for Ukraine, that the nation had actually been invited to join NATO, and that assistance to it would only expand.

2.

On the day of the first round of the presidential vote, a mini-table tennis tournament was held in Zelenskyy's office. It was won by Vladislav Krasinskyi, a correspondent for RBC-Ukraine. The winning prize was to play a game with Zelenskyy. Before their game, the correspondent made an offer: if Zelenskyy were to lose, he would give RBC an exclusive interview.

On April 17, 2019, Zelenskyy gave the promised interview. By prior agreement, he was not sent a copy for approval. (In 2015, journalist and people's deputy Serhii Leshchenko submitted a bill to abolish the mandatory approval of interviews. The bill did not pass at that time, and in 2020 Leshchenko himself prohibited *Babel* magazine from publishing an interview he gave without first seeing a copy for approval. "Leshchenko is a member of your team," Krasinskyi said to Zelenskyy, pushing for the right to publish the interview without approval. "He is not a member of my team, different people come and help," Zelenskyy replied. But he did give permission to publish the original text without editorial approval.) He said many things of interest, but he was especially often reminded of one promise:

> **Are you prepared to take on political responsibility? If someone like Svynarchuk is found in your team, would you resign?**
> I believe President Poroshenko should have jailed Svynarchuk. He couldn't have done it himself, but he should have come out and said, "It is my request, I am appealing to all law enforcement agencies, to all judges, etc. . . . ."
> **Would you resign?**
> If there were someone like Svynarchuk, I think a president should resign. He's a partner, that's important. Was he a partner of Svynarchuk? Of course, not just resignation, but then a criminal investigation of this issue. But if Svynarchuk was on his team, and he didn't know what he was stealing, then he should have put Svynarchuk in jail. You understand well where we live, and what goes on. People can slip through.

Oleh Svynarchuk, a long-forgotten figure because Ukraine has much more serious problems now, was a Ukrainian businessman, the head of Poroshenko's headquarters in the Cherkasy region, was responsible for Ukraine's military exports after Poroshenko's victory, was the first deputy secretary of the National Security and Defense Council (NSDC) of Ukraine, and on this occasion took his mother's more respectable maiden name—Hladkovskyi. (Svynarchuk in Ukrainian suggests something swinish.) He was accused of embezzlement, fired, arrested, and released on a bail of 10 million hryvnia. Before the election's second round, Zelenskyy promised to ask Poroshenko a question: why aren't the swine behind bars?

We recall this story mainly because a corruption scandal also arose around Yermak. The young filmmaker and performance artist Geo Leros (a deputy in the Rada from the Servant of the People faction) published some *kompromat*, that is, compromising information, usually of a salacious kind, that is common in Ukraine. In the spring of 2020, he supported an appeal to Zelenskyy from a small group of deputies who called for the creation of an advisory council with the participation of separatists from the ORDLO territories (an abbreviation adopted in Ukraine for the occupied part of Donbas, referring to separate districts of Donetsk and Luhansk regions). Yermak strongly objected. "Apparently, Andrii Yermak thought he was better and more experienced than everyone else. Thus did he begin squeezing out any group that might deliver alternative thoughts to the president," Leros declared. He announced that he was collecting dirt on Yermak, and the very next day received a compromising tape showing Andrii Yermak's younger brother Denys (born in 1979) actually trading in appointments, citing his family ties. Yermak demanded to know the origin of the tapes and how they had reached Leros. But Leros refused to reveal the informants. In response Yermak stated that he had earlier blocked an appointment that Leros had tried to push through his office (presumably the nomination of Ilia Sahaidak to the post of deputy minister), so now the parliamentarian was taking revenge on him: "They are battling not only me—they are battling the Ukrainian government, the presidential team," he said at a briefing. Denys Yermak made his own statement: He did not deny that it was his voice on the tape, but he claimed that the discussion was not about appointments, but rather about projects that he planned to propose in a fully official manner. Several anonymous sources said the tape scandal could be guessed to have originated with the previous head of the Office of the President Andrii Bohdan, who had been "sidetracked by similar methods."

3.

All this and subsequent attempts to bring down Yermak led to nothing. He will depart his post either when the war is concluded or when Zelenskyy goes. That will happen when a radical change of style takes place. For now, he suits the current style perfectly.

We now come to a fundamental consideration that concerns politics in general, but Zelenskyy's politics in particular. The peculiarity of the narrator king is that he builds a story for his nation, obeying all the laws of genre, whether consciously or unconsciously, but doing it in such a way that it is believable, and people want to follow along. He creates a kind of theatrical mask for reality, for reality is always messy, and almost always illogical. In the narrative that Zelenskyy is creating for Ukraine there is a need for a mysterious, demonized figure endowed with all kinds of powers, and Yermak fits such a role perfectly. He never allows himself a single personal statement, and he always says just enough to be interpreted in opposite ways—as an agent of Russia, and as the chief patriot of Ukraine in Zelenskyy's entourage.

Far be it from me to think, of course . . . although why? In fact, I would be terribly happy to learn that there is a special person in Zelenskyy's team responsible for all the drama, for everything is very clearly organized, and one is tempted to see an author's hand behind everything. I even suspect, or sometimes hope, that if some day Zelenskyy finds the time to read this book, at least in his retirement, and it is of interest to him, that he will reveal this secret to me. That he will personally, secretly identify for me the consultant from the Block team who is structuring the plot of his presidency. However, it is most likely that this plot is being built according to the laws of the genre itself—or is controlled personally by the Creator. But what a grand idea it would be to keep within the administration a person who, so to speak, writes the history of modern times! For Putin there was Vladislav Surkov who appointed himself chief demon. He is a gifted man, but he has bad taste, so he appointed himself as the main figure. As a result, his demonism was provincial, smacking of something from an Institute of Culture, and with his *Nashi* organization taking the form of ironic postmodernist proto-fascism. The difference, however, is that in Russia it was all played out seriously, with gusto, and without the slightest self-irony.

From the very beginning, Zelenskyy's entire presidency in Ukraine has been an art project that, like any true art, must be played out with deadly risks. In this art project, in this plot of a new Ukrainian statehood, the role of an omnipotent, omniscient, strictly covert administrator is crucial. He says only what is allowed by protocol; he assists the president at all stages of his work; but he never takes the initiative. He is labeled a Russian agent, the chief corruptor, the main fighter against corruption, a representative of the security forces, and the architect of all Ukrainian politics. But he decides nothing and only ensures the smooth functioning of all the stage machinery. (Incidentally, why is Yermak most often suspected of backstage connections with Russia? Because in Ukraine today this is the worst possible suspicion, and the most influential politician is obliged to cast just such a shadow. A man without a shadow is suspicious. It is better to cast a long one.)

There is no question that Ukrainian politics is a dramatic play. But it is, at least, well written and impeccably directed, a full season of an ongoing TV series with a competent scriptwriter and worthy props. For all the staged, or, if you like, serialized, nature of Ukrainian politics, it has no such failures as the Prigozhin rebellion in Russia (which, even if it was designed to entertain the population, was full of wild logical and logistical inconsistencies). Whereas a figure like Yermak is flawlessly conceived.

Yermak attracts a great deal of negativity, being a kind of black hole. As it should, this hole draws in all the negative emotions that otherwise might have gone to Zelenskyy. The version that Yermak is an agent of Moscow is based on the fact that his father is most likely connected with the Russian security services, his mother was born in Leningrad, that he himself is well acquainted with Dmitry Kozak, and that he has participated in negotiations with Russia on many occasions. But upon thoughtful examination, this version does not stand up to criticism, for there is no evidence of Yermak's family's ties to the Russian security services, except for his father's work in Afghanistan. All attempts by Ukrainian political analysts (in particular, *Focus* magazine in 2020) to reveal Yermak's ties with Kozak appear to be purely speculative. Not a single fact has been unearthed, but for Yermak's own hints that his contact with Kozak was more constructive than with other Russian representatives. Still, the scenario that makes Yermak look like an agent of Moscow is unusually attractive. It is interesting to follow. It is interesting to speculate about. It puts no obligations on Yermak. It endows his character with a genuine, not Surkovian, demonism.

A thoroughly suitable observation, as a neighbor in Ithaca used to say. While I was proofreading this book, Vladislav Surkov once again published a poem in *Russian Pioneer*, the regular outlet for his literary activity. Even in his Kremlin period, he did not hide his penchant for writing; he was capable of writing songs for Vadim Samoilov of the Agatha Christie rock band, or penning a novel.

Poems like this:

> not a word
> blind prophets
> leaf through holy books
> where not a line is written
> no letters, smudges, nor hidden obscene gestures
> reduce yourself silently
> to a point out at sea
> to ruination to extremes
> of muted non-existence
>
> disappear don't stop
> let time flow and overflow
> 'til tomorrow itself
> Let the world begin and be what it will

I suspect all mysterious figures, including the Lord, can be explained apophatically (apophaticism is a form of theological thinking), that is: God can be defined through what he is not.

So, in regard to the question of the ideal administrator: Andrii Yermak does not write poetry. Or, if he does, he does not show it to anyone.

4.

The more mysterious the figure of the supreme administrator, the more insignificant his role in politics. It is rather like the Masonic mysteries: the more noise there is around them, the lower the belief that they exist in reality. Neither the power of the Freemasons, nor their involvement in the great esoteric mysteries, nor the world government with its web of global connections ever show themselves. But for the Freemasons the myth of a secret society looks flattering and fascinating, and you couldn't dream up a better legend for the world as a whole. The myth of the secret society is a new variant of religious feeling, its degeneration, if you will. There is a technical executor behind the figure of a powerful administrator, but his reputation already puts him halfway down the road to success.

The reader is entitled to exclaim: the Kyiv leadership consists of simulacra! But the reader will not be quite right. The leadership in Kyiv consists of professionals, including professional scriptwriters. The fourth season of *Servant of the People* is directed with exceptional talent, and all of its main characters—the Trickster Leader, the Mighty Demon, the Servant of the People—all fulfill their roles to perfection, regardless of what their functions actually are. The only thing missing is the femme fatale. She would have been perfect for the role of mediator. In conspiracy novels this role determines much. In the Russian story she is usually a Jew. In the Ukrainian version she might be Polish, or something of that nature. They slipped up on this one. Maybe after they see this book they'll find one? There are plenty of femme fatale beauties in key positions in the EU, aren't there?

To top off his demonic reputation, in 2023 Andrii Yermak threw all his energies into the preparation of a summit in Saudi Arabia that was designed to enlist the global South in the Ukrainian cause. This was a sort of response—asymmetric, of course, since it was well-thought-out—to the Russian-African summit, although it is possible that the get-together in the Konstantinovsky Palace in St. Petersburg was an attempt to get ahead of the game. After all, the Saudi meeting was announced far in advance, and intelligence forces never sleep. Russia wanted to return to its old stomping grounds by engaging Africa, while Ukraine was finally intensifying its work in the south and east, while also keeping an eye on the Arabs. Arestovych admitted that no proper work with the third world had been established throughout the twenty years of Ukrainian independence.

It goes without saying that the Saudi summit raised tensions and expectations all over the world—the idea was to put forth a peace plan, but Zelenskyy warned that no peace plan and no negotiations could include the participation of Putin. If Ukraine ceases to receive aid, he seemed to suggest, we will make do with our own efforts. If we lose, we will die—life isn't eternal anyway.

But the real goal was not a peace plan, but rather to attract more non-aligned countries to Ukraine's side. If so, then this was an especially revealing error. The fact is that Third World countries are bad allies: the poverty-stricken have no principles, pragmatism comes first (as Vladimir Putin incessantly proclaimed during his first term as president). Pragmatists have no allies. And the Non-Aligned Movement is in no position to be picky when choosing allies. Third World countries are promising tug-of-war targets, but here's the catch: they are the first to betray. Neither Russia nor Ukraine have any strong feelings for them, aside from the usual shaman's contempt for secular culture.

And friction will soon begin with America. We have already mentioned that Zelenskyy tends to shed directors. Which is why Yermak—how's that for intuition?!—focused his efforts on finding new allies, often unexpected ones. Incidentally, I would not be surprised if he is also engaged in contacts with the Russian opposition, including the oligarchic opposition. Such allies should not be neglected, even considering Russia's general toxicity in the modern world. Furthermore, the parallels with Latin America, mainly in its mythological, poetic, and passionate literature, have long been obvious. Ukraine may find very influential friends there.

5.

Although Ukrainian politics is completely unpredictable, and the future of the world is far from clear, one thing is certain: the standard move of "feeding someone to the masses" is not applicable in this tale. What I mean is this: Virtually every major official in Russia lives with the firm understanding of his inevitable persecution at the end of his career. He will be thrown to the masses from the tsar's porch to deflect the people's anger.

This has happened in Ukraine, too, but it hasn't been common under Zelenskyy. I hope he will not embrace tradition to such a degree because problematic issues are increasingly accruing to Yermak, and, by Russian standards, he would be the perfect figure about whom to shout, like Fyodor Rostopchin, Moscow's Governor-General during Napoleon's invasion: "People! This man here is the scoundrel who . . ." (insert any failure or mistake). But Zelenskyy won't do that because of one particular acting, producing, and human trait he has: his self-centeredness. That's why he will never name Yermak as the culprit of some comprehensive problem: Only he, personally, can be the root cause of everything that happens. For the same reason, Zelenskyy will never claim Russia is to blame for everything: he does not attach that much importance to Russia. He won't even criticize Russian ideologists who constantly blame the insidious Anglo-Saxons of being behind everything. Zelenskyy does not consider Russians smarter than Ukrainians, never, not in the least. And he does not consider Yermak superior to himself. Yermak will lose his position only when he comes out of the shadows, or, God forbid, starts publishing poetry.

"Yermak is with me for a reason. I trust him," Zelenskyy has said.

At a press marathon on November 21, 2022, a reporter from Ukraine's Channel Five asked Zelenskyy if he saw any similarities between Yermak and Vitalii Zakharchenko, the Minister of Internal Affairs under Yanukovych who is considered responsible for the Maidan shootings. Who would have doubted it: Zakharchenko now works for Rostech, a Russian state corporation.

"There is no point in comparing the stories of Zakharchenko and Yermak. First, Mr. Yermak killed no one, and never gave such commands. Secondly, Mr. Yermak, on the contrary, brought home people who, by the way, the owner of your channel, the former president, Mr . . ."—then he catches himself, because, actually, he is a "comrade"—"whom comrade Petro Poroshenko should have brought home as part of his operations."

And he added: Andrii Yermak is now negotiating with "the leadership of the best intelligence agencies of different countries," and "chiefs of staff of various presidents," which, according to Zelenskyy, indicates his confidence in the man running the Office of the President.

"They know everything about him. His phone, believe me, has been tapped and listened to by all the heads of every intelligence agency—they wouldn't sit at the same table with him."

Look how he constructs Yermak's image of being all-knowing and mysterious! I love it.

The plot about deceived trust definitely does not fit Zelenskyy. "The tsar is good, the boyars are bad" is not a Ukrainian theme at all. The Ukrainian theme is that the tsar is good, the boyars are reliable, and the people are even better. Zelenskyy needs only one thing from his retinue—that it not betray him. His retinue can rely on reciprocal guarantees.

I think, by the way, that the character of Chuiko in *Servant of the People* is based on the Soviet myth of the All-Powerful Administrator. All of us, and Yermak certainly, watched the youth-oriented science-fiction movie *Moscow-Cassiopeia* as children. In it the great Russian actor Innokenty Smoktunovsky played Director of Special Duties, who was sent out into space ahead of all the other characters.

That's Yermak. With that eternal irony about his own omnipotence showing on his good-natured, always deceptive, always slow-moving face.

But, of course, the cast of characters would not be complete without the Double Agent. And this, as the reader has already guessed, is by no means Yermak.

Arestovych

1.

I think Oleksii Nikolaievich Arestovych is the most interesting thing that happened to Ukraine following Zelenskyy's election.

I'm not hiding it—just go and try to hide it: I'm an Arestovych fan! I am a "cheese" for Arestovych. I must explain to the reader what *syrikhi*, or "cheese," is. No, it's not something that has disappeared from the market shelves, but it is something that did disappear: the uncritical, fanatical admirer, which has vanished as a class. There are no absolute idols anymore. Everyone has been compromised. Everyone has been debunked. "Cheeses," my young reader, was the name for fans besotted with love and fanaticism. They followed the tenor Sergei Lemeshev, who lived on Moscow's main drag, Tverskaya Street, opposite the Post Office, in a building that housed a cheese store that was a cult destination in Soviet times. On occasion you could get more than the routine "Russian" and "Poshekhonsky" cheeses there; but what were always there were fans waiting for their beloved tenor, the democratic singer of popular songs and classics. They were there on duty to catch a glimpse, to see a responsive smile, to toss him a bouquet of violets, which was always the cheapest bouquet. The great actress Alla Tarasova, the tenor Ivan Kozlovsky, and later pop star Alla Pugacheva all had *syrikhi*, "cheeses." These dedicated fans were treated with disdain, but also with respect, because they sacrificed themselves by being on duty no matter what the weather. I was a fan of Arestovych when it was fashionable, and I remain one now that he has, as I predicted, become a universal enemy. And, I must say, I prefer this state of affairs—if only because it is more familiar. Truly, we love in our idols a perfect version of ourselves.

This man's biography plays no role in anything, because no one knows it. The more mythologized it is, the better. But somehow it happened that all the important names and problems of the new century left their mark on this biography. Arestovych has been demonized like no other, and he takes genuine pleasure in that. There is nothing so nasty that he would not repost it on social media. There are no caricatures that he would not circulate, and no gossip he would not hasten to spread. He himself has diligently inflated the myth of his demonic nature since the very beginning of the war. It really is difficult to argue with him—he confirms every vile thing said about him in advance. In one of our conversations, I asked him point blank: Do you understand that the more merit you have now, the sooner you will be declared a traitor?

"I definitely do," he nodded. "It's already begun. Generally speaking, a modernist is a traitor by definition."

And that is an excellent formulation—precisely because a modernist is doomed to abandon any immanence such as blood, soil, nationality, age, kinship, and homeland—anything he did not choose himself. Arestovych is the only consistent modernist in the field of Ukrainian politics (and Russian, of course, because Russia today is overwhelmed by such impenetrable, putrid archaism that any non-conformist statement there smacks of suicide). Arestovych is an embodied challenge to his environment and context, and, for a man of forty-eight, his behavior has been strikingly unbecoming of his age. Usually by this age, people have become dependent on reputation, avoiding strident statements, and spend their time seeking a quiet position. But the peculiarity of today's generation of forty-somethings—including Zelenskyy—is that they were forced into secondary roles for too long: the last Soviet generation had to grab as much as it could, and then get their fill of wielding power. And when they were forced out of power because they had already bored everyone to tears, a war began. As such, instead of being able to enjoy the expected bonuses of power, Zelenskyy's peers received unprecedented responsibility. As they say, fear your wishes—they come true.

Zelenskyy, it seems, was not so much stimulated by this responsibility as stunned. He was not prepared for his experiment to deliver such results. Arestovych, on the other hand, swims in it like a fish in the Dnipro River. He resembles his beloved hero Gorbovsky, created by his favorite writers, the Strugatsky brothers: "Gorbovsky was curled up in front of the console, strapped to the chair. His black hair fell over his eyes, and he bared his teeth with every jolt. The jolts were continuous, and it seemed as if he were laughing. But it was not laughter. Sidorov had never imagined that Gorbovsky could be so . . . not strange, but somehow so alien. Gorbovsky was like the devil. Valkenstein looked like the devil, too. He hung prostrate over the atmospheric fixer console, twitching his outstretched neck. It was remarkably quiet. But the hands on the instruments, the green zigzags and spots on the fluorescent screens, the black and orange spots on the periscope screen—all of it was tossing and turning in a merry dance, and the floor jerked from side to side like a shortened pendulum, and the ceiling fell and bounced back up again." What a merry dance. Arestovych once said that Ukraine now looks like Mexico in Eisenstein's unfinished movie—a carnival of skeletons, a dance of death. They have determined that they are already dead, so now they can have fun. It's a state behind, and beyond fear. And Arestovych is having fun as if he were in that creepy carnival, which, according to Eisenstein's plan, was to be the finale of his *¡Qué Viva México!*

2.

I doubt that war solves moral problems. Rather, it drives them further into the depths. It is highly doubtful that war reminds the world of half-forgotten virtues such as patriotism or solidarity. (It actually draws patriotism into question, at least as concerns those on the attacking side.) It advances people who are professionals, and this is its second positive consequence.

In normal times—and especially in such rancid epochs as the 1990s—people like Arestovych either remain in fifth and tenth roles, or in those spheres where they attract no attention (because there is always a war being fought on some invisible front, and that is a territory for meritocracy whether you like it or not). Such a person could not possibly have stepped forward in Ukraine in the times of Yanukovych or Poroshenko. But the election of Zelenskyy, as we recall, marked the coming of an age of professionals—when those for whom it is impermissible to purr began to chirp, and the cobbler took up stitching boots.

It is curious that this triumph of professionalism that replaced the age of total and tedious dilettantism began in the sphere of show business. Perhaps that's because professionals are more noticeable there. But it's one of those things that, once you start, others will follow. Arestovych was the second professional to find himself in the right place at the right time. In February 2022, he rapidly became the most famous Ukrainian after Zelenskyy. His fame quickly spread throughout all Ukraine, then throughout all of Russia, and by March—throughout the world. There are few individuals on the planet who could wear this global fame with such magnificent self-confidence.

I struggle to remember how I first heard of him, but when people recommended that I listen to Arestovych, they usually said: He made the most accurate predictions of the annexation of Crimea in 2014, and the advent of war in 2022—both times three years in advance. I also struggle to say just what he actually did. Formally, he was an advisor to the Office of the President. But the status of advisor in Ukraine is a special topic: these positions are occupied by irreplaceable people who do everything simultaneously. Sometimes they have no other position only because it is troublesome to state out loud what they do. Arestovych is a chief motivational manager. He doesn't comfort, lull, or generally relax his listener. His task is constantly to remind people why they are fighting and enduring hardship, why this is something Putin needs, and why it is Ukraine's duty to resist it. Roughly speaking, he is a manager of the world picture. There is no such position officially, and there can be none, so he is an advisor (make that "former advisor," but, as they say, there are no former advisors). Roughly speaking, his task, like the task of any normal political ideologist in power, is to establish the coordinates of life: floor-to-ceiling, left-to-right. And it is precisely this job that is most in demand during times of military turbulence.

RUSSIAN PUBLISHER'S NOTE: the Ukrainian Security Forces and the Ukrainian Military Forces quietly snickered.
AUTHOR'S RESPONSE: . . . And after the Ukrainian Military Forces—the Ukrainian Security Forces. Who, by the way, were also in need of psychotherapy.

For the sake of appearances such work must not be done ostentatiously. In times of war nothing should be done merely for the sake of the report, which is the usual way of doing things in Russia. During war, efficiency is important, and nature knows no one more effective than quick, courageous, and adventurous mavericks. Most of the Red Army commanders and heroes of the Russian Civil War of 1917–1922 (Grigory Kotovsky, Aleksa Dundić, Kamo [Simon Ter-Petrosian], Nestor Makhno, Vasily Chapaev, Mikhail Frunze, and Mykola Shchors) belonged to this type of individual. Their lives after the war ended took tragic turns—death came to them faster in peacetime than it ever had done at the front.

In times of great upheavals, figures like this make their appearance regularly. They are universal, well-read in literature and sociology, fond of math, can fix a car, beat somebody up, and never repudiate the high-minded title of adventurer. (One remembers that Che Guevara, icon of leftists all over the world, said: "Many will call me an adventurer, and that I am . . . only one of a different sort: one who risks his skin to prove his truths.") Arestovych is a trickster for the sophisticated, a synthesis of Ostap Bender, Sherlock Holmes, Harry Potter, and a bit Zelenskyy. Arestovych is a new type of hero: like the character from "The Internationale," he has been everything.

He was born in Georgia, in Kakheti, on August 3, 1975. His father was an officer who served in the German Democratic Republic, and later headed the admissions committee at the National Defense Academy in Kyiv. His mother was an accountant. His older sister Olesia, now a notary in Kyiv, is the wife of Andrii Korniichuk, formerly an officer of the Upper Rada administration, and former secretary of Ukraine's delegation to the Parliamentary Assembly of the Council of Europe. His older brother Serhii is a businessman. Arestovych's biography is known mostly from his own words and is striking for its grand extremes. In regard to his range of interests and diversity of talents, he is comparable only to another great propagandist, the Russian journalist Alexander Nevzorov (and even their interests are similar—biology, and equestrian sports). Arestovych's worldview, however, unlike Nevzorov's, is characterized by consistency. The main difference, in fact, is that he has one.

Arestovych entered the biology department of Kyiv University and dropped out after a year, becoming an actor in the Black Box studio theater. He graduated as a military interpreter at the Odesa Institute of Land Forces (later renamed the Military Academy—academies proliferated everywhere in the post-Soviet period). He served in the Main Directorate of Intelligence, and the Department of Strategic Research of the Ministry of Defense of Ukraine and participated as an interpreter in a peacekeeping mission in the Balkans. He resigned from the army in 2005, explaining that the country's leadership (Viktor Yushchenko, who was brought to power by the first Maidan) began to interfere in the work of the military. He acted in commercials. He played supporting roles in seventeen comedy films and TV series (he is especially reproached for the female role of Lucy in the 2011 movie *Don't Be Afraid, I'm Nearby.* Arestovych not only refuses to renounce this role, but he willingly posts photos of himself wearing a woman's wig). He created his own film and commercial-making company, Aegis Artist Group (aegis referring to the shield carried by Athena).

He was an active opponent of Ukraine's Orange Revolution (2004–2005), seeing in it the triumph of the ideas of nationalism, which always seemed provincial to him. In Moscow, he met Alexander Dugin, the number one Moscow occultist, a representative of far-right conservatism, and he joined Dugin's Eurasian movement. In 2008, he became disillusioned with Dugin and began organizing Crimea's defense against a Russian invasion. He announced the creation of the Down with Everyone party, but it turned out to be unviable. After 2014, when the hostilities began in eastern Ukraine, he first announced the creation of the People's Reservist movement, then served as a scout in the 72nd mechanized brigade, speaking only sparingly about his trips across the front line. He participated in the work of the trilateral contact group that developed the Minsk agreements. When Andrii Yermak became the head of the presidential administration, he made Arestovych his adviser, although Arestovych quit a year later, saying he was tired of bureaucracy. From the beginning of the Russian invasion, he became a leading military expert on Ukrainian television, and, on regular television broadcasts with Russian human rights activist Mark Feigin, he painted a picture of military operations that was unwaveringly optimistic for Ukraine. Many Ukrainians of both sexes, as well as Russian liberals, both in Russia and abroad, admit that they do not fall asleep without listening to Arestovych.

He broke with Mark Feigin in July 2023, nobly thanking him for his cooperation.

"Why don't you work with him anymore?"

"I won't wash my dirty laundry in public, but I'll be honest: Mark managed to surprise me. That's not an easy thing to do."

(I won't retell the rumors about Feigin's dissatisfaction with Arestovych's growing popularity: Since they didn't stoop to a public showdown, why should we bother?)

On January 14, 2023, commenting on a missile that struck a residential building in Dnipro, Arestovych said that, according to one version, the missile had been shot down by the Ukrainian air defense. Mykola Oleshchuk, the Commander of the Ukrainian Air Force, responded that the Ukrainian Armed Forces "do not have firearms capable of shooting down this type of missile." Forbes published a report that, "Subsequently, Arestovych declared that 'no air defense missile could have caused even half of such destruction,'" and explained his initial words as the result of fatigue. Putin's press secretary Dmitry Peskov immediately took advantage of Arestovych's error—suggesting that they admit it themselves—and a wave of hatred arose. Arestovych immediately resigned from his advisory post: "I want to demonstrate an example of civilized behavior: a fundamental mistake, which means resignation," he wrote in Telegram.

True, he apologized without any self-deprecation. "I always trust my listeners and I am confident that I am engaging with adults who can add two and two, not with twitchy kindergarteners who are accustomed to passing off their own feelings as someone else's thoughts. Therefore, I allow myself the luxury of not being afraid to speak freely, without choosing words, and hoping that adults will not fall into hysterics from certain combinations of them, but will be capable of determining the essence and subject of what is being expressed. It is dangerous to build a country in which you have to tremble over the combination of words."

But this is precisely the kind of country Ukraine is bound to be—like it or not. It is a nervous time. Since January 2023, Arestovych seemed to be liberated from the duty to comfort people, instead discovering a new duty: to criticize and stir up trouble. The whole situation contributed to this, since in his previous capacity he had begun to irritate too many people, and whatever you cannot overcome, you must be prepared to lead. In his Apeiron courses of psychological and ideological training—another of his countless areas of activity—Arestovych teaches something like this: if the ninth wave is coming at you, you've got to ride it.

3.

This motley jumble of biographical data—do not mistake it for self-promotion—reminds me first of all of my description about one of my own heroes, who is also a trickster. Every revolution and almost every war brings characters of this kind to the surface. The Russian journalist and political opportunist Ivan Manasevich-Manuilov was one. As was Roman Malinovsky, who fooled Vladimir Lenin himself. And Casanova. And Cagliostro. And Tom Edward Lawrence, better known as Lawrence of Arabia.

Such people shine brightly, disappear suddenly, and then films are made about them, and they—aristocratic old men with lively sparkling eyes—attend the premiere. They may have to borrow a tuxedo for the event, because in their old age they, who once cast diamonds about, can't afford dinner every day.

"To begin with, I wish to emphasize," he said modestly, "that I have been associated with the struggle of the working class throughout my entire career. I was expelled from the university in the fifth year for participating in a strike. I was sent to Kursk province, but due to shell shock in the Russo-Japanese War, I obtained permission to go abroad for treatment. My mother fell at the feet of police officers, kissing their boots. I went to Turin, where I studied history and did historical research. There I grew close to the Garibaldians. Do you know the Garibaldians? Fighters for the liberation of the Italian working class, Spartak, and all that . . . I attracted the attention of the police, and was forced to flee to Russia, where I grew close to activists in the Bolshevik underground. I carried out assignments for them in Serbia and Bulgaria. You understand? Brothers, courageous young men, and all that. But all very secret!" he raised his finger. "Please note! For the sake of secrecy, I had to meet with the First Assistant to the Minister of Foreign Affairs of Bulgaria,

Miridonov himself! I later prepared a brochure about this, but the tsarist government would not publish it. Anyway, you understand, for considerations of conspiracy . . . In 1917 I immediately took the side of the rebels, immediately! I left for Tiflis on special assignment. I was in charge of financial aid for the Bolshevik underground. After that, I was transferred to Leningrad—where, on special assignment, I identified former players who were dangerous from the point of view of the counterrevolution, and reported specially to Comrade Ogranov. This was my path, the path of one who ardently sympathizes with the cause, not perfect in everything, perhaps, but sincerely striving . . ."

Thus speaks Ostroumov, the title character of my novel *Ostroumov, or the Sorcerer's Apprentice*. But there have been many such characters and novels: *Ibicus* by Alexei Tolstoy, where the hero by a prophetic coincidence was named Nevzorov; Ehrenburg's *Julio Jurenito*, and Babel's Benia Krik tales. According to Mark Lipovetsky's just observation, the trickster is always an agent of progress. He is the protector and bearer of "irony and mercy," as Fitzgerald put it. His demonic nature is nothing more than an ironic mask designed to weed out fools, and fools hate Arestovych with a passion, accusing him of underestimating Ukrainian culture and slandering the nationalists with whom he himself became so close at one time. (With Dmytro Korchynsky, for example, a true jokester, and activist in the extremist Right Sector group.) Some of his statements almost bring him in direct line with Nevzorov, who also at one time positioned himself as a Russian nationalist, and a friend of the writer Alexander Prokhanov and the painter Ilya Glazunov. ("I look at the issues of restoring historical memory, justice, struggle, victories and defeats, the formation of nations, language(s), and the closing of historical wounds as a soldier would look at a louse.") But if Nevzorov never expounded a philosophical system, and never offered reliable military forecasts, limiting himself merely to scathing revelations, Arestovych, first of all, frequently discussed his worldview, and second, gave no less than three extremely accurate predictions of future military and/or political events:

1. In 2003, he predicted that Crimea would be annexed by Russia.

2. In 2008, he predicted the inevitable Russification and secession of Donbas.

3. In 2019, he predicted a large-scale war between Ukraine and Russia (and although many predicted it, including the author of these lines, only Arestovych clearly dated it to the end of 2021–beginning of 2022). He himself claims that making this forecast was simple: Russia had a relatively small window left in which to blackmail the world with nuclear weapons, and Putin urgently needed to come up with new bait to replace the fading consensus about Crimea.

As late as September 2024, polls suggested that approximately half of Ukrainians (49 percent) would not forgive Zelenskyy were he to make peace on Russia's terms.

Arestovych's worldview rests on three pillars: post-Soviet modernism, Vernadsky's doctrine of the noosphere (he himself repeatedly called himself a religious person and believes in the divine act of creation), and the Strugatsky utopia. This utopia describes the world of the future as a space of "joy and curiosity," that is, as a world in which it is more important for people to work than to live, and where the joy of knowledge is stronger than the joy of expansion. Arestovych calls the Soviet Union the best thing that happened to humanity in the twentieth century, and not because he likes mass repression or the imperial idea of Big Brother, but because everything else was even worse than the mature (or late) USSR.

Arestovych maintains an absolute, soldier-like, loyalty to Zelenskyy. In August 2022, Arestovych gave an interview to Dmitry Gordon and said that if Zelenskyy, keeping his promise, does not put forth his candidacy in the next presidential election, he will announce his own candidacy. However, he repeated, that is only on the condition that he does not cross paths with the current president. The war, of course, nullifies pre-war promises, but there is a chance that Zelenskyy will eventually tire. What are Arestovych's chances?

Personally, I would be happy to see him as president, but I am almost convinced that this is impossible. And this confidence fills me with a curious joy: Arestovych has a huge road ahead of him, and holding power would iron out his interesting wrinkles in an undesirable way, and impose too many serious obligations on him.

Actually, this whole book (at least in concept) is about how God forces man to perform in a divine drama, and fulfill tasks put forth by God. About how one is or is not suited to this role. About how a person unconsciously fits into a niche prepared for him, and about how it is up to the spectator to learn to recognize the intent of the drama, and to extract from it its prime concept. For history is a visual expression of the divine plan for mankind; it has no other meaning.

4.

On July 12, 2023, following the NATO summit at which Ukraine received significantly less than it wanted, but the maximum of what was possible, Arestovych published a text that clearly marks a new stage in his turbulent biography.

> The fact that there are weak leaders in the West today who are incapable of making serious decisions does not negate the simple fact that we depend on these leaders rather more than entirely.
>
> Our main mistake, the irreparability of which yesterday struck us as might a bad stench, is that we relied on the politics of emotional blackmail, the politics of performance, the politics of courageous, hard-set jaws.
>
> But we should have been (choose any moment: February 25, 2022, 2019, 2014, 2008, 1991, 1648) engaging in a policy of improving our partnership qualities and acquiring real sovereignty.
>
> Over the course of historical time, we have had two such periods— Mazepa and Skoropadskyi.
>
> Everything else is a fairytale about "heroism" masquerading as "partnership."
>
> It is easier to be heroes than to engage in genuine systemic construction.
>
> But any military man knows: heroism is a consequence of failure.

You can estimate the number of our failures by counting the instances of our mass heroism throughout our history.

It's natural that our partners who support our economy, our Defense Forces, and have their own (!) goals in foreign policy are rather surprised at our position, which is that we are emotionally blackmailing them, demanding that they replace their goals with ours—and at the same time, for just a second, pilfer their taxpayers' money, which they take from their own people and send to us.

1. The Americans are not going to defeat the Russian Federation (lest it fall, lock, stock, and barrel to China).

2. We demand our victory and the break-up of Russia—paid for by American money.

3. We pilfer American money—Americans demand we stop.

This is an outline of what is happening now in Vilnius, and an outline of what is happening with this war and with our entire foreign policy in general.

And foreign policy is an extension of domestic policy.

It is not without reason that the "fight against corruption" is NATO's primary demand for Ukraine.

If we were to improve our true sovereignty systematically, primarily by improving the economy, we would then receive, small perhaps, but legitimate tools for influencing our partners' positions, and a share of independence in our decisions and goals.

Alas . . . the eternal curse of Ukraine is at work.

As soon as the popular Russian radio commentator Alexei Venediktov reposted this—dare I say it—campaign platform, Arestovych predictably began receiving criticism, and many of the comments were written at least as well as his. I am prepared to accept several of them:

All his life Liosha has been able to write beautifully what the masses expect from him. Writing is not doing. He never did anything and never was anyone. He merely changed his shoes at the necessary time. He once was a *porokhobot*, literally, a bot for Poroshenko, then he fell in love with Zelenskyy. Now he has launched his own presidential campaign. He is a man without principles, like anyone who comes from a military family. A narcissist. He always disables comments on his account, he only accepts likes. [...] He is not Ukrainian, he doesn't care who he's showing off to. Today he'll make Ukrainians fall in love with him, tomorrow he'll appeal to Russia and will have the same success there.

Some wrote immediately that Arestovych's text was "scaldingly honest" and full of sincere pain for Ukraine. Others said he was stunningly false and full of coquetry (this is a standard reproach of anyone who is able to speak clearly), while playing into the hands of Russia. The latter is entirely true because any radical criticism of Ukraine, especially in derogatory tones, plays into Russia's hands. But what are we to do about that—nothing? As they say, if you're afraid of Putin, don't go to the outhouse.

If we try objectively to consider what was said, without taking into account the instant, knee-jerk reactions, we cannot deny Arestovych's main skill: He doesn't reflect, but anticipates the mood of the masses and expresses it with remarkable clarity. The text is aimed not so much at Ukrainians—most of them are traumatized by the war and are in no mood for an objective conversation about the future—but at Europeans and Americans. Of course, the entire world is fatigued with the military agenda; Ukraine has managed to maintain interest in itself for an astonishingly long time thanks to the unprecedented stupidity and atrocity of Russia's military leadership, and its civilian lies. We all remember a scene from *The Unbearable Lightness of Being*—Milan Kundera's death made many people reread it, and were convinced of the frightening reoccurrences that the very first page of the novel warned us about:

As I have said, the Russian invasion was not only a tragedy; it was a carnival of hate filled with a curious (and no longer explicable) euphoria.

She took fifty photographs with her to Switzerland, which she had made herself with all the care and skill she could muster. She offered them to a high-circulation magazine. The editor gave her a kind reception (all Czechs still wore the halo of their misfortune, and the good Swiss were touched); he offered her a seat, looked through the prints, praised them, and explained that because a certain time had elapsed since the events, they hadn't the slightest chance ("not that they aren't very beautiful!") of being published.

"But it's not over yet in Prague!" she protested, and tried to explain to him in bad German that at this very moment, even with the country occupied, with everything against them, workers' councils were forming in the factories, the students were going out on strike demanding the departure of the Russians, and the whole country was saying aloud what it thought. "That's what's so unbelievable! And nobody cares anymore."

But the editor moves on to examine photos from a nudist beach article.

Ukraine soon will be displaced by a new topic, although not definitively; and for Ukraine a time will come for other leaders. When that happens, many will recall the phrase that every heroic feat is another person's failure. It is an effective phrase, but false, for the world is not yet so comfortably organized that everything in it works. Great feats will be necessary as long as unbridled evil and aggressive ignorance exist. No sovereignty could save any non-nuclear state from Russian aggression, be it Hungary or Kazakhstan. In fact, for the Baltic states even NATO membership is no 100 percent guarantee. Zelenskyy, too, had no other option but the politics of performed heroism. Every individual seeking power—and this is their main distinguishing feature—seems to think that there are many options up on high. But there almost never are. In any case, in wartime there is no alternative to heroism.

But that's not what interests Arestovych right now. He is thinking about investing his popularity in power, about transforming moral capital into political capital. The war gave him this chance; there will be no other. He himself is probably convinced that he is taking action not for the sake of power, but for the good of Ukraine. And that may very well be so. It was precisely for the sake of political struggle that he shifted away from comforting and patriotic rhetoric to alarmist and critical rhetoric, although he was always critical of Ukrainian nationalism and narcissism. Does he have like-minded and potentially influential supporters? In the intellectual sphere—definitely. Here is what the Ukrainian philosopher Andrii Baumeister wrote immediately after the NATO summit:

> The NATO summit in Vilnius was an important, severe, and sobering lesson in political realism for Ukraine and the world. Ukraine's policy of "hard pressure" and "strong rhetoric" in regard to its partners was revealed to be entirely inadequate, and was a resounding failure. This is the failure of the "Andrii Melnyk" collective with its loud, rude statements, retroactively declared to be "effective" and "successful." Even the British Defense Minister began asking Ukraine's leaders for at least minimal gratitude . . . The political West has reminded us, and the whole world, of its preeminent art: the art of pathos, loud, elliptical, sometimes very pleasant, but often completely meaningless formulations. Ukraine now understands the form and style in which the conversation about the nation's membership in the EU will take place. There is a wide field of application for "homework," and "terms and conditions." You can be sure of that.
>
> As in Bucharest in 2008 when Ukraine and (then) Georgia were told "no" in the form of "yes." And now there was almost a direct "no." Doesn't this look like a signal to Moscow? As if to say, we are being very careful, we don't want to worry you, please don't worry!
>
> Angry and pathos-filled statements are a weapon from the arsenal of yesterday.

As we see, the conclusions of the popular philosopher are no different from Arestovych's memorandum, and in some ways they are harsher. But Baumeister has no intention of getting involved in an electoral struggle, his scholarly career is in excellent shape. Arestovych, on the other hand, is clearly not one to limit himself to psychological workshops. For me personally, his entry into Ukrainian politics would be a joyous event—he is at least a radical opponent of nationalism, a man of swift reactions and a fan of the Strugatsky brothers. But, as we know, these three qualities, individually and collectively, guarantee no one of anything. Many of Arestovych's traits make us wary even today, and one of them is the excessively rapid, although entirely adequate, change in his rhetoric.

Zelenskyy asked Ukraine to believe in a somewhat reckless, but cheerful and open-minded country that was ready to experiment. Arestovych offers the image of a nation that failed to win a war (although it managed not to lose), and, in this sense, replicated the systemic mistakes of its past history: too much pathos, too little work, too little sovereignty. This is not a matter of Ukraine inflating its self-image, but rather amplifying the demands that need be made on it—and that is not something everyone can get behind. Ukraine has grown fond of its heroic image, and it will not easily part with it. Today's sober gaze might easily be mistaken for temporary disappointment, panic, or even withdrawal. Abstinence following heroism is usually very painful.

A candidate from the military, or at least from among the military analysts, will have the best chance to assume power after Zelenskyy (provided he has enough sense to leave the presidency in time). This was the case in Armenia after a much smaller war. It is a dead-end choice, despite all the talent a potential military man might have. There is hope that everything will turn out all right, but the initial reactions to Arestovych's statements show that people willingly believe him when he offers comfort and raises the country's self-esteem, but not at all when he takes the denunciatory route. He would have an excellent chance of coming to power if the elections were held among the Russian liberal intelligentsia, but their opinion is met with either indifference or hostility in Ukraine. As such, we will have to wait until 2029, when Ukraine will either become disillusioned with the military, or completely enchanted with it. Beyond that, depending on the duration of the war, many interesting twists and turns are in store.

However, leading the opposition may be an even more favorable option for Arestovych. Especially since there will be more than enough reasons to criticize him: the language problem, which has gone nowhere; the notorious corruption, which also has a high chance of going nowhere; and the war, which may not go away in the next few years unless God gets bored with the Russian government. I don't think anyone has any illusions anymore. It is clear to everyone that the name "Putin" means "war," despite the peaceful pauses that Russia needs more than Ukraine, and which certainly will not be employed for peaceful development. As we can see, all these problems give the Ukrainian opposition a wonderful field for criticizing the authorities—provided that the opposition in Ukraine survives and possesses the same rights. Wartime is unpredictable in this sense. It will be interesting to see the arguments that Arestovych will put forth for peace, although the atmosphere in the country may change by then, and fatigue will take its toll. But I think the role of leader of the opposition—an eternal one, with no chance to take power—is much more likely for him.

And much more advantageous, we might add. Arestovych as a leader might turn out to be unbearable, but Arestovych as a mouthpiece, or leader of the opposition, would be as much in his proper place as Zelenskyy is in his. He is guaranteed a significant part of the support of the intelligentsia. Most important is that it will be very interesting, since everything connected with this phenomenally gifted man is interesting.

And the fact that I hope to remain an ardent supporter of his is also a guarantee that he will eternally fail to come to power. Those on whose side I fight usually lose, albeit handsomely, while making history. This pattern has led me many times to a sincere desire finally to go over and play on the side of the Russian authorities. However, their instincts are as good as mine, and they certainly would not accept me.

Thanks be to God who protects us from our worst temptations.

5.

Here are some excerpts from my streamed conversation with Oleksii Arestovych on July 30, 2023.

If you remember, we talked about how you would go from being everyone's favorite to being everyone's enemy.

I've always occupied that space. Many people do not understand why they criticize me in Ukraine. They think I am an enemy of

Ukrainian society, an enemy of the Ukrainian idea, they do not know that I am an enemy of any society, and that any idea but my own is alien to me. They don't realize how profitable it is to deal with an enemy. An enemy is always honest—at least one like me. Enemies always tells it like it is. They are the only ones who can save some societies from themselves. War is an opportunity to do some work on yourself.

Are you sure that after this war Ukrainian society will not become nationalistic and slip into archaism? War never improves morals.

War is a good reason to do evolutionary work on oneself. But for many people it is an opportunity to let themselves degrade salaciously, to remove every last restriction, to blame everything on the war using the principle of "War wipes the slate clean." Let's toss off humanity's last hundred years. Yes, war destroys morals. Like the hero of Alexei German's film *Hard to be a God*. He no longer wanted to be an earthling, he didn't want to be a Communist, he wanted to slash and burn. A lot of people have thrown themselves into that. On the other hand, there is still plenty of common sense, as well as of people who crave the weird.

The Americans are demanding elections in March 2024. What's your view of that, and will you participate in them?

We need to clarify things right away: what Americans? Right now this is a society that is almost undergoing an ideological civil war. They dislike each other much more than they dislike their external opponents. If there will be elections—yes, of course, I will participate. If you're going to talk the talk, you'd better walk the walk. If I set out to build [something akin to the Strugatskys' science-fiction novel] *Noon Universe*, the best tool for doing so is political power. My role is to write the prologue to *Noon Universe*.

Might you become the voice of all the Russian speakers in this election campaign?

No, there are too many of me to become the voice of just Russians and just Russian-speakers. I have a lot of Ukrainian-speaking supporters. For me, the language issue does not top the list, even though they hang that label on me, or label me as a bogeyman. I am not scooping up the remnants of Medvedchuk's Opposition Platform for Life party. Of course, I defend Russian-speakers, and of course I am ready to work with good Russians, as I would with any good people—Chinese, or Americans . . . I want to stand between people and the system, the system of those who eat, humiliate, and kill. I want to break it. And build a society of creative free people, built on trust, joy, and curiosity. As you understand, I am an ambiguous person in Ukraine today. An unambiguous person would be Zaluzhnyi. Everyone chews him up. He withstands continuous attacks of political proposals. Thank goodness I have the opportunity to talk with him one-on-one, and as far as I know, he distances himself from politics. He is unconditionally a military man in the loftiest sense of the word. He is concerned about the military dangers that threaten Ukraine for the next twenty years, and he wants to conduct a radical restructuring of the national security system, in particular, the armed forces. Military literature is scattered all over his office, and each day he finds time to read for another five or ten minutes, at least enough to read one more paragraph.

How did Zelenskyy survive in the current situation? When war becomes the routine, perhaps another person is needed?

Zelenskyy withstood this situation because he is a very strong man, and very ambitious, and his set of qualities suited the situation perfectly. He is a politician of a transitional period, if you look at it from height of history. He is duty bound to bring about the transition from the old Ukrainian republic—which is actually USSR-2, only much less efficient—to the new one. And history will praise him for agreeing to be a figure of transition. Fifty years from now, when assessing his performance, posterity will tip the balance in his favor. The smart ones always realize that voluntary crucifixion as a mode of transition is a costly thing, that is, if he understood that. And he did, as far as we know.

The inevitable question: Don't you think corruption is the underbelly of the national character, that it is a way of survival, a tradition, almost a folklore, a folk craft? There was no corruption in the Third Reich, and that's worse . . .

Corruption as a survival mechanism. Yes, it is a tradition. Without corruption people would not have survived. It was even necessary to corrupt all those Poles, Muscovites, and Turks. Domestic corruption, accommodating a relative, giving $300 to a doctor, slipping $100 to a kindergarten to admit your child. It's like having a drink for the road. But if it's blood money stolen from the budget, that is no longer a matter of national character. That is a question of national survival. In Ukraine, from the very beginning, ever since the '90s, the authorities have created a system in which a talented person cannot compete with them, because they use the state [for their own purposes].

Putin says there would be no war if it wasn't for Maidan. We know this is a lie, and yet: how do you assess Maidan today?

It is too complex a phenomenon. Even then I said that Maidan frightened politicians on both sides of the West-East border. It was a struggle of some oligarchs against others, a people's assembly, an uprising, an attempt to prevent Ukraine from changing course. It was a historical challenge for the people. The self-organization and self-defense there were very interesting. Wonderful cultural structures were born. It was a very specific atmosphere, where five hundred organizations, often despising each other, trod the same ground—but no one stepped on anyone else's feet, and everyone worked toward a common cause. I called it a chronoplasm. On December 31, 2013, I was doing a live broadcast from Maidan, and at that moment the clouds parted behind me and a pillar of light descended—I saved it somewhere in my photos. Maidan showed what a new Ukraine could be, what new social forms it could offer to the world. As for the rest . . . Of course, like any phenomenon, it was part conspiracy and part inspiration—including input from Russia and from the people's struggle for national self-determination. I agree with the definition of Revolution of Dignity. It's just that we haven't brought it to completion yet.

What are the most dangerous political forces in Ukraine today?

Those who want to establish a mono-ethnic and monocultural project. I do not consider any of them to be of consequence and, frankly speaking, I react to them with great irony. Ukraine needs to build a new civilization, then spread the experience, including to the

West. I won't hesitate to say it frankly: the West is in a dead end, its potential for development has been exhausted, it has no vision of the future. The great bright West, to which everyone prays, has been gone for over a hundred years. And that is interesting: as the Chechen General Dudayev said, the more enemies, the more interesting things are.

Is it possible to fight fascism and not be infected by it? In general, will this all last for months, years or decades?

I think that somewhere before the spring of next year, a question will arise about the ability of the Russian Federation in its current form to support technological warfare. It already lacks sufficient combat equipment, it has already become something between an army and a militia. They can conscript seven million more, but that does not translate to victory in war. It is quite possible to avoid being infected, we may even have a certain amount of immunity.

Will the West pressure Ukraine to compromise for "territory in exchange for peace"?

We hear such public statements, and not from the least important people—NATO's chief of staff, one of Reagan's national security advisers, and, then, the Kissinger Doctrine ... Zelenskyy already answered brilliantly: "If you want, we are ready to give up [the Russian city of] Belgorod."

It is unrealistic to think that, today, the Ukrainian defense forces could go back to the borders of 1991. We cannot return those borders in our current form. We lack the weapons, military equipment, and quality of military training. We need radically to change the rearguard system in Ukraine, or increase the support of the West, which is not yet evident. However, for example, we can take Crimea. We don't care about anybody pushing some button.

It seems to me that if you lose the election, you would look great as the leader of the opposition.

I will always be at the most effective position for achieving my goals. Whether that will be the nation's highest post, or whether it will be a faction in the Upper Rada, or leadership in the opposition. I will write my prologue in any case and at any place.

How do you keep yourself in a state of mental balance when the whole world is complaining of depression?

There is a good metaphor: We get in a car and drive to Odesa, and along the highway there are people spitting, throwing cans, trying to shoot at us, holding placards saying: "Don't go to Odesa, go to Mykolaiv! Our happiness is in Mykolaiv! Only scoundrels and FSB agents go to Odesa!" Will that make us turn toward Mykolaiv? Will our mood sour? Personally, I'll only feel better. I eat all that for breakfast.

Do you think Putin is feeling a sense of victory or failure right now?

On the one hand, he realizes that he has failed, and that the state machine which he built is not capable of solving his political aims and historical tasks of restoring the USSR. On the other hand, looking at the West, which, God forgive them, frankly saved him during Prigozhin's march on Moscow, he realizes that these suckers can be milked for a very long time. And the broad masses in Russia can be abused for a long time to come, no one will object. He personally does not suffer, he has no less caviar on his slice of bread because of all these sanctions. So he failed in his general goal of changing the map of the world, the history of the world forever, which was what he tried to do. But he hopes to drag the campaign out at least to a draw. Putin's political clock is still ticking, but as a historical figure he is now absent regardless of the outcome of the war. Russia as a world power is done for. Putin finished off historical Russia, it technically still remains, but its history is over.

Another inevitable question: I don't believe this is a colonial war.

Anti-colonial discourse is one of the leading idiocies being foisted upon us. Ukraine was never a colony; moreover, it was, in large part, one of the creators of the Russian Empire, the Soviet Union and the holder of the keys. There was never anything close to colonialism. It was a symbiosis, a project of Feofan Prokopovich in the early eighteenth century. He needed to establish an Orthodox statehood, and he understood there would never be any statehood in Ukraine. He needed a strong, serious economic state that could pay for their privileges, their way of living—and at the same time he wished to protect Orthodoxy, because he was a fanatical fighter for Orthodoxy against Catholicism, although he studied in Europe for nine years at the best universities. He was bringing his project into being. He was simply looking for a new Byzantium and he spent three years persuading Peter the Great and his entourage to proclaim Moscow the center of Orthodoxy. They were smart guys too, and they said, "You speak well of unifying Orthodox lands. What are the foundations of dynastic law?" They were very serious about all this. Then he suggested changing the name: An Orthodox emperor can unify lands. And he persuaded them. So where the hell is the colony? We created all this, we rightfully own all the merits and all the shortcomings. When we admit this, that will be the next step of our maturation, it will mean that Ukraine has removed its short pants. For now, however, they are trying to sew us into these short pants, and even people like Timothy Snyder are booed when he says "everything is not so simple."

Is there already a global split in humanity? According to what criteria?

The global split in humanity has been going on for a long time. Everything is like in Bromberg's Memorandum: humanity is divided into two unequal parts according to a criterion unknown to us. I can say what it is, though: there are people who support communication and cooperation; there are people who support a war of all against all as a natural state, people who want civilization to follow the path of fear and control, and who would strengthen that by digital means. And there are people who believe that you must follow the path of joy and curiosity, and turn into a free search group. That was especially clear during COVID. Either Leviathan, fear and control—or trust and joy. This is especially clear throughout the history of the church. Christianity offered three main ideas: the ideas of salvation, transformation, and co-creation. When the church relied on the idea of salvation, it lost out to the secular authorities: the world is a complete horror show and we must be saved from it, because we ourselves are a horror show. So the church, instead of being an ethical controller of the secular state as it had long been, sought to offer a new perspective. It lost its bearings and as a public institution began appealing to people's worst instincts. But Christianity has two more ideas: there is the notion of transformation, or transfiguration—God became man so that man would become God. And there is also the notion of co-creation with God. And the *Noon Universe* is, roughly speaking, a continuation of the Christian idea, where the emphasis is on man's acquisition of divine qualities, and on co-creation with God and the Universe.

In many families, the wives are for you, and the husbands are against.

And often the opposite.

Well, somehow it turns out that in the world of Slavic cultures a smooth-talking person is considered a windbag, while gloomy, silent people are considered reliable.

This is not a Slavic story, it is a criminal story. In a country where a third of the men served time in prison, the culture took on criminal connotations. Let's take the attitude to Zelenskyy, that actors are "clowns." That is silly. In the West, for example, actors are world ambassadors and generally figures of the first rank. How can I put this more delicately: All politics are decided in Hollywood. Or take contempt for waiters, although the service sector all over the world has long been in charge of things. In our society, the so-called salt-of-the-earth-type men are considered the reliable ones: it is best when they have a bald head, and a neck as thick as a thigh, like a horse—someone like [Russian general Sergei] Surovikin. His last name even means 'harsh' in Russian. No one notices that when they pray to this collective figure they are building a kind of Jabba the Hutt from *Star Wars* to their own detriment. They think it's courageous. But I always say: if anyone wants to compete with me in masculinity, including the saltiest of the bald men, come on, I'll always be happy to let you see how deceptive appearances can be.

XXIV. INTERLUDE

PLAYING SOLITAIRE. I'm writing this book like this: I'll write two or three pages, watch the news, then play solitaire. Most often it's Spider Solitaire, so that it lasts longer. This wasn't the case in the beginning, or rather, it didn't happen like this all that often. Now, after each dose of news, I have a question for the universe: Does any of this make any sense at all? Sometimes—and more often than not—solitaire suggests "yes," and then I continue working. Sometimes it's "no," and then I continue working even harder so because I have to give meaning to the universe without receiving any reaction from it.

Nobody commissioned this book from me. I came up with the idea myself, so to speak, as a pleasant way of passing eternity. (The originator of this expression is my neighbor in Ithaca. He lived two streets over from me, and I'm writing another biographical book about him. It will also be of no use to anyone.) None of my former Russian friends will believe that I am writing Zelenskyy's biography without a commission and even without a contract, although for a long time now I have cared little about what my late friends think of me. All that remains alive in them is their hatred, including toward me, and this is not very interesting. Sometimes, when, as part of my university work in preparation for lectures, I happen to review some of my "Public Lessons" or conversations with schoolchildren, I automatically ask myself the question: who did this all bother so much? But it was they, my former friends, those who were incapable of doing anything like this, who were so bothered. Now, through their combined efforts, they have created a situation for the world where nothing makes sense, and in order to accomplish anything at all, you must play solitaire.

The poet Osip Mandelstam told his wife: Stalin turned us all into people-in-waiting. This is a very accurate psychological—if not psychiatric—diagnosis for people living in an interim era. A purely social understanding of this diagnosis, in which everyone is waiting for someone to come for them, would be superficial. One could say "people-waiting-it-out" because an era of terror is always a time of deferred calls and responses. Terror comes to the fore, forcing people to fear for themselves when they should be fearing for humanity. Time lived under a dictator is wasted time because: Firstly, it is an era of personal impotence. A person is tied hand and foot. Anything can be done with him, but he himself cannot do a thing. This is a time when everyone, including the dictator (he is as unfree as all his subjects), are objects of history; it simply has no subjects. Secondly, under a dictator, you can't say anything out loud, you can't write anything, except to hide it away in your desk drawer—or in tamizdat, where no one really needs it. Discussion of the situation is postponed until it moves into the past and becomes much less convenient for analysis. Everyone who studies terror settles scores with the past, or discusses it in isolation, since public discussion is impossible even in a kitchen format. Russia is waiting for the moment when it will again be pulled together into a consolidated audience, but will there be anyone to consolidate? And most importantly, where? This is unknown. In today's Russia everything is guesswork.

Ukraine is different. First, it will obviously survive not only spiritually, but also territorially. No matter how the Ukrainian situation develops subsequently, it will be a nation with whom it is prestigious to have friendly relations, and the restoration of which is honorable. Furthermore, it will be a nation that won a spiritual victory precisely at the moment when its president refused to flee Kyiv at that moment when it fell under attack. Ukraine's victory is a matter of time, and this also creates an unpleasant situation of delay: everyone is waiting for the obvious to be stated. Ukraine has already won—spiritually, intellectually, and also in purely military terms, because an enemy many times superior to it not only could not crush it, but also has given back some of what it had taken. The only thing that Russia can offer the world has already been demonstrated in Donbas—a criminal mess, infinitely far from the insipidly archaic ideal, where torture is committed "in basements." The whole world is waiting for the losing country to admit its defeat, although it will neither admit nor even notice it. "He did not notice the obscenities hurled at his king," as the Soviet novelist Vasily Aksyonov wrote prophetically. Russia earnestly pretends that the worse things are, the better they are, and in this sense it really cannot lose, since its situation cannot become so bad that the people will rebel and restructure the state. Russia has only one path—to keep sinking further until personnel shortages and general degradation destroy the economy, the transportation system, and the entire anemic infrastructure. Complex systems are vulnerable, but the Russian system is very simple. Before the whole world, as it degrades and descends more deeply into complete savage cruelty, Russia destroys Ukrainian cities with impunity and kills civilians. There are few things more depressing in the world than the spectacle of absolute, self-aware, brazen evil, with which nothing can be done until it destroys itself.

Solitaire means patience. Leo Tolstoy played solitaire, according to his wife Sofia Andreevna, when his work was not going well. That is, when his thoughts encountered an insurmountable obstacle. When an idea began to take shape or the desired tone was found, Tolstoy had enough professional skills to develop it. But when a thought encountered an obstacle, or the material did not lead to adequate stylistic design (roughly speaking, any old style seemed false when applied to new material), he would try to get a hint from the universe. He could win, he could lose, and he could deal a new hand, but his mind, in the meantime, bit into the obstacle. There is a sensation that if the Lord does not find a solution or style—He engages in a game of solitaire. In the end, it's not just Tolstoy who experiences creative crises.

The world feverishly searches for logic in chaos. But God has a lot of time, while Ukraine must act here and now. While I'm playing solitaire, Zelenskyy is talking and acting. Zaluzhnyi is building a defense, and the Ukrainian Armed Forces are implementing a counteroffensive plan. People must live before they are able to formulate the how and why for themselves.

In general, this book—like any other, but this one in particular—is a mode of self-therapy: There was practically nothing left of fifty-five years of my Russian life (except texts—although the texts themselves mean nothing). I cut myself off from this life, and beginning a new one—that is, integrating myself into American literature, building American connections—is impossible without very strong motivation. For me this was precisely an attempt to recharge my batteries—this book has no other purpose, for it is guaranteed to bring me nothing but bumps and bruises. A person whose life has practically no meaning left can be recharged via a person whose life, lacking any prerequisites in the past, is filled to the brim with meaning. In the near future, the very survival of humanity, including mine, depends on that person, and no one else in the world. That's just how it happened. Lightning struck him out of the blue. He did nothing to bring this on, and he did nothing to deserve it. And I think he would be happy if this cup had somehow passed him by, but no one asked him. It fell to him to confirm that the world had meaning and purpose, and he did that. He has already done it, regardless of this story's ending. There are many ways he can still deflate his main success—but never completely.

Furthermore, I write this book not knowing how it will end. The worst-case scenario is that no one will be left to read it at all. What consoles me is that you must live your life until you reach a final conclusion about how you lived, and how you should have lived. The interlude is over, my soul has been relieved. Thank you for your attention. Let's move on.

PART TWO

TRAGEDY

The New Year's *Evening Block* in 2022 turned out to be surprisingly unfunny, but how's this for paradoxical instinct: Zelenskyy took part in it. For two years he had not joined his team's New Year's shows, apparently not wanting to be associated with his previous image as a comic. But now he showed up, with Yermak, of course. (They also joked about this: "Who did he come with? Oh, you didn't even need to look.")

All the jokes from that show land differently today: A mother-in-law comes to visit and when they're putting her in a taxi to go home, they ask: "To Bucha? By taxi? That costs three thousand . . ." Ilya Lagutenko's song declaring, "Just be patient, it will be more fun . . ." (The old gray-haired Lagutenko. Oh, Lord, how old everything is, and worn out like jokes about mothers-in-law.) Still, Zelenskyy visited his friends and heroically feigned having fun, although we now know that at this time British and American intelligence were bombarding him with reports about the concentration of Russian troops on the border. Perhaps only one joke—also a sad one—contains enough truth to give the humor authenticity: "How I loved you!" as the actor portraying a recent fan tells him. "Then one day I fell out of love." Perhaps the evolution of the people's attitude toward Zelenskyy is depicted here with unprecedented authenticity. It's not for nothing that at the very beginning, *Block 95* gave voice to the president's thoughts, accurately imitating his famous hoarseness: "It's been a long time since I've seen so many people . . . not carrying placards."

Still, he had to have unprecedented intuition to come to the shooting of the New Year's *Block 95* segment: it is now clear that it was a farewell. Because the coming Year of the Tiger forever separated Zelenskyy from his comic image, and Ukraine from the Russian context. This was probably the last Ukrainian New Year's show in Russian.

The main symbols of the special military operation (as the war is called in Putin's newspeak) were two Latin letters—V and Z. They were painted on the sides of trucks, on the armor of tanks and combat vehicles, on the facades of theaters whose leadership supported the "special operation." No one knew the origin of these symbols.

The Z was dubbed a half-swastika—the talk was that they weren't honest enough to employ a full-fledged symbol. People recalled the runic Wolfsangel sign which translates as "wolf's hook," and was used in the symbolism of several Wehrmacht divisions. It was also assumed that Z stood for "for victory" ("za pobedu" in Russian) but then it would have been easier to write the Russian "z." Even though the Russian "z" ("з") suggests the number three, it would have been more patriotic. Furthermore, the troika is also a well-known symbol—from the trinity to the Uvarov triad. Various decoding options were proposed: *Zadanie Vypolneno* (mission accomplished), and *Zapad Vzyat* (the West is seized), but then, again, it would have been more natural to use the Cyrillic alphabet. After all, Z is the last letter of the Latin alphabet, suggesting that there is nowhere else to go. A romantic version briefly made the rounds about the sign of Zorro, the Spanish nobleman and defender of the poor who gained fame in the twentieth century thanks to the books of Johnston McCulley, films starring Douglas Fairbanks (and subsequently, Antonio Banderas). Zorro drew the "sign of Zorro"—the fatal Z—in the air and on walls. But the peak of his popularity came in 1975, when he was played by Alain Delon. But what does the old hero of Spanish legends have to do with the Russo-Ukrainian confrontation? In the end, the point of view prevailed that V and Z were simply the easiest to draw, just as three boxy Russian letters comprising an obscene word are always carved into elevator walls, not because people are constantly thinking about the male organ, but because it is easiest to carve into plastic with crosswise strokes. It may be that design matters for the war were commissioned through some PR agency (the names of political strategists Igor Mangushev and Andrei Ilnitsky were occasionally mentioned, but without evidence), and, having decided on making some easy money, the agency settled on the simplest, and, at the same time, most unorthodox solution. Basically, however, looking for anything rational in the Russian war of 2022 is a rather hopeless task. There were no reasons for it, except for those that will be presented as best we can in the third part of our book. Even the eternal retention of power by Vladimir Putin would have been quite possible without military action—nothing threatened his power, it could have gone on rotting for at least another thirty years in a half-suppressed state. After all, any escalation is always an acceleration of the historical process—the midwife of history, as they say.

In fact, it seems to me that the key to the secret may be the Ukrainian word *bozhevilnyi*, which refers to a person not in his right mind, that is, someone in the grips of God's will. When a person is deprived of a primitive earthly mind, he becomes entirely dependent on God's providence, and God's providence was to give this war the initials of its main character—Volodymyr Zelenskyy, and his magical assistant Valerii Zaluzhnyi.

It's so fantastic and absurd—like everything in this savage war that dramatically throws the world back a century—that it looks authentic. Of course, this is unrealistic and suicidal, but God marks the rogue, sometimes with her own hand. The key to Russia's defeat in this war is that it chose the initials of its main enemy as a symbol of victory. Perhaps the designers were preparing for The Hague in such a secret way so that, in the event of an inquiry, they could say they were winking at the Ukrainian side!

Be that as it may, the initials of Volodymyr Zelenskyy and Valerii Zaluzhnyi adorn the armor of Russian tanks, howitzers, and infantry fighting vehicles. Russian soldiers and officers go to the front in the name of Zelenskyy. Combat aircraft take to the air in Zelenskyy's name. And all of them, in the best traditions of the popular Soviet children's writer Arkady Gaidar, seem to shout: "Salute the boy!"

No, the aggressor cannot win a war like this. By starting this war, he shot himself in the foot, and by choosing such symbols, in the head.

I. PREPARATION

In February 2023, the *Politico* portal published an investigation stating that Russia had begun preparing for a large-scale invasion in the spring of 2021. Jon Finer, Deputy National Security Adviser to the U.S. President, says he discovered a dangerous concentration of Russian forces on the Ukrainian border in March and April. Avril Haines, director of the National Intelligence, already suspected that the troops were not gathering for the sake of diplomatic pressure. "I only underestimated the scale of the invasion," he said. In Geneva at the June 2021 summit, the conversation behind closed doors was not about cyberattacks, as analysts had assumed, but about Ukraine. Putin calmed everyone down, but on July 12, 2021, he published an article titled "On the Historical Unity of Russians and Ukrainians," posting it on the Kremlin website simultaneously in Russian and Ukrainian.

Who actually wrote this article is still unknown, although Ukrainian analyst Oleksandr Kochetkov clearly saw Surkov's shadow here, his return to the public sphere. "There are specifically some Surkovian tricks in there," he said. In Ukraine the article's main thrust was rightly considered to be an attempt to falsify history in order to legitimize military action—a search in the distorted past for a justification of aggression today. Doctor of Historical Sciences Alexei Miller (not to be confused with the head of Gazprom) saw in Putin's theses on the historical unity of the Slavs a compilation and combination of nineteenth-century historians Sergei Uvarov and historian/politician Nikolai Ustryalov. It is doubtful that Putin is familiar with the views of Uvarov or the works of the Eurasianist Ustryalov, but someone may have told him about them. The essence of Putin's article is the assertion that "Soviet national policy took a great Russian nation consisting of the triune peoples of Great Russians, Little Russians, and Belarusians, and established the status of three separate Slavic peoples—Russians, Ukrainians, and Belarusians—on a state level." The Ukrainian language, he asserts, is not a language, but a "dialect," and we have always been connected by linguistic affinity. As such, the formation of Ukraine was a Bolshevik project: "Thus, modern Ukraine is entirely a creation of the Soviet era. We know and remember that to a large extent it was created at the expense of historical Russia. It is enough to compare which lands reunited with the Russian state in the seventeenth century and which territories of the Ukrainian SSR seceded from the Soviet Union. The Bolsheviks treated the Russian people as inexhaustible material for social experimentation. They dreamed of a world revolution, which, in their opinion, would abolish nation-states altogether. Therefore, they arbitrarily cut borders and distributed generous territorial 'gifts.'"

Professional historians dismantled Putin's theses over the following week, and Zelenskyy responded in the spirit of *Block 95*, also speaking in two languages: "It's nice that the man knows the Ukrainian language (*laughs*). I think when the President of the Russian Federation starts writing in Ukrainian, it means we are doing everything right. I didn't have time to read the whole article, but I saw some profound work. Putin really put a lot of time into it. One can only envy that the president of such a large country can afford himself that time. For some reason, Putin doesn't have enough time to meet with me. I didn't realize what he was spending his time on, but now I see the results. Although we could discuss what he wrote about. Perhaps I could provide him with material for a new article. We are forgotten when people talk about the victory over fascism, but in other cases they recall that we are a fraternal people. I don't think it's a brotherly thing to do. It's more like Cain and Abel."

The remark about the historical unity of Cain and Abel turned out to be prophetic. The British ambassador to the U.S., Dame Karen Pearce, remarked: "It was clear that things had gone very wrong." Russia's September exercises, labeled "Zapad," or West, according to Pentagon observations, were much larger than the previous year's. In September, the American intelligence community came to the unequivocal conclusion that preparations were being made in earnest for an invasion.

On November 2 and 3, CIA Director William Burns held talks in Moscow. He flew in on Biden's personal instructions with a single (carefully hidden) purpose: to make it clear to senior Russian officials that America was aware of the plans for Ukraine and was not inclined to consider them a diversionary maneuver. "I spoke to Putin on a secret phone," Burns recalled in February 2023. "He was then in Sochi, in self-isolation amid a new wave of COVID. The conversation was strange, but very direct. I explained everything that the President had instructed me to. [Putin] responded with long-familiar accusations against Ukraine, and expressed firm confidence that Russia would be able to impose its will on it. His circle of advisors had narrowed greatly, so that some of them were slightly surprised by my information about his plans. I came away confident that he had made his decision. The window of opportunity to influence the situation was closing—at least that's how he saw it. Without the ability to influence Ukraine, he could not consider himself a strong leader. He saw Merkel leaving and Macron distracted by his own elections. On the way back, I called Zelenskyy from the plane. He listened to me very carefully and soberly." In fact, on November 2, Zelenskyy met in Glasgow (at a conference on climate control) with Tom Sullivan, deputy head of the State Department, and received a warning that Russia was preparing a large-scale invasion. Secretary of State Blinken recalled that "Zelenskyy accepted this information stoically."

On December 3, in an attempt to stop the war, American intelligence dared to take an unprecedented step—it leaked to the *Washington Post* a detailed map of the beginning of hostilities, culled from a combination of data. "It was seven in the morning in Washington, three in the afternoon in Moscow, and it was nice to think that many around Putin would have trouble sleeping that night," says Emily Horne, a spokeswoman for the National Security Council, not without gloating. Moscow did not react, and Washington began developing sanctions.

In mid-January, Zelenskyy was informed that an invasion was imminent. However, as Burns emphasized, Ukrainian intelligence had done its part well, and Zelenskyy had no illusions about the possibility of avoiding conflict. He advised the Americans that he did not intend to address the nation with a warning yet, so as not to create panic. The Americans warned of Putin's three-stage plan: a land assault on Kyiv, the capture of Hostomel airport, and an attempt to capture or force Zelenskyy out of the country in order to install a puppet government. On February 10, the U.S. consulate in Kyiv closed. Most of the allies were evacuated, those remaining moved to Lviv.

Five days earlier, my wife and I had received a U.S. work visa in Kyiv; I was supposed to begin working at Cornell on February 21. We submitted documents for the visa on January 5, they were processed for a month, and we finally received a message that we could come to pick up our passports. We spent a week in Kyiv, visiting friends there. Most of the Kyiv residents insisted that they were quite ready for war, yet didn't believe it would come. It was then that I became convinced that it is impossible to prepare for war. That is, when they really start firing missiles at you, you understand that no speculative preparation—even if it is based on the most accurate intelligence data—has anything to do with real war, with the understanding that someone is coming to kill you personally. Two weeks later, literally on the eve of the war, we called Kyiv from the States. Our friends continued to prepare and not to believe. Yuly Dubov, Russian oligarch Boris Berezovsky's right-hand man in the '90s, and now a political emigrant and writer living in London, a very informed person possessing a heightened sense of danger since those very '90s, had warned me: "There will be a stampede at Sheremetyevo after the 20th. It's best to fly out on the 20th."

On the morning of February 24, my friend Masha Starozhitskaya and her daughter called me from Kyiv. They laughed. It was a normal nervous reaction. We called each other every day, but from the next day on no one was laughing anymore.

II. ON THE EVE

On December 15, 2021, Putin presented NATO with his ultimatum. Going over the head of Ukraine, he addressed the North Atlantic bloc, and above all, the United States. The demands were harsh and obviously un-workable: long-term guarantees that NATO would renounce any advance to the East; a rejection of the decisions of the 2008 NATO Bucharest Summit stipulating that in the future Ukraine and Georgia would become members of NATO on the grounds that it contradicted the commitment of the leaders of all OSCE participating states "not to increase their own safety at the expense of the safety of others"; and the renunciation of an official agreement by the United States and other NATO countries not to deploy attack weapons systems posing a threat to Russia on the territory of the latter's neighboring countries, both members and non-members of the alliance.

On January 26, the States submitted a written response to the Russian Foreign Ministry, which predictably did not satisfy Putin. "We have not seen adequate consideration of our three key demands regarding the prevention of NATO expansion, the refusal to deploy attack weapons systems near Russian borders, and the return of the bloc's military infrastructure in Europe to the state of 1997, when the Russia-NATO Founding Act was signed," he said at a press conference after a meeting with his like-minded friend, Hungarian Prime Minister Viktor Orbán. On February 17, U.S. Ambassador to Russia Sullivan was presented with a Russian memorandum: "We note that the American side has not offered a constructive response to the basic elements of the draft agreement with the United States on security guarantees prepared by the Russian side. The packaged nature of Russian proposals was ignored, from which 'convenient' topics were deliberately selected, which were then 'distorted' to the purpose of creating advantages for the United States and its allies." Then the Russian Ministry of Foreign Affairs—exactly a week before the invasion—gave the assurance that, "There is no 'Russian invasion' of Ukraine, which the United States and its allies have been officially announcing since the fall of last year, and there are no plans for one. Statements, therefore, about 'Russia's responsibility for the escalation' cannot be regarded as other than an attempt to exert pressure on, and devalue, Russia's proposals for security guarantees." The usual arguments for Russian rhetoric were immediately cited: a coup d'état took place in Kyiv, a legal referendum took place in Crimea, and there is a civil war in Donbas.

Everything was obvious—at least to those who wanted to understand. Promises not to invade Ukraine weren't worth the paper they were printed on. That was understood in the United States. Zelenskyy knew that. In mid-February, a large-scale evacuation began in and around Kyiv—unfortunately, not as large as it should have been. To what extent Zelenskyy was aware of the inevitability of a Russian attack is still debated: most likely, like any normal person, he understood, but did not believe it.

In any case, his address to Ukrainians on January 19, 2022, brought him a new wave of criticism later on. It evoked bewilderment even in the aftermath, and by late February this attempt to reassure the population a month before the invasion looked strange. As we have seen, he was fully informed not just about the likelihood, but about the inevitability of a Russian invasion by November 2021. And yet, at the end of January, he suddenly declared:

> All the news and informational space is filled with the same messages: the war with Russia, the fact that the invasion might start tomorrow or at any moment, and it is "already a certainty." And that is different from the "certainty" that was predicted a month ago and the "certainty" that was predicted last year. It's also certain that we're supposedly not ready. But supposedly we won't be left all alone. And what, exactly, is the news? Hasn't this been a reality for eight years? Didn't the invasion begin in 2014? Is the threat of large-scale war affecting us only now? These dangers have been around for more than a day. And they haven't gotten bigger. What has gotten bigger is the hype surrounding them. Now they are actively attacking not our land, but your nerves. So that you will be in a constant state of anxiety. All our citizens, especially the elderly, need to understand this. Exhale and calm down. Don't run out for buckwheat and matches. What should you do? Just one thing: keep a calm, cool head. Maintain confidence in our armed forces, our army, our Ukraine. I begin every morning digesting information about the real situation in Donbas

and along our borders. We know all the possible threats, and we understand all the possible actions we may take in response. This is not news. We rely on ourselves first and foremost. Not because we do not have support—we do. But because we have dignity and pride. That is why we have partners. The level of their support, and of the international coalition is higher than ever. And this is not news.

We know about everything and we are ready for everything. But we are doing everything so that in the end we won't need that. We're doing everything we can to find a diplomatic solution. We're doing everything to bring peace to Ukraine.

What should you do? Just one thing. Keep a calm, cool head. Maintain confidence in your armed forces, your army, our Ukraine. Don't get yourself worked up. React to everything wisely, not emotionally. Use your head, not your heart. Do not shout, "All is lost," but know that everything is under control, and everything is going according to plan. Don't give in to constant, anxious thoughts: "What will happen tomorrow? What will happen in the future?" Be firm in your knowledge.

Let me tell you: On January 22 we will celebrate Ukraine's Day of Unity. We will open the Zaporizhzhia bridge. Over the next year we will build the largest highway in Ukraine from Uzhgorod to Luhansk. We will build roads, bridges, schools, stadiums, cars, airplanes, and tanks. We will immunize most of the population. In April we will celebrate Easter, in May we'll enjoy the sun, shish kabobs, weekends, and Victory Day. And then in summer we'll take the annual exams. We will enter universities, plan vacations, cultivate vegetable gardens, get married, and celebrate weddings. And then, in the fall, we hopefully will cheer on our national team at the World Cup in Qatar. In winter we will prepare for the New Year holidays.

In this year as always, the whole family will gather around the table on December 31, and I am sure that in my New Year's address I will say: "Dear Ukrainians, I told you—we are good!" We did not panic. We were not provoked. We were calm and strong and we are ringing in the next New Year. Without panic. Without terror. Hopefully without viruses. And I sincerely believe—without war.

Oh, how many times he was later reminded of those shish kebobs—both in Russia and Ukraine. Zelenskyy has absolutely no luck with shish kebobs—and all because of his damned creativity. On June 21, 2021, Ukrainian Press Day, he resolved to invite the country's leading journalists to his Zalissia residence for kebabs, grilling them personally, and the opposition howled that Zelenskyy was hand-feeding the press. In fact, the president's right to throw a barbecue with those he likes personally is not disputed by anyone, but everyone had their own list of those whom Zelenskyy should absolutely have invited! (He mostly invited TV people, which is understandable given his profession: Dmitry Gordon and his wife Olesia Batsman, Savik Shuster, Oleksii Gazubei, Natalia Vlaschenko, Serhii Shcherbina, Oleksandr Martynenko, Yurii Bogutskyy and Nataliia Moseichuk.) Vlaschenko told me that, although all the conversations were "off the record," nothing fundamental was said, but the kebabs were good, and they drank little. Zelenskyy doesn't like to drink, although he sometimes enjoys a glass of dry red wine. ("I can drink a bottle of vodka," he confessed in an interview with Dmitry Gordon right after his election, but somehow he's never been seen doing it. In one episode of *Block 95* he taught Pierre Richard how to drink vodka. But as a person who once spent two days with Richard in 1992, I think Richard himself could teach Zelenskyy more.) Diana Panchenko (a host on The First Independent news channel who was not invited) wrote on her blog, "That's what Ukrainian journalism is all about—eating meat from the president's hands, being happy that it wasn't you who was shut down." It's an understandable reaction. The kebab fiasco in his pre-war speech, as it turned out, was much more serious. It is clear that Zelenskyy needed to reduce panic, and it is clear that he failed to do so—just as the TASS statement in the USSR on June 13, 1941, in an almost verbatim, identical wording about rumors of an impending war, only strengthened everyone's belief that war was imminent. Zelenskyy is most often criticized precisely for this—while seeking to calm Ukrainians, he failed to take proper measures to evacuate the Kyiv suburbs which the Russian army already entered just a week after the outbreak of war, and, in fact, generally lowered the vigilance of his citizens.

In Zelenskyy's defense, we can only say that evacuations were already underway a week before the war started, albeit at an insufficient pace. As for the weakening of vigilance, I was in Kyiv in early February, and all of my friends were talking about certain war. Traditionally, proclamations made by the Ukrainian authorities are given less credibility than rumors. As for Zelenskyy's motives, I will risk making an assumption based, again, on an understanding of the specifics of his profession. I have already quoted here a conversation between the Russian poet Nikolai Gumilyov and G. K. Chesterton in 1917, when Gumilyov declared the need to recruit representatives of the creative professions into presidential or prime ministerial posts. Representatives of the creative intelligentsia—there's nothing to be done about it—are distinguished by performative thinking. This, in the terminology of British thinker John Langshaw Austin (*How to Do Things with Words*), is a mode of statement that does not describe, but models reality. In other words, it literally orders the rain to fall, the wind to blow, and the people to march. Such performatives are a characteristic feature not so much of strong-willed leaders as of artists endowed with creative imagination. Without faith in the power of the word, neither the poet nor the actor will achieve anything. "I said so—and so it became," is a normal attitude for a humanitarian, and even more so for a screenwriter. Leo Tolstoy sincerely believed that the tale of the War of 1812 would remain in the memory of the people precisely as he wrote it. Objective reality is, after all, an oxymoron: the world remains as we have filmed, drawn, and described it. I think, since I am generally able to put myself in the shoes of another artist, that Zelenskyy tried to put a curse on reality. And an artist who does not try to achieve this is a bad artist. It's not Zelenskyy's fault that reality this time turned out to be more stubborn, and that, on New Year's Eve 2023, Zelenskyy spoke entirely different words:

> This year wounded us in the heart. We have cried all our tears. We have shouted all our prayers. Three hundred eleven days. We have something to say about every minute of it. But most words are superfluous.

They're unnecessary. We don't need explanations, embellishments. We need silence. In order to hear. We need pauses. To understand.

The morning of February the 24th.

Hostomel. Bucha. Irpen. Borodianka. Kharkiv. The Mryia [the destroyed jumbo cargo jet].

Kramatorsk station. Toy.

Chernihiv.

Mariupol. Drama Theater. The word "Children" written.

Olenivka.

Odesa. Multistory building. Girl. Three months old.

Vilniansk. Maternity ward. Baby. Two days old.

Azovstal.

It's impossible to forget. And it's impossible to forgive. But it is possible to win.

We stood on our feet because something kept us going. Our spirit.

Defense of Kyiv.

Kharkiv.

Mykolaiv.

Chornobaivka.

Snake Island.

HIMARS.

Antonivsky Bridge.

"Cotton" pops.

Crimean Bridge.

Neptune.

Cruiser Moskva.

Russian warship.

Izium, Balakliia, and Kupiansk.

Kherson.

And we pray that Kreminna and Svatove will stand, Melitopol, all of Donbas, Crimea.

We fight and will continue to fight. For the sake of the main word: "victory."

It will definitely come. We have been approaching it for 311 days.

We have put much strength into it. But at the moment when it seems you can't go any further, remember what we have already been through.

I want to say to all of you: Ukrainians, you are incredible! See what we have done and what we are doing!

How our soldiers have been crushing this "second army of the world" since the first days.

How our people stopped their equipment and infantry columns.

How an old man used his hands to stop a tank.

How a woman knocked down a drone with a jar of tomatoes.

How enemy tanks, armored personnel carriers, helicopters, shells were stolen during the occupation.

How we fundraised for Shahed hunters, naval drones, armored vehicles, ambulance vehicles, and Bayraktar drones in several hours.

How we withstood all threats, shelling, cluster bombs, cruise missiles, darkness and cold.

How we supported each other and the state.

Everyone is important in war.

Whoever holds a weapon, the steering wheel of a car, the helm of a ship or plane, a scalpel, or a locator.

Everyone who is at a laptop, who drives a combine harvester, a train.

Who is at a roadblock and a power plant.

Journalists and diplomats, utility workers and rescuers.

Everyone. Who is working. Studying at a university or school. And even those who are just learning to walk.

All this is for their sake. Our children. Our people. Our country.

The whole of Ukraine immediately called this appeal historic. It indeed was very powerful, as, indeed, almost all of Zelenskyy's wartime speeches are. It's worth comparing to the words he spoke on January 19, 2022, to see how radically his style changed. Only the belief in performative constructions did not disappear. Zelenskyy still believes that the spoken word has material power. He predicts that 2023 will be the year of victory for Ukraine, along with the restoration to the borders of 1991, the year of the return of refugees and territories. Even if he himself thinks differently, this is precisely what needed to be said. We had already seen that an actor who is able to convince himself has a magnetic effect on his spectator.

Unfortunately, he was mistaken about the participation of the Ukrainian national team in the Qatar World Cup. On June 1, the Ukrainians defeated the Scots (3:1) in a qualifying match, but on June 5 they lost to Wales in an extremely dramatic match. Many were certain that Ukraine would get the benefit of the doubt from the referees during the qualifying matches, but first, midfielder Oleksandr Zinchenko's goal was disallowed (allegedly he shot before the whistle), then a ball flew off forward Andrii Yarmolenko's head into the Ukrainians' own goal, and then at the end of the first half a penalty was not called although the reason that Yarmolenko fell was unclear. As such, there were no Ukrainians at the championship in Qatar. The world was already rooting for them in much more brutal circumstances, and perhaps their place in the sports news would only have blurred everyone's impression.

In January 2022, Western embassies (primarily the American one) began evacuating their staff, and discouraged citizens from visiting Ukraine. Zelenskyy (in a conversation with Anthony Blinken) called this measure excessive. On February 13, Biden called Zelenskyy and warned that the invasion would begin within a week. (U.S. intelligence called February 16th; Russian propagandists laughed loudly in response—"Russia didn't show up for the war.")

On February 21, following an appeal by State Duma deputies (at the initiative of the Communist Party), Vladimir Putin signed a decree recognizing the Donetsk and Luhansk People's Republics, in other words, doing what all official patriots had been fervently urging for seven years. At the Russian Donbas Forum in Donetsk on January 28, Russian journalist Margarita Simonyan shrieked hysterically (I suspect it was an authorized move, because Russian propagandists do not open their mouths without authorization): "The people of Donbas want to live at home, and want to be part of their, and our, enormous, great, generous homeland. We are obliged to provide this for them. Russia, Mother Russia, bring Donbas home."

Mother Russia responded. By recognizing the Luhansk and Donetsk People's Republics, Russia cut off any potential retreat routes (which it had already ruled out anyway): Russian troops entered the republics that were not officially recognized by anyone else.

On February 21, Vladimir Putin denounced the Minsk agreements in a televised address. At the same time, he named his conditions for peace with Ukraine: recognition of the Russian referendum in Crimea, Ukraine's refusal to join NATO, and Ukraine's complete political neutrality and demilitarization. It was obvious that no one would agree to these conditions. Denys Shmyhal, then Prime Minister of Ukraine, said so much out loud.

III. FEBRUARY 24

Here are a few select quotes from Vladimir Putin's address to the citizens of Russia on February 21, 2022:

> Modern Ukraine was created entirely by Russia, or rather by Bolshevik, Communist Russia. This process began almost immediately after the revolution of 1917, and Lenin and his associates did it in a very crude way in relation to Russia itself—by separating, tearing away from it, a part of its own historical territories. Of course, no one asked the millions of people who lived there about any of this.
>
> Then, on the eve of, and following the Great Patriotic War, Stalin annexed to the USSR, and gave to Ukraine, several lands that previously belonged to Poland, Romania, and Hungary. At the same time, as a kind of compensation, Stalin gave Poland part of the original German territories, while, in 1954, Khrushchev, for some reason, took Crimea from Russia and gave it to Ukraine also. In fact, this is how the territory of Soviet Ukraine was formed.

From the point of view of the historical destinies of Russia and its peoples, Lenin's principles of state-building turned out to be not merely a mistake; it was, as we say, much worse than a mistake. After the collapse of the USSR in 1991, this became absolutely clear.

In fact, as I have already said, Soviet Ukraine emerged as a result of Bolshevik policy; nowadays we could even call it "Ukraine named after Vladimir Ilyich Lenin" with good reason. He is its author and architect. This is fully confirmed in the archival documents, including Lenin's strict directives on Donbas, which was literally squeezed into Ukraine. And now "grateful descendants" demolish Lenin's monuments in Ukraine. They call it decommunization.

You want decommunization? Well, we are quite happy with it. But there is no need to stop halfway, as they say. We are ready to show you what real decommunization means for Ukraine.

Despite well-known problems, Russia has always cooperated with Ukraine openly, honestly and, I repeat, with respect for its interests; our ties have been developing in various areas. At the same time, it is striking that the Ukrainian authorities preferred to act in such a way as to take all rights and advantages in relations with Russia, but without accepting any obligations. Instead of partnership, a parasitic attitude began to prevail, which on the part of official authorities in Kyiv sometimes took on an absolutely unceremonious character. It suffices to recall their permanent blackmail in the sphere of energy transit, and the banal theft of gas. I should add that Kiev tried to use dialog with Russia as a pretext for its bargaining with the West, blackmailing it while making it appear that Ukraine was drawing closer Moscow, while extracting preferential treatment for itself: otherwise, so to speak, Russian influence on Ukraine will grow.

At the same time, I want to emphasize that from the very beginning the Ukrainian government began building its statehood on the basis of denying everything that unites us, and sought to distort the consciousness and historical memory of millions of people, entire generations living in Ukraine. It is not surprising that Ukrainian society experienced the growth of extreme nationalism, which quickly took the form of aggressive Russophobia and neo-Nazism. Hence the participation of Ukrainian nationalists and neo-Nazis in terrorist gangs in the North Caucasus and the increasingly shrill territorial claims made against Russia.

It is also important to realize that Ukraine, in fact, has never had a stable tradition of genuine statehood. And since 1991, it has followed the path of mechanically copying other people's models, detached from both history and Ukrainian realities. Political state institutions have constantly been reshaped to please the quickly formed clans with their own selfish interests that have nothing in common with the interests of the people of Ukraine. (*One wonders: Did Russian oligarchs and their clans have much in common with the interests of the people of Russia? I ask that parenthetically, but how could I possibly be so meticulous as to comment on every word?—D. B.*)

The whole point of the so-called pro-Western civilizational choice of the Ukrainian oligarchic government was, and is, not to create better conditions for the well-being of the people, but to keep billions of dollars stolen from Ukrainians and hidden by the oligarchs in Western bank accounts, while slavishly rendering services to Russia's geopolitical rivals.

There is no stable statehood in Ukraine, and political and electoral procedures serve only as a cover, a screen for the redistribution of power and property among various oligarchic clans. (*But any election is just a cover for the redistribution of property, right? And all this democracy of theirs? Who had ever seen that before?—D. B.*)

Maidan did not bring Ukraine closer to democracy and progress. By conducting a coup d'état, the nationalists, and the political forces that supported them, finally brought the situation to a dead end, and pushed Ukraine into the abyss of civil war. Eight years after those events, the country is divided. Ukraine is experiencing an acute socio-economic crisis. (*And now brotherly Russia will help to overcome it.—D. B.*)

In fact, it all boiled down to the fact that the collapse of the Ukrainian economy is accompanied by outright robbery of the country's citizens, as Ukraine itself was simply driven by external control.

This is carried out not only on orders from Western capitals, but also, as they say, directly on the ground—through an entire network of foreign advisers, NGOs and other institutions deployed in Ukraine. There simply is no independent court in Ukraine. At the request of the West, the Kiev authorities gave representatives of international organizations priority rights to select members of the highest judicial bodies—the Council of Justice, and the Qualification Commission of Judges. (*Who is talking about an independent court? Russia? Where 99.9 percent of convictions are handed down from above, always coinciding with state directives?—D. B.*)

Ukraine's entry into NATO is a direct threat to Russia's security. The point is not our political regime, nor anything else. They simply don't want such a large, independent country as Russia to exist. This answers all questions. It is the source of traditional American policy in regard to Russia. Hence the attitude toward all our proposals in the sphere of security.

Russia has done everything to preserve the territorial integrity of Ukraine (*Oh, especially in Crimea.—D. B.*). In this regard, I consider it necessary to make a long-overdue decision—to immediately recognize the independence and sovereignty of the Donetsk People's Republic and the Lugansk People's Republic. And we demand from those who seized and hold power in Kiev to cease hostilities immediately. Otherwise, all responsibility for the possible continuation of bloodshed will be entirely on the conscience of the regime ruling on the territory of Ukraine.

A READER'S COMMENTARY. Some ten years ago I had the occasion to encounter the topic of the industrialization of Ukraine in the late nineteenth century while working on a research project. One of the indirect reasons for that was that a well-known Swiss engineer asked if I knew the name of Stephen (Stepan) Tymoshenko. "I don't," I admitted at the time. "How could that be?" the engineer responded in surprise. "He is a Ukrainian, the author of *Theory of Elasticity*, and a Stanford professor for more than thirty years. Do you also not know why the Swiss-born Mayer mounted construction in Kharkiv?"

> So I started collecting information about industry in Ukraine. Between 1888 and 1900, fourteen major steel mills were built in Ukraine, and all but a plant in Bryansk had "Western" parents. All the advanced technologies flowed into what books and archival reports refer to as the Southern Region. The basis for this was laid by the policy of Russia's first Prime Minister Sergei Witte's policy to attract foreign capital. In a 1955 edition of one of his works on the statistics of industry in pre-revolutionary Russia, you can find Lenin's thoughts, for even the most qualitative and scrupulous work did not lack in quotations from him: "The Southern region of the mining industry is in many respects diametrically opposed to the Urals. The purely capitalist industry that has grown up here in recent decades knows neither tradition, nor class, nor nationality, nor the insularity of a specific population. Foreign capital, engineers and workers have been and are relocating to Southern Russia in masses, while in the modern era of this fever (1898) entire factories are being transported there from America."

Modernism and archaism, right?

So Ukraine was largely created by foreign capital. Not by Russia, not by Russians, and not by Lenin.

Zelenskyy understood that he must respond to this appeal immediately, for to leave it without commentary would mean agreeing that Ukraine does not have the right to its own statehood. Zelenskyy responded early on the morning of February 22:

> Dear citizens of Ukraine! Great peoples of a great country!
>
> We and our state have no time for long lectures about history.
>
> I will not talk about the past. I will talk about reality and the future. Ukraine stands behind me. Within its internationally recognized borders. And they will remain as such. Despite any statements and actions of the Russian Federation.

Just as we will remain calm and confident.

For this I want to thank all our citizens.

You prove it once again: Ukrainians are a smart, wise nation.

Despite everything you keep a cool head and react calmly in a balanced and mature way. We have been ready for everything for a long time.

But there are no grounds for your sleepless night.

This evening we held a meeting of the National Security and Defense Council of Ukraine. Ukraine unequivocally assesses the recent actions of the Russian Federation as a violation of the sovereignty and territorial integrity of our State. All responsibility for the consequences of these decisions rests with Russia's political leadership.

Recognizing the independence of the occupied areas of the Donetsk and Luhansk regions may indicate Russia's unilateral withdrawal from the Minsk agreements, and the rejection of decisions made in the Normandy Format. This undermines peace efforts and destroys existing formats of negotiation.

With today's and tomorrow's possible decisions, Russia legalizes its troops, which, in fact, have occupied the regions of Donbas since 2014.

A country that has supported war for eight years cannot support peace, as it claims. I have discussed the situation with French President Emmanuel Macron, German Chancellor Olaf Scholz, US President Joseph Biden, British Prime Minister Boris Johnson, and European Council President Charles Michel. I also plan to speak with Turkish President Recep Erdogan.

What happens next? We want peace, and we are consistent in our actions. Today the Ministry of Foreign Affairs of Ukraine sent a request to the member states of the UN Security Council on the basis of the Budapest Memorandum with a demand to hold consultations immediately. I have initiated the convening of a meeting of the UN Security Council and, a special meeting of the OSCE. We insist on fully adequate work from the OSCE SMM to prevent provocations and further escalation. An emergency summit of the Normandy Format has been initiated. We expect clear, effective steps of support from our partners.

It is very important to see now, who are our real friends and partners and who will go on trying to scare the Russian Federation with words. We are committed to a political and diplomatic settlement, and will not give in to provocations. Our borders are reliably protected, a system of territorial defense has been created.

Our partners support us. In accordance with Article 51 of the UN Charter, Ukraine reserves the right to individual and collective self-defense.

We clearly distinguish between provocations and attacks of the aggressor's forces.

The truth supports us. And we will never hide the truth from you.

As soon as we see a change in the situation, as soon as we see an escalation in danger, you will know all about it. There is no reason for chaotic actions now. We will do everything to keep it this way. We are committed to peaceful and diplomatic paths. We will follow them and only them.

But.

We are on our own land.

We fear nothing nor anyone.

We owe nothing to anyone.

And we will give nothing to anyone.

Of this we are certain.

For it is not February 2014, but February 2022. Another country. Another army. The same goal.

That is peace.

Peace in Ukraine!

Glory to Ukraine!

This statement is both strong and weak at the same time: as they write in chess notation—"?!" Strong because it is short, it is lacking in hysteria and panic, and it does not present Ukraine as a victim, which is how Russia always presents itself. Russia generally acts from the position of the poor and offended: we were not asked, we were not listened to, we were deceived. Weak—because he offered a civilized answer, without a shadow of the usual mocking humor, remaining carefully within diplomatic boundaries in response to all the back-alley rhetoric, and blustery claims of "we will show you." That's not how it works. "It won't pay with SS-man," as Saul Repnin said in the Strugatsky brothers' sci-fi novel *Escape Attempt* when a captured concentration camp guard responds rudely in response to humane treatment.[2]

Of course, Zelenskyy had no hope that this would stop anyone. He wanted to prevent panic (there was none), and besides, leaving Putin's statement completely unanswered would have been unmanly. So he answered only with general, non-specific words.

Meanwhile, on February 22, even optimists had no doubt that Russia would begin hostilities any minute. In the evening, Zelenskyy called the leaders of the parliamentary factions to Bankova Street. It was the first meeting of all parliamentary leaders since inauguration day. The meeting was attended by General Zaluzhnyi, the head of the security forces Ivan Bakanov, and the head of military intelligence Kyrylo Budanov. Yuliia Tymoshenko insisted on immediate mobilization. Defense Minister Reznikov believed an escalation of the situation was possible in Donbas, but not a full-scale conflict. Budanov's speech was the most radical. He warned about the imminent outbreak of war, but there was a feeling, the meeting participants said, that the president did not believe him. After the meeting, Zelenskyy made a new televised address: "Today there is no need for a general mobilization. We need quickly to finish bringing the Ukrainian army and other military formations up to full strength. As the Supreme Commander-in-Chief of the Armed Forces of Ukraine, I issued a decree on the call-up of reservists for a specific period." He also announced the complete unity of all political forces in Ukraine: "All parties are now of the same color—yellow and blue."

---

2 TRANSLATOR'S COMMENTARY: This is a direct quote from the Strugatsky brothers' novel. It is in bad, I would even say, incomprehensible English. But the author said his book is full of commentaries and remarks from editors and readers, so he saw no reason why I should not add my own.

The Ukrainian press has repeatedly reconstructed Zelenskyy's last days of peace and first days of war: on February 22 (it was unusually warm in Kyiv, +10° Celsius) the Secretary of the National Security and Defense Council Oleksii Danilov, driving his personal Audi, arrived at Bankova Street at about 8 P.M. and reported to Zelenskyy that "there is a high danger of his physical elimination" (I quote from *Ukrainska Pravda*). Zelenskyy listened carefully to the report and went to the next meeting.

Ukrainian intelligence had at their disposal maps captured from paratroopers from Pskov. They said, "To be distributed February 20," but the "20" was crossed out, and "22" replaced it. Usually maps are issued two days before an event. What caused the delay? Could it be that American intelligence had correctly predicted at attack on February 20, so the Russians chose to catch the Americans in a lie by not attacking on that date? On the morning of February 23, seeking to emphasize the particular tension of the situation, Biden personally received Ukrainian Foreign Minister Dmytro Kuleba and Ukrainian Ambassador to the United States Oksana Markarova in the Oval Office of the White House. *Ukrainska Pravda*, recalling that meeting a year later, wrote: "Despite the promise of support, it was less like encouragement offered to an ally, but more like meeting a child with cancer. In the person of Kuleba, Biden said goodbye to all of Ukraine." Still, it was too early to say goodbye to Ukraine. Meanwhile, the Security Council of Ukraine switched to round-the-clock operation. By 10 P.M. on February 23, the Upper Rada voted to declare a state of emergency. At this time, the Armed Forces of Ukraine had already reactivated military warehouses and were preparing airfields.

At five o'clock in the evening on February 23, Zelenskyy met with representatives of big business. All the richest people in Ukraine showed up: Hennadii Korban, Borys Kolesnikov, Rinat Akhmetov (who flew in from abroad), Serhii Tihipko, Oleksandr Feldman, Vladislava Molchanova, and Maksym Temchenko. The oligarchs, who asked not to be named, shared their impressions with *Ukrainska Pravda* and the Oligarch portal. There were three main impressions:

- Zelenskyy, on the eve of the invasion, believed he would be able to resolve the situation;
- There was no direct contact with Putin, all attempts to establish contact yielded nothing, the presidential administration asked for any possible mediation;
- Zelenskyy did not ask for any emergency donations (unlike during the first wave of COVID), but called on the oligarchs not to leave the country, and to shield the national currency from a precipitous fall.

Everyone supported him unanimously. It was noted that he was nervous, but held firm; his face looked unhealthy, as if he were suffering from prolonged insomnia. Informants said that the mood of the businessmen was one of alarm. They assessed the situation more realistically than the political leaders, and gave no credence to the notion of compromise with Russia. Apparently, they understood that compromise for Russia was unnecessary and even dangerous. "It seems they don't believe anything will be full-scale," one source said. The fact is that until the very end it was common for a normal person to believe things would not lead to war, but "normal" people have not been entering the business world for a long time—modern businessmen are ready for whatever may come. Zaluzhnyi, incidentally, informed everyone that the army was in full combat readiness and would meet any development with dignity. The Surkis brothers—Ihor and Hryhorii, football magnates sitting directly opposite Zelenskyy—whispered to those sitting near them that it would begin at 4 A.M., but they didn't say that out loud. Later, in hindsight, many criticized Budanov for saying nothing overt about the war—"Instead of jabbering, we could have evacuated our families." To that criticism Budanov responded that he could not say anything directly, but had made everything unambiguously clear.

At nine in the evening, Zelenskyy retired to his office, inviting his speechwriter Yurii Kostiuk, Andrii Yermak, and press secretary of the presidential office, Daria Zarivna, to join him. He spent two hours with them preparing an appeal to Russian citizens in Russian, and at 11 P.M. he recorded it:

Today I attempted to initiate a telephone conversation with the President of the Russian Federation. The result was silence. Although there should be silence in Donbas. Therefore, today I want to appeal to all citizens of Russia—though not as president; I am addressing Russian citizens as a citizen of Ukraine. You and I are separated by more than two thousand kilometers of common border. Your troops are stationed along it today. Almost 200,000 soldiers, thousands of combat vehicles. Your leadership approved their advance—into the territory of another country. This step could be the beginning of a major war on the European continent. The whole world is talking about what could happen any day now. A reason for it might occur at any time. Any provocation, any outbreak can set everything on fire. They tell you that this flame will liberate the people of Ukraine. But the Ukrainian people are free. They remember their past, and they are building their own future. Building, not destroying.

Ukraine in your news and Ukraine in real life are two completely different countries. The main difference between them is that ours is real.

This is our land, it is our history. What will you fight for and with whom?! The people of Ukraine want peace! The Ukrainian authorities want peace. We want it and make it. Doing everything we can. We are not alone. This is true. Ukraine is supported in this by many countries. Why? Because this is not about peace at any cost. We are talking about peace and principles, about justice, about international law, about the right to self-determination, about the right to determine one's own future, the right of every society to security, and the right of every person to live without threats. This is all important for us, it is all important for the world. It is important for you too.

We don't need war. Whether cold, hot, or hybrid. But if troops attack us, if they try to take away our country, our freedom, our lives, and the lives of our children, we will defend ourselves. We won't attack, we will defend! As you advance, you will see our faces, not our backs—our faces.

War is a great misfortune. This misfortune comes at a high cost—in every sense of the word.

I know that this appeal of mine will not be shown on Russian television. But Russian citizens must see it, they must know the truth. And the truth is that you need to stop. Before it's too late. And if the Russian leadership does not want to sit down at the negotiating table with us for the sake of peace, it may sit at that table with you.

Do Russians want war? The answer depends only on you—citizens of the Russian Federation.

I was there when Eduard Kolmanovsky's song, "Do Russians Want War," based on a poem by Yevgeny Yevtushenko, was taught in schools. Parodies were written about it. One of them, "Russian Kittens are Sick," sounded very much like the original title in Russian. Yevtushenko, when he wrote it, could be absolutely sure that Russians did not want war. It was autumn of 1961, and the Second Thaw was underway (following the first from 1956 to 1958). He had just returned from his first trip to America, where everyone asked him this question. The singer Mark Bernes, when he recorded it in the spring of 1962, also believed that they did not want war. Additionally, those who distributed this record—it was still a 78 at the time—to the delegates of the World Moscow Congress for Peace and Disarmament on July 9, 1962, also believed this. We all believed that the elders in the Kremlin might want war but that as a whole Russians never would.

But the veterans of World War II gradually disappeared. Those who remembered the war grew old. And there were fewer and fewer reasons for unity. And the ability to think critically about propaganda dissipated in the '90s, as it had, in fact, even in the '80s. Those who worked in the '90s in independent television (which, in fact, was entirely dependent on the owner) wanted to remain in the profession, and so took up military propaganda. As such, by February 24, 2022, approximately one third of Russians wanted war, and over the coming year this figure increased to 75 percent. Maybe they didn't want war as such, but they believed that once it had started, it had to be carried out to the end. And how could Russia end a war if not with victory?

They very much wanted greatness. They had nothing against Ukraine. They even considered it sweet and touching. They liked dumplings, vodka, and folk songs. But they had lost the habit of objecting, and many had lost the habit of thinking. Those who tried to think assured themselves: this is my country, and I have no other. The people above surely know what's best and we don't know everything. What if Ukraine really is preparing to attack Donbas, and we miraculously arrived just in time? The plot of "We miraculously arrived in time" was worked out in Prague in 1968, and in Afghanistan in 1980, and in Pristina in 1999, and in Ukraine in 2022—the convulsions of an empire at ever-increasing intervals. (Will there be something in 2048? Or will there already be nothing at all?)

At four in the morning on February 24, Putin addressed his subjects, announcing the start of a "special military operation" (the word "war" was not only not uttered, but was banned in Russia).

We see that the forces who carried out a coup in Ukraine in 2014, seized power and retained it with the aid of, in essence, decorative election procedures, have finally abandoned peaceful resolutions of the conflict. For eight years, an endlessly long eight years, we did everything possible to ensure that the situation was resolved through peaceful, political means. All in vain.

What I think is important to further emphasize: Leading NATO countries, in order to achieve their own goals, support the extreme nationalists and neo-Nazis in Ukraine in everything, who, in turn, will never forgive the Crimeans and Sevastopol residents for their free choice of reunification with Russia.

They, of course, will go to Crimea, just as they did to Donbas, waging war, in order to kill, just as special killing squads from gangs of Ukrainian nationalists, Hitler's accomplices, killed defenseless people during the Great Patriotic War. They also openly state that they lay claim to a number of other Russian territories.

The entire course of events and analysis of incoming information shows that Russia's clash with these forces is inevitable. It is only a matter of time: they are preparing, they are waiting for the right moment. Now they are also claiming to possess nuclear weapons. We will not allow this to happen.

At the same time, our plans do not include the occupation of Ukrainian territories. We will not force anything on anyone. Furthermore, we recently heard how voices are increasingly raised in the West that the documents signed by the Soviet totalitarian regime cementing the results of the World War II should no longer be implemented. Well, how are we to answer that?

Let me remind you that neither during the creation of the USSR, nor after the Second World War, did anyone ask the people living in certain territories included in modern Ukraine how they themselves wished to organize their lives. The basis of our policy is freedom, freedom of choice for everyone to determine their future and the future of their children independently. And we consider it important that this right—the right to choose—should be available to all peoples living on the territory of today's Ukraine, to everyone who wants it.

(*That is, they come and ask, do you understand? They ask Ukrainians where they want to live. To do this, they'll have to bomb a little, but nobody has ever asked them this question before.—D. B.*)

In this regard, I appeal to the citizens of Ukraine. In 2014, Russia was obliged to protect the residents of Crimea and Sevastopol from those whom you yourself call "Nazis." The residents of Crimea and Sevastopol made their choice to be with their historical Motherland, with Russia, and we supported this. I repeat, we simply could not do otherwise. (*He repeats this for the third time, and, taking into account the previous appeal, for the sixth time.—D. B.*)

I must also appeal to the military personnel of the Ukrainian Armed Forces.

Dear comrades! Your fathers, grandfathers, and great-grandfathers did not fight the Nazis, defending our common Motherland, so that today's neo-Nazis could seize power in Ukraine. You swore an oath of allegiance to the Ukrainian people, not to the anti-human junta that robs Ukraine and mocks these very people.

Do not follow criminal orders. I urge you immediately to lay down your arms and go home. Let me explain: all servicemen of the Ukrainian army who fulfill this requirement will be able to leave the combat zone freely and return to their families.

I will strongly emphasize once again: all responsibility for possible bloodshed will be entirely on the conscience of the regime ruling on the territory of Ukraine.

Now a few important, very important, words for those who may be tempted from the outside to intervene in the events now taking place. Whoever seeks to interfere with us, and even more so, to create threats to our country or to our people, should know that Russia's response will be immediate, and will lead you to consequences that you have never encountered in your history. We are ready for any development of events. All decisions necessary in this regard have been made. I hope I will be heard.

The following comparison then appeared in the press throughout the world, but how can we not also quote it—it is phenomenal in its clarity:

We long suffered from a terrible problem, a problem created by the Versailles Treaty, which grew worse until it became unbearable for us. Danzig was and is a German city. The corridor was and is German. Both of these territories, according to their cultural development, belong exclusively to the German people.

As always, I tried peacefully to achieve a review, a change in this intolerable situation. It is a lie when the liberal world says we want to bring about change by force. On my own initiative, I have repeatedly suggested that these intolerable conditions be reconsidered. All these proposals, as you know, have been rejected—proposals to limit weapons and, if necessary, disarmament; proposals to limit military production; proposals to ban certain types of modern weapons. You know the proposals I have made for the restoration of German sovereignty over German territories. You know the endless attempts I made for a peaceful settlement. All of them were in vain.

This is from a speech delivered in the Reichstag on September 1, 1939. Oh, it's no coincidence that Hitler's cap is said to be preserved in the main cathedral of the Russian Ministry of Defense.

We tried our best. We tried peace. We were all deceived. Roughly speaking, they cheated us.

We have no other choice left, and now we will kill everyone. Responsibility lies with those who are killed.

IV. DAY ONE

At half past five in the morning, missile attacks hit Kyiv.

The Russian Federation attacked in four directions: Odesa and Kherson from the territory of Crimea; Kyiv from the north; Kharkiv from the northeast; Ukrainian-controlled Donbas from the southeast.

Oleksii Danilov called members of the National Security and Defense Council on their mobile phones. He warned the Speaker of Parliament Ruslan Stefanchuk about the need to introduce martial law in the country.

Zelenskyy immediately went to his office. He made his first call—on his mobile—to Boris Johnson, informing him that Ukraine would not surrender. The first conversation over a secure channel occurred with Biden. The Rada opened a session at 8 a.m., and by nine they had adopted laws on general mobilization and martial law. The deputies asked for an audience with the president. Arakhamiia replied that this was unlikely, but he sent Zelenskyy a text message. Zelenskyy replied that he was waiting for faction heads at his office. About nine heads of factions gathered on Bankova Street. Journalists were waiting on the ground floor; Mykhailo Podoliak and Oleksii Arestovych came out to them. On the fourth floor, Zelenskyy proposed that the speaker of the Rada move to the west of the country; Poroshenko and former speaker Razumkov opposed: "The Russians will say the authorities have fled." It was decided to leave Ruslan Stefanchuk, chairman of the Upper Rada, in Kyiv, and send Deputy Speaker Oleksandr Kornienko to one of the neighboring regions. At this moment, officers from the presidential security service entered and reported that Russian sabotage and reconnaissance groups were already operating in the Pechersk region in the center of Kyiv. Zelenskyy was taken to a bunker.

Roman Akravets and Roman Romaniuk in *Ukrainska Pravda* wrote then that the president's decision not to leave Kyiv was based on two premises. First, Zelenskyy believed the reports of his own security service, and not the alarmist reports of Western intelligence services. He was promised that the Russians would not be able to take Kyiv (and, as we now know, they could not). Secondly, the bunker was built during the Soviet era and was designed to withstand a direct hit from a nuclear projectile. Zelenskyy rightly judged that it would protect him more reliably than any European capital. The core of the team was always in the bunker with him. Yermak, his first deputy Kyrylo Tymoshenko, Minister of Infrastructure Oleksandr Kubrakov (called the "shadow prime minister"), and the head of the Servant of the People faction, Davyd Arakhamiia, were often present.

A decision was made to evacuate the Cabinet of Ministers. The ministers of internal affairs, health, infrastructure, energy, and defense remained in Kyiv. *Ukrainska Pravda* wrote then that there is no better metaphor for Ukraine than this train, taking ministers to an unknown destination, with a single guard armed with a single pistol. I would say this was a metaphor not only for Ukraine, but for the entire world. For the world, at noon on February 24, 2022, the lone guard was Ukraine. But it fulfilled its duty.

The first journalist to visit and photograph the bunker in detail was then thirty-eight-year-old Dmytro Komarov. The funny thing about this is that I knew Komarov as a teenager just starting out as a reporter, and I warmly approved of his idea for a blog about hitchhiking. Komarov thus traveled the whole world, with almost no money, visiting the most exotic places, first becoming one of the best bloggers in Ukraine, then becoming perhaps the most famous television journalist (perhaps alongside Dmitry Gordon and Natalia Vlaschenko, but for a younger audience). Today he is almost a tycoon, and I, to borrow Bulat Okudzhava's words, have remained a "lone craftsman." I'm a little shy around Komarov. I don't think he would even recognize me. This is because there is no vertical mobility in Russia, unless, of course, you climb into that career elevator that requires you to enter on your hands and knees. There are plenty such career elevators in Russia—from Russia Today to the Leaders of Russia movement—but in all these instances you must swear your loyalty and recalibrate your biography entirely. That does not suit me at all, but, hey, I'm not offended. I have fewer temptations.

Komarov made a television film, *The Year*, about Zelenskyy's year of work under war conditions. Zelenskyy was shown in the bedroom, at a desk with a photograph of the family and a bust of Churchill, in a wardrobe where a formal suit hangs in anticipation of peacetime. Until that time comes, Zelenskyy will wear camouflage, as befits the Supreme Commander-in-Chief.

This is a powerful film, probably the best that has been made about the war so far—a two-hour report from the main hot spots. Komarov was the first journalist to drive into Bucha in a tank, not yet knowing what he would see there, and he and his group were the first to photograph corpses on the streets. The camera recorded irreversible changes in his face, voice, and intonation—he was the first to discover all this. Komarov was the first to film a mass grave in Izium. He was the first to ask the Ukrainian military what would happen if the Russians entered Kyiv. They answered: the Ukrainians would blow up all the bridges, including the famous Paton Bridge. The entire Boryspil Airport had already been mined and the landing strip was covered with oil so that not a single enemy plane could land.

Komarov asks Zelenskyy: "How did you say goodbye to your wife on February 24?"

"Listen, I know how to make films myself," says Zelenskyy. "There was no profound eye contact or long goodbyes. I knew we might not see each other again. She knew that too. I really love my family, if you don't know. But I knew I had to do my job, and everything else is secondary right now."

This episode, thanks to the *Washington Post*, went down in history, and is mentioned in many sources, including an interview with Olena Zelenska. She wakes up because there is no one next to her in bed, and she sees her husband putting on a black suit. To her silent question he answers: "It has begun." In fact, that night, if Zelenskyy did lay down, he laid down for an hour, but no more. Both Washington and Kyiv already knew for sure that Russian shelling was about to begin.

"When did you speak your famous phrase about taxis and ammunition?"

"On the morning of February 24. My first call to Biden. I also told him that if the president leaves, that's no [legitimate] state."

The easiest way to step into the position of a hero is from two points (in fact, it's only possible from these two points). Either there is a monolithic human wall behind you, and you embody its main qualities. Or a human wall stands in front of you, and you stand alone against it. In Russia, the second version of heroism is much more common—the first is practically non-existent there. Because there is absolutely nothing heroic about standing behind a crowd and driving it to slaughter—"forward, eagles! I've got your backs with my breast!"

At this key moment of the war, when Zelenskyy said, "I need ammunition, not a taxi" (the second most famous phrase of the war was the response of the Ukrainian border guards: "Russian warship, go fuck yourselves!"), the fate of the war and the fate of the world were decided. For a systemic politician in Zelenskyy's place could have assessed his chances and left. This would not have made Ukraine's resistance any less desperate, but there would have been more desperation in the resistance. Zelenskyy chose neither compromise nor flight. Zelenskyy chose a military confrontation, the position of David vs. Goliath, and it is unlikely that at the time even he understood the grand scale of the choice was making.

Incidentally, it is not difficult to explain this choice from a purely psychological perspective, precisely because Zelenskyy was not alone for a second on that day. At all times there were people around him who depended on him, ranging from staff to security, from deputies to ministers. Zelenskyy's entire previous life was a team game, he was the soul of his class, the captain of his team, the engine and manager of the Block, and a film producer. He had assembled a team here too in his presidential post. While harpies were already quoting the people of *Block 95*—"It is difficult to get into the Block, but it's even harder to get out"—this team was united, seamless and reliable. Zelenskyy could not leave his team. It was normal and natural for him to send his wife and children to the west of the country (they returned immediately following the withdrawal of Russian troops from Kyiv), but he himself could not publicly show weakness. An actor is alive as long as people are looking at him. Of course, this behavior was not acting, it was purely heroic, but it is easier for an actor to become a hero because he can perform it.

And then he pronounced the most important phrase of this war: "The fight is here; I need ammunition, not a ride."

Whether he said that personally to Biden or to a high-ranking American intelligence officer who had proposed immediate evacuation, no American journalist could confirm. But the Ukrainian embassy in Britain was the first to repeat it, and then the *New York Times* wrote that this phrase of Zelenskyy's would go down in the history of Ukraine, regardless of whether it survives this war or not.

Surely there will be people who will say that Zelenskyy did not speak these words, because no one but Biden heard it. They will probably assume it was all invented by PR people or Ukrainian diplomats in London. But what he actually said is not so important: the verbal dressing of victory will come, if only there is a victory to describe. It is important that Zelenskyy never left Kyiv for a second. On February 25, he posted a late-night video from Bankova Street: "The faction leader is here, the prime minister is here, the head of the presidential office is here, Podoliak is here, the president is here. Civil society is here. We all defend Ukraine. Glory to our defenders and protectors! Glory to Ukraine!" This video needs to be rewatched in moments of despair. What faces they all have there, what courage! And, you know, this is still a time of complete uncertainty, Kyiv is being caught in a pincer movement, enemy reconnaissance groups are snooping around the city; they are positioned in the center of Kyiv. The first thought of any normal person would be: if they can do it, so can I! In the history of the world of the last decade, I know nothing more motivating than this homemade video from Kyiv that night, filmed on a phone by Zelenskyy's press secretary Serhii Nikiforov.

"Have you tried talking to Putin?"

"They kept telling me he wasn't ready. I worked through any intermediary I could, tried scheduling a conversation through several international partners—but he wasn't ready. Now I'm no longer ready to talk to him."

When Zelenskyy recalled those days in August in an interview with the *Washington Post*, he said: "The day would start at 5 A.M. during these first days, and end deep at night. We slept for a couple of hours in clothes, because honestly, we had to be ready at all times. Not because it's something heroic—it was a psychological state. You just can't afford to relax. And when you don't relax, your brain is working and can make quick decisions. Something about the military, something about civilians, something about territorial defense, while you need to keep planning for this and that. [. . .] It was a constant barrage of problems and decisions—bam, bam, bam. Suddenly they seized a nuclear power plant, suddenly they were shooting, this is something we need to get on air fast. We were doing everything, including informational policy. Frankly speaking, this is called crisis management."

He is asked, "When was the moment when you were sure the defense of Kyiv would hold?"

"We didn't know. We knew we would fight. Why? It was logical. If we rally and unite, if people believe me as president, if the military unites with the people, then it is logical that they can't take a city of many millions. They don't have enough forces, they won't be able to take it. Because if one million people walk out with nothing but a Molotov cocktail in their hand, it's unstoppable. I understood that a city like Kyiv—simply to take it, it's impossible. How? It's very difficult, very difficult, if they come into the middle of the city. Everyone understands that the minute they come into the middle, and go into the center of the city onto the Maidan [Independence Square], and start a war within the government quarter—from that moment, we are going to burn them. Because a battle inside the city—it is very difficult, it is very difficult. They needed way more equipment and people. So they had a chance either to shoot us, as they did in Mariupol, where they simply destroyed everything, or they can come into the city—but they would need tons of forces. Or they can get rid of me . . ."

Russia at this time was attacking Kyiv from two sides. Then Vladimir Putin would say he was asked to withdraw troops from Kyiv to ensure negotiations, as a gesture of goodwill. Who might ask for this, and who the Russian President would listen to in this situation, is a mystery. The attack on Kyiv faltered, and this was the first success of the Ukrainian Armed Forces. After that, the West believed Ukraine would be able to successfully resist the invaders.

The Russian plan was to enter Kyiv three days after the start of the war. The city was defended only by the 72nd brigade (most Ukrainian troops were busy in Donbas). On February 24, 2022, Russian troops landed at Hostomel airfield. At the same time, they intended to enter from Belarus via Chernobyl, but the chairman of the Ukrainian border service, Serhii Daineko, gave the order to blow up all bridges on the border. Russian military expert Viktor Litovkin arrogantly explained that by claiming it was, "so the population won't escape that way."

The BBC published a detailed chronicle of this attack on Kyiv: "According to the General Staff, nine battalion tactical groups (BTGs) of the Russian army began the attack on Kyiv through the Chernobyl zone on the morning of February 24. Another 10 BTG remained in reserve in the Homel region near the Belarusian-Ukrainian border" (a single BTG contained from 600 to 800 fighters, but on the eve of the invasion the groups were strengthened to 1000).

The *New York Times* received from the Main Intelligence Directorate of the Ministry of Defense of Ukraine a schedule of the advance of Russian troops to Kyiv: the starting line was the Homel Oblast, then crossing the Pripyat River, the village of Belaya Soroka (on the border with Ukraine), and finally, Stoianka (a village near Irpen five kilometers, or three miles, from the outskirts of Kyiv). This entire 200-kilometer route was supposed to take thirteen hours.

The Ukrainian General Staff commented in a statement: "Faced with resistance, the enemy was forced to deploy into battle formations and fight their way toward the capital. For three days, until the end of the day on February 27, the lead units of the Russian Armed Forces, advancing from the Chernobyl line, arrived and consolidated at the border of the settlements of Stoianka–Hostomel–Demidov." The landing force in Hostomel was destroyed on the night of February 25, but the Russians sent up reinforcements. The column of Russian equipment advancing toward Kyiv reached the fifty-sixth kilometer by March 1 and consisted of four battalion groups, which the Russians put into action on February 28. "Thus, the huge column that was supposed to capture the Ukrainian capital consisted of 10 reserve BTGs brought in from Belarusian territory. According to rough estimates, it consisted of up to 10 thousand soldiers, about 100 tanks, and 400 infantry fighting vehicles and infantry fighting vehicles," the BBC calculated.

The battle for the village of Moshchun (three kilometers, or just under two miles from Kyiv) led to the village being razed to the ground, but the Russians were stopped there for the first time, and driven back. Another BTG was destroyed in Rakovka (slightly north of Moshchun). The Russians advanced until March 19, when they were stopped and began to dig in. On April 2 they left Irpen and Bucha.

V. MARCH

Zelenskyy's March 3, 2022, press conference was, frankly, frightening to watch. The Russian press did not miss an opportunity to mock him. No matter how many times they referred to him as being drunk, it was clear that he wasn't drunk, but simply dead tired. Speaking intelligibly and quickly, with clear formulations and impeccable self-control, he had difficulty keeping himself from falling asleep during overly long-winded questions (and several times during pauses he simply blacked out). Anyone who has ever had to struggle with sleep could see that before us was a person who had not slept a wink for several days. He allowed himself only one emotional attack—then, it seems that after that, he never addressed Putin personally, nor did he allow himself any personal intonation in all their communications. The Bucha events took place at the end of March 2022, and

Zelenskyy broke down seriously—or, if you prefer, he froze in hatred. The Russians ceased to be people for him, they ceased even to be enemies—they now resembled alien invaders, from whom one would not expect human reactions.

But on March 3, Zelenskyy still seemed to believe it was possible to stop and play everything back: "Vladimir Putin, leave our land. If you don't want to leave now, sit down with me at the negotiating table. Not from thirty meters away, like with [French President Emmanuel] Macron and [German Chancellor Olaf] Scholz. I'm your neighbor, you don't need to hold me at thirty meters distance! Sit down with me and talk. What are you afraid of? We're no threat to anyone.

"I am an open person, I know all the issues that President Putin, his entourage, and the Minister of Foreign Affairs raise. We need to speak without being offensive, without conditions—we need to speak like people, and like men. I am ready to discuss all issues. About Ukraine, about the problems of the Russian language, about occupied or non-occupied Donbas. About the status of Donbas, about the DPR, LPR—about everything that is happening."

The very notion of speaking man-to-man, the very mention of a neighborly conversation was evidence not only of President Zelenskyy's endless naïveté, but proof of the shock he had experienced along with all of Ukraine. This shock was not nearly as great in Russia. The propaganda there had prepared the population for war, and precisely for Russian aggression which Russia allegedly had been forced to undertake. But the level of propaganda in Ukraine under Zelenskyy had decreased. They preferred not to believe in the war until the last moment. Zelenskyy says with sincere surprise that Russia doesn't just want to bring Ukraine to its knees, it wants to destroy Ukraine, to see that it simply doesn't exist. In extreme bewilderment, he asks: "What do you even want? What must we do to get you to stop killing our children?" He soon will understand: there are no such sacrifices that Ukraine must make, no such concessions. He is faced with the same looming iron wall that crushed the world in 1939: Russia's only demand is that no one be left.

"But we can't leave our territory! We can't say we are part of Russia, that there is no Ukraine," Zelenskyy repeats, probably already understanding deep in his soul that the conditions are this, and nothing else: They, Ukrainians, simply must not exist. The only way for Putin to remain in power forever is through war. The only possible outcome of the war is not a compromise, but a complete and unconditional surrender of the rest of the world, not immediately, gradually, but of everything. You can't sit still on this planet. And this new Reich possesses nuclear weapons that it is ready to use: it has nothing to lose. Some still believed that Putin was being a scaremonger. Zelenskyy soon realized that Putin was truly driven into a corner, and the force that drove him there was much more serious than NATO. This force was time. The only way to resist modernity, to stop the future, and to ensconce yourself on the throne forever is by imposing war on the world, tossing more and more new generations into the furnace. Zelenskyy did not yet understand that his only fault was that he belonged to this future. He was a rejection of the archaic, he stood for the unwillingness to live in a world of eternal confrontations, executions, and denunciations. "What does he want? We are not terrorists, we don't rob banks," Zelenskyy repeats, not at all trying to look menacing and decisive at this moment. He asks childish questions, like a schoolboy being pursued by street thugs. He was just walking home, bothering no one, and these punks caught up with him on the way. He doesn't even have anything for them to take away from him, they don't need his lunch money. Their way of life is nothing but mockery and violence, they don't know how to do anything else. I remember well how my son, who was attacked by just such a gang, asked me in sincere confusion: "What did I do to them?" How can you explain? You did nothing to them, yet you did everything: Your mere existence in the world threatens their sense of being, and they understand that. They don't know, they don't want to learn, and they never will learn what you are capable of doing. It is impossible to teach them lofty emotions or expose them to complex pleasures. The great Soviet storyteller Alexander Sharov, in his novella *Old Manuscripts*, wrote of a young scientist who learned to eavesdrop on the thoughts of a pike. The young pike thinks just one thing: "I want to eat carp. I want to eat carp." Then he starts listening to a three-hundred-year-old pike, thinking that she might have gained some wisdom, had seen enough of life, and had finally begun having real thoughts about something. But all he heard was something repeated in wildly rapid speed, with an insane intensity, racing around in her ichthyoid brain—"I-want-to-eat-carp-I-want-to-eat-carp-I-WANT-TO-EAT-CARP!!!"—and nothing else. It would be naïve for a carp to ask why he is to blame. It is naïve to expect that in the aggressor country there will be honest journalists who will listen sympathetically to the leader of Ukraine. Here is how the website of Russian Channel One reacted to this terrible press conference: "The question about his use of various kinds of drugs is among those that journalists ask most frequently of the former head of the office of the President of Ukraine, Ondrii Bohdan."

"While I was alongside him, there was no problem. As to what is happening now . . . we need to do some research. This is a medical symptom, you can't hide it. I see that he has changed physiologically, his face is different. His speech is different, his words are different, he has different facial expressions. He's not the same at all. He searches for words, and tries to remember words," noted Bohdan.

And then, naturally, there are the opinions of experts—in this case, drug addiction specialists. Even they admit that Zelenskyy's speech is quite adequate. But he has difficulty concentrating, and occasionally just shuts down. "They'll probably say again that I haven't slept for several nights." And of course, who's going to believe this? The users' comments—I admit that, unlike experts, they were not paid a penny—are unanimous: "He is on drugs. This is no president. Compare him with ours."

Soon enough this "comparison with ours" ceased to suit even commentators on government websites. For, unlike Zelenskyy, who spoke with difficulty, but honestly and clearly, Putin had nothing to say aside from the regularly repeated and long since exposed lies. And soon he stopped speaking altogether—nothing could justify the obvious military collapse. Beginning in April, Zelenskyy began to win this fight, first on points, later by knockdowns.

The turning point was the events in Bucha, a Kyiv suburb, which Russian troops entered on March 15 and abandoned on April 2.

VI. BUCHA

I was in Bucha at the end of June 2022, and an aura of disaster still hung over the city: there are places where something truly terrible happens, and the horror that accumulates there does not dissipate. This is how I remember the town of Spitak, where the most destructive nine-magnitude earthquake in the history of Armenia happened on December 7, 1988, during the Armenian-Azerbaijani war. Life in Bucha in the summer was incredibly active. Journalists were constantly being brought in from all over the world. Father Andrii, who survived those ten days, showed off the courtyard of his church, built just before the war but not yet painted, and in his church there hung photographs of the Bucha victims in place of icons—exhumations, inspections, and reburials. The churchyard was still dug up, but right there, in the church, the same Father Andrii joined new couples in wedlock and baptized new children. By June, more than three hundred refugees had returned to Bucha. Mayor Anatolii Fedoruk, who hid among his neighbors during the occupation (many knew that, but no one gave him away), showed what was left of his house. Let us clarify, very little remained of the house, since, upon leaving, the Russian troops shot it up with grenade launchers. Right there was a mutilated Mazda that the Russians hadn't been able to open to drive away, so they just trashed it in order to make themselves feel better. Next to the skeleton of the half-burnt-out house stood unharmed plaster rabbits and mushrooms, while Fedoruk treated journalists to cognac and cherries in his surviving gazebo. "We'll rebuild," he said cheerfully, although there was no cheerfulness in his eyes. And the more that Bucha, with its weddings and christenings, tried to show that everything was not so scary after all, and that it was still possible to live there, the more obvious it was that all this was an attempt to hide the irreparable: most of the residents not only did not recover from the trauma, but never really even grasped what had happened.

The dead were buried, houses were rebuilt, refugees returned—and yet, one felt with extraordinary acuteness that quite recently things had been very bad here. I know this smell of disaster from the city of Shusha in the war zone of Nagorny-Karabakh and Beslan after the terrorist attack on a school. And the smell is not so much from something burning as from sheer horror. Horror hung in the air. It is a heavy matter, like mercury, and it won't go away for a long time. It is the smell of absolute helplessness, and utter confusion. The feeling that no one will save you. At the same time, Bucha was a wealthy suburb, a prestigious area. The houses here were good and the land was expensive, and people returned here confident that no one could run them out of here. And no one did run them out. Indeed, the Russians were driven out, turned back from Kyiv. But the decision to allow people to return here was naïve. You can bury the dead and clean the houses, but you cannot return here.

It was all like an excursion to Auschwitz, only this was in wartime. In general, everything is done much faster in modern warfare: the enemy may still be advancing, but excursions are already being carried out. Thousands of foreign journalists have worked in Bucha, and everything that happened there has been carefully documented. Many people—out of psychological self-preservation—would like to think these reports are propaganda. They are not propaganda.

The population of Bucha before the war was approximately 40,000. The majority managed to escape, and about 5,000 remained in the city. Residents of Bucha left in their cars under Russian fire. Russian special forces appeared in the suburb on February 25, considering it a suitable base for an attack on Irpen. The Ukrainians recaptured the suburb twice, but eventually surrendered it on March 3. I quote the online magazine *Kholod*, which prepared a review of the world media: "In all, 461 dead were found in Bucha. Of these, 73 bodies were exhumed from the largest mass grave at the Church of St. Andrew in the presence of high-ranking European officials Josep Borrell, Ursula von der Leyen, and Ukrainian Prime Minister Denys Shmyhal. Forty of those buried were identified as civilians, and many of the bodies showed signs of gunshot wounds. On

April 4, the *New York Times* published satellite images of Bucha taken in mid-March. "A review of videos and satellite imagery by *The Times* shows that many of the civilians were killed more than three weeks ago, when Russia's military was in control of the town, and have been rotting in the street ever since.

"One video filmed by a local council member on April 2 shows multiple bodies scattered along Yablonska Street in Bucha. Satellite images provided to *The Times* by Maxar Technologies show that at least eleven of those had been on the street since March 11, when Russia, by its own account, occupied the town."

Intercepted conversations between Russian soldiers were published. They openly admitted that they "did in a lot of civilians," and that there was an order to shoot everyone—"civilians and non-civilians." All this has been studied by hundreds of journalists and verified by hundreds of experts. I believe none of the Europeans was interested in falsifying these data—after this information mere "indignation" and "concern" were no longer possible. Journalistic investigations from Bucha appeared in all major world media, and around the world they no longer caused concern or indignation, but shock. That shock has not passed to this day.

While the world—and partly the Russian opposition—was seeing Russia as a state rife with corruption, official impunity, and oligarchic luxury, in actuality, it was quietly transforming into a bastion of new fascism, an archaic, full-blown cannibalistic state, that was fanatically hostile to everyone. One could have guessed this after hearing Elena Kostyuchenko's 2015 conversation about the brutal covert war in Donetsk with Dorzhi Batomunkuev, the Buryat member of a tank crew, but, at that time, some hoped that these were just isolated cases. Not everyone, even back then, could kill so easily and without the slightest doubt. The Buryat, it seemed, harbored no hatred: "Subconsciously, you know you're fighting the same sort of person as you, in the same sort of tank. Made of flesh and blood. But on the other hand, you understand that he is your enemy. The people I killed were far from innocent. They killed civilians and children. The scum sits there shaking all over, praying that he won't be killed. He starts to ask for mercy.

God alone is your judge. We took a few Ukrainians prisoner. Everyone wants to live when you've got their back against the wall. But they are the same sort of people as you, they have mothers too."

Seven years later, such thoughts no longer occurred to anyone—or no one admitted them.

BBC published several "house chats" from Bucha—this is a common phenomenon in Ukraine. Although the city constantly had internet problems, dozens of murders were recorded in this correspondence among neighbors. The Russians presented their withdrawal from Bucha as an act of goodwill to create an environment of mutual trust at the negotiations in Istanbul.

No one in Bucha, no one in the world understood what had been going on. What was the source of this pathological fury and senseless reprisals against civilians? Either they saw an enemy in every Ukrainian, regardless of gender and age, or they were angry at the cleanliness and wealth of local housing: The standard of living in Bucha is high by Ukrainian standards, but by Russian standards it could seriously shake a fragile soldier's psyche. "Inhuman beasts" is a description that appears more often than others in household chats and reports of Ukrainian journalists. No one was prepared for what they learned, not even those who followed Russian propaganda. No matter how much it dehumanized the Ukrainians, it never went so far as to call for killing everyone. "Don't feel sorry for them, my president!" wrote the Russian science-fiction writer Sergei Lukyanenko. But who really listened to Sergei Lukyanenko? There are no writers or propagandists in Russia with substantial authority; it was not a matter of propaganda, nor of the substances that were allegedly pumped into the soldiers before battle. After all, there were no battles: the army stood at a standstill in the city. This was just how they had fun.

The people who committed atrocities in Bucha have been identified— they called their relatives at home. Many called from mobile phones taken from residents of Bucha, so it was not difficult to identify the interlocutors. The mother of one of the infantrymen from Pskov responded to a correspondent from *Important News* who contacted her on WhatsApp:

It seems to me that only the lazy aren't writing about this bullshit)))

Everybody has already figured this out

Depending on which version interests you, Zelenskyy already came up with everything about this, what and how it happened

If a person has a head on his shoulders and common sense, how can you believe this horror about Russian soldiers? They don't even mock prisoners, let alone civilians)))

You'd be better off figuring out who slits the throats and shoots our prisoners on the road, and give that information to the Red Cross—plus what the Ukrofascists do with the ones they didn't kill)))

That would be a good job for you as a journalist.

Many world media outlets covered the story of Ivan Skiba, who was shot but not killed. I quote from *Important Stories*: "They stripped us all and looked for tattoos. They shouted: 'You are Banderites!'" Then the soldiers took everyone's cell phones. The men were forced to line up one after another, hold the jacket of the person in front, and, at gunpoint, were led to house 144 Yablonska Street, a four-story office building where the Russian occupiers set up their headquarters. There the men were forced to take off their boots and jackets. They made them kneel, some had their hands tied. One of the detainees, twenty-eight-year-old Vitalii Karpenko, was shot dead immediately. Ivan Skiba saw this. Skiba and another man, Andrii Verbovoi, were taken into the building. A bucket was put on Ivan's head, and they began hitting it with a rifle butt and a brick. Skiba can only guess what happened to Verbovoi. He never heard his voice again. Most likely he was killed.

"After that, they took me out again, and made me kneel," recalls Skiba, who was returned to the detainees. "The soldiers discussed among themselves what to do with us. One said: 'Fuck 'em up, only take them away so they're not lying around here.'" One of the prisoners was released because, as Skiba says, he was "weak-hearted" and admitted he was a member of the terrorist defense. He is currently under investigation; the Ukrainian authorities have accused him of treason. The remaining men were led around the corner of the house. Skiba recalls that there were two soldiers, they looked very young. Next, the men were placed facing the wall, and the shooting began. Skiba remembers the words of one soldier: "You're all fucked, you fucking Banderites!" A bullet hit Ivan from the side, passing through him, and he collapsed to the ground. "They finished off anyone who showed signs of life." Skiba fell next to a dead man who was already lying on the ground before they arrived: "I tried not to breathe, only steam was coming out of my mouth. I had no shoes, so I took the shoes off the dead guy who was lying there before we came."

Skiba ran from the scene of the execution, climbed over three fences, and ended up in a private house that had already been visited by the invaders. Everything in the house was turned upside down. He found a jacket, a hat, and some alcohol so he could treat the wounds.

For 10 to 20 minutes, Ivan lay on the sofa, trying to warm up, but this was prevented by soldiers, who again burst into the house. "I said I was the owner of the house, my family had evacuated. My face was covered in blood, I said, 'It was incoming fire.'"

The soldiers took Ivan back to headquarters in house 144, where he was given medical assistance, then led to a bunker where about two hundred civilians were hiding from the shelling.

On March 7, the Russian soldiers took everyone outside. The women and children were released first. Then the men. "They told us: 'We have come to free you!' As if to say, we're good guys. Don't take up arms, and we will let you go. I think they wanted the bunker themselves to hide from the shelling."

There are dozens of such articles. The total number of people killed in Bucha is estimated by the Ukrainians (as of summer 2023) at 422 people, but these figures are not final and are being revised upward. They find new mass graves, record testimony, and look for specific culprits from among the Russian military. Arestovych published a list of eleven military units directly involved in massacres of civilians.

The clumsy, mediocre lie of Russian propaganda that those killed in Bucha were victims of Ukraine's terrorist defense force has been repeatedly analyzed in detail by Mediazona, Meduza, and Insider. As always, the statements are haphazard: those killed died as a result of Ukrainian shelling; there were no deaths; those killed appeared after the Russian army left (although they are visible on satellite images from mid-March); the Ukrainians did this to themselves in order to have sanctions placed on Russia. Everyone! They killed everyone themselves just to have sanctions put in place! After these murders, the shamelessness of the propagandists should no longer surprise anyone— it's the idiocy that surprises one. Are they hoping for leniency in a future tribunal? It is doubtful, however, that this will be a mitigating circumstance. I am quite familiar with Russian propaganda, but I don't remember Russia doing such a mediocre job of lying, neither in Soviet nor post-Soviet times.

Zelenskyy called the day of his visit to Bucha the most terrible day in his life, perhaps also because he reproached himself for delaying the evacuation. And after this day, it was impossible not to notice the changes that took place in Zelenskyy's intonation and appearance. Ukraine and the world saw a new man—mournful, as if sprinkled with ashes, but also much more firm, filled with a samurai's readiness for revenge.

His appeal of April 3rd is perhaps the most tragic of all. I quote him with a minimum of ellipses, because, as he said himself, every word is important.

Today this address will be without greetings. I do not want any unnecessary words.

Presidents do not usually record addresses like this. But today I have to do just that. After what was revealed in Bucha and our other cities the occupiers were expelled from. Hundreds of people were killed. Tortured, executed civilians. Corpses on the streets. Mined area. Even the bodies of the dead were mined!

The pervasive consequences of looting. Concentrated evil has come to our land. Murderers. Torturers. Rapists. Looters. Who call themselves an army. And who deserve only death after what they did.

I want every mother of every Russian soldier to see the bodies of the murdered people in Bucha, in Irpin, in Hostomel. What did they do? Why were they killed? What did the man who was riding his bicycle down the street do? Why were ordinary civilians in an ordinary peaceful city tortured to death? Why were women strangled after their earrings were ripped out of their ears? How could women be raped and killed in front of children? How could their corpses be desecrated even after death? Why did they crush the bodies of people with tanks? What did the Ukrainian city of Bucha do to your Russia? How did all this become possible?

Russian mothers! Even if you raised looters, how did they also become butchers? You couldn't be unaware of what's inside your children. You couldn't overlook that they are deprived of everything human. No soul. No heart. They killed deliberately and with pleasure.

I want all the leaders of the Russian Federation to see how their orders are being fulfilled. Such orders. Such a fulfillment. And joint responsibility. For these murders, for these tortures, for these arms torn off by explosions that lie on the streets. For shots in the back of the head of tied people.

This is how the Russian state will now be perceived. This is your image.

Your culture and human appearance perished together with the Ukrainian men and women to whom you came.

I approved a decision to create a special mechanism of justice in Ukraine for the investigation and judicial examination of every crime of the occupiers on the territory of our state. The essence of this mechanism is the joint work of national and international experts: investigators, prosecutors and judges. This mechanism will help Ukraine and the world bring to concrete justice those who unleashed or in any way participated in this terrible war against the Ukrainian people and in crimes against our people. [. . .]

Everyone guilty of such crimes will be included in a special "Book of Torturers," will be found and punished.

Ukrainians!

I want you to realize that. We drove the enemy out of several regions. But Russian troops still control the occupied areas of other regions. And after the expulsion of the occupiers, even worse things can be found there. Even more deaths and tortures. Because this is the nature of the Russian military who came to our land. These are bastards who can't do otherwise. And they had such orders.

I want to be understood correctly. We do not blame the West. We do not blame anyone but the specific Russian military who did this against our people. And those who gave them orders. But we have the right to talk about indecision. About the path to such Bucha, to such Hostomel, to such Kharkiv, to such Mariupol. We have no indecision. No matter whether we are in a certain bloc or non-aligned, we understand one thing: we must be strong.

Fourteen years ago, Russia's leader in Bucharest told Western leaders that there was no such country as Ukraine. And we prove that there is such a country. It was and it will be.

We will not hide behind the strong of this world. We will not beg anyone.

Honestly, we shouldn't have asked for help with weapons to protect ourselves from this evil that came to our land. All the necessary weapons should have been given to us anyway—without requests. Because they themselves realized what evil had come, and what it had brought with it. [...]

There are the standards of the Ukrainian people. And there are the standards of the Russian occupiers. This is good and evil. This is Europe and a black hole that wants to tear it all apart and absorb it.

We will win this war. Even if individual politicians are still unable to overcome the indecision they will pass on to their successors together with their offices. [...]

No, this was not at all the Zelenskyy that Ukraine had elected in 2019. But Ukraine was not the same, and the world was not the same. On February 24, 2022, he still did not understand this. By April 3, he had no doubts left.

VII. FECES

There must definitely be a chapter about shit, no matter how awkward it may look. Bucha was not only tortured and shot up. Bucha was so polluted that further life there would be possible only for those able to overcome abomination and squeamishness.

The philosopher Alexander Filonenko told me about one fact that struck him almost more than all the other Buchan atrocities: In the houses occupied by Russian soldiers, everything but the bathrooms were smeared with feces. Probably, Filonenko explained, these latrines seemed too clean and shiny to Russian soldiers to easily perform their natural needs there.

There is always a lot of shit in war. George Orwell wrote about this more accurately than others in *Homage to Catalonia*: "Sometimes it gave you a sneaking sympathy with the Fascist ex-owners to see the way the militia treated the buildings they had seized. In La Granja every room that was not in use had been turned into a latrine—a frightful shambles of smashed furniture and excrement. The little church that adjoined it, its walls perforated by shell-holes, had its floor inches deep in dung. In the great courtyard where the cooks ladled out the rations the litter of rusty tins, mud, mule dung, and decaying food was revolting [. . .] [The village] did not possess and never had possessed such a thing as a lavatory or a drain of any kind, and there was not a square yard anywhere where you could tread without watching your step. The church had long been used as a latrine; so had all the fields for a quarter of a mile round. I never think of my first two months at war without thinking of wintry stubble fields whose edges are crusted with dung."

Enough has also been written about the sacred—and I do not exaggerate—attitude of Russians toward feces. Here is Andrei Sinyavsky ("River and Song," 1984), one of the greatest experts on Russian literature and the Russian character:

> Wherever won't a Russian defecate! On the street, in an alleyway, in a park, in a telephone booth, in a building entryway. There is some comma in our whimsical nature that pushes us to neglect the conveniences of civilization and relieve our needs in a relaxed, cheerful manner, despite the fear of being caught red-handed—in a park, a bathhouse, a movie house, or the footboard of a tramcar . . .

However, nothing in Rus' is as desecrated as our "monuments of folk architecture," protected by the authorities from the lawlessness of the church—until special orders are issued. Is a deserted place conducive to intimacy? What else can a lonely person do in an empty place? He'll take off his pants, feel like Voltaire for a minute, and run. And this isn't just stupidity or barbarity. On the contrary. One senses in it a persistent will in the fight against an enemy, and our passion for proving in practice that matter is primary, and the human mind is fearless. Oh, how the daring Russian soul just loves a risk. And how much bold invention and inexhaustible inventiveness there is! In one thirteenth-century cathedral I was fortunate enough to discover the flirtatious trace of one truth-seeker, who left a neat pile right beneath the cupola, on a dizzying beam stretching from one corner to the other: he wasn't worried about falling . . . What kind of *idée fixe* and determination must one hold under one's belt in order to climb up there, balance yourself, and risk your life?

But even before Sinyavsky—to be sure, with less talent—the Soviet classic Maxim Gorky pontificated on this topic, in an essay about Lenin, no less:

I recall this loathsome fact: In 1919, in St. Petersburg, there was a congress of the "poor folk from the countryside." Several thousand peasants had come from the northern provinces of Russia, and hundreds of them were placed in the Romanov Winter Palace. When the congress ended and these people left, it turned out that they had not only polluted all the palace's bathrooms, but also a huge number of the most valuable Sevres, Saxonian, and Oriental vases, using them as chamber pots. This was not done out of necessity—the palace latrines were entirely in order, and the water supply was working. No, this hooliganism was an expression of the desire to spoil and discredit beautiful things. During two revolutions and a war, I hundreds of times observed this dark, vengeful desire of people to break, distort, ridicule, and defame the beautiful.

That is, they apparently didn't shit in the toilets—they were too beauti-ful. It would have been a shame to shit in such luxury, to say nothing of not even having to squat.

Stanislav Lem, in a letter to his translator (published in the collection *Resistance of Matter*, 2002), also noticed this feature of the Russian con-sciousness—using the example of soldiers who had come to liberate the Poles:

> No animals demonstrate the, so to speak, FECAL FIXATION, that the Russians demonstrated when they permeated and clogged bombed-out living rooms, hospital wards, bidets, and water closets with their excrement, defecating on books, carpets, and altars. It was the "excretization" of the entire world, which they now COULD— what a joy (!)—raze to the ground, grind into dust, and cover with shit. On top of that, they could rape and kill (they raped women after childbirth, women after heavy operations, they raped women laying in pools of blood, they raped and shat). Moreover, they FELT COMPELLED to steal wristwatches. One sad little ill-bred soldier of theirs lying among Germans in the hospital no longer had such an opportunity because his predecessors had taken everything that could be taken. He burst into tears from the insult of it while simul-taneously shouting that if he didn't get a WRISTWATCH immedi-ately, he would shoot the first three people he met.

Lem explained this feature of Russian behavior—as well as the behavior of Russians in general—by the fact that they are a people "with truncated values."

> Betraying one's relatives, betraying friends to be tormented, lying at every step, living in falsehood from cradle to grave, trampling on the traditional values of culture, alongside the fossilization of certain for-mal aspects of this culture. It all becomes obvious that this raping, demolishing, and shitting is one side of a coin, while the other is

Soviet puritanism, Victorianism, "national allegiance," "patriotism," "communist morality," etc.

All this was labeled as Russophobia in 2002. Today it looks like a very delicate statement of the obvious.

Bucha was utterly befouled, on purpose, and with pleasure. The occupiers were not embarrassed by the fact that they were shitting right next to their own sleeping quarters. As suggested by Sinyavsky, the defiling of Bucha was an act of defiance in principle: it was a sacred act to break in and befoul everything but those places that were intended for it. As I was finishing this book, a message came from the village of Bohorodychne in the Donetsk region, which had been liberated from the Russian occupiers (it is about 40 kilometers, or 25 miles from Izium): "They ran away so quickly that they even left half-cooked pasta on the stove. And shit. Mountains of shit. They shat everywhere—in the school where they lived, in houses, even in the church of the local monastery. Here they established a privy right behind the altar." Ukrainian military journalist Oleksii Kashporovskyy reported this on September 11, 2023, on his Facebook timeline.

Shitting behind the altar is not mere common negligence, and not even blasphemy. This is service to a new, unprecedented religion, the desire to present to God and people not so much the best, but rather the only thing that exists. This is the only trustworthy Russian export item. Bucha—like this entire war as a whole—represents the shit that so generously has spilled over Russian borders; it is an export, this expanse of human waste. Actually, Russia has exported nothing else for the longest of times. Oil is the devil's excrement, as the Spanish essayist and novelist Carmen Rigalt put it. However, in 2016, the American Pacific Laboratory learned how to distill excrement into gasoline using hydrothermal liquefaction, so their common chemical nature is no longer a secret to anyone.

There are two opposing trends in Russian society. On one hand, there is the sacralization of feces, whereby its significance is exaggerated. To pollute means to mark, to annex, to make something one's own. On the other hand, with the obvious anal fixation characteristic of infantile communities and similar individuals, the process of defecation itself is extremely uncomfortable and dirty, so making a restroom clean is somehow blasphemous. Look at you, you want to take a sterile shit! No! The process of producing shit should stink, be shameful, and unembellished by anything civilized; for civilization, as opposed to culture, as Spengler noted, is a concept hated by conservatives, the guardians of tradition. Civilization strives to make everything bearable, to paint it up, to clean it up; but life should be unbearable, as it is in its chthonic depths! The essence of life is its unbearable nature. Politics, hygiene, competition, the press, independent courts, basic cleanliness—all this is precisely an attempt to surround the shameful process of life (as shameful as defecation) with all sorts of little frills, bows, and souvenirs. No, it is shameful to shit in a clean place! Life should be dirty, life should be reduced to shit; hence the sacrality, but hence also the extreme inconvenience. Russian service to any cult, incidentally, is generally surrounded by many complications—hence the persistent resistance of the Church to any attempt to translate liturgical texts into Russian, to make them at least somewhat understandable. But it must not be clear! Furthermore, you are not allowed to sit during the service, there must be no benches in a cathedral! Ambiguity and inconvenience must be oppressive. And that's how it is in Russia during the performance of any cultish rite, right up to an interview with the boss, or the purchasing of food. The seller performs a sacred act, sustenance is delivered through him, as Orthodox believers ask for in their prayers. But that is precisely why the seller and the store security guard must be rude: everything sacred is carried out with maximum rudeness, inconvenience, and humiliation.

This strongly contradicts the European, and, to some extent, Ukrainian, mentality. At the train station in Przemysl, Poland, where refugees were met, fed, and allotted apartments, I spoke with a woman from Mariupol. She was youngish and very concerned about cleanliness and tidiness, even in this hot refugee summer.

"Most of all," she said, "I was afraid to leave the basement to go to the restroom." I couldn't go in a bucket in the basement, I was too ashamed.

I would go up to my apartment on the first floor. More than anything I feared they would kill me in my restroom: dying without panties is simply unthinkable!"

This inability to defecate in public, and the fear of death in the toilet, is a phenomenon of a diametrically opposed nature. It is better not to defecate than to defecate just anywhere and anyhow. Suffer it until the last minute to avoid public defecation. It is no coincidence that Putin labeled the Russian military operation in Ukraine "denazification," about which an anecdote immediately appeared: Putin, grunting, gloomily tells reporters: "Defecation has been completed."

"Vladimir Vladimirovich, did you mean denazification?" they timidly ask.

"No."

Defecation has not yet been completed, but no one has any doubts about its nature anymore.

VIII. NEGOTIATIONS

Bucha put an end to the negotiation process, which, according to the testimonies of several witnesses, had reached a decisive point by the end of March. The delegations had prepared everything for the meeting of the heads of state. But Zelenskyy said no.

These negotiations, which took place at the Regnum Carya Hotel in Belek, near Istanbul, did not evoke much optimism from the very start among Ukrainian or Russian commentators. They were attended on the Russian side by figures of the second, if not third rank: the former Minister of Culture, now presidential adviser, the historian Vladimir Medinsky, former State Duma speaker Boris Gryzlov (who found his way into history solely with the phrase "parliament is no place for a discussion"), Deputy Defense Minister Alexander Fomin, Deputy Foreign Minister Andrei Rudenko, and the then-chairman of the State Duma Committee on International Affairs Leonid Slutsky, known mainly for his harassment of, and his habitual way of, addressing women as "cute little bunny." Ah, my bias shows again! Surely he is also known for something else, since he was entrusted with leading the Liberal Democratic Party of Russia (LDPR) after the death of Vladimir Zhirinovsky? But no, nothing. None of these people had the power to decide anything. According to the evidence from the Ukrainian side, they constantly had to coordinate each position taken. Meanwhile, Medinsky is no beast, I knew him well, he taught at MGIMO at the same time I did (I taught the history of Russian literature, he taught the history of Russian diplomacy). The students loved him, and we often took smoke breaks together. He is an utter cynic, but no beast. In another era, no one would have suspected him of being a beast—terrible times have revealed everyone's essence, leaving no illusions! The average age of the Ukrainian participants was ten years younger. The Ukrainians were represented by the head of the Servant of the People faction Davyd Arakhamiia, Defense Minister Oleksii Reznikov, Deputy Foreign Minister Mykola Tochytskyy, and Advisor to the Presidential Office Mykhailo Podoliak, later one of the main public speakers on the Ukrainian side. The negotiations included (although this was not advertised) the banker, oligarch, and one of Putin's so-called wallets, Roman Abramovich, on the Russian side, and Oleksii Arestovych on the Ukrainian side.

It is from the words of Arestovych, spoken in April 2023 (on Vasily Golovanov's TV program), that we know that Russia's starting demands were virtually impossible to meet: Ukraine's non-aligned status, the recognition of the annexation of Crimea, the reduction of the army to fifty thousand soldiers, the renunciation of heavy weapons—in short, voluntary paralysis for Ukraine. But gradually, as Ukraine showed the will to resist, and NATO showed amazing solidarity, the demands of the Russian side began to soften, and soon (after a meeting in Homel and two in Brest) a direct dialogue between the ministers of internal affairs was scheduled. They had almost already agreed on a non-bloc status, the issue of Crimea was frozen and postponed, but then Zelenskyy made a second decision that changed the course of the war. The first was his refusal to evacuate, the second was his radical withdrawal from any negotiations with Russia after the entry of Ukrainian troops into Bucha.

By the beginning of April (when the Russian army left Bucha), the positions of the parties had become closer—and this was the closest rapprochement during the entire war. Russia's demands in the final wording sounded something like: "Ukraine abandons the desire to return Crimea and Donbas by military means; the security guarantees that Ukraine will receive (from Western allies) do not apply to the territory of Crimea and Donbas; Ukraine is declared to be a permanently neutral state, protected by international legal guarantees; and Ukraine would like Russia not to object to the country's accession to the EU." The Ukrainian wording was: "Discuss the issues of Crimea and Donbas separately and solidify in the agreement the positions of Ukraine and Russia on Crimea, and within fifteen years, conduct bilateral negotiations on the status of Crimea and Sevastopol. The Donbas problem should be resolved on the level of the presidents of Russia and Ukraine. Indicate in the agreement that during these fifteen years the countries will not use armed forces to solve the problem of Crimea (Kyiv still does not recognize Russia's sovereignty over Crimea). Ukraine is ready to agree to a non-aligned and non-nuclear status if there are clear guarantees from a number of countries. It undertakes not to enter into military-political alliances. International military exercises on the territory of Ukraine can only be carried out with the consent of the guarantor countries. The decision on the guarantee agreement must be made via an all-Ukrainian referendum. Potential guarantors are the UK, China, USA, Türkiye, France, Canada, Italy, Poland, and Israel. Some countries have already given preliminary consent to this."

According to Ukrainian delegation member Davyd Arakhamiia, and in accordance with the Vienna Convention, "an agreement concluded under pressure would not be considered valid, so it must be concluded after the withdrawal of troops."

I quote from an overview in *Novaya Gazeta*, which has long been banned in Russia, but continues to be published in 999 copies. Alexander Mineev: "The end of the Special Military Operation is being discussed all over the world." Officially, Zelenskyy halted and banned all negotiations with Moscow only after the annexation of four Ukrainian regions (on September

30, 2022, Russia approved the annexation to its territory of the Donetsk, Luhansk, Zaporizhzhia, and Kherson regions—Russia never controlled the latter, then soon lost it completely). Then Zelenskyy said he would not negotiate with President Putin on anything, ever. But Bucha had already placed Russia outside the negotiation process, outside the European context, outside human criteria. After that the world saw a new Zelenskyy. I think the turning point was real, by which I mean to say it was not a performance on his part. This was a man who had peered into hell, and he had very little in common with his former self.

Waffles from the Crimean children's resort of Artek are often served on the presidential train, and Zelenskyy tells journalist Dmytro Komarov: "Artek will soon be ours again." Komarov continues:

"What changed in you?"

"I realized I could kill," Zelenskyy said. "And that I want to kill them."

IX. THE COURSE OF THE WAR

War, in principle, is a rather tedious matter. That is, I can't imagine how one can write about war in an interesting way. The only war bestseller in which peacetime is absent even in the form of flashbacks is *All Quiet on the Western Front*, but even it is dominated by trench talk, food, a visit to a brothel, and quite a lot of blood and guts. This was probably the first such naturalistic depiction of war—not battles, during which, as a rule, one turns off reflection and memory, but of life in the trenches. No matter how many war books you consider, whether they are satirical, like *Catch-22*, or moderately bombastic, like *A Farewell to Arms*, or realistic, like *In the Trenches of Stalingrad*—the main thing is absent: the actual fighting. It is present either in reports, that is, as described at headquarters and in directives, or in isolated images, like strobe flashes at night. A person does not think at times like this.

Russian poet Novella Matveeva spoke of "the boredom of wars." The main emotion of all war epics is fear and boredom, boredom experienced between attacks of fear. War is endless discomfort and endless monotony.

War is more boring than any industrial production novel, because there, at least, something is still created. In war, a soldier is deprived of personal will, for he is constrained by the orders of his superiors, and the general is not much freer. Only a maniac, who usually proudly calls himself a "dog of war," is capable of loving war as a source of bloody scenes and perverted pleasures associated with the dismemberment of an enemy. Several such maniacs are immortalized by Russian writer Eduard Limonov in an essay called "Dogs of War." But Limonov also disdains ornamental flourishes: "WAR STINKS. Barracks stink, the soldiers' socks, their shoes, and their uniforms stink. Because a soldier cannot shower twice a day, as do the odorless, sterile inhabitants of European capitals. The ingredients of war perfumes are: the smell of cold, burned-out houses, the smell of corpses, the smell of urine. November 1991 near [the Croatian city of] Vukovar. A Corpse Identification Center is cordoned off with wire. As soon as I open the door of our BG-167-170, my nostrils are filled with the sweet, greasy smell of corpses. Despite the strong sub-zero temperature and the diesel fuel deliberately burned in the fires, the smell of corpses prevails."

But this war consists of more than just stench, murder, lies, tricks, and geopolitical calculations. This war ends seven centuries of Russian history, compromising once and for all this method of government and territorial growth. This war is a huge festering boil, a confirmation of everything that perceptive individuals have long suspected; the final triumph of justice, regardless of the ending. It mathematically proves the need for the collapse of a system that puts the homeland above truth, and the nation above humanity. It confirms the fears of dissidents, the conjectures of outcasts, and the fears of neurotics—of everyone who is supposed to feel at least a little more than the average person. The fate of this war will not be decided at the fronts. In fact, no one really knows what is happening there. This is probably what has happened in all wars: you know nothing until your city is captured; hence the great confusion emanating from all major clashes. One need only recall the hell of Moscow on October 16, 1941. Objectivity—which is not always so objective—is provided only by American or European correspondents who occupy, perhaps, not a neutral, but at least not a completely biased, position. (And it is precisely the cool, objective tone of these journalists remaining above the fray that irritates both sides: there can be no neutrality today!) Russian journalists, even the most liberal ones, have no access to Ukraine. Ukrainians see only the heroism of Ukrainians and the endless bloodthirstiness of Russians. Even more important, no military victory of the territorially and numerically superior Russia can mean the enslavement of Ukraine. Ukraine has decided for itself that it exists, as it were, in a posthumous space. It acts like a samurai—this war is taking place in a metaphysical realm. One nation no longer fears death, for it has already accepted death internally. The other nation has not yet been born.

This war has only one meaning: it demonstrates that Russia in its current state cannot do without war. This war, no matter how blasphemous it may sound, pleases two categories of people. The first are the maniacs, those very "dogs" who were bored and lacked grandeur without access to a big meat grinder. The second are the alarmists, who, despite all the stability in Russia in the early 2000s, sensed an unsteady quagmire, tremors, aromas of collapse and disintegration. Alarmists like me said from the very beginning that Putin's Russia was many times worse than Brezhnev's, but people objected: Oh, come on, the borders are open! And the opposition media is able to broadcast! And we have the right to private property! (As if shutting down any media source, sealing the borders and confiscating all private property is not a matter of two minutes.)

This war has neither geopolitical (generally a pseudoscientific term) nor economic meaning, while conspiracy theorists who talk about the intrigues of the entire world against Russia don't believe a word they say themselves. This is not a war to establish the new colonization of Ukraine (which is impossible by definition—the nation would have to be destroyed to the last Ukrainian). It is not a war for the decolonization of Russia, as other supporters of its normalization and routinization claim. (Russia has never been colonized by anyone, for it was already colonized by the fanatical sect of Chekists. It has all the signs of "internal colonization," as Alexander Etkind put it. The United States has never expressed a desire to capture and control this distant and fundamentally uncontrollable space.) This war is the only way to keep existing for a thoroughly immoral state that has lost all means of development aside from repression and mobilization. This war is a confirmation of the Russian philosopher Pyotr Chaadaev's worst and most radical insights. It highlights in a new way all previous Russian wars, and debunks all historical myths. It leaves nothing standing of the most stable Russian cult, that of the Motherland, which is always written with a capital letter, always right, and always justifies everything. During this current war Russia has lied so much, and has suppressed its own citizens so severely that we need not even discuss its war crimes—which it denies in the most pathetic of ways. You will know them by their fruits, and these fruits are extremely evident. This is generally the most obvious and transparent war in the last seventy years. You can argue (if you really want to argue) about whether houses in Kryvyi Rih and churches in Odesa were destroyed by Russian missiles or by fragments of Ukrainian air defense missiles falling on them, but some things are indisputable. And, by that, I mean the total dehumanization of those supporting the war, the astronomical prison sentences for members of the Russian opposition, the false deeds, the cannibalistic rhetoric, and the utter shamelessness of Russian propaganda. Against this background—which is customary in Russia—any Ukrainian excess, any idolization of Stepan Bandera, and any nationalist rhetoric cease to matter, just as all the mistakes of Dubček and his associates dissolved against the backdrop of Russian tanks in Prague. Never before have W. H. Auden's lines from 1968 received such weighty proof:

> The Ogre does what ogres can,
> Deeds quite impossible for Man,
> But one prize is beyond his reach:
> The Ogre cannot master speech.

> About a subjugated plain,
> Among its desperate and slain,
> The Ogre stalks with hands on hips,
> While drivel gushes from his lips.

There is just one meaning of this war: Regardless of all retreats and counteroffensives, regardless of the outcome of all battles and negotiations, it demonstrates the dead end of Russia's special path, and the incompatibility of such a path with the existence of the rest of the world. This is a war against human existence as such. And by leading the resistance to this anti-human project, Zelenskyy is defending not only Ukraine. It would appear now that all observers agree that the stakes are much higher. He is defending the Mankind project itself, which has never before been exposed to such danger.

So this is not a boring war, no. Nothing is ever boring when Zelenskyy is present.

X. IN PLACE OF A BLITZKRIEG

Volumes will be written (are already being written) about the Russo-Ukrainian war. I am not a military analyst, I analyze the course of the war here only to the extent that it allows us to trace the evolution of Volodymyr Zelenskyy in the years of 2022 to 2023.

In a conversation with Arestovych, Pavel Leschinsky, a journalist for the Lithuanian portal Nra.lv, said: "Humanity has always known wars, but it's hard for me to remember another war that was so ethically clear. There is a victim, there is an aggressor. There is defense of one's home and there is an attempt to seize it." Arestovych replies that Ukraine made a stupid blunder by blurring the clarity of the war somewhat, but in general, especially taking into account the colossal unprofessionalism and rudeness of Russian propaganda, we have to admit the exceptional conspicuity of the division of roles in this war. Throughout 2022, Russia persistently and rapidly broke through the bottom—both in terms of military skill, and in terms of excessive, inexplicable brutality, demonstrated first in Bucha, and then exacerbated by further failures since then. It would be wrong to say that only Ukraine learned to fight—Russia also learned something and made it extremely difficult for the Armed Forces of Ukraine to break through its defenses. But it was unable to formulate the goals of the war, or, at least, indicate the approximate end point. Attacks on civilians and civilian infrastructure did not become less frequent. The rhetoric regarding Ukraine, its army, its top officials and the countries that support it only became more obscene. We will focus on five aspects of this topic:

- The main battles of the war, and the successes of the parties;
- The number of casualties among the military and the civilian population;
- The nature and extent of Western assistance;
- The evolution of Ukrainian and Russian societies;
- Changes in the character and behavior of the leaders of the two countries.

On March 24, 2022, Zelenskyy spoke remotely at the NATO summit in Madrid.

It was a strong speech.

Dear attendees!

I am addressing you from Kyiv, our capital, which has been fighting for a month already, just as our entire country has.

Yes, it is true—we are not in the Alliance. Not in the most powerful defense union in the world. We are not one of the thirty states under the umbrella of joint protection. Under the umbrella of Article 5. It feels like we are in a "gray zone." Between the West and Russia. But we are defending all our common values. And we are a radiant people! And we have been defending all these values for a month now!

A month of heroic resistance. A month of the darkest suffering.

A month of unpunished destruction of a peaceful state, and along with it—the whole architecture of global security. All this is before the eyes of the whole world.

Over the decades, Russia has accumulated considerable resources, military resources, manpower and equipment, air bombs, missiles.

They invested insane amounts of money in death while the world invested in life. But Ukraine is holding up courageously! At the cost of thousands of lives. At the cost of destroyed cities. At the cost of almost ten million migrants. Three and a half million of them are already in your territories, in the territories of NATO countries. I am grateful for your support of these people. And people, unfortunately, continue to leave their homes. They are fleeing the terror that the occupiers brought with them.

The very first hours of the invasion meant brutal missile strikes for us. During this month of war, Russia fired more than a thousand different missiles at our cities. Made hundreds of air raids.

On February 24, I addressed you with a perfectly clear, logical request to help close our skies. In any format. Protect our people from Russian bombs and missiles. We did not hear a clear answer. Ukraine does not have powerful anti-missile weapons, we have a much smaller air force than Russia. Therefore, their advantage in the sky is equivalent to the use of weapons of mass destruction.

You see the consequences today—how many people have been killed, how many peaceful cities have been destroyed.

The Ukrainian army has been resisting for a month in unequal conditions! And I have been repeating the same thing for a month now. In order to save people and our cities, Ukraine needs military assistance without restrictions. As Russia uses its entire arsenal against us without restrictions.

It destroys all living things. Any objects—from houses to churches, from food warehouses to universities, from bridges to hospitals.

Ukraine asked for your planes. So we would not lose so many people. And you have thousands of fighter jets! But we haven't been given any yet.

We asked for tanks. So that we can unblock our cities that are now dying—Mariupol, Berdiansk, Melitopol, and others. Cities where Russia is holding hundreds of thousands of people hostage and artificially creating famine—no water, no food, nothing there.

You have no less than 20,000 tanks! Ukraine asked for a per-centage, one percent of all your tanks to be given or sold to us! But we do not have a clear answer yet.

The worst thing in a war is not having clear answers to requests for help.

Ukraine never wanted this war. And does not want to fight for years. We just want to save our people. We want to survive! Just survive! Like any nation, we have the right to that. The right to life. The right to this one percent.

I do not blame NATO. You are not beholden [to us]. It's not your fault. It's not your missiles, it's not your bombs that are destroying our cities. This morning, by the way, there were phosphorus bombs. Russian phosphorus bombs. Adults were killed again and children were killed again. I just want you to know that the Alliance still can prevent the deaths of Ukrainians from Russian strikes, from Russian occupation, by providing us with all the weapons we need.

Yes, we are not in the Alliance. And I am complaining about nothing. But Ukrainians never thought that the Alliance and the Allies were different things.

That in matters of life and death you can be a force separately, but together—no. That NATO could fear Russia's actions. I am sure you understand that Russia does not intend to stop in Ukraine. Does not intend to and will not. It wants to move further.

Against the eastern members of NATO. The Baltic states, Poland—that's for sure. Will NATO stop worrying about this, about how Russia will react? Who can be certain of that? And do you have confidence that Article 5 can work?

"Budapest" hasn't worked for us. Our Budapest Memorandum. It has not worked for peace in Ukraine.

And I will tell you honestly—[the] Budapest [Memorandum] is not working for peace in Ukraine today either. Yes, we receive help from individual members of the Alliance. I am very grateful. Ukrainians are sincerely grateful for this. To each of you who gives what you have, for supporting us.

But what about the Alliance? The question of Article 5 is fundamental. I just want you to know that this is on our minds. And I sincerely hope, for your sake, that we are wrong in our assessments and in our doubts. And that it is true that you have a powerful

Alliance. If we are wrong, the world is safe. But if we are even just one percent right, I ask you to reconsider your attitude. Your own estimates.

And to truly take measures in matters of security, security in Europe and, consequently, in the world.

You can give us one percent of all your aircraft. One percent of all your tanks. One percent! We can't simply buy them. Such supplies depend directly only on NATO's decisions, on political decisions, by the way.

MLRS systems. Anti-ship weapons. Means of air defense. Is it possible to survive such a war without these?

Consequently, when all of this is finally available, it will give us, and you as well, one hundred percent security. The only thing I request of you . . . after such a month of war. This is a request for the sake of our soldiers. After such a war against Russia . . . Never, please, never tell us again that our army does not meet NATO standards.

We have shown what our standards are capable of. And how much we can contribute to the common security in Europe and the world.

How much we can do to protect against aggression against everything that we value, everything you value. But NATO has yet to show what the Alliance can do to protect people. To show that it truly is the most powerful defense union in the world. The world is waiting. Ukraine is waiting. Our proposals are on the table. Our requests are on the table. We need peace now. The answers are up to you.

I am thankful to those who help us! Thank you!

Glory to Ukraine!

It was a very emotional speech, almost free verse, but unlike the goal of poetry, the speech had the purpose of bringing about immediate action. Boris Johnson supported Zelenskyy more fervently than anyone. Johnson insisted on providing Ukraine with sufficient military aid to contain Russia's onslaught, and proposed considering the matter of Ukraine's place in NATO over time.

An enhanced package of just such armed assistance was approved, and Ukraine received a multi-year program of support. Total military aid to Kyiv received from NATO countries was estimated at $65 billion. But Zelenskyy needed at least an invitation, at least a road map, at least clearly defined conditions for entry into NATO. This did not happen either in Madrid or, a year and three months later, in Vilnius. By the end of summer 2022, that is, before the total destruction of Mariupol, some NATO leaders hoped to maintain channels of interaction with Russia. The turning point occurred in the fall, when Ukraine began to take revenge.

After the blitzkrieg failed in its plan to capture Kyiv in three days, and Ukraine in ten; after the physical elimination of Zelenskyy failed and the formation of a puppet pro-Russian government ceased to be relevant, Russian strategy changed. God knows what made Vladimir Putin believe that Ukraine would greet him with flowers. Perhaps every leader, spoiled by a long tenure, loses access to objective information and becomes a hostage to his own environment. One way or another, after minor personnel changes and castigations invisible to the world, Russia switched to Plan "B," that is, to slowly wear down the enemy in the hope that the West's patience would run out and military assistance would stop, while Ukraine's own population would overthrow the government or force it to capitulate. (Was there a risk of termination of Western assistance? Zelenskyy told journalist Dmytro Komarov point blank that without the first significant victories of the Ukrainian Armed Forces, no one would have seriously invested in this assistance.)

Mykhailo Podoliak announced that there were ten attempts on Zelenskyy's life in the first weeks of the war. The *Times* (London) wrote about three. In the first week of the war, the Russians captured Kupiansk and Berdiansk, occupied Kherson, and the Zaporizhzhia nuclear power plant. In Kherson Russian tanks were met by protest demonstrations of civilians (they were brutally dispersed, including with tear gas, but they came out again and again shouting, "Kherson is Ukraine!" Full-fledged police terror was established in the city. Russia claimed it had returned to the city forever, but it did not enjoy the slightest support among the local population. In early March, the city of Volnovakha in the southwest of the Donetsk region was completely destroyed, and the same fate awaited Mariupol which had been blockaded since the first days of the war.

Snake Island in the Black Sea in the Ochakov district of the Odesa region is very small (0.2 square kilometers), but it controls the approaches to three ports. On February 24, the following dialogue took place between sailors of the Russian cruiser Moskva and Ukrainian border guards:

"Snake Island, we are a Russian warship. To avoid bloodshed, we propose you lay down your arms and surrender. Otherwise, you will be hit. Do you hear me, Snake? Over."

"Russian warship, go fuck yourself!" replied border guard Roman Hrybov, who later patented this phrase. It adorns many Ukrainian badges, T-shirts, and billboards.

Snake Island was captured by Russia (according to Zelenskyy 13 border guards died, 82 were captured, 19 were exchanged). On April 13, the Russian cruiser Moskva sank after being hit by a Ukrainian Neptune missile, and on June 30, Snake Island itself was completely liberated.

It was not possible to completely capture the Donetsk region. Facing difficulty and sacrifices, Russian troops reached the borders of Luhansk. In April 2022, there was continuous shelling of the city of Rubezhne, and amid this hell, the National Guard of Ukraine picked up two boys, brothers aged five and nine, on the street. There were no adults with them. They said their father had gone to work in Poltava, and that their mother had gone to buy groceries but did not return, so they were looking for her. They were taken to a hospital in Sievierodonetsk. These children ended up in Dmytro Komarov's film *The Year*. The five-year-old boy, whom everyone called Petrovich, became a favorite in the hospital, and, when he was shown on TV on February 24, 2023, throughout the whole of Ukraine. Indeed, he is an absolutely charming boy and he speaks beautifully. He said that a rocket fell near their house, "and only small pieces of the house remained." It was absolutely impossible to watch, especially when he asked to be taken to his father. But he did not cry, he held himself together well. His mother was found later: the Russians had grabbed her right on the street when she was out trying to buy food, and they had taken her to one of the captured administrative buildings, where she was suspected of being a Ukrainian spy. Then they let her go, thank God, but when she returned home, her house was demolished and her children were nowhere to be seen. Thanks to the film, however, they were found and reunited. This episode with Petrovich, who talks about the remaining small pieces of his house, should be shown to everyone who considers the fate of the children of Donbas and Luhansk, children whom the Russians ostensibly came to protect with protection of such a nature. I seriously doubt that this Petrovich will ever forget, much less forgive, what happened to him, although everything did end well for him. At least for the time being. Meanwhile, the Z-poets wonder why no one loves them the way Soviet citizens loved the patriotic writer Konstantin Simonov during World War II. And this is why: Simonov once wrote, "The major brought in a boy on a gun carriage. His mother had died, and the son was not able to say goodbye to her. Those ten days will be counted in his favor as ten years in this and the afterworld . . . I must look on with eyes that had wept there in the dust as that boy returned with us and kissed a handful of his country's earth." As for the Z-poets, here is what they write for modern children: "The village is lucky today. The soldiers cleared the village. Another village will be just as fortunate; our soldiers will enter it any minute. Then the military broom will clear a third village, and the world will be clean, without any fascists." This poem is called "Children," and you can sense the difference. The author, a forty-nine-year-old director and a graduate of the Literary Institute, says he has felt happiness only during this war, in it he felt needed for the first time in his life. He is terribly proud of himself.

Someone might ask me: Don't you feel sorry for the children of Donbas? Those who have died since 2014? Yes, it's terribly painful, unbearably painful. But who started the hostilities in Donbas? Wasn't it Igor Strelkov who told proudly and floridly, in his restorationist manner, how he triggered the beginning of the war? Didn't he write about how the locals didn't want to fight, and he literally had to chase them with bullets? Did anyone rebel against the new government wherever there were no Russian *ikhtamnets*—

"those who are not there"? Did Maidan degrade Donbas to the state which it now is in? And is it the Ukrainian government that mobilizes there now without consideration either of age or health status? Donbas was used, and now it is completely destroyed. Read Viber chats from Rubezhne, they are widely available on the Internet: "When the so-called liberators came into our neighborhood, the first thing they did was run from apartment to apartment to find new clothes, and threw their old rags out right outside the doors. Thank God, there were many witnesses"; "Soldiers of the Luhansk People's Republic lived in my apartment, and every day they took something from it, whether a telephone or a slow cooker." On the Russian, not Ukrainian, site rubezhnoe.com, this information goes right through the roof. This is Petrovich's homeland. So many messages about pillaging, and of what kind! The Meduza, Important Stories, and Signal portals wrote about the notorious washing machines, refrigerators, and toilets that were transported by truck to Russia—all with photographs taken on stolen phones. This war is well documented, and no one was particularly shy.

Perhaps the most tragic story was that of Mariupol. The city was blockaded on March 2. Azovstal, a metallurgical plant where about two thousand Ukrainian military personnel were concentrated, refused to surrender. The Rossiya channel aired a documentary by Russian journalist-propagandist Andrei Medvedev about Mariupol, where he constantly mentioned Ukrainian atrocities against civilians. (The Ukrainians made their own film, *20 Days in Mariupol*, directed by Mstislav Chernov; it premiered at the 2023 Sundance Film Festival.) Before the war, 450,000 people lived in Mariupol. Three hundred fifty thousand people fled the city when the fighting began. And here I am faced with the problem that ultimately forced me to take on the biography of my hero, rather than to write a novel about recent events.

Director and cameraman Chernov, photographer Yevhen Maloletka, and producer Vasilisa Stepanova were the last journalists to remain in occupied Mariupol. Twenty days later they escaped, and after another eighty-six days the city was . . . no, not seized, but was utterly destroyed by Russia. Razed to the ground. Now they are restoring it with horrible pageantry. They trotted out the popular Moscow actor Yevgeny Mironov to perform there, and he promised to take patronage over the city's restored theater, posing for pictures with survivors. But who cares about Mironov?! One of Putin's doubles went there and hung out with residents, not even maintaining hygienic distance! True, he went there during the night so that people, God forbid, would not see or say too much, and no one would be able to shout out that he had destroyed the city.

The children of Mariupol were dragged to a concert in Moscow's Luzhniki stadium to mark the anniversary of the so-called "special operation," as a result of which people were specially deprived of anything human that they had left. So here's the problem (I watched Chernov's film, I could do that in the States): No evidence, no chronicle conveys the horror of Mariupol. I believe that Mariupol is, in general, the worst catastrophe of this war, for everything is so compact. See for yourself: three hospitals in the city were completely destroyed, and four were partially destroyed. That is, one survived. Nine-tenths of the housing was destroyed. The number of those killed and those who died from wounds is estimated at 75,000. This is approximate, we do not know the exact numbers. Humanity has already decided how to talk about such things: prose doesn't work, fiction is offensive. The Soviet-Belarusian writer Ales Adamovich once suggested that what is needed is not prose, but super-prose, not writers' "speculation-imagination-condensation-standarization," but the voices of surviving witnesses, their documentary recordings. Nothing else will work. But here's a terrible paradox: these artless eyewitness stories don't work either, precisely because of their bare simplicity. A person who has experienced horror is, as it were, paralyzed, frozen. He observes without comprehending, and the result is a briefing rather than a narration. It might terrify you, but it does not force you to imagine and experience it all as it was. Apparently, the only way to talk about war is to not be in a war. War destroys the ability to experience and empathize. One grows accustomed to it, it wears you thin. Otherwise, no one would survive.

Russian television, when Chernov's first reports appeared via the Associated Press (no more than half an hour, because the Internet disappeared almost immediately in the city), called it all a "production with extras." When

Chernov showed the full, 95-minute film, it became clear to everyone that this was not a matter of production or editing. This is how Russia liberates a city without shooting at civilians. The most terrible thing there is women giving birth as bombs fall. Russia struck a maternity hospital on March 9. One woman in labor was wounded, and she later died along with her child. It is most unbearable to look at children in these circumstances, but it was precisely the children of Mariupol who had lost their parents that the Russian authorities dragged to a concert at Luzhniki. And these children there thanked a Russian soldier with the call sign of Angel for saving them as he did. This "Angel," as it turned out, was a man named Yury Gagarin, a former businessman and FSB employee (he is in uniform in some photographs on social media). The girl who thanked him on stage at Luzhniki was a teenager from a troubled family, thirteen-year-old Ania Naumenko, whose mother was mortally wounded when she left the basement to get cigarettes. Her stepfather fled in the first days of the occupation, and the fate of her brother and sister (from other fathers) is unknown. All this—Angel's biography and the girl's story—was later unearthed by Russian and Ukrainian journalists, and even a news story in occupied Donbas exposed the story of Angel. The bombs struck the very heart of Russian—and Donetsk—life, and unleashed ungodly deeds. The life of this one single girl, who was accustomed from early childhood to surviving without maternal care and who therefore adapted to the blockade more quickly than others, could serve as the basis of our proposed novel, but what cynicism would be required to write such a novel! Here's the thing: those who died were not saints, and the attackers were not just Orcs, although many of them derived pleasure from committing atrocities they never paid for. This war has served only to reveal polarization—the extreme dehumanization of some, and the fantastic ability of others to endure. But aside from this, it also has revealed the unimaginable vitality of those who previously had survived with difficulty. It was people like these among the combatants who comprised the majority—the rest managed to escape either from occupation or from mobilization. What a finale the scene in Luzhniki would make to our novel, when Ania Naumenko, confused, begins to recite: "Uncle Angel saved hundreds of thousands of children in Mariupol . . . oh, I forget the rest!" So the emcee prompts her, trying not to save hundreds of thousands of children, but trying to save the situation at hand: "Go on, give Uncle Angel a hug! Don't be embarrassed!" What embarrassment?! Nothing has embarrassed anyone for ages! Ania Naumenko clings awkwardly to Uncle Angel, who was once on the wanted list for doing illegal business, and even he finds it somewhat awkward.

Many of the children from Mariupol were taken to Russian orphanages where conditions of torture are common, all under the pretext of rescuing them. Meanwhile, the Ukrainian authorities never gave permission for the removal of their citizens from Ukrainian territory, and are now engaged in intensive searches for them. Daria Herasymchuk, Zelenskyy's adviser on children's rights, said that 16,226 children were taken to Russia—and these are just those whose names are known. In Crimea alone there are 43 camps where children from Ukraine are subjected to psychological indoctrination. It was for these kidnapped children that Vladimir Putin, together with Russian Commissioner for Children's Rights Maria Lvova-Belova, were put on the international wanted list, and warrants were issued for their arrest. This was done by the International Criminal Court in The Hague personally by Judge Tomoko Akane, who, in turn, was immediately placed on the wanted list in Russia. There is little chance she will ever go to Russia, however, while it is much more likely that sooner or later Putin will have to travel to a territory that recognizes the ICC. For the time being he even must participate in the BRICS summit remotely, for who knows what grand idea might come to someone there in South Africa.

But these are all distractions so as not to talk about Mariupol. On March 16, Russia struck the Mariupol Drama Theater, where thousands of people were taking refuge at that time. The deaths of 1,348 residents of Mariupol, including 70 children, were documented there. There was no water, food, or electricity in the city. There were more than 500 civilians at the Azovstal factory which was defended by the Azov battalion. Zelenskyy conducted negotiations with the UN to organize their evacuation. Only on May 19 did the defenders of Azovstal begin to surrender—there were about 2,000 of them (Russian Minister of Defense Sergei Shoigu put the figure at 1,908).

Officials in Russia competed among themselves in their barbarous thoughts, demanding the execution of the trapped individuals. Putin's press secretary Dmitry Peskov promised that prisoners of war would be guaranteed humane treatment. Macron tried to persuade Putin to stop shelling the city. Putin responded that the shelling would stop after Ukraine surrendered. Some of the Azov fighters (about 300 people) were transferred to Ukraine in an exchange, more than 50 died in the explosion of a colony in Eleonovka, in the Donetsk region (the DPR claimed that Ukraine fired at the colony, while Ukraine stated that the Russians blew it up to hide the traces of the brutal treatment of prisoners. Experts determined that, judging by the destruction, the charge was placed inside the building). Twenty-four more (of which nine were women) went on trial in the Russian city of Rostov, although the Geneva Convention prohibits public trials of prisoners.

Only someone with an active imagination can imagine what these people experienced by way of hunger and cold in a blockaded city under constant shelling, amid the equally constant filtration that revealed the identity of Ukrainian military personnel. As for someone lacking such an imagination, we could never wish such an experience upon them. It can only be compared to the conditions of the Leningrad blockade in 1941. Meanwhile, Russia described this all as liberation. All the documentation and evidence was labeled as falsified and trumped-up, as Banderite propaganda. Zelenskyy constantly and desperately looked for mediators to negotiate humanitarian corridors, and guarantees for those who surrendered. At this time, he generated unprecedented international activity, emphasizing in all his speeches that there were two ways to save the residents of Mariupol and the Ukrainian military—a military path and a diplomatic path. But there were not enough weapons to pursue the military path, one was compelled to resort to diplomacy. Speaking before the parliament of South Korea (speeches before parliaments took place almost daily at that time), he said: "The worst situation is in Mariupol. Mariupol has been destroyed. There are tens of thousands of dead there. But even despite this, the Russians do not stop their offensive operation. They want to make sure that Mariupol is a demonstrably destroyed city. Through missile and air strikes, Russia has already destroyed hundreds of infra-structure facilities responsible for economic and social life in Ukraine. Among them are oil depots, airports, food warehouses and various other enterprises. Nine hundred thirty-eight educational institutions and 300 hospitals have been destroyed."

It was very difficult at this time for Zelenskyy to combine his search for a way out of the situation, while maintaining his personal dignity, and continuing the constant attempts to convey to the world the truth about the catastrophic situation. He could not complain and could not press for pity. He had to act in a tragic role, not a sentimental one. He had to become an emblem of heroic resistance, and emphasize the readiness to resist no mat-ter what—a task that no mere politician could cope with. Zelenskyy coped, becoming the face of a nation struggling desperately. It seemed impossible to imagine that three years ago this man could make any audience laugh, and entertained Ukraine with comic stand-up routines. It was an unthink-able transformation, grotesque, and unprecedented in history. I remember, perhaps, only one person in a similar situation—Georgy Vasilyev, one of the composers of *Nord-Ost*, the musical that was attacked by terrorists in Moscow in 2002. He remained with the hostages in a hall overflowing with explosives. He had to console the hostages, negotiate with the militants, and seek guarantees from the authorities. By his own admission, he had written off his own life. But Vasilyev was responsible for a thousand people, while Zelenskyy was responsible for forty million. And he managed publicly to present the surrender of Mariupol—a heavy, demoralizing defeat—as a demonstration of incredible resilience, a moral victory, for even among the most ignorant and dismal regimes existing on Earth, not a single one would support Putin in his systematic, three-month destruction of the city, accompanied by his mocking of its heroic defenders. Previously, the Azov battalion had an ambiguous reputation in the eyes of the world. They were, after all, comprised of nationalists and far-right activists, and were not part of the regular army, but were a kind of free-standing militia; but now "Azov" became synonymous with courage throughout the whole world, while the Azovstal citadel was seen as something like the Brest Fortress which heroically held off Hitler's forces for a week at the beginning of World War II. The Azov brigade, created in 2014, was perceived ambiguously in Ukraine itself at that time—but when Zelenskyy brought many of its members home in 2023 following a prisoner exchange negotiated in Türkiye, they were greeted as saints. Margarita Simonyan, head of the Rossyia Segodnya media group, posted on Twitter regarding Turkish president Recep Tayyip Erdogan, who brokered the return of the brigade members to Ukraine: "Mother," she wrote in reference to all of Russia, "must we swallow this too?"

Zelenskyy at this time had to take on the roles of savior, defender, and supplicant. He had to remind the world what it would be up against if it did not now help stop the most dangerous aggressor in history. He stopped joking and punning a long time ago, his speech became dry and abrupt, and he was no longer ashamed of the hatred he felt. In the Easter days of 2022, Russia shelled Odesa, killing a mother and daughter as the father survived by going out to the store. The whole of Ukraine, in fact, the whole world, gazed upon Odesa resident Yurii Hlodan, who had lost his wife and three-month-old daughter, while Zelenskyy shouted into the camera: "Here you see the Easter days we are having! Amazing! Seven missiles arrived in Odesa today, seven missiles. We shot down two. One rocket hit a multistory building. Eight people—right now, right at this moment—eight people are dead, 18 or 20 are injured. A three-month-old child was killed. The war began when this child was a month old. Can you imagine? What is going on? The stinking scum. What else can you call them? There are no other words. Just scum. And on days like these! They don't give a damn about anything. Who is their god? What are they talking about? What are their values? What is their world like? The Russian world, a Christian world? The Middle Ages. I have no strength left. Just seven missiles tossed at Odesa. Their beloved Odesa. They call it 'Odesa-Mama,' it's their favorite, it's where they loved to come."

This was no nervous breakdown. It was not impotent anger. It was unbearable suffering, and there was no need to imitate it. Zelenskyy knows how to understand and imagine someone else's tragedy. It's his profession.

A professional politician would have found other words. He found "stinking scum," the strongest phrase that could be said while remaining inside the bounds of decency. Before the whole world he was losing hope of maintaining mutual understanding and good neighborliness with the Russians, at least with some Russians. This was a renunciation of all of Russia and forever, because everything being done was being done on behalf of all of Russia, with no divisions into who was good and who was bad. And there were no ideological divisions in Ukraine at that moment. No one could have guessed at what price unity would be bought.

Another important process also took place at this time, also launched by Russia, and it was especially sinister in terms of its prospects. Of all deteriorations, the primary one is the loss of nuance, a flattening out. War leaves no shades, and it compels you to choose between two. That same ethical clarity led not only to the fact that one side finally turned black and the other white: it also led to the fact that Zelenskyy, a complex, ambiguous man with a rich inner world, was forced to begin thinking in flat coordinates. All that remains is what is beneficial to Ukraine, and what is good for Russia. Not only did the space for compromise disappear, but also the space for ambiguity. And for him, whose political victory came under the sign of this very ambiguity, who was expected to escape simplistic black-and-white coordinates, there was now no other value system left.

Sergei Berezhnoi, once a St. Petersburg science-fiction writer and critic, and now a Kyiv journalist, warned me back in 2019 that Zelenskyy would have to rule in a divided society, then Berezhnoi himself did everything in his power to ensure that the split into supporters of the old Poroshenko and the new Zelenskyy grew worse and more radical. Immediately after his campaign victory, however, Zelenskyy called for unification, and it seemed that things were working out for him against the backdrop of COVID. Now, however, Russia left him no other choice. Zelenskyy had to acquire authoritarian traits of a kind he had shown a penchant for in his infancy back in his producer days. They now turned out to be necessary and essential.

XI. THE JULY SCANDAL

The largest instance of reshuffling in the Ukrainian security forces during the war was the resignation of Ivan Bakanov and Iryna Venediktova, the acceptance of which was signed by Zelenskyy on July 17, 2022. Bakanov was the head of the Security Forces of Ukraine (SBU), Venediktova was the prosecutor general.

Bakanov was considered a close friend of Zelenskyy's. He made a rapid career, like many of his mates from school and the Block. From 2017 to 2019 he was chairman of the Servant of the People party, subsequently the first deputy head of the Ukrainian Security Forces (chief of the anti-corruption department), and from May 27, 2019, he was the acting head of the security forces (replacing Vasyl Gritsak, who pointedly did not greet Zelenskyy during the inauguration; he was considered a hawk, and insisted on a visa regime with Russia). Zelenskyy spoke about the large number of traitors in the security forces in April 2022, demoting General Andrii Naumov (dismissed from the security forces nine months earlier) and Serhii Krivoruchko, the former head of the security forces department in the Kherson region. On the same day, an announcement was made about the detention of Oleh Kulinich, the head of the Crimean department of the SBU, who had temporarily moved to Kherson.

In another televised address, Zelenskyy explained the resignations:

As of today, 651 criminal proceedings have been registered regarding treason and collaboration activities of employees of prosecutor's offices, pretrial investigation bodies, and other law enforcement agencies. In 198 criminal proceedings, the relevant persons were informed of the suspicion. More than 60 employees of the prosecutor's office and the SBU remained in the occupied territory and are working against our state. Such an array of crimes against the foundations of the national security of the state, and the connections that have been recorded between members of the Ukrainian security forces and the Russian intelligence services, raise very serious questions for the relevant leaders. Each of these questions will receive a proper answer.

Looking ahead, let's note that Ukraine did not find reason to continue action against Bakanov. A case was not filed against him, and he remains in Ukraine. (In Russia they hastened to report that he was under investigation and had escaped.) Many of Zelenskyy's opponents who demanded radical purges perceived this as an encouragement of high treason. In general, it would be naïve to think that one belligerent side can be better than the other in everything: repression, suspicion, and even collaboration are contagious.

Kulinich was Bakanov's advisor. Many Ukrainian media sources repeated the story that he was part of the same criminal group as former Deputy Secretary of the Security and Defense Council Volodymyr Sivkovych, who moved to Russia in 2014. The recruitment of Ukrainian officials was carried out by the 5th service of Russia's FSB, and was personally supervised by the head of the 9th directorate of the operational information department of the 5th service of the FSB of the Russian Federation, Ihor Chumakov. There was much talk in both Ukraine and Russia about the fact that Ukrainian law enforcement agencies were packed with Russian agents. The State Bureau of Investigation came to the conclusion that many personnel decisions—for example, the dismissal without explanation of the deputy head of the SBU Ruslan Baranetsky in July 2021—were carried out in direct contact with the leadership of the FSB. The text describing the suspicions raised against Sivkovych, released by the Russian security forces, directly links his activities with the Russian special services. For example, Kulinich, at the instigation of Sivkovych, lobbied for General Naumov's appointment to the SBU instead of Baranetsky. Let us recall that Zelenskyy fired Naumov in that very same July 2021.

Those media outlets taking a balanced position were careful not to accuse Bakanov of betrayal, and blamed him only for his inexperience. If you don't want to root out treason later, you shouldn't appoint childhood friends to prime operational positions. But there are also plenty of those—they grew especially active in April 2023—who accuse Zelenskyy of conniving with spies, blaming him for not finding the time to speak openly about Bakanov's connections to the FSB. "Supporting and protecting Yermak, Tatarov, Demchenko, Bakanov, Kulinich, Naumov, Hetmantsev in close proximity to the president, and protecting Sivkovych from criminal prosecution, is an eloquent response. Zelenskyy is afraid that if he surrenders all the scoundrels, they won't remain silent, but will betray him themselves," writes Ukrainian journalist Yurii Butusov, founder and head of the All-Ukrainian Fund for the Defense of National Security. Butusov's influence on Ukrainian society is not great, but he is not alone in his accusations. Ukraine entered the stage of a witch hunt, but it could not do otherwise. All future failures would be explained away by Russian espionage—and if Zelenskyy did not surrender his own people, attacks would have begun on him. In essence, he was a hostage to the situation. Either he would have had to feed someone to the clamoring crowd—or become food himself. In general, he was not inclined to surrender his people, and what strategy he would have to choose regarding the inevitable radicalization of patriots was still a question at that time.

By mid-2023 this radicalization had reached the point where hatred of Russians had become omnipresent. Still unable to deal with Putin and his team, Ukrainian society attacked Russian liberals. This may be predictable, but it is significant.

XII. KORBAN

One of Zelenskyy's main internal problems in the summer of 2022 was the matter of Hennadii Korban. The published (more precisely, leaked), unsigned order to deprive several Ukrainian oligarchs of citizenship was never verified, except for the fact that Korban was indeed not allowed into the territory of Ukraine after traveling to visit his family, and his Ukrainian passport was confiscated. On July 28, 2022, Zelenskyy officially confirmed that Korban had been deprived of his citizenship "on the basis of current legislation" (without specifying which clause of this legislation he violated; according to the Constitution of Ukraine—a document of direct effect—no one can be deprived of Ukrainian citizenship). At the time this chapter was being written, Korban was in Poland, although there was no exact information about his whereabouts. He claimed that a criminal case had been opened against him and a number of his employees. At the same time, he continued to be the head of the defense headquarters in Dnipro. His Telegram account, a year after he was deprived of citizenship, accepted all complaints about municipal problems, such as clogged sewers or burnt-out lighting—and these city problems were solved as best they could be.

The situation with Korban—the reasons for which remain "under wraps"—was the first evidence of a widely discussed belief that Zelenskyy was beginning to clean Ukraine out and, in place of local initiatives, thanks to which Ukraine survived, was beginning to encourage the establishment of a vertical power structure. Dnipro's Mayor Borys Filatov described this precisely in a letter he wrote defending Korban: it was signed by more than a hundred businessmen and public opinion leaders in Dnipro.

Using Korban's example, it is perhaps easiest to show the fundamental differences between the Ukrainian oligarchy and the Russian one—and at the same time the reasons why Russian methods of "de-oligarchization" in Ukraine are unlikely to work.

Hennadii Korban received me on June 27, 2022, in his office on 58 Starokazatska Street where Dnipro TV, the city's main TV channel controlled by him, is located on the ground floor. He immediately said he had many complaints against Zelenskyy (primary among them the fact that, having been warned about the exact time of the start of hostilities, Zelenskyy refused to believe this information and did nothing, thus leading to the tragedies of Irpen and Bucha). But he was prepared to pursue these claims only after the war because, for the time being, the Supreme Commander-in-Chief was beyond criticism. At the very least such criticism must be expressed only behind the scenes.

Dnipro's mayor Borys Filatov was present at the meeting—the only doctor of jurisprudence among Ukraine's mayors, a motorcyclist, a diver with three hundred dives, and the main Netsuke collector in Ukraine—and he told me: You don't quite understand how Ukrainian politics works. The president here does not decide everything; in essence he decides nothing. Everything is determined by *gromady*, an untranslatable word that suggests citizens' meetings, and grassroots initiatives on the community level. Zelenskyy, apparently, did not understand this immediately. And, when he did, he did not want to accept the fact that local decisions were made by strong leaders. He—and those around him, primarily the head of the administration Yermak—took action that can still be explained by wartime laws: that of establishing an autocratic vertical strategy. The question is how successful this will be, and will it lead to Ukraine transforming into a kind of Russia, lead to its gradual infection with Russia's main diseases. Unfortunately, when fighting an aggressive, totalitarian enemy, you are in regular and close contact with it, so that even the freest country is forced to adopt its opponent's sins and vices. As such, Russia was infected by Germany and the idea of national exclusivity. By 1947, the era of the struggle against cosmopolitanism, Russian ideologists led by Leonid Leonov argued vociferously that Europe had given birth to fascism, that Europe was not able to resist it, and only the Soviet Union, with its experience in creating a new kind of human, was able defeat the worst evil in history! From there it was one step to the notion of racial purity, i.e., state anti-Semitism, and that step was taken. You ask: why did Britain avoid infection? Well, for all the six years of World War II, no German soldier set foot on British territory. There it was a war in the skies, on the sea, and in foreign territories. Russia, in the meantime, picked up germs that required a long period of recovery. *Pravda* in 1951 was not far from the *Völkischer Beobachter*. The idea of national exclusivity, unthinkable in a multinational state during the Great Terror, no longer surprised anyone after Stalin's toast to "the Russian people."

"We are not fighting with Russia in order to become Russia," declared the prominent Dnipro science-fiction writer and journalist Yan Valetov. Whether he will be heard is an open question.

XIII. OPERATION INTERVIEW

Another high-profile scandal of August 2022 was an interview that Volodymyr Zelenskyy gave to the *Washington Post*, published on August 16, 2022.

The interview by Isabella Kurshudyan was huge, and it contained several sensations at once. First, Zelenskyy for the first time provided the motivation for his desire to be elected: "The second party in the country was the party of the Russian Federation. If I hadn't—not specifically because of me—but if I hadn't run for president, this party would have been the first." (This refers to the For Life Opposition Platform, led by Putin's godfather Viktor Medvedchuk.)

Second, Zelenskyy for the first time directly began not just to thank the West for its help, but to sharply criticize it for the inadequacy of this help:

> And, of course, we did not receive anything from the point of view of security guarantees. Security guarantees are provided not only by Ukraine's membership in NATO. It's not just about safety, although I believe that the [Membership Action Plan] in NATO would have been [one of] those exact preventive sanctions that I constantly talked about at all meetings. Preventive sanctions mean to do something to make the Russians afraid to attack—because they will attack, so do something about it. But this did not happen, unfortunately.
>
> I'm not complaining. We've already passed the stage of complaints in our lives. This is not necessary. We're stronger now than we were before the invasion. We are just stronger. Our position is more correct, and I believe that this is the most important thing, because only an internally strong country can somehow resist. Partners can only help us de-occupy territories, but only the people of Ukraine can stand up and persevere.
>
> These security guarantees, which I constantly mentioned to all leaders, they provide you with access. I am grateful to the partners for the weapons we are receiving now, but if you're not a NATO member, you can't get them. Let's be honest. You can say a million times, "Listen, there may be an invasion." Okay, there may be an invasion—will

you give us planes? Will you give us air defenses? "Well, you're not a member of NATO." Oh, okay, then what are we talking about?

Now I am really grateful to many partners who, despite the fact that we are not NATO members, understood what is happening and that Ukraine is the first step on Russia's bloody path, and that this is not going to end just like that. The fact that we are being given these weapons, let's be honest, this is not only for us, it is also for them. After all, they have already understood that the Russian troops will not stop, they will move on. Therefore, here on our territory, Europe and the West are protecting themselves, too. I speak quite diplomatically as in it's not just about them but they are protecting themselves, too. Although everyone has their own price. And so access to these weapons, NATO's [Membership Action Plan], these NATO programs, the accession of Ukraine to NATO, all this would make it possible for us to upgrade ourselves.

Next, Zelenskyy spoke for the first time about the fact that, at the beginning of the hostilities, the West was quite ready to turn a blind eye to it, just as it had closed its eyes to Crimea. Had Ukraine not demonstrated the ability to defend itself, there would have been no one rallying around it in the West:

> Of all those who called me, there was no one who believed we would survive. Not because they didn't believe in Ukraine, but because of this demonization of the leader of the Russian Federation—his power, his philosophy, the way he advertised the might of the Russian army. And so [they thought], with all due respect to the Ukrainians: "They won't bring it, they'll be finished off in two or three days, maybe five, and then it will all end."

> Why did even some European leaders say "three days"? Because some Europeans did not plan to rally around Ukraine. Everyone wanted to just [wipe their hands of this]. Like, okay, this is Ukraine's problem. Let's just turn a blind eye to this for a few days. In a few days, the Russians, whatever they may be like, will occupy Ukraine.

And then we'll come to an agreement with them somehow. I am sure that such thoughts have arisen, because this war in Europe, in the center of it, does not benefit anyone.

For the Russian Federation, we were like an appendix that needed to be removed, but they didn't understand. They thought we were an appendix, but we turned out to be the heart of Europe. And we made this heart beat. These countries have united around us—thanks not only to us but also because the society in these countries was not ready to give up the concept of freedom simply because it is Putin, who is feared and has been demonized in the West. The West itself demonized him, they painted him to be so very terrible, with a nuclear weapon in his hands. Do you remember these posters with Saddam Hussein? Sometimes we too are afraid, but Ukraine showed the devil isn't as scary as he is made out to be.

When asked why he did not warn anyone about the impending invasion, but, on the contrary, tried to calm people down, Zelenskyy answered crisply:

If we had communicated that—and that is what some people wanted, whom I will not name—then I would have been losing $7 billion a month since last October, and at the moment when the Russians did attack, they would have taken us in three days. I'm not saying whose idea it was, but generally, our inner sense was right: If we sow chaos among people before the invasion, the Russians will devour us. Because during chaos, people flee the country.

So did you personally believe full-scale war was coming?

Look, how can you believe this? That they will torture people and that this is their goal? No one believed it would be like this. And no one knew it. And now everyone says we warned you, but you warned us through general phrases. When we said give us specifics—where will they come from, how many people and so on—they all had as much information as we did. And when I said, "Okay, if they're coming from here and it's going to be heavy fighting here, can we get weapons to stop them?" We didn't get it. Why do I need all these warnings? Why do I need to make our society go crazy? Since February, even from January as there was a lot going on in the media, Ukrainians transferred out more money than Ukrainians abroad received in assistance.

And so, as you probably remember, since the full-scale invasion started and until now, all I've been asking is to close the sky, because if the sky was closed, we wouldn't have all these deaths. I have no complaints—up to the point when someone starts telling me, "But we were sending you signals." Up to that point, I have no complaints. But when one is claiming they were sending us some signals, I tell them, "Send us weapons." I was absolutely right, and I'm sure about it even now. Everyone wants Ukraine to win, but no one wants to wage war with Russia. And that's it. That's a full stop. And that's why we had to decide how to stay strong. If no one wants to wage war with them, everyone is scared to fight them—excuse me, then we'll be deciding how to do that, whether it's right or wrong. But the war will go farther, deeper into Europe, so please send us weapons, because we are also defending you. And they started sending it.

First of all, the tone in which Zelenskyy spoke to the West here was sensational. This was no longer the tone of a supplicant. Later, many reproached him for his bitter ingratitude: as if to say, we give you everything, although we don't have to, but you demand more, and are dissatisfied at the same time! Yes, they are dissatisfied, because Ukraine is protecting the West, and if it doesn't protect it, Russia will become a dangerous neighbor. The plan to join NATO is good, but that's a piece of paper. If you knew everything so well and reproach the West for not heeding your warnings, why didn't you do anything yourself? Zelenskyy, now, had the right to use such a tone, for in August 2022 it was already clear what kind of war was being waged.

But the West got the message: Ukraine began to receive weapons, and not only Bayraktars, but also HIMARS. This was Zelenskyy's personal diplomatic success, a direct result of his demands. From the first days of fall 2022, a period of triumphant Ukrainian counteroffensives began.

The first was a rapid 70-kilometer march near Kharkiv, when thirty settlements in the southeast of the region, including Izium, were liberated within a week.

XIV. THE SEPTEMBER OFFENSIVE

This was Russia's largest defeat since the Kyiv retreat, which, in turn, was Russia's largest military defeat since World War II. It was a mad retreat that certainly cannot be justified by surprise or treachery, for everything happened in the middle of a war unleashed by our own Russian nation. It began on August 29, 2022, and continued until November 11, when the Ukrainian Armed Forces entered Kherson without a fight. This was the same Kherson about which it had been said that "Russia will be here forever." Russia was there precisely from March 3 to November 10, that is, the new Russia lasts just seven months and a week. Russia managed to include Kherson in its territory and included it in the Constitution, after which it bombed and shelled this territory for another two months—and continues to attack it now.

"Maybe it doesn't sound like what anyone expects now. Maybe not as in the news. But you need to understand: no one will just leave if they don't feel pressed by strength," Zelenskyy said in an evening televised address on November 9. "The enemy does not bring us gifts, docs not make 'gestures of goodwill.' We fight for everything we get. And when you are fighting, you must understand that every step always meets resistance from the enemy, it always means the loss of the lives of our heroes. Therefore, we move very carefully, without emotions, without unnecessary risk."

Back on July 10, Iryna Vereshchuk (Minister of Occupied Territories, a stubborn woman who would not evacuate from Kyiv on February 24) called on all residents of the southern regions occupied by the enemy to leave by any means: hostilities and de-occupation had begun. In order to cut off Russian forces in Kherson from other territories, Ukrainian artillery shelled and rendered the Antonivka Bridge unusable (from July 27). One of the most charming Ukrainian demotivators dates back to this time—truly, every stage of the war was accompanied by new memes, sometimes cynical, almost always witty. A naked couple; the girl moans: "Darling, don't hit me!"— "Then where do I hit?"—"The Antonivka Bridge!!!" The book's Russian publisher didn't think this a very witty meme. That's a shame. I really like it.

The counteroffensive simultaneously developed around Kherson and the Kharkiv region, where it began with the liberation of Kupiansk, the almost completely destroyed Balakliia and Izium. Sviatohirsk and Liman were liberated next. By mid-October, Ukraine controlled most of the Kherson region. A comparison of footage of protest demonstrations, how Russians were greeted in Kherson, and the hugs with which Ukrainians were greeted was very eloquent, but these images were not shown on Russian television. It is known that when Soviet troops entered liberated cities during World War II and the initial rejoicing subsided, the identification of collaborators began. Staying in the occupied territories of the USSR was revealed in all questionnaires and hampered career growth until the end of Soviet power. It was not customary to write about this in military prose: literary generals like Konstantin Simonov could afford it in the story "His Wife Arrived."

"The Germans were here for a month. This is no village where at least some food supplies might be hidden, or buried away. This is a city after all. Bread was baked here in bakeries, and distributed to bakeries. Food was distributed via ration cards; water was drawn from wells, electricity was received from a power plant. You can't imagine that the Germans arrive today, and tomorrow people no longer need water, bread, electricity, or anything else!"

"'What is the big deal about electricity!'" the chairman interrupted Lopatin. "The electric power plant is a military target, we could easily get by on paraffin stoves! And that mechanic is a traitor! He could have blown it up, but he chickened out!"

"Would you have blown it up?"

"Absolutely."

The chairman said it so simply that Lopatin believed him.

"I have an order to identify every single accomplice of the fascist occupiers, and rest assured that I will carry it out. I have a conscience! I may not eat, and I may not sleep. But I will do that!"

Zelenskyy specifically highlighted this danger, and that is another of his defining differences from Soviet leaders. His speech on October 3, 2022, addressed the problem of the work of the Ukrainian security forces in the liberated territories:

> The work of transport, post office, police, normal supply of water, gas, electricity is being restored—as much as possible. The occupiers left many mined areas, many tripwires, almost all infrastructure was destroyed. The damage is colossal.
>
> But life is returning—it is returning wherever the occupiers were driven out. We also make social payments—pensions, salaries. In particular, to the teachers who remained loyal to Ukraine and did not switch to the curriculum of the occupiers.
>
> This is actually very important. Russian propagandists intimidate people in the areas still under the control of the occupiers that Ukraine will allegedly consider almost everyone who remains in the occupied territory as collaborators. Absolute nonsense.
>
> Our approach has always been and remains clear and fair. If a person did not serve the occupiers and did not betray Ukraine, then there is no reason to consider such a person a collaborator. These are elementary things. If the teacher remained a Ukrainian teacher and did not lie to the children about who is the enemy . . . Or if a person remained a Ukrainian employee of the Ukrainian utilities service and, for example, helped preserve the energy supply for people, then such a person cannot be blamed for anything.
>
> Hundreds of thousands of our people were in the temporarily occupied territory. Many helped our military and special services. Many simply tried to survive and waited for the return of the Ukrainian flag.
>
> Of course, there were those who betrayed Ukraine. But such cases are quickly established by the Security Service of Ukraine and

are not massive. Russia did not meet mass support in Ukraine, and this is a fact.

The fact that he spoke these words and considered them to be especially important against the backdrop of reports of victory makes him a new type of leader. Naturally, there would be no discrimination against returning POWs—only respect, the joy of repatriation, aid in psychological rehabilitation, the return to their families, and to the front, if they are able and want to. Everyone wanted to, and everyone trusted everyone. Komarov's film *The Year* ends with a scene of the greeting of returning prisoners, and the penultimate episode shows the return of the Ukrainian army to Kherson. Women tell how frightening it was. They cry. Then they pull themselves together. Why are we talking about this? We should be happy! They laugh. Never in Ukraine have we laughed and cried so much as in this triumphant autumn.

Enormous evidence of Russian atrocities was found in the liberated territories: mass graves of people shot with their hands tied, and signs of torture. A cemetery was discovered in Izium containing 445 civilian graves, as well as a mass grave of the Ukrainian Armed Forces. Dmytro Lubenets, the Upper Rada Commissioner for Human Rights, said that many Ukrainian military personnel were shot after being tortured. Zelenskyy visited the towns of Izium and Balakliia immediately after they were liberated. He addressed foreign journalists who had gathered in the city in huge numbers—there were more than a hundred: "You saw Bucha. Have you seen Mariupol? Now you see this," he said. "How many more such atrocities must Russia commit for the world to stop it?" This call had never looked so realistic.

On September 29, Zelenskyy addressed the peoples of the Caucasus (primarily the Chechens, for it was they whom Ramzan Kadyrov had most diligently mobilized for the war with Ukraine. This was not supported by grassroots enthusiasm; mass unrest occurred in Dagestan, and Zelenskyy chose to play precisely on the reluctance of the Caucasians to become cannon fodder). I think one of the features of Zelenskyy's presidential behavior is precisely his desire to reach out to those who are least able to hear him; throwing a stone into the midst of one's opponents in hopes of provoking the strongest possible response. This is also a sign of his actor's instincts.

He recorded an appeal on Krepostnoi Lane in Kyiv near the memorial plaque to Imam Shamil which had been erected through the efforts of the Dagestani community. The speech took place at the Masalova estate (her actual house was demolished long ago; a new one now stands there). Shamil had visited Kyiv on his way to Mecca. After seven years of persuasion, Alexander II had finally given him permission go on the Hajj pilgrimage. Shamil, whose reconciliation with the emperor was supposed to break the resistance of the mountaineers, was made a nobleman and received a life-long allowance. Since the shortest route to Mecca lay through Kyiv, Shamil stayed there from December 1867 to May 1869. "We know how to preserve the memory of heroes," Zelenskyy said.

The address was received quite favorably in the Caucasus, although a blogger on the Caucasian Knot website using the pseudonym "Chechnya Inside," noted that Zelenskyy's speech could have been more emotional. In the Caucasus, he wrote, we well remember Russian shells and cluster bombs. I think the mention of Shamil, although a strong cultural move, will not work in the current Caucasus precisely because, through the efforts of the Kadyrovites and other new authorities, the memory of spiritual heritage in the Caucasus has largely been trampled. Zelenskyy addresses those who cannot understand him. Some are hostile to the name of Shamil because he surrendered to Russia; for others, he means nothing, because they simply have not heard of him.

This is the problem with most of Zelenskyy's appeals to Russians: He seeks to take into account a cultural context where there has been no cultural context for so long. There is something else—embitterment, mental illness, and a fundamental disconnection from any roots, for our age has abolished all of Russia's previous history. Paradoxically, it is more alive for Zelenskyy and his team than for Russians. Genuine cancel culture rules the roost in Russia, not in Europe. Pushkin's monuments are not being toppled in Europe—his legacy has simply been nullified. For duped Russians it means nothing, and it is pointless to reach out to them. Those who remember Pushkin understand everything anyway. The notion of negotiations is meaningless simply because negotiations presuppose the understanding of speech—and the situation with this in Russia in 2022 was bad. The Chechen blogger is right—these days you need more emotion.

Russia's response to the Ukrainian offensive was barbarism—a generally strong, intense response. Russia deliberately began to destroy Ukrainian infrastructure, providing Ukraine with a truly besieged winter.

In his speech on Ukrainian Independence Day on August 24, 2023, Zelenskyy found especially grateful words for Ukraine's power engineers, electricians, and repairmen:

> Last winter, we experienced massive missile attacks and the threat of blackout. There were different moments. When cities remained in darkness. When it was cold. There was also indomitability. And when our people worked and turned the power back on, there were loud shouts of "Glory to Ukraine!" "Glory to Ukrainian electricians!" and glasses were raised to our air defense and power engineers. And this is absolutely true. Our power engineers worked around the clock. During air raids. Sometimes under fire. Always in danger. Always knowing how much people are waiting for electricity in hospitals and defense enterprises. And how much every family is waiting for light and warmth.

It really was a feat comparable to something accomplished on the front line. Ukraine's Minister of Energy Herman Halushchenko was a lawyer by training, and how he miraculously prevented a complete blackout in Ukraine is a mystery. Russia fired tens of thousands of missiles into Ukraine after the beginning of the war; there were over 16,000 massive attacks, and in nine cases out of ten these missiles were aimed at civilian targets, primarily at electrical substations. On October 10, 2022, Russia carried out the largest missile attack on the entire Ukrainian territory since the beginning of the war—eighty-four missiles, half of which were intercepted. But the remaining ones that landed were enough to cut off power to eleven regions, including Kyiv. A satellite image of pitch-black Kyiv circulated in the world media. By morning, power had been restored to about a thousand settlements.

On October 22, another rocket attack—smaller in scale, but using the much-publicized Sarmats—left one and a half million homes without electricity. Forty percent of Ukraine's energy system was critically damaged. After the shelling on November 15, 2022, a quarter of the Ukrainian population was left without electricity. On November 23, Russia was recognized by the European Parliament as a terrorist country (a sponsor of terrorism), because its main victims were now civilians. But this was a measure of moral influence; no fatal consequences for Russia could possibly have resulted from this. So, a terrorist country, what else?

Most amazing is that Zelenskyy found the proper words at this time. Even Russia seems to have become bored with repeatedly demonstrating the demonic nature of its regime. Zelenskyy did not interrupt his national television therapy for a day. It remained diverse, and never fell into dissonance with the audience.

October 10:

> It is a tough morning. We are dealing with terrorists.
>
> Dozens of missiles, Iranian "Shaheds." They have two targets.
>
> Energy facilities throughout the country. Kyiv region and Khmelnytskyi region, Lviv and Dnipro, Vinnytsia, Ivano-Frankivsk region, Zaporizhzhia, Sumy region, Kharkiv region, Zhytomyr region, Kirovohrad region, the south of the country.
>
> They want panic and chaos, they want to destroy our energy system. They are incorrigible.
>
> The second target is people.
>
> Such a time and such goals were specially chosen to cause as much damage as possible.
>
> Please stay in shelters today. Always follow the safety rules. And always remember: Ukraine existed before this enemy appeared, and Ukraine will exist after it.

October 22:

We continue to neutralize the aftermath of today's terrorist attacks on our infrastructure. The geography of this new massive strike is very wide: Volyn, Odesa, Khmelnytskyi region, Kirovohrad region, Dnipropetrovsk region, Rivne region, Mykolaiv region, Zaporizhzhia region and other places.

The main target of terrorists is energy. Therefore, please be even more careful than before about the need to consciously consume electricity. The stability of the power industry of our entire state depends on each city and district of Ukraine.

Please limit the use of appliances that use a lot of electricity. And especially during peak consumption hours in the morning and in the evening.

In part of the territory of our country, where electricity was cut off due to today's strike, it has already been possible to restore the power supply. Electricity has already been partly restored in the Odesa and Khmelnytskyi regions, and in most of the Rivne region as well. There are positive reports from other regions as well. But in many cities, in many districts, recovery work is still ongoing. We are trying to return power to people as soon as possible.

I want to thank everyone who is involved in this work: energy workers, utility and local government workers, government officials and businesses that also help. Together, we are now showing that Ukrainian life cannot be broken. Even if the enemy can leave us temporarily without power, it will still never succeed in leaving us without the desire to make things right, to mend and return them to normal.

And even now—partially in the dark—life in our state, in our Ukraine, is still civilized. Unlike Russia that brings us this terror. Even with electricity they still have the same barbarism there as in ancient times. Only barbarians can bring such evil to the world.

Russian propagandists are lying when they say that this terror against our infrastructure and people can somehow slow down the operational actions of our military, or create difficulties for our defense.

Ukrainians are united and know for sure that Russia has no chance of winning this war.

He had a phenomenal ability in a situation where one quarter of the nation had been plunged into darkness, to divert his listeners' attention to thoroughly unexpected, seemingly extraneous topics:

> Ukraine was very well represented this week in Frankfurt at the largest book fair in Europe and one of the largest in the world. This is not just an event for the publishing business and writers. It is one of the key European discussion platforms and an influential informational event.
>
> The First Lady of Ukraine presented her projects supporting education and the cultural sphere there. In particular, the Books Without Borders initiative will provide children of our forced migrants with books in the Ukrainian language. And also the Ukrainian Bookshelf project, which is already represented in twenty countries of the world.

No one was bothered by this reference to books and the First Lady's cultural projects. Everyone understood that you will go crazy if you constantly think only about rocket attacks and casualties. They are barbarians, we are cultured. We are bleeding, yet we attend the Frankfurt Book Fair. Alexander Pushkin's uncle, dying, said: "How boring Katenin's articles are!" Pushkin considered this unforgivable pettiness, but I consider it heroism. This is a magnificent contempt for death, which cannot succeed in distracting cultured people from their cultural work.

On November 15, Zelenskyy spoke via video link during the G20 forum in Bali. There he first presented his Ten Points—his conditions for peace in Ukraine, which Russian Foreign Minister Sergei Lavrov immediately called unrealistic. Russia at this time was not averse to sneaking away to gain a foothold in the already captured territories. Zelenskyy, however, continued to reject outright any negotiations with Putin or Putin's people. The ten conditions were:

- Radiation and nuclear safety;
- Food security;
- Energy conservation;
- Release of all prisoners and deportees;
- Implementation of the UN Charter, and the restoration of territorial integrity and world order;
- Withdrawal of Russian troops and the cessation of hostilities;
- The return of justice (meaning trials for war criminals);
- Counteracting ecocide;
- The exclusion of further escalation; and,
- Commitment to the end of hostilities.

Radiation safety was the number one issue after Russia seized the Zaporizhzhia nuclear power plant. Putin continued to threaten the deployment of nuclear weapons if Russia was threatened. Whatever he considered a threat—whether it was the loss of Crimea, or an invasion of Russian territory—was not specified, but his message to the world was for them to freeze in its tracks.

The winter of 2022–2023 was relatively warm in Ukraine, and in Europe as a whole. The average European temperature was 1.2 degrees C. warmer than the norm. Russia could not freeze Ukraine out, and could not bring about mass protests. In the winter and spring, Russia tried in vain to take Bakhmut (thanks mainly to the Wagner forces, Yevgeny Prigozhin's private military company under the command of Dmitry Utkin). Bakhmut was not so much taken as utterly destroyed by the end of May 2023; Avdiivka was almost encircled, but was never captured (of the city's 35,000 residents, only 1,500 remained, and the housing stock was 90 percent destroyed).

Many military experts mentioned that Russia had changed its tactics. By the spring of 2023, Russia controlled 18 percent of Ukrainian territory (versus 27 percent in March 2022). Having rejected taking new territories, and barely holding on to captured ones, Russia began a campaign of continual rocket attacks. In Kyiv the number of air alerts reached dozens per night. On June 6, an event occurred that seemed finally to convince Russia's sympathizers that there were no red lines it would not cross: the Kakhovka hydroelectric power station was destroyed, and forty thousand people on both banks of the Dnipro River (fourteen cities and towns) found themselves in the flood zone. Immediately before the explosion—on May 30, 2023—Russia adopted a resolution "temporarily not to conduct technical investigations into accidents of hydraulic structures in the occupied territories of Ukraine that occur as a result of military operations, sabotage, or terrorist acts." At the same time, the application of part of the clauses of the Federal Law "On the safety of hydraulic structures" was canceled. Subsequently, one can argue as much as one wants that the dam of the Kakhovka hydroelectric power station was destroyed by Ukrainian shelling. Even if all international experts did not agree that the hydroelectric power station was blown up, and even if the nocturnal explosion at 2:50 A.M. was not recorded by European observers, this Russian ruling in itself points to the culprits. There was no discussion on this issue among specialists. Zelenskyy immediately convened an emergency meeting. By three o'clock in the afternoon, 1,500 people had been evacuated from the flooded territories exclusively by the Ukrainian army.

Volodymyr Zelenskyy's address on this day was short and extremely gloomy. In general, despite the enormous disasters that had befallen Ukraine, he still did not lose his ability to empathize, and he avoided developing a professional psychological barrier:

> This day, which began with an urgent meeting of the National Security and Defense Council, continued with a meeting of the Staff. We are waiting for a meeting of the UN Security Council.
>
> The disaster at the Kakhovka hydroelectric power plant caused by Russian terrorists will not stop Ukraine and Ukrainians. We will still liberate all our land. And each Russian act of terrorism increases only the amount of reparations that Russia will pay for its crimes, not the chances of the occupiers to stay on our land.
>
> First of all, I am grateful to all our first responders, military, representatives of local communities, each of our regions, who are now helping people from our southern regions flooded by the Russian terrorist attack.

Second, the government at all levels is doing everything to save people and provide drinking water to those who used to receive it from the Kakhovka reservoir. Kryvyi Rih and the entire Dnipropetrovsk region, cities and villages in Kherson, Mykolaiv and Zaporizhzhia regions—no matter how difficult it is, we have to help people.

Third, I am grateful to everyone who is currently evacuating people from the towns and villages flooded by water from the Kakhovka reservoir. It is very important now to take care of each other and help as much as possible.

Fourth, the whole world will know about this Russian war crime, the crime of ecocide. This deliberate destruction of the dam and other HPP facilities by the Russian occupiers is an environmental bomb of mass destruction. For the sake of their own security, the world should now show that Russia will not get away with such terror. And I am grateful to all leaders and states, all nations and international organizations that have supported Ukraine and are ready to help our people, and our de-occupation efforts. The Prosecutor General has already appealed to the Office of the Prosecutor of the International Criminal Court to involve international justice in the investigation of the dam explosion.

Fifth, it is only the complete liberation of Ukrainian land from Russian occupiers that will guarantee that such acts of terrorism will not happen again. Russia uses anything for terror—any object. The terrorist state must lose.

I want to say a few more things separately. Regarding our south and Crimea. We will find a way to restore normal life on our land after the expulsion of the ruscists. This applies to water and everything else. This applies to all our regions—from Kherson to Dnipropetrovsk, from Mykolaiv to Crimea.

The fact that Russia deliberately destroyed the Kakhovka reservoir, which is critically important, in particular, for providing water to Crimea, indicates that the Russian occupiers have already realized that they will have to flee Crimea as well.

Well, Ukraine will get back everything that belongs to it. And it will make Russia pay for what it has done.

Glory to all our people who are fighting and working for the sake of our country and our people!

Today, just like yesterday, I would like to celebrate our heroes in the Bakhmut sector. Well done, warriors! The 3rd separate assault brigade and the 57th separate motorized infantry brigade—thank you! Thank you for moving forward!

Glory to Ukraine!

Here we must make a small digression. When I read a lot of reports in a row, let's say by the Russian journalist Anna Politkovskaya, who was murdered in 2006 for her writings about Chechnya, I can be irritated by the monotony. The Chechens have always been chivalrous, sympathetic, and noble; and the federal powers have always been bad. I do not wish to fall into one-sided propaganda by claiming that the Ukrainians have always behaved impeccably. Wish as I might to protect myself from accusations of being bought, commissioned, a follower of Bandera, etc. I know I'll never be able to. Russia is not in the proper mood right now to be able to evaluate a book about Zelenskyy objectively. And, yes, I do not pretend to be objective. Ultimately, the leader of Ukraine is defending my values, my ideas about the creative intelligentsia, and the honor of our profession. For some reason this presupposes some kind of bias on my part. There is no question that the Ukrainians themselves investigated the actions of the Tornado volunteer battalion and sentenced them all to severe terms for torture. Ukrainian officials have often repeated that cases of prisoner abuse or extrajudicial killings will be investigated. And there is no reason to doubt this, for Ukraine has a vital interest in maintaining its international image. But Russia has an amazing ability to color situations in black-and-white tones. It engages in such horrors that, by comparison, Ukraine looks like a saint in the eyes of the world. Even if someone previously had doubts about that. The incident of the Kakhovka hydroelectric power station, where Ukrainian volunteers rescued victims, and the Russians tried to stop them with regular shelling, is one of those extremely clear-cut situations.

Perhaps the environmental disaster in the city of Oleshky, provoked by Russia (not only the explosion of the Kakhovka Dam, but also the invasion itself, which put the hydroelectric station under attack), provides us with an opportunity to finally formulate Russia's main characteristic, its specialty, so to speak: Its purpose is to provoke extremely ambiguous situations in its own internal policies, while in external affairs, it gives total ethical clarity to everything it touches.

Inside Russia, an ethical attitude toward absolute geographical determinism prevails: One does not choose one's homeland, we have but one homeland, the homeland is like a mother to us (even if it behaves like the cruelest stepmother). You can break the law for the sake of your homeland, not to mention your personal well-being—the homeland stands higher than truth. The Motherland violates divine and human laws every step of the way, but it resists fascism and thereby justifies any of its initiatives occurring in a timespan stretching from the previous two hundred, to the next one hundred years. The state stands even higher than the homeland (a reviewer of the newest Russian history book by Vladimir Medinsky, that member of Russia's negotiating team, wrote that the purpose of studying history is to convince young people that they have no homeland other than the Russian State. Hey, grab this flag and go!). The Russian state may be bad, but it is the only form of state (given our vast territory, geographical location, and harsh climate) that guarantees us the presence of a homeland and its functioning; we can only do what we do and nothing else; and any change undermines our sovereignty, that is, the right to do whatever we want. As such, any action aimed at improving our homeland automatically leads to its destruction, and, because of this, Russia must always mourn its best people. It destroys them with fanatical persistence in order, ultimately, to appropriate them posthumously. This is where the main ambiguity lies: any liberator is, by definition, a destroyer; any enslaver by definition a benefactor; and, consequently, Russia is still unable to formulate its attitude to the Decembrist movement (1820s) and Lenin (1920s), or to say goodbye to Stalin.

In foreign policy, on the contrary, Russia demonstrates a fine ability to whitewash and ennoble everything it touches. The Afghan mujahideen were indisputably an unpleasant bunch, but in the light of the Russian invasion they resembled ideological fighters. Nationalists like Dzhokhar Dudayev hardly brought prosperity to Chechnya, but compared to Russia's protégé Ramzan Kadyrov, Dudayev and his protégé Akhmed Zakayev were almost angels, and the guerrilla leader Shamil Basayev was a people's hero. Viktor Yushchenko was a bad president in Ukraine, which even the initiators of Maidan 2004 do not doubt, but compared to Viktor Yanukovych he is a noble idealist; even Viktor Yanukovych, who refused to suppress the Maidan uprising by force in 2014, looks like a humanist compared to Vladimir Putin, which is why Putin considers him a weakling and pointedly avoids any communication with the man who now lives as a refugee in the Russian city of Rostov. Russia's handling of the territories adjacent to the Kakhovka hydroelectric power plant—seizing them in order to flood them—is a kind of ideal model of Russia's behavior in war—and not just this one. Wherever Russia brings its so-called "Russian world" to the territories it seizes, it establishes "torture in basements," ruin and degradation. This is what it did with Donetsk and Luhansk. This is how it destroyed Mariupol. This is how it captured part of the Kherson region. The consequences of the Kakhovka disaster could have been far more significant—not fourteen villages, but hundreds could have been flooded. However, even now the consequences are not clear. We don't know how many fish died, or how many animals perished, although no one even asks these questions in light of the death of over fifty residents, mainly the elderly. This flooding was followed by the usual blatant lies—it's all because of their HIMARS, we have nothing to do with it—although hydrologists all over the world have thoroughly substantiated the impossibility of destroying the dam via missile attacks. In fact, Russia's actions are not just villainous, they reflect a demonic plan that emerges more and more clearly.

XV. BAKHMUT. PRIGOZHIN

I will not provide a detailed discussion here about Yevgeny Prigozhin and his so-called rebellion. This is not a book about him nor is it about the

Russo-Ukrainian war, but about a single turning point in Ukrainian history, and about the man who became the face of this extremely important era. But Prigozhin, and no one else, is the face of Russia in this war, its most striking character (no hero, of course). We must see who is fighting on behalf of Russia. He died (if he really died, which seems to be officially confirmed, but who believes the Russian powers-that-be?) precisely as I finished editing this chapter. My custom is to pay attention to such coincidences.

Again, however, we will not go into the details of Prigozhin's biography: much has been written about him undeservedly. Let us dwell on the activities of Wagner, his private military company functioning on Ukrainian territory for a relatively short period, October 2022 to June 2023. After that Wagner and its Wagnerites disappeared from Ukraine, probably forever.

Ilf and Petrov's brilliant conclusion is that their Ostap Bender is symmetrical to their Koreiko, a great schemer of the new era, one who knows neither sentimentality nor self-irony. Humor is not alien to him, but it is the humor of a bull terrier. There is zero reflective thought or, more accurately, this reflection consists of a feeling of mystical superiority over the rest of the world, the feeling of a predator not so much toward an herbivore, but toward grass, toward flowers. Why the hell all this stuff grows makes no sense to him. In making money and deceiving suckers, Koreiko is, if not more talented, then certainly more successful than Bender. He amasses seven million, while Bender ends up with just one, and even that is taken away from him. But there is something similar between them. Both are schemers and scammers, only from different eras. Bender is interested in the beauty of the scam; Koreiko is focused on results. But it is curious that both draw pleasure from taking risks. It's not that Koreiko enjoys taking risks, he generally prefers a quiet life. But a scam, preferably with a fatal outcome for his enemy, gives him an adrenaline boost. This is the little thing that still amuses and touches him: you can't live with no entertainment at all. Otherwise you'll end up like the hapless Berlaga from the same novel.

Prigozhin was just this kind of bull terrier on the Russian side. There is a certain symmetry in the two "captains," Zelenskyy coming from the KVN comedy show, and Vladimir Putin coming from the KGB. We have talked about this. Ukrainian General Valerii Zaluzhnyi spoke of Russian General Valery Gerasimov with respect, and, although most likely all is not well with Gerasimov's sense of moral reflection and propriety, he was at least a professional. Zaluzhnyi seriously warned against underestimating him. In this entourage, Prigozhin would appear to be Arestovych's double—the only figure equally successful at PR while also possessing a penchant for grand schemes. Of course, Arestovych is a lighthearted player, an intellectual. Prigozhin is a murderer with the psychology of a criminal. That is, the embodiment of everything that Arestovych hates. But they are antipodes, and their relationships are bound to be antagonistic. In any case, Prigozhin was the only prominent such figure on the Russian side. No one managed to outshine him either in villainy, or in impudence. He was Russia's only example of self-organization, and was a good example of the kind of self-organization that Russia fosters.

The private military company named Wagner was created in 2015. At first it was called Slavic Corps, but then was renamed in honor of the call sign of its commander Dmitry Utkin—"Wagner." We already mentioned it in the "Wagnergate" chapter. The owner of the personal military company (PMC), Yevgeny Prigozhin (1961–2023), was close to Putin, and was used for some of the latter's dirtiest deeds, from participation in wars, to the liquidation of undesirables (one of which he himself eventually turned out to be). After Prigozhin's death, which was never fully confirmed, he was often lauded as the most talented representative from among Putin's elite. It is difficult to talk about talent in his case—even as a PR man, and the creator of a troll factory, he always acted extremely rudely and, so to speak, in-yer-face. Compared to the rest, however, who generally cannot string two words together, and are extremely cowardly, he is at least brazen. That is, he reflects certain thieves' virtues. The role of Prigozhin under Putin—I started talking about this long before 2022, and now it has become a commonplace—is closest of all to the role of Rasputin under the last tsar, and there is no mysticism in that either. We have already mentioned that when history becomes too obvious, that only speaks of the stupidity of the observers, who can be reached in no other way. Russian history, in its cyclical repetitions and striking coincidences, is visual to such an extent that the Lord, its main author, seems utterly disappointed in the analytical abilities of the audience. The figure of Prigozhin is important to us in order to picture the level of the rabble Zelenskyy must confront.

The similarity with Rasputin is based on the fact that, at critical moments in Russian history, when, by definition, no representatives of the common folk can find their way into power, something resembling an official representative of the masses appears at court. The very concept of the "deep people" was introduced by Vladislav Surkov although he never really explained it. We are left to decipher it. "Deep" precisely because these people are not represented in any way, either in politics or in public life. Perhaps they are described in culture, for it is precisely they who make up the face of Russia as its neighbors see it. "Deep" also means darkness, brutality, a long, deep fall, etc. Under Nicholas II, such "deep people" were sectarians who expressed the desire of the masses for an informal, unofficial kind of spirituality. In post-Soviet Russia, prisoners became these deep people. They were the most active and, at the same time, brutal segment of the population. Prisoners in Putin's Russia are anyone who has shown economic initiative, spoken out against the authorities politically, or simply committed a crime—not an economic or military one, but an ordinary crime, and not in the interests of the authorities, but for reasons of drunkenness or brutality. All of Russian society is steeped in and permeated with prison psychology—partly because all the most significant people were imprisoned under Stalin. Partly because the entire structure of Russian society, always closed off and based on incessant violence, is no different from sectarian or prison life. In essence, there are two forms of self-organization in Russia—the mafia or the sect. The Wagner PMC showed all the signs of a totalitarian sect. Prigozhin received the authority to recruit prisoners in order to mobilize the population: if they kill—good, that will make it easier for the homeland. But if they don't kill, they can be released so that they can continue their favorite activities—robbery, rape, less often, murders—in freedom. The military units of Ramzan Kadyrov, or Prigozhin's released prisoners exist in order to solve internal problems, that is, to potentially suppress any uprisings.

The problem is that Vladimir Putin is accustomed to relying on the worst individuals, and the Kadyrovites and Prigozhinites, just like their leaders, are very unreliable allies. They have no ideological reasons to fight. There is nothing patriotic about them (especially since Kadyrov is a patriot exclusively of his own enclave). This means that in the event of any personal risk, they will choose to protect their own interests, not those of the state. The intelligentsia or fanatics like Igor Girkin-Strelkov serve in Russia for ideological reasons. The homeland has no need of intellectuals—it successfully got rid of them, liquidated them, one might say, as a class. Fanatics receive no better treatment. Girkin-Strelkov long walked under the sword of Damocles, as a result of which he was accused of extremist calls to action and was imprisoned. He, however, has not lost hope of competing for the presidency, and, under certain conditions, he does have a chance for Russia is trending in a negative dynamic, and is unlikely to be able to reverse it.

Prigozhin did not recruit prisoners just for war, of course. He dreamed of his own personal army, like any oligarch, and prisoners were the exact same expendable material for him as the superficial people (antonym of "deep," that is, official people) are for Putin. Did he really intend to seize power? Perhaps. But in general, in an era of unrest, it is simply useful to have a personal armed detachment on hand: for protection, for suppressing the disgruntled, for fighting off neighbors should Russia suddenly fall apart. Prigozhin's army was tested in Syria where Putin sought to gain geopolitical weight, and in Ukraine, where it demonstrated a complete, as was to be expected, lack of motivation. In general, the paradox of war is that atrocity alone is not enough. You also need training, cunning, and solidarity. Prigozhin was by no means idolized by his troops, contrary to the legend. The naïve attempt to create a myth about the "people's favorite" was intended for timid underdogs who call themselves intellectuals. In Ukraine, the attitude toward Prigozhin's army was initially contemptuous.

Prigozhin's army fought mainly near Bakhmut, a mining town 80 kilometers, that is, 50 miles from Donetsk that, in peacetime, counted 70,000 residents. "In war, a certain location, sometimes quite distant from the most strategically important point, emerges as the place where the maximum efforts of the warring parties are applied, and becomes the arena of legendary battles," said Israeli military analyst David Sharp in a conversation with *Novaya Gazeta Europe*. "This was the case in Verdun during the First World War, or Stalingrad in the Second World War. Had the Germans managed to cover the hundreds of meters remaining to the Volga, it would not have changed a thing." It might have changed something in a spiritual sense, but laying down so many lives in Stalingrad—"For us there is no land beyond the Volga"—was in fact not a military, but an ideological necessity. No one would take a single step back from the city named for Stalin, formerly Tsaritsyn! Bakhmut did not have such ideological significance. Prigozhin here put up resistance because of his own desire to show off. The city was taken in the usual Russian way, especially characteristic of this war, that is, by razing it to the ground. Zelenskyy visited the city on December 20, 2022, presenting awards to its defenders—apparently not because Bakhmut was of such strategic importance, but because he wanted to challenge the Russians, who time and again announced their capture of the city (there were at least a dozen such statements between October and March).

In general, Zelenskyy often visits the front lines. In the summer of 2023 alone he visited the Vuhledar-Marinka line, where he celebrated with military personnel on Marine Corps Day; Bakhmut on the day of special operations; the area of Donetsk just seven hundred meters from the enemy; and the Melitopol line, where he gave awards to soldiers of the 3rd operational brigade. He visits the front lines at least twice a month. The Russian Z-press (and that is the overwhelming majority of the press) regularly ridicules this as PR. Of course if he had not gone to the front, it would have meant he was cowardly hiding in the home front. No one has responded to this shrieking for a long time even in Russia, because Putin's manner of fighting the war from his bunker has long been ridiculed even by the most zealous propagandists. Of course, Zelenskyy's trips to the front primarily solve a morale rather than a military problem (although it is a thin line between them). A narrator king has a responsibility to create a narrative, and to tell his warriors how proud he is of them. Most likely, the tone of Zelenskyy's conversations with the soldiers over time has greatly decreased in humor, and increased in pathos, for in the second year of the war he didn't joke at all: "The lightness is gone," as Olena Zelenska said.

Prigozhin repeatedly stated that the task of Wagner was not to capture Bakhmut (which was attacked for five months and destroyed), but to grind down the Ukrainian army. It's no pity to grind down your own—you can go out and recruit more. According to the underestimated official data alone, 2,504 Ukrainians died in Bakhmut from the end of February to the end of March, while according to Mediazona, a total of more than 70,000 Russians were killed and wounded in Bakhmut from May 2022 to February 2023. Prigozhin, either giving vent to his discontent, or attempting to create the image of a worthy soldier who speaks with respect of his enemy, said that the resistance of Ukrainians had no equal in the last century. That is, the Battle of Stalingrad was inferior to the one in Bakhmut. "Prigozhin of Bakhmut!"—the elderly bard of the Russian General Staff, Alexander Prokhanov, admired breathlessly. By May, Prigozhin once again stated that Bakhmut was completely under the control of the Wagnerites, and that they could leave, giving way to regular units. We will probably never know what the real contribution of the Wagnerites was to the destruction and storming of Bakhmut, but quantitatively they made up no more than a quarter of the Russians who fought there; true, three quarters were merely drafted, untrained privates.

During the Bakhmut battles, Prigozhin regularly blackmailed and insulted the Russian army authorities. His famous phrase "Shoigu, Gerasimov, where are the shells?!" was spoken in Bakhmut. Prigozhin shouted in his videos that if he was not given weapons immediately in the necessary quantity, he would withdraw his people and expose the front. Apparently, it was then that Putin began thinking about liquidating Wagner (an act that was not prescribed in Russian legislation and, therefore, could not officially exist). An army unit that does not obey command and exposes the front when it sees fit adds a fair amount of absurdity to the course of an already senseless war. The authorities wanted unity of command.

It is curious that Zelenskyy never once paid the Wagnerites the honor of mentioning them directly. For him, this unit, which spoke louder than others about its atrocities, was simply not worth acknowledgement, even during the days of the Wagnerian mutiny in Russia, which showed the whole world the army's complete unwillingness to defend Putin. Zelenskyy, of course, is not a purist and was not brought up in an elite school—block 95 in Kryvyi Rih was a restless place where strong characters are forged. And yet, if we talk about Zelenskyy's psychological portrait, there are things that he withdraws from. The semi-criminal morals of Kryvyi Rih's street life were one thing, but penal battalions risen from hell (and Russian prisons are hellacious, and they turn everything they touch into hell), are a whole other thing. Every time Zelenskyy had to speak out about Wagner or answer questions about it, you could see him wince, how angry and disdainful he was, how everything in him rebelled against this vile kind of thieves' patriotism, and lawlessness on all levels. Still, he did not identify any fundamental differences between the owner of Wagner and Russia. The Russian government was as illegitimate for him as a private military company. If we talk about how Zelenskyy changed during the war, we must take note of three stages that he passed through: mistrust, hatred, and disgust. Following in the steps of its narrator king, Ukraine went through the same stages.

Zelenskyy and Prigozhin have their own history. First, the fall of 2019 brought Wagnergate, or, Operation Avenue, which we have mentioned previously. This was a muddy story, as is everything connected with Prigozhin. Second, an even murkier case was the murder of Wagnerite Yevgeny Nuzhin with a sledgehammer. But in this situation literally every existing statement must be questioned. It is not surprising, since the death of Yevgeny Prigozhin himself was not confirmed reliably by anyone, his funeral took place in secret, and videos of his resurrection popped up here and there with the speed of mushrooms. The initial version is as follows: on the night of November 13, 2022, a video was leaked online in which a man who identified himself as Yevgeny Nuzhin was killed with a sledgehammer. Before this, Nuzhin tells the camera that he went to the front with the goal of going over to the Ukrainian side and fighting the Russians. On a street in Kyiv he was kidnapped and taken to a basement where he was "tried" at a kangaroo court. After that he was hit on the head with a sledgehammer. It was unclear whether this was murder or a staged act.

It was established that Nuzhin was born in Kazakhstan in 1967, served in Russia's internal troops, was convicted to twenty-four years in prison for murder (and causing bodily harm to another victim), was moved among several prisons and colonies, had access to a telephone in prison, and appeared on social media. In July 2022, he was recruited by Prigozhin in the Ryazan prison colony, but almost immediately surrendered, saying in an interview with Ukrainian journalists that he condemned the invasion. (At the same time, he supported the annexation of Crimea on social media and regularly posted Russian patriotic symbols, including supporting the full-scale invasion after it took place.) In an interview, he said that Wagnerites are used as cannon fodder, that brutal morals prevailed in the group, and that traitors are "neutralized" without trials, that is, they were shot. How he got back to the Wagnerites is unknown. Some sources told journalists that the Wagnerites kidnapped him straight from Kyiv, but the main version was that he was turned over to Russia in an exchange. This version was clearly directed against Zelenskyy, since he repeatedly, personally and publicly, gave security guarantees to Russian prisoners. To justify this act of his, a rumor was spread (a good dozen colleagues repeated it to me) that the Wagnerites, for Nuzhin alone, offered 50 Ukrainian prisoners who, should the deal be refused, would be shot. That is, everything involving Nuzhin's service with the Wagnerites and his capture served as proof that his story was not fabricated, and explained why the Russians wanted him so badly. In fact the name Nuzhin in Russian sounds exactly like the word *nuzhen*, meaning "necessary" or "needed."

If Zelenskyy allegedly agreed to give up Nuzhin for fifty or so Ukrainian prisoners, thereby saving their lives, no one would have questioned him. But the whole story smacked of a bad literary scenario. Prigozhin was something of a hack writer (like most Z-patriots, he suffered from this disease in a severe form—he supervised the script for a propaganda film, *Hot Sun*, was especially involved in the functioning of his own media, and even published a children's book titled *Indraguzik*. Can you imagine that? *Indraguzik!* There is nothing worse than failed creative people—they ferociously hate those who have succeeded. Journalists sent Zelenskyy a question: did he really extradite Russian prisoners against their will? There was no answer, and I suspect Zelenskyy was not even aware of this story. Most likely, the very fact of Nuzhin's existence became known to him only as a result of this request. Putin's press secretary Dmitry Peskov, when asked for a comment, said it was none of Russia's business. Everyone started talking about the fact that the Wagnerites and their patron had been granted the right to reprisal, and that the Russian government had lost its monopoly on violence. Nuzhin's body was not returned to his relatives, allegedly, as they explained themselves, because the person handing it over would automatically be confessing to the murder. Whether there was a murder, whether Nuzhin was kidnapped, whether he was going to defect to the Ukrainians from the very beginning, or whether the whole legend was launched with the aim of discrediting Zelenskyy—no one now will say. But lawlessness is a situation where there are no actual and logical limits, where literally anything is possible! As the Russian publisher Maria Vasilyevna Rozanova said, the Kremlin elders recognized limits at least, and they did not find particular pleasure in being bad, deliberately bad, or worse than everyone else. Now that Prigozhin himself is no longer with us (again, let's keep a question mark here), Zelenskyy's response to his plane crash has a different ring: "This is none of our business."

Zelenskyy responded in exactly the same way to Prigozhin's notorious rebellion on June 24, 2023—the main event in Russia's human and historical wasteland. Whether this was actually a rebellion is not at all clear. Prigozhin himself said he "blew his lid." He was offended that his group's achievements in Bakhmut had been underestimated, that his anarchists were forced to swear allegiance to Defense Minister Shoigu, that his own status was unclear, so he, allegedly, headed for the Russian capital on a "march of justice." He got almost as far as Tula, but for some reason turned around there. One version was that he was planning to overthrow Putin.

Another was that he was going to remove Shoigu from his post. Still another was that this was Prigozhin's way of hightailing it from the front before Ukrainian General Oleksandr Syrskyi mounted a successful counteroffensive. All these versions are equally possible, none are convincing, and the main symbol of the failed rebellion emerged when one of Prigozhin's tanks got stuck in the gates of the Rostov circus. Zelenskyy made a brief Russian-language statement on this matter:

> Everyone who chooses the path of evil destroys himself. Whoever sends columns of troops to destroy the lives of another country and cannot stop them from fleeing and betraying when life resists. Whoever terrorizes with missiles, and when they are shot down, humiliates himself to receive Shahed drones. Whoever despises people and throws hundreds of thousands into the war, in order to eventually barricade himself in the Moscow region from those whom he himself armed. For a long time, Russia used propaganda to mask its weakness and the stupidity of its government. And now there is so much chaos that no lie can hide it. And all this from one person, who again and again tries to scare everyone with references to the year of 1917, although he is incapable of bringing about any other results. Russia's weakness is obvious. It's a full-scale weakness. And the longer Russia keeps its troops and mercenaries on our land, the more chaos, pain, and problems it will have for itself later.

Zelenskyy's reaction to Prigozhin is complete and utter disassociation. He doesn't understand, and doesn't want to understand, the phenomenon. Prigozhin is another life form entirely. He would never have encountered anything like it if this life form had not overflowed its laboratory beaker and had not gone on to conquer living human space. It is difficult to imagine anything more typical of today's Russia than Prigozhin, or anything more demonstrative than his methods of waging war. All this is a consequence of the monstrous decline of morals in Putin's Russia.

The worst thing is that someone must do something about all this. And that someone had to be Zelenskyy.

Prigozhin spoke honestly about him to his press service in November 2022, saying, "Although he is currently the president of a country hostile to Russia, Zelenskyy is a strong, confident, pragmatic, and nice guy."

Imagine him saying that! These guys could drive anyone crazy.

XVI. COUNTEROFFENSIVE

Everyone in Russia, Ukraine, and the West discussed the fact that Ukraine's counteroffensive would begin at the end of spring 2023, or in the first week of summer. It appeared to be inevitable. Everyone was encouraging it, and it seemed most of all to resemble the constant demands on Russian General Kutuzov in the war against Napoleon—it's time to mount a general battle, how much longer can you wait! Kutuzov was forced to engage in this battle, although he still had to abandon Moscow. That said, it is generally accepted that in the Battle of Borodino "the hand of the strongest enemy was laid upon the French." The Ukrainian counteroffensive was necessary to prove the combat capability of the Ukrainian Armed Forces, and the quality of the weapons supplied to them, to raise morale, and simply for reasons of the basic laws of drama, which in this war—as it turned out—meant more than military theory. This counteroffensive, by definition, could not have been victorious, for Ukraine received much less weapons than it asked for, and the weapons were not the kind that it asked for.

On July 14, the *Washington Post* published a summary of a conversation between its correspondents Konstantin Khludov, Sergei Morgunov, and Karina Khrabchuk with Ukrainian general Valerii Zaluzhnyi: "Conducting a counteroffensive with the goal of regaining territory, defeating Russia, and minimizing Ukrainian losses requires resources that are still in short supply. Western officials said Ukraine had enough tools to succeed, but Zaluzhnyi sharply criticized his colleagues who argued that Kyiv did not need F-16s. Their own military would never fight like that. And Western allies, citing fears of an escalation of war with Russia, have imposed a condition on the longer-range missiles and other equipment they have provided so far: they cannot be used to strike Russian soil. Therefore, according to Zaluzhnyi, he uses Ukrainian-made weapons for frequent strikes across the border, which Kyiv will never officially recognize as its own."

Two weeks earlier, Zaluzhnyi told Isabel Khurshudyan:

> To save my people, why do I have to ask someone for permission what to do on enemy territory? For some reason, I have to think that I'm not allowed to do anything there. Why? Because [Russian President Vladimir] Putin will . . . use nuclear weapons? The kids who are dying don't care.
>
> This is our problem, and it is up to us to decide how to kill this enemy. It is possible and necessary to kill on his territory in a war. If our partners are afraid to use their weapons, we will kill with our own. But only as much as is necessary.

On August 20, 2023, Zelenskyy announced that Ukraine would receive forty-two F-16s from the Netherlands. He posed for a photo with Dutch Prime Minister Mark Rutte in front of these fighter jets. As befits a narrator-king, in Denmark Zelenskyy posed in the cockpit of a fighter jet with his wife. This caused predictable hysteria in Russia: the undemocratic Danish authorities did not allow almost anyone but Danish journalists to ask questions! Danish Prime Minister Mette Frederiksen entered the cockpit of a fighter plane barefoot! Half of the fighters transferred to Ukraine are no good! All this was accompanied by a refrain: a Ukrainian clown is posing for photographers! (And at this moment the Russian clown forgets which hand his watch is on.)

But despite the transfer of fighters and the promise to transfer long-range artillery, the counteroffensive, as Zaluzhnyi warned, was slow and would not be the last. Ukraine had to chew through three lines of Russian defense. And although Zaluzhnyi claimed he was moving forward every day, even if sometimes by just 500 meters, the pace of the offensive did not suit him or the West. On August 25, Zaluzhnyi participated in a meeting with NATO generals on the Polish border. Ramstein, an international assistance group for Ukraine, which meets regularly, and is not named for Till Lindemann's musical group, but for the airbase where the team met for the first time on April 26, 2022, convenes monthly, suffers no doubts and constantly emphasizes its readiness to support Ukraine until the end of hostilities.

XVII. VZ AGAIN

Zaluzhnyi. Syrskyi. Podoliak
1.

For many in Ukraine and beyond, the initials of VZ today refer primarily not to Volodymyr Zelenskyy, but to Valerii Zaluzhnyi—another symbolic coincidence in the history of this war.

The three most famous and influential figures in Ukrainian defense are Minister Oleksii Reznikov (retired on September 5, 2023), Commander-in-Chief Valerii Zaluzhnyi, and Head of the Office of the President of Ukraine Mykhailo Podoliak. Much was written about the reasons for the resignation of fifty-three-year-old Reznikov. Corruption scandals were cited as the main motive, but I think that here, as in most of Zelenskyy's decisions, stylistic considerations were primary. Reznikov was a lawyer, a civilian, emphatically intelligent; his successor, the Crimean Tatar, financier and tough negotiator Rustem Umerov, is sixteen years younger and much more pugnacious.

Naturally, representatives of the Armed Forces of Ukraine have emerged during the war as prominent figures, whom Ukraine treats with adoration, as Israelis do their army. This is the natural course of things, it couldn't be otherwise, and it's good that the ambitions of the Ukrainian military leaders are not far-reaching. They could easily become the president's chief rivals in a struggle for power, were there to be a power struggle in Ukraine. Fortunately, that has not been a distraction so far.

Zelenskyy's role in the leadership of the army is assessed differently by different sources, but he trusts his military, and does not interfere in the management of troops. Here, as in the economy, he prefers to rely on professionals. It is as if Zaluzhnyi was deliberately put forward for the main role in the leadership of the Ukrainian army to provide contrast with his Russian colleagues. On July 8, 2023, he celebrated his fiftieth birthday. He was born in Novohrad-Volynskyi, in the family of an officer. He graduated from the Odesa Higher United Command School (1997) and the National Defense University of Ukraine (2014). On July 27, 2021, he was appointed Commander-in-Chief of the Armed Forces of Ukraine.

As befits the commander-in-chief of a fighting army, Zaluzhnyi is a secretive man. That is why his few interviews (primarily with the American media) are especially valuable. The portrait that emerges from them is attractive and frightening at the same time. But the most attractive thing about him is his absolute directness. In regard to Zaluzhnyi, the word "cunning" is most often used. But there is nothing particularly tricky in this war: Ukraine needs as many weapons as possible, and it will be able to manage them. Its task is to chew through Russian defenses and regain captured territories. This cannot be done without long-range artillery and aviation. I am no military expert, whose job it is to write textbooks based on the material of this latest war, and to explain the significance of raids on enemy territory (dozens of articles have been written about Zaluzhnyi's raids, his tactics of fighting a superior enemy have been analyzed in detail). I am merely interested in the personality of the man in whom Ukraine places its greatest hopes today.

"The most important experience that we had, and the one that we professed almost like a religion, is that Russians, and any other enemies, must be killed, just killed, and most importantly, not be afraid to do it. And that's what we do."

"I trust my generals. Since the beginning of the war, I fired ten of them because they weren't committed. Another one shot himself."

"Russian mobilization worked. It is not true that their problems are so terrible that these people will not fight. They will. Their tsar sent them to war, and they went. I studied the history of the two Chechen wars—the same thing happened there. They may not be as well equipped, but they still pose a challenge to us. The Russians are training about 200,000 fresh soldiers. I have no doubt that they will have another try at Kyiv."

I suspect that both Zaluzhnyi and Zelenskyy came to the same conclusion about what, for them, was most important: there is nowhere to retreat to, there is no compromise, and there cannot be. While the whole world subtly tries to convince Zelenskyy that all wars end in negotiations, he stubbornly stands his ground. While the whole world unobtrusively explains to Zaluzhnyi that he was given all possible weapons, and NATO simply has no more, he continues to repeat: I need 100 aircraft and 6,000 HIMARS, and we will return to the borders of 1991.

Zaluzhnyi in Ukraine is called "our Napoleon" (and Zelenskyy, as we recall, is "our little Churchill," although the "little" was dropped). On the commander-in-chief's fiftieth birthday, the Kholodnyi Yar 93rd detached mechanized brigade dedicated a song to him and recorded a video. I must say, it is a powerful spectacle—utterly unlike anything you would find in Russian officialdom or the Russian criminal world. "We don't want anyone else's meadow, we'll fight for our own until the end. No one can stop our advance. Through fire we move toward our goal. We'll liberate our Ukraine. We'll break our enemies' backs." And the chorus: "If Zaluzhnyi gives us the order—we will be in Moscow." (A fine expression of freedom, as the great Russian writer Andrei Platonov might have said. In an interview with Yanina Sokolova's *Rendezvous* program, Zaluzhnyi admitted he had a dream of riding in a tank down Moscow's famed Arbat street. "But we'll be careful. It's a historical place.") The song is sung, the soldiers themselves playing guitars, drums, and wind instruments, by a very motley crew ranging in age from twenty to fifty, with a predominance of forty-year-olds. The average age of the Ukrainian army is thirty-eight, they try not to let young people into battle. They do not panic—they have a calm confidence and a complete readiness for anything. Russia was able to raise a huge army, only it's not really theirs. The song picks up: "All our boys are friends—he, and you, and me. Our father is Zaluzhnyi, the Ukranian Armed forces—our family." The reference to another popular song was clear: "Our father is Bandera, Ukraine is our mother, we will fight for Ukraine!"

Ukrainians are especially proud that Zaluzhnyi is "completely ours." He is a general with no Soviet experience. He did not serve in the Soviet army, and received his military education exclusively in Ukraine. Before the war, his wife Olena was a financier at Ukrgasbank. They had been married for twenty years, with two daughters. His best friend is Chief of the General Staff Serhii Shaptala. Zaluzhnyi calls Generals Montgomery, Bradley, Adams, and Patton his idols. Like them, he was on the cover of *Time*—the first and, so far, only time a Ukrainian military man has had that honor. Zaluzhnyi was first called the Iron General not by the Ukrainians, but by the American publication *Politico*, after the Russians retreated from Kyiv in April 2022. At the same time, Zaluzhnyi's rejection of an authoritarian Soviet-like style was emphasized for the first time.

In an interview with Dmytro Komarov, Zaluzhnyi admitted: "The commander-in-chief is not supposed to talk about his weaknesses. But I can admit that I cried once during the war—when a mother was looking for her son, a helicopter pilot. He had died over Mariupol. And I had to tell her that."

In 2023, a military secret came to light (Ukrainians dole out such sensations very carefully, so the secret, of course, was leaked deliberately): The notion of blowing up Kyiv's bridges in the event of a successful Russian attack on the capital was discussed in March 2022. Zaluzhnyi received a call from Ivan Bakanov (then the head of the security service; removed by Zelenskyy on July 17, 2022. Subsequently, any unpopular decisions could be blamed on him). Bakanov suggested blowing up the bridges. Zaluzhnyi replied: under no circumstances. That would be a betrayal of everyone who remained on the left bank.

During the 2023 summer counteroffensive, Zaluzhnyi regularly had to explain to the West, Ukrainian citizens, and secret Russian well-wishers why it was moving so slowly. The Russian defense lines, built over a six-month period after the retreat from Kherson, were called "Surovikin's lines," although the line of Russian General Surovikin was only one among many. It stood on the left bank of the Dnipro, and consisted of four lines of defense. There was also the Wagner Line (one-and-a-half kilometers in the Bakhmut area of a planned 217 kilometers reaching from Luhansk to Svitlodarsk), the so-called "notch line" of Belgorod governor Vyacheslav Gladkov in Russian territory, and anti-tank obstacles in Crimea. According to the British Institute for Defense Studies, the Russian defense lines are among the biggest fortifications in history. According to the Royal United Services Institute, the Russian defense consists of three lines. The first is located along the line of contact and contains infantry combat positions with trenches in the form of fox holes. Next are several lines of obstacles consisting of anti-tank ditches four meters deep and six meters wide; followed by concrete pillboxes, and guns dug into the ground. The depth of defense is about thirty kilometers, or under twenty miles. "Defense lines are punctuated by minefields, like cheese and meat in lasagna. According to Z-military correspondent Dmitry Steshin, "everything is mined there,'" correspondent Pavel Vorobyov writes with gusto in News.ru. Here I inevitably recall Soviet writer Samuil Marshak declaring in 1945: "We are mining everything, from shed to barn . . . A German woman approaches us. What is your name?—'Minna!' she says." Russian, Ukrainian, and Western experts were unanimous that it would be extremely difficult to overcome the Russian defense lines built from October 22 to February 23. The breaking of the Surovikin line in the Zaporizhzhia region began to be reported only on August 30. Zaluzhnyi introduced into action almost the last of his reserves, and the breakthrough was conducted by the 82nd air assault brigade of the Ukrainian Armed Forces, numbering two thousand warriors, equipped with British Challenger tanks, Marder and Stryker infantry fighting vehicles. If the encirclement of the city of Tokmak had been completed shortly thereafter, the next task would have been the liberation of Mariupol. In any case, it was possible to gnaw through the Russian defenses, albeit at huge costs. Zaluzhnyi avoided declaring victories, arguing that there were still multiple offensives ahead, and that it would hardly have been possible to reach the borders of 1991 during the spring of 2024. (Arestovych believed that by this time it would only have been possible to drive the Russians out of Crimea, and it would not be possible to return to the previous borders without a manifold increase in the supply of long-range artillery.)

If Ukraine manages to take Mariupol and show the world what happened there during and after its capture, the world will have to endure a serious shock. I am greatly tempted to wait for the results of the counteroffensive, but this book is not about the counteroffensive, which will be written about later in textbooks. Zaluzhnyi has become the most popular person in Ukraine and could easily win the presidential election if he wanted to, but he does not intend to compete with Zelenskyy.

Still, after the war ends, regardless of the pace of the liberation of Ukrainian territories, Zaluzhnyi may turn out to be one of the most popular generals in the world. How he will use this capital, and whether he will want to invest it in politics, is unknown. What is known is that his name has become a symbol of hope. One wants to avoid pathos here, for pathos is not characteristic of him. God bless him and he will do the rest.

2. Podoliak

Podoliak, an advisor to Yermak, is one of the main voices of this war. German magazine *Focus* puts him in third place in the ranking of the most influential Ukrainians. This is explained by the fact that in today's Ukraine— and I suspect in the rest of the world, too—there is nothing more valuable than fresh, reliable front-line reports. The time when Ukraine needed a comforter has passed. Today it needs an expert (by the way, Arestovych clearly sensed this and in spring 2023 he turned from a comforter into a furious critic).

Podoliak has had a stormy biography. He was born February 16, 1972, and is a physician by training, a graduate of the Minsk Medical Institute. From the early '90s, he worked as a journalist in Belarus, and was an outspoken critic of Lukashenka, who from the mid-'90s built a training ground for the world in which both Putin's Russia and Yanukovych's Ukraine would soon find themselves (even if Yanukovych looks rather endearing compared to the other, last two dictators of Europe). Podoliak was expelled from Belarus without trial or investigation. They simply came to his home and told him to pack up in half an hour. He was deported to Ukraine without the right to visit Belarus for five years. Podoliak has repeatedly noted that he is grateful to Lukashenka for the deportation: it made it easier for him to call a spade a spade. I think this is precisely the kind of biography that *Novaya Gazeta* columnist Ian Shenkman had in mind when he scandalously wrote in mid-2023 about the journalists of our generation that we are all beneficiaries of this war. He said this as a provocation, but in essence it is true. This war gave our generation a kick in the pants, without which many would not have been able to leave Russia, or make up their minds about what was transpiring. We kept waiting everyone out: first seeing off the democrats of the first wave, then the nomenklatura, then the old KGB forces. All of these people drove matters to the point where people had to save themselves and, if possible, humanity. Our "we will take things from here"—to quote a popular song by Viktor Tsoi—came about only because there was no one else left. By the way, in Ukraine today, most processes are controlled by people born between 1970 and 1975.

In Ukraine, where the situation with vertical mobility was excellent at that time, Podoliak was not sidetracked, and he headed up the *Ukrainian Newspaper*. He also found himself in the opposition here, speaking out sharply against Viktor Yushchenko. He ran into an interrogation by the Ukrainian Security Forces, which demanded that he reveal the sources of his investigation into the Yushchenko poisoning (allegedly it was organized by his comrades-in-arms). Then he created the Observer website and a "reputation management" company. I roughly understand those to be custom political crusades (or battles against them). But among the journalists of the '90s—in Ukraine this began in the 2000s—there was practically no one who did not participate in such campaigns. It was a kind of professional school, albeit an extremely cynical one.

Conflicting things are said about Podoliak. It is said that he worked for criminal authorities, including ones from Donbas. It was believed that he served Poroshenko as a political strategist (he denies this). In 2020, Yermak invited Podoliak to be his adviser, which once again confirmed his extreme pragmatism, not to say cynicism: He needed an effective person, even if it was with an ambiguous reputation, and so Podoliak began to oversee the work of the Presidential Office with the press.

Podoliak participated in the unsuccessful February–March negotiations and covered their progress. He regularly gives interviews to the Anti-Corruption Foundation (FBK), founded by Alexei Navalny, and liberal Russian journalist Yulia Latynina, meets with Russian journalists, and arouses pathological hatred among propagandists. They call him *Podliak*, a word that plays on his name and suggests a "scoundrel." He has the reputation of a person who easily shifts his positions—he called Yermak a dark demon one year before going to work for him. But I don't think he is motivated by money. In the end, Podoliak is busy today with deadly serious work, and even if he were a pure pragmatist, life would be more valuable to him than money. It seems to me that Podoliak, as an exemplary PR man, has a flair for understanding the future, and this flair told him that Zelenskyy represented the most promising and, at the same time, coherent force in Ukrainian society. He came to work for Yermak at what was not the easiest of times—Zelenskyy's negative rating, as we remember, was growing rapidly. As such, Podoliak joined the team because it interested him. He loves professional challenges, and there is certainly a professional challenge to confronting today's wave of ridiculous, but very loud Russian propaganda.

If we are to speak of cunning, Podoliak takes a cunning approach to his work: he prefers to tell his listeners and interlocutors unpleasant things. Being a professional PR man, having chosen this profession because of a deep affinity for it, and possessing an excellent understanding of people, he is convincing precisely with his objectivity. It can be said that he was the first to formulate the main lesson of this war: its outcome and the memory of it will be determined not by military confrontation, but by morality. Russia has much of everything, it will have tactical successes, it will attack more than once (I well remember the panicky mood of the summer of 2022, when Russia, after the rollback from Kyiv, went on the offensive in Donbas). Russia may even win, but this victory will mean the defeat and capitulation of the whole world. "Moreover, reaching an agreement with Putin, in fact, pushes him to achieve other goals using blackmail methods. He came in, exhibited an absolutely barbaric way of waging war, destroyed a thousand small and medium-sized cities, including Mariupol. He killed many thousands of people, including children. If after this you still pretend it is possible to come to certain legal agreements with Putin, then this suggests that Russia can continue to use the technique of maximum direct pressure on any market, on any country. Europe, if it follows this path, will be forced, step by step, to make concessions, not only regarding the territories of other countries, but also in something more significant. Russia will claim victory in a local European war and will claim a greater leadership role on the European continent," he told Meduza, and this was heard. Actually, this notion was already floating in the air. Over and over again Podoliak repeats: if we don't resist, you will have to resist. At this point one can't establish who was the first to say this to the Europeans, he or Zelenskyy, but it has become part of Zelenskyy's rhetoric.

Can Ukraine lose this war? In a military sense, it would be quite easy: the complete seizure of territory (most likely without complete control, but with mass extermination of the population), in extreme cases a nuclear blast. None of this is a problem. It is quite possible to defeat Ukraine in a purely military sense—all you have to do is halt Western military assistance. But this is the very case when coming to terms with Russia's victory means relinquishing your own future and covering yourself with eternal shame. A quote attributed to Churchill: "You were given the choice between war and dishonor. You chose dishonor, and you will have war." Podoliak, wearing his eternal mask of a calm, reasonable, even somewhat florid theorist, quotes to the world on behalf of Ukraine the words from Maurice Maeterlinck's *The Blue Bird* as they sound in the Russian translation: "Those who go with their children will die. Those who don't go will die a few seconds later."

"All that the leadership of the Russian Federation is doing now is pushing its strategy to the point of absurdity. As I understand it, this is something like a fantastic suicide attempt for the entire country," goes another of Podoliak's formulas that have been picked up by others. Russia does not have a picture of the future, Ukraine does, and this is the only guarantee of victory. Throughout his career, Podoliak has never been afraid of losing. He likes to take risks. He is only afraid of humiliation and boredom—a normal trait for an adventurous schemer endowed with good instinct.

I may not want to have Podoliak as either an enemy or a friend. But I would definitely like to be allies with him. This would mean that the future is on my side.

3. Syrskyi

Oleksandr Syrskyi was born July 26, 1965, in Russia, in the Vladimir region. He is a graduate of the Moscow Higher Combined Arms Command School. He served in Ukraine and graduated from the Academy of the Ukrainian Armed Forces in 1996. His 72nd mechanized brigade of the Ukrainian Armed Forces received the Black Cossacks insignia. The Black Cossacks were an equestrian division from the times of the Ukrainian Republic, that is, 1918, and they were dressed in experimental black uniforms. They successfully drove out the Bolsheviks and took Kyiv on August 31, 1919. They all wore a cockade in the form of a skull with crossbones and top knots. I'm thinking a skull with a top knot might make a very effective patch. There's no imperial aspiration in that, is there, dear reader?

In 2014, Syrskyi became the first deputy head of the Main Command Center of the Armed Forces of Ukraine. Soon he headed the joint headquarters of the Armed Forces of Ukraine. He was the commander of a group that covered the Ukrainians' exit from the Debaltseve cauldron. Some Russian publications credit Syrskyi with commanding the BARS group: I don't know if this is a deliberate confusion, but BARS is a group of Russian volunteer soldiers, actively covered by the Z-press. That happened to be Syrskyi's call sign—it is possible that the Russian volunteers appropriated it for the sake of show, and, indeed, Syrskyi fights successfully. The Russians decipher BARS as the Special Combat Army Reserve. Syrskyi doesn't decipher his call sign in any way, he just tries to live up to it. For his work in Debaltseve he received the Order of Bohdan Khmelnytskyi, III degree. Syrskyi is the only colonel general in the Ukrainian army: this rank was assigned to him on August 23, 2020, after which it was no longer assigned to anyone. In February 2022, it was Syrskyi who was responsible for the defense of Kyiv and the Kyiv region. After this, Zelenskyy appointed him commander of the ground forces.

In 2013, Syrskyi underwent training in Brussels and, while there, developed a passion for decentralized command, or mission command, a strategy that Prussian Field Marshall Neidhardt von Gneisenau began developing in 1813, and which was perfected by Helmuth von Moltke in 1866 and 1870. In practice, it looks like this: a task is presented to the unit commander. He personally plans how it will be carried out. Military analysts in the United States, Great Britain, and the Netherlands have proven in detail the effectiveness of this method, although they do not always employ it, because the inertia of an army's chain of command is very strong. If every mid-level commander were to decide how to carry out combat missions and received expanded powers, what would be the result? Total chaos, as the writer Mikhail Veller might put it! The Swedes implemented this strategy when the Swedish-Danish-Norwegian Nordbat 2 battalion was tasked with stabilizing the territory of the former Yugoslavia within the UN forces. Sweden, as you know, did not wage war for two hundred years and during this time managed to greatly democratize its army. Mission command gave its officers the right to personally interpret orders and regulate their own powers. In the conditions of the former Yugoslavia it was necessary to react quickly, to make decisions on the spot. A rigid command structure would not have coped with their task of regulation, since they were defending an extremely militant and energized population. Nordbat 2 was effective, and NATO headquarters began discussing the fact that the natural development of freedom and democracy in the world would lead to the encouragement of initiative from below within armies, which would seem to be hostile to democracy by definition. But there you have it. Theoretical works, and special studies appeared, and a doctrine was formulated—the so-called five points of decentralization: mutual trust, conscious discipline, communicating a clear picture to subordinates, competence, willingness to take risks.

In December 2022, Syrskyi gave an extremely rare interview to *The Economist*. The most famous phrase there is, "Underestimating Russia is setting yourself up for failure." The key theme, however, was Syrskyi's requirement for commanders to find non-trivial solutions. He stated that Kyiv was on the verge of being encircled and admitted that he was urgently forced to form battalions of military school cadets. The war, from his point of view, will be long, but he has no doubts about Ukraine's victory. "We have studied the enemy. For every poison we have an antidote."

Syrskyi has a reputation as an ascetic and a gym fanatic. However, Zelenskyy also believes that the gym is the best way to relax. Syrskyi played a key role in the liberation of Izium and received public praise from Zelenskyy. He is now operating near Bakhmut and is confident that he will turn the situation around. It was Syrskyi who raised the Ukrainian flag over Balakliia. Syrskyi's main trait is described as excellent tactical training, the ability quickly to assess the situation, and unfettered ambition. All these are invaluable qualities in times of war, and preconditions for bad character in times of peace. Syrskyi's character is a difficult one, but he fights in an exemplary manner—the American press began calling him a genius.

Zaluzhnyi and Syrskyi were put on the wanted list in the Russian Federation, a PR move that the Russian authorities often resort to. Furthermore, the judge of the international criminal court who put Putin on the wanted list was in turn put on the wanted list all over the world. Podoliak described this succinctly: "Open House in the asylum."

And he added: you don't need to go looking for them [Russians committing crimes]. They will come to you and answer all your questions.

We see from this quick sketch that two categories of people succeed with Zelenskyy: diligent students and risk-takers. However, you can skip the words "with Zelenskyy," for, indeed, only these two categories of people succeed. The rest, to be honest, imitate vigorous activity.

XVIII. Z, GODDAMMIT!

There are three ways to talk about this war. We can talk about the suffering of civilians, the heroic volunteers, and the impeccable solidarity that united the population. Of course, there will be facts that contradict this version. Doubters would talk about predation, selfishness, and invincible corruption, which I demagogically justify. Meanwhile, a regular reader writes to me, it is precisely because of corruption and the theft of medicines in Ukraine that it is impossible to obtain anesthesia to fix a tooth! For every thesis about the unity and inspiration of the Ukrainian population, there is an antithesis about predation and how the war has corrupted its morals. For every story about children weaving nets, there is a story about muscular, bearded men escaping conscription and flooding into Europe. But it is possible, at least over the course of many pages, to talk about destroyed homes, separated families, and the victims of war, primarily because the Russian army hits peaceful cities more often than military targets. Many such stories are mentioned here, and in total, about 400,000 war crimes of a wide range have been documented in Ukraine, from murder or rape of civilians to looting. Modern warfare is recorded in detail. One of the leaders of his generation, Russian director Ilya Khrzhanovsky, the creator of the grandiose *DAU* project, and subsequently the artistic director of the Babyn Yar Museum, said, while leading me past the huge mirror in the main installation of this museum, about the project of a complete three-dimensional chronicle of the Second World War: "We now have new methods of reconstruction, so to speak, of the entire data array—to replicate the entire event in absolute completeness. There are testimonies of all witnesses, and, with the help of a computer it is possible to determine down to the millimeter all the points where the executions took place, by the positions of the shadows in the photo, timing it down to a second. Almost all the events of the twentieth century are exhaustively documented. So we are entering an era of establishing the full truth about how things were; absolutely objective truth, not interpreted by historians. A revelation of incredible power awaits us. That is, we will, for example, actually learn the whole truth about the war. For many it will be a shock. Forensics—also known as computer forensics—is the main tool in solving crimes today. It is time to apply this to military crimes. We have brought together millions of documents that will be stored and analyzed here, in the main building of the museum, in the form of a huge mound, under a dome with an area of nine thousand square meters. When this kind of history of the war is written, the need for ideological interpretations will disappear altogether."

Additionally, as Olena Zelenska rightly notes, Ukrainians—and she personally—do not want to see themselves as victims. They complain to no one. They are faced with an extremely difficult task of asking the West for help, or rather, provoking it for this help, so as not to be humiliated. This situation is unbearable, and you have to be Zelenskyy to get out of it without falling into the position of a supplicant, and at the same time avoiding reproaches of ingratitude.

The story of this war for Ukraine is not a story of suffering, although the memory of the victims will always be sacred. It is a story about how the power grid and military equipment were quickly restored after being destroyed, how they extricated themselves from hopeless situations in conditions of almost total lack of funds and weapons, how they learned to surpass the enemy in determination and cunning, how the generation of managers and post-industrialists were forced to get used to guerrilla warfare and shooting, and how they, supposedly pampered and lazy, managed to do all that. It so happened that people were pampered and lazy in places where they didn't have to work. But in Ukraine, which was actually building a new society, work was imperative. These people emerged as very strong professionals in the war. They themselves will write about their combat experience. They are the ones about whom Zelenskyy said: "Young, beautiful, and strong—free people who grew up in a free country; that's the Ukraine I believe in." It would be possible to focus on the atrocities of the occupiers, on the chaos and lawlessness that the "Russian world" brings with it. And then Zelenskyy's Ukraine would stand forth in stark contrast, for here, too, there are inexhaustible reserves of creepy and grotesque stories.

Incidentally, *Evening Quarter* continues to be broadcast, and they make rude, furious jokes about the so-called Russian world. In one marvelous episode a drone hovers over a Russian trench and Boklan, portraying a Russian mobster, says:

"It's time to pray!"
"Do you know any prayers?" asks Kazanin.
"I do! We are Russians, God fucking damn it! God is with us!"

This is a very accurate depiction of the Russian religious worldview, written using the most sacred formulas of the contemporary Russian language. Such dialogues comprise Serhii Loznitsa's great and terrible film, *Donbas*, a feature based on documentary stories posted online by supporters of the "Russian world." It would take more than one volume to collect them, and there surely will be someone to do this.

I've been interested in the people on whom Zelenskyy has relied—people of his generation and, perhaps, of his type. The People, in contrast to the Z-people whom the Putin era produced in abundance.

RUSSIAN PUBLISHER'S NOTE: Here in the margins we have a dialogue with my Russian publisher who asked, "Didn't they exist before?" This is an interesting question, because I remember the seventies well and the wild dominance of the extremely cruel *gopota*, or lowlife thugs. The seventies (and even the sixties) were not an idyllic time; the contrast and conflict between the people and the intelligentsia seeped into all the best texts, from Vasily Aksyonov's *Victory* to Natalya Ryazantseva in Ilya Averbakh's film *Alien Letters*. But this shadow, this underbelly of society knew its place. The *gopota* of the Putin era is a *gopota* that demands its rights, one that considers itself and, probably rightly so, an elite. Things like this have never happened before, and they will have to be dealt with for a very long time, and very crudely.

Z-people kill their own and others out of despair, for, once again, nothing has worked out for them—neither on a global scale, nor on a national scale, where they are feared but despised, because they hate the future and do not want to move into it, because they are capable of shining, and even then only with a putrid light, only in the darkness of the Putin era. The only way for them to avoid being found out is the endless prolongation of this miserable era.

In contrast, Z-People are a generation of thirty- and forty-year-olds whose chief worry is *nezalomnost'*—a term that roughly translates as inflexibility.

This inflexibility is even more important than independence. For people of the Z-Generation bravado is more valuable than money, so as to avoid the more bombastic formula of, "Honor is more valuable than life." They will live freely, openly, cheerfully and at ease in the truest sense of the word. No one will force them to do anything. In them all the best and worst traits of the national character are developed harmoniously, and they will bow neither to the East nor to the West. They are the Ukrainian character's main reserve, its gold fund, its first detachment of renewal. They are capable of much, they stand firmly on their feet, are professionals in their field, and do not interfere in those of others. They are fast learners. They never forgive anything and are capable of remembering goodness. They are consequential individuals.

Talking about Zelenskyy means talking about them.

Nothing may come of them, as is true of anything in this world. They may disappear into sluggish new generations, or may not find a place for themselves in peaceful life. They may go crazy from post-traumatic syndrome, escape to Europe and get lost there. But this has happened with every war generation: not all veterans can fit into the new world they defended, and they don't always have the strength to rebuild and equip it. They have already done the most important thing—they justified their generation, which suffered the greatest crisis of the century. They did not die out during the pandemic, did not break down during the war, and did not grow weak after it ended. The phrase—what doesn't kill me makes me stronger—cannot be spoken about everyone, alas, but it can be spoken about them.

In order to keep the future from coming, homeostasis throws every generation of true, established modernity into the furnace of war. The current generation of Ukrainians truly did not perish in fire, did not drown in floods, and the copper trumpets of praise were of no interest to them. They are the first modernists who had a chance to survive and establish new rules—to build a world in which knowledge is more interesting than thievery, and solidarity is held in higher esteem than domination. This is what Zelenskyy and his TV hero Goloborodko have in common. These are the people whom president Zelenskyy eventually became, for he had no interest in being president of the former Ukraine.

XIX. APPEALS AND TRANSFORMATIONS

Observations on Rhetoric

The Russian word *obrashchenie* has two meanings: speech directed at a specific individual, and transformation, as a werewolf might do. Zelenskyy's speeches are a chain of appeals and transformations. He edits them himself and sometimes writes them from start to finish. At the same time, he has had quality speechwriters ever since the days of the Block. Let's take a look at his rhetoric and its dynamics.

Zelenskyy speaks a lot, addressing Ukrainians and the world community almost every day, truly fulfilling the main function of the narrator king—informing people of the how and what of things. We can outline his main rhetorical techniques based on the speeches he has made in the last year. We will do it as neutrally as possible, since oratorical techniques can and should be goal-oriented: Zelenskyy has a specific task—to attract to his side as many leaders, donations, and ordinary sympathizers as possible, and at the same time to support among Ukrainians the spirit of being prepared for anything and everything. All is fair in love and in war, said John Lyly and everyone else who is not too lazy to repeat it. That is, there are no dishonest tricks in love and war; in a sense they are all goal-oriented, but there is nothing to be done about it.

1. Zelenskyy likes to emphasize that Ukraine is solving the problems of the whole world, that Russian aggression is not merely a Ukrainian problem, and that Ukraine protects all wives, husbands, children, and old people from an unpredictable aggressor armed with nuclear missiles. Russia, on the contrary, insists on localizing the discourse, which is also a very old (and rather dirty) technique: "Bug off, this is a dispute among Slavs," etc. "Have a drink and a bite to eat, Pops, don't let this nonsense worry you." Zelenskyy and his team have succeeded in popularizing the main narrative: that this is not a dispute among Slavs, it is the leading edge of a struggle between the world's archaism and the world's modernity. "Any war is a common global challenge—a threat to the world, and not just the suffering of those

against whom this aggression is committed." (Address to the Organization of American States, June 22, 2023).

Moreover, Zelenskyy manages to present the future restoration of Ukraine as, again, a global task. All of Europe will participate financially in this. ("And, of course, I thank Switzerland, Germany, France, Italy—every country where we have agreed on key principles for recovery.") Ukraine promises to turn into a pan-European, or even a worldwide, construction site, where young people from all over the planet will go to work for reasons of material gain, interest, and prestige. Ukraine has a chance for the first time in the world, again with the intellectual and financial participation of the whole world, to build a collective utopia, an ideal state. It was historically more difficult for Russia—as prescribed in "The Internationale" Russia was to destroy itself "to dust, and then" (although, as always, it did not destroy everything, leaving intact all the most horrible things, of which the secret police was paramount). Zelenskyy never tires of attempting to seduce Ukrainian and global listeners with these pictures of a European utopia, because Russia did the destructive part of the work. Ukraine, even if against its own will, is doomed to start much from scratch, although the world is very tired of insoluble conflicts and crises. An utterly destroyed Ukraine is the perfect construction site. We all remember Emerson's phrase that "every wall is a gate." From Zelenskyy's rhetoric (which is forced upon him, but how else does one come to terms with the spectacle of a ravaged country?) we can learn that every ruin is a construction site. "The key Ukrainian principle is simple and fair, namely: no ruins will be left in Ukraine. We will rebuild everything, restore everything, and we know exactly what steps need to be taken in what timeframe and with what forces to defeat Russian aggression and rebuild our country."

Zelenskyy never tires of reminding the world that we all must build a collective utopia, and that everyone will be allowed to participate, even Russians who have proven their anti-war position. What might this be compared to in literature? It will be—and it will be!—something like the collective construction of an aquatic plant in "The Girl on the Cliff," a fantasy story by Soviet-Russian writer Vadim Shefner:

18th Correspondent. I was surprised that such primitive tools were used on the island. One might think we had returned to the first half of the twentieth century. What museum did you get these shovels, picks, and crowbars from?

Andrei. I didn't get them anywhere. They commissioned them themselves based on old drawings from some Leningrad factory, and they themselves brought them to the island.

18th Correspondent. Who are "they"?

Andrei. Volunteers. They come from all over the world.

20th Correspondent. But there are doctors of labor security on the island. A doctor's word is law.

Andrei. They don't listen to doctors. Anyway, there are so many volunteers that they work for no more than an hour. Nothing in it is harmful to the health.

21st Correspondent. Do injuries occur on the island as a result of the use of imperfect tools?

Andrei. There are no major injuries. But there are bruises and calluses. Yesterday, a man from Chile injured his toe with a shovel.

21st Correspondent. I hope he was immediately evacuated to a hospital on the mainland?

Andrei. Not immediately. For his honorable wound, his friends allowed him to work another hour out of turn.

Russia has always supplied the world with great utopias. But who would have thought it would be like this in the twenty-first century?!

2. Zelenskyy repeats this notion in every speech he addresses to the world community, and in every third speech delivered to Ukrainians: "Ukraine will definitely be able to protect Europe from any Russian forces, and it doesn't matter who commands them. We will protect. The security of Europe's eastern flank depends only on our defense." (June 24, 2023, the day of the Prigozhin rebellion.) Without us, the world will collapse—Zelenskyy successfully and with good reason implants this notion into the minds of his fellow citizens and allies. Ukraine is not just a part of Europe, it is its leader and showcase: "It is here, in Ukraine, that the world will see

what Europe is capable of. Here, in Ukraine, we will have the maximum of Europe in Europe—the maximum possibility of what European values are capable of, what European and global cooperation is capable of." In truth, Zelenskyy managed to turn the war into a powerful catalyst for the Europeanization of Ukraine: the sole chance of depicting a catastrophe as a global wake-up call, and an incentive for Europe. At least in Zelenskyy's portrayal of it, Ukraine has transformed from a potential weak link in the European family into a major symbol of European values. "What does it mean to be pro-Ukrainian? It is to be pro-European. You are in Europe today. You are an integral part of a calm, civilized Europe."

3. He has shifted the center of gravity to Putin's personality. This is a seemingly controversial technique, since even in Russia, with its rather bastardly cult of personality (as goes the personality, so goes the cult), people can guess that Putin is not the point. But the task of every leader is to present a problem as something that can be solved. Whether it is possible to reeducate the Russian population or reform the Russian empire is still unclear, but removing Putin is a completely solvable task. Even if the Ukrainian army or the Russian opposition cannot do it, sooner or later it will happen in the natural course of things. "The longer this person remains in the Kremlin, the more disasters there will be." (This is true, but what happens if you remove this person from the Kremlin? It certainly won't be worse, but you can't expect any quick improvements either. A wasted nuclear field is in no way preferable to a nuclear state.)

RUSSIAN PUBLISHER'S NOTE: Taking control of such a field is not that difficult, but Putin benefits from the myth of the savaged field following him.

AUTHOR: I agree, but this myth is extremely convincing. The screenwriters Pyotr Lutsik and Alexei Samoryadov, the main prophets of the late Russian '90s, depicted just such a world. I can imagine it following the destruction of all institutions and the failure of all braking mechanisms, both external and internal. Is such an outcome better than dictatorship? I suspect they are as incomparable as a villain and a villain's corpse.

4. The creation of new news channels, and a bold positive agenda. The president of a warring state, in principle, cannot complain of boredom, but there is the monotony of catastrophe—whether it be epidemic, plague, or war. There you have the great tedium of the end of the world. At such times, finding joyous, or at least encouraging, news is a task unto itself, something Zelenskyy's speechwriters cope with quite professionally. This might involve the graduation of officers from six military universities (as on June 23, 2023), the announcement of new large-scale supplies of weapons, or new promises about rapprochement with NATO. As a rule, Zelenskyy will begin an address by saying the day was momentous and difficult, but then he immediately moves on to comforting news—such as: we have advanced in several directions; new sanctions have been imposed on Russia; or Ukraine has achieved new successes at the Global Forum, etc. This Global Forum, where the world community must decide the fate of Russia and determine the bloc status of Ukraine, has emerged as a national project that is the equal of a counteroffensive. The very mention of the Global Forum pleases the ear, for it almost has the same ring as the Nuremberg Tribunal. It will confirm that the world community's agenda today is being formulated not by the UN, but by Ukraine. And this is true whether others like it or not. The Global Forum, if it takes place, will only secure this status.

5. Constant—and very dramatic—emphasis of the global nature and scale of the spectacle that is unfolding before our eyes. Hence what Zelenskyy has repeated literally from the first day of his presidency: "The eyes of the world are fixed on us"; "The whole world is looking at us"; "A global drama is unfolding before the eyes of the whole world," etc. There is nothing to object to here: the only positive aspect of what is happening is the significance of this tragic era.

RUSSIAN PUBLISHER'S NOTE: An era is always significant.
AUTHOR: I would not say so. No matter how you describe them, the 2000s were insignificant. They were zeros in every way.

Also positive, no matter how terrible it sounds, is the entertainment value. We are not mere ordinary people, we are participants in a mystery play about the world. We have been invited by the Almighty to participate in a feast. Not just Ukraine, but the whole world is participating in the next (and perhaps final) battle of good vs. evil. It is dangerous. But we are fascinated.

6. Specifics. In almost every address with a domestic agenda, and in many speeches for international audiences, Zelenskyy names the names of specific officers. Not just senior command personnel, but lieutenants, senior sailors, privates—participants in the war whom he never fails to reward personally. This is not the propaganda of heroic resistance, and certainly not the typical kind of exhortation, so common in Russia right now, to immediately surrender one's life for the sake of the Motherland. There is, in Ukraine, none of the necrophiliac propaganda so common in Russia. It's not even close. Russian propagandists prefer to talk about heroic deaths, for, there, the ideal citizen is a dead citizen: there is no need to feed him. Zelenskyy, in every daily address, prefers to glorify at least one living person. And such a mention is an incentive more reliable and powerful than any military reward, not to mention one of a financial nature.

Almost every evening, in my addresses, I thank our warriors—particular units, particular brigades, which distinguished themselves the most on the front line or in the defense of our sky in a day or in a week.

And today—more personal words of gratitude to particular warriors.

We should all remember that our defense, our active actions, and the independence of Ukraine are not something abstract. These are very particular people, particular actions of particular heroes, thanks to which Ukraine exists and Ukraine will continue to exist. Thousands and thousands of our strongest, bravest, most accurate people . . .

Take our soldier Yaroslav Kan, a paratrooper. He fought in the most fiercely embattled spots of the front. Bilohorivka, defense of Lysychansk, defense of Soledar. Battles for Svatove, Kreminna, Bakhmut . . . Four wounds! Now, he is undergoing treatment, and recovering. And ready to return to the front again. It is extraordinary human power! Thank you, Yaroslav! (June 3, 2023)

7. Rhythm. Zelenskyy's syntax will change in full accordance with the circumstances surrounding the deliverance of his speeches, and the topic he is speaking about. Following the destruction of the Kakhovka hydroelectric power station dam, when more than one hundred cities and towns were flooded, Zelenskyy's speech became abrupt and choppy:

> The situation with drinking water in our cities and communities. Leaders on the ground and in the government know the drill. We have solutions, resources and funds. We will do everything to provide people with drinking water despite this disaster. There may be inconveniences, but we will do everything. Today, I held a separate meeting on water supply and safety of people in the cities and communities of the Dnipropetrovsk region—I was there personally. Kryvyi Rih, Marhanets, Nikopol, Pokrov and other communities—we discussed them.
>
> The situation with infrastructure and environmental damage. The damage caused by the Russian act of terrorism is very significant, this is clear to everyone. But it should also be clear that there are no alternatives other than maximum recovery and maximum reconstruction. It may be Russia that will be left devastated after Putin, but not Ukraine.
>
> And one more thing. Mandatory. Security. I am in constant communication with our military. The commanders of Khortytsia, Tavriia, all those involved in the hottest areas. Donetsk region—very tough battles. But there are results, and I am grateful to everyone who ensures these results! Bakhmut—well done. Step by step. I thank each of our warriors! Avdiivka, Marinka, the entire east, the situation in the south, the situation after the Russians blew up the dam of our native Kakhovka—we see every detail. But it's not time to talk about that today.

8. Establishing a positive context for Ukraine, one of purely positive associations. Ukraine means grain and food security for the whole world;

Ukraine means solidarity; Ukraine means caring for children. The world's first associations with Ukraine are participation in the grain program, the cohesion of the nation, and the readiness to defend the world and be a buffer between Russia and the West. It should be noted that with the prodigious help of Russia, Zelenskyy finally managed to erase the most durable association with Ukraine in the world consciousness: corruption. But Ukraine is very open to external monitoring, and there are some things more serious than nepotism and theft. The heroism of the defenders of Ukraine, and the wit of its president, who is popular with journalists and diplomats throughout the world, have completely expunged from the world's consciousness the negative images of the Ukrainian oligarchy, Ukrainian vulgarity, and Ukrainian nationalism, which is especially unpopular, for example, in Israel and Poland. Essentially, Zelenskyy has always insisted that corruption is a worldwide problem; that there is no exclusive Ukrainian corruption. These days—regardless of how extensive it is—it is mentioned in polite society no more than a congenital physical defect might be. That is, it may be there, but you don't advertise it.

9. Personal details, aspects of his own biography, and measured regular references to his own family's life. "Sometimes my son is present in my office (*Kyrylo is ten years old.—D. B.*). Sometimes, anyway . . . And what interests him most here are these chevrons. The soldiers, volunteers, and relatives of our soldiers give them to me. At the front and in Kyiv, in hospitals, at award ceremonies for heroes in the Mariinsky Palace. This chevron board is filling up, but very slowly, because Kyrylo takes one every time. I'm happy that he takes an interest in this. In our heroes, our defense, these Ukrainian chevrons. For some time now I have wanted to make a special series of posts on my social media about these chevrons. About where they come from. Who gave them to me? What divisions are they from? Today we will begin making such posts."

What are these chevrons? They are a collection of gifts given to Zelenskyy by different units, sometimes sent by relatives of the dead and the living. There is a real life behind each chevron. At the time of this writing, the wall of Zelenskyy's office was decorated with fifty-three chevrons: the

Kraken special forces, the 110th separate mechanized brigade, the 36th detached marine brigade, the 38th detached marine brigade (two wolf heads on a black background with the inscription *Victoria amat fidelis*—"Victory loves the faithful"). Here also is the chevron of the Edelweiss 10th detached mountain assault brigade, which became famous during the defense of Soledar. Here, too, is the badge of the Patriotic Cats charitable organization from Kherson.

The cats standing alongside the wolves are a cross-section of the Ukrainian national character today, and it's no surprise that Zelenskyy gives the best items in the collection to his son. I have noticed that he raises the topic of his family no more than once a quarter, being well aware how sentimental and at the same time intimate it sounds. This topic cannot be turned into a bargaining chip.

10. Humor. This would seem to go without saying, yet, at the same time, Zelenskyy's addresses contain surprisingly little of his trademark humor, even of the darkest nature. Sometimes he'll make a dark joke about "unsheltered shelters" that people could not get into. Sometimes in response to a question about pro-Russian sentiments in Europe, you'll hear a familiar intonation almost drawn from a KVN sketch. "What does pro-Russian mean? Supporting terrorism? I don't see Americans moving to live in Russia, and I don't see Russians themselves switching to Soviet-style cars."

Here, however, we must express a paradoxical and, perhaps, cynical thought. By definition, there is something tragicomic in the very situation where the leader of a nation is obliged to make daily appeals. This has never happened anywhere. Try to imagine Stalin forced to address the nation every day during the war: he would have died in a week. His entire image—about which a separate book could be written—rested on the poetics of silence, on the fact that "the tsar's voice must not be wasted on trivialities." Moreover, he avoided appeals in critical moments because he himself was scared to death. On June 22, 1941, Molotov addressed the country, but on October 15-16 of the same year, during the days of the famous Moscow panic, no one addressed the people at all! Stalin's guard Rybin left us memoirs, and, on the morning of October 16, Stalin allegedly drove through the streets, saw monstrous looting underway, ordered the car to stop, and went out to talk to the people. (About what? Was he going to try to stop the looting of a populace abandoned by the authorities to the mercy of fate? Think what you will, but he was no idiot.) They asked him when we would send the enemy packing. "When the time comes, we'll do it," he answered, then went back to the Kremlin, and decided not to leave Moscow. Quite amazingly, the crowd that gathered around Stalin that day did not leave a single testimony to this amazing gesture, and we do not have a single memoir on this topic but for the testimony of one security guard. Knowing Stalin, who always suspected the people of wanting to overthrow him, we can't take this story on faith, although what won't a person do under the influence of stress? We also know quite well that Putin in critical circumstances—be it Beslan or Prigozhin's march on Moscow—hides from the press and makes no public statements. During the war, he has addressed the nation with programmatic speeches a few times, and repeated the same thing in all these speeches: we don't start wars, we end them, we were surrounded, we were left with no choice, etc. Repeating this every day would be an utter farce. But forget Putin! Churchill, with whom Zelenskyy is most often compared either approvingly or ironically, used his famous gift of oratory no more than once a week. I really don't know a single world leader, including the extremely talkative Fidel Castro and Aleksandr Lukashenka, who could withstand the regime of daily televised addresses. Maybe Arestovych, but he lost it, becoming the butt of countless jokes about there are only "two or three weeks" separating the country from victory. True, his broadcasts lasted an hour, and Zelenskyy's addresses lasted a maximum of ten minutes. Still, Zelenskyy's record as a stand-up performer of speeches is unprecedented.

Every day he answers the most painful questions, whether they refer to panic over a potential bombing of the Zaporizhzhia nuclear power plant, or Russian attempts at a counteroffensive. He understands his mission as president precisely—this again speaks to the matter of the narrator king—as conducting a narrative, and partly as offering psychotherapy. The situation whereby the president is compelled—and considers it his duty—to address the country every day is, of course, not just abnormal, it is exceptional. Zelenskyy works not only as a Ukrainian Churchill, but also as a Ukrainian Levitan, painting the landscapes that the world needs to see. Especially in the irrational, often insane state in which Ukraine currently finds itself, this is not as pathetic as it is funny in that grotesque and lofty understanding of the humorous that we have discussed in relation to *The Servant of the People*. After all, the very core of *The Servant of the People* and its current real-life sequel, watched by the entire world with delight and horror, is its fundamental message: "Citizens! Things are very bad for us now." We are in a crisis as the defrocked Russian deacon Andrei Kuraev formulated it, and crisis is the normal state of a thinking Christian. It is difficult for us. It will be even more difficult for us. Our case is unprecedented. We understand everything about ourselves. And yet, there is nowhere to retreat to.

This intonation of those who are doomed to victory—since defeat will lead to the destruction of Ukraine, and perhaps the demise of Europe as a whole—creates an incomparable grotesqueness, prevents Ukraine from slipping into tedious pathos, and makes Zelenskyy much more humane than all other world leaders. This happens because, please note, the human situation is precisely the situation of one who is doomed to triumph. He is the king of nature, and the conqueror of the elements. He is mortal and immortal. He is funny and frightening. The need to address Ukraine every day from this position—for Ukraine also occupies an ambivalent position, becoming more irreproachable in the eyes of the world the more it suffers the severest of trials—compels Zelenskyy to speak time and again about the central, fundamental contradiction of human nature. This contradiction is magnificent. And it's funny, nothing can be done about it. I'm sure that in a future biopic about Zelenskyy, many gags will accrue to this inevitable appeal. Zelenskyy, like Scheherazade, must speak while he is alive, and he lives while he speaks.

Finally, the last point is also significant, although it doesn't concern rhetoric, but rather Zelenskyy's position as a whole. Joseph Brodsky, a fairly typical poet of the Russian world, for all the exceptionality of his talent, respected might. As such, he gave strong advice to strong people, and dealt with the masses in condescending platitudes. But it is instructive to heed some of Brodsky's advice. Speaking to graduates of the University of Michigan in 1988, he said:

> At all costs try to avoid granting yourself the status of the victim. No matter how abominable your condition may be, try not to blame anything or anybody: history, the state, superiors, race, parents, the phase of the moon, childhood, toilet training, etc. The menu is vast and tedious.

Brodsky usually spoke in serious tones to students, especially those who were graduating, for they were in a position of strength—the future was on their side. He wanted to please this future, or at least come to an agreement with it. With immigrants (who most often occupy a weak position in relation to locals) he spoke condescendingly, half-seriously, and often repeated himself. But graduates of the University of Michigan are the ones who will decide the fate of America, and therefore, in part, the world. Brodsky instructed them not to complain. "Try to respect life not only for its amenities but for its hardships, too . . . Remember: that's life speaking to you in the only language it knows well."

For the president of a country at war with a huge and, moreover, nuclear neighbor, there would be nothing easier than to shape at least part of his speeches—let's say, the ones for export, the ones designed not for a Ukrainian, but for a foreign audience—as bitter complaints. "Oh, look what they are doing to us!" But never, even when the truth about Bucha was coming to light, did Zelenskyy descend to this level. From the very beginning he spoke not only with Russia, but with the world as well, from a position of strength. This can only be achieved by possessing complete internal readiness for death. We are prepared for the worst, therefore it is impossible to intimidate us. We have no choice, and that's why we are heroes. I don't know whether Zelenskyy has read Ruben Gallego's famous book *White on Black*, but it was there that this child who survived a Soviet orphanage for the disabled formulated one of the main theses of our time: "I am a hero.

It's easy to be a hero. If you don't have arms or legs, you are a hero or a dead man. If you don't have parents, rely on your own hands and feet. And be a hero. If you have neither arms nor legs, and you also managed to be born an orphan, that's it. You are doomed to be a hero for the rest of your days. Or die. I am a hero. I simply have no other choice."

Zelenskyy has never employed victim status. His rhetoric, vocabulary, intonation belong to the victor. And this presents a dazzling contrast against the backdrop of Russia, which is constantly wailing and complaining: "we are alone against everyone . . . everyone turned away from us . . . we were forced . . . we had no other choice . . . the hostile environment . . ." Russia is a killer that moans and complains eternally about its difficult childhood. This intonation of a sentimental sadist is present in all the prison ballads, and all of Russia's patriotic lyric poetry is sustained in the same tearful intonations of those prison chansons. Z-poets continue to complain endlessly that they are not recognized in the world and are underestimated by the Russian authorities. Z-patriots endlessly moan, not rising from their sofas, and mourning their dead heroes, because traditionally no one in Russia cares about the living. Ukraine, fighting an enemy infinitely crueler and infinitely more superior in numbers, speaks of itself in the intonations of the immortal pirate, Captain Jack Sparrow, an insolent trickster who knows it is unseemly to mourn himself. "Smile, your enemies are looking at you," was something the Russian poet Andrei Voznesensky liked to repeat. Those who truly feel bad don't complain.

All that's left is to win the war, says the skeptic with a mawkish smile.

Well, you know, I'm not so sure that's even necessary. Because it's already happened.

XX. INTERLUDE

Jellied Meat

On April 26, 2022, amateur poetess Natalya Geut—she has some five hundred poems on the stihi.ru website—posted her "Letter to the EU," which went viral. To save space, I quote it in prose format.

While the jellied meat trembles on the table and water quickly fills the bath, I write a letter to you in the EU to share some news. All is good here in Russia. No, we aren't starving at all. We drink champagne from Crimea and eat caviar from Kamchatka. We forgot your McDonald's long ago, all the guests have fled. After all, nothing tastes better than potatoes fried with a pinch of salt. The Mercedes gathers dust in the garage, I drive our homegrown Lada now. It is so much better for taking seedlings to the dacha. Your dollars are of use no more, we now hold rubles in high regard! A dollar won't even buy you a gyro sandwich at the nearest stall. Your sanctions petered out long ago. Don't let the American fool intimidate people. We will not betray Putin, we are not ukrainers, we are not suckers. Everyone is united for Russia, so don't you joke with us. You bathe just once a month? Well, well . . . Your gasoline is too expensive? Eggs and sour cream too costly for your budget? Come visit us, we'll fire up a Russian bathhouse, set the table, and serve a shot of vodka for you, poor Europe. We'll give you food to take home, we'll give you wine from the cellar. Because our people are invincible. We'll hold a wake for your EU. Hang tight . . . you'll see tough times yet. Winter will come, it's just around the corner. God always judges by deeds, but God is always with Russia . . . with us!!!

Natalya Geut is probably a good woman. She's the author of a poignant text titled "Keep your Children Safe from War." She is inspired by patriotism and national pride, and were it not for the war, she would still be living a normal life. Putin himself could live the average life of an average KGB officer, an ideal dacha neighbor who would even lend you his lawn mower—only if you damage it, he'll kill you. Otherwise, he's the life of the party. But this jellied meat, the true face of Russia, is what fascinates me. Russia today is jellied meat, which stands in contrast to freezing, unwashed, starving Europe. The heroine of the poem takes a bath, pampers her heels in it (such people always say "heels," because they deserve it), and the jellied meat is not just waiting—it's actually trembling. It is always trembling.

She is happy to have her jellied meat. But the happiness it provides her is not complete without imagining pictures of suffering Europe. Europe no longer has Russian gas, that swamp fuel that the swampy Russian compost produces in unlimited quantities, a shifting quagmire of earthen jelly, a trembling, frozen swamp of Russian reality, in which all organic remains are preserved in meritorious immutability. Neither earth, nor water, it is a swamp, and it produces gases as regularly as an intestine overflowing with heavy food. We sit in the jelly, we eat the jelly, we think amid the jelly—and our thoughts are trembly, and gelatinous, like interim states that overwhelm our poetry: a mixture of pride and shame, disgust and tenderness, the desire to escape, and the hope to remain. This kind of jelly can only cause delight if you imagine an impoverished, frozen Europe, wishing to do us reverence, whining at the door: Let me in, I want someone like Putin, too, someone just as gelatinous! Come in, Gayropa, we don't mind! We'll feed you, give you something to drink, teach you something about life, and give you something to take home! It is with terrible clarity that I see this bathtub in which she sits—also a kind of jelly, water on top, meat below, and the water is getting cold. It's such a pity to get out.

I would call Natalia Berezova's ten-minute film *My Life* the best Russian cartoon of the post-Soviet period. It is the monologue of a pig, his school essay. "An uncle told me that when I grow up, I should be a good fellow. Or meat jelly? No, best to be a good fellow." There is no contradiction here: a good fellow, according to Russian standards, is a jellied fellow. Until you are refrigerated for your boss's table, you are not yet completely done for. I can hear indignant cries: what a Russophobe! In Ukraine they eat jellied meat no less! Of course, who will argue? There is even a special recipe for Ukrainian-style jellied meat, although there's nothing specifically Ukrainian about it. But eating it does not mean becoming it, and that's the key difference. In Russia, when everyone was wrapped up in living a healthy lifestyle, there was a punning slogan: a person is what he eats. In some communities, people are truly determined entirely by their menu—its cost, its prestige . . . Meanwhile, a person is what they think or do. But when they think nothing or do nothing because both are forbidden, they even lose those skills. That's when they become what they eat. Then they are jellied. That is, they stink and tremble.

To be honest, independent of the dish itself, which since childhood has aroused my suspicions with its slippery, gelatinous quality somewhere between a liquid and a solid, the word combination of "jellied meat" is extremely unpleasant in itself. Were it not the name of a popular dish, an indispensable element in modest feasts during the winter holidays— New Year's or Revolution Day on November 7th—it would sound like a punishment, a civilized version of a familiar phrase: listen, this jellied meat can't be beat, or, you can't beat this jellied meat! It sounds like a synonym for death, and that is just what death is—jellied meat is made from a thickened broth from a dead pig, or, that is, from those parts of the pig, the head, hooves, and bones, which in themselves are not suitable for food. They're only good for jellied meat, which, incidentally, is called *kholodets* in Russian. Thus jellied meat was imported to Russia. And it rhymes perfectly with the last name of that now completely forgotten deputy prime minister of the era of mature Putin, the model official Olga Golodets, who oversaw the problems of education and healthcare, and said we do not need many people with higher education. Golodets and *kholodets*, jellied meat, are the two main states of a nation that considers potatoes with salt to be the highest happiness, and doesn't need any Mc-Donald's. The nation can feed itself full by what it raises in the garden. Every spring people lug seedlings out to their six hundred square meters at the country dacha, and scorch-burn everything on the land with fire. God is with us. While Russia wages war with its closest neighbor, until recently one of its most beloved relatives, and while it kills civilians and destroys infrastructure, dispersing its own young people around the world as unplanned refugees or driving them to slaughter—we dine on jellied meat, and we're just fine. A distinctive feature of jellied meat is that it always trembles, and there was a joke about this: Putin opens the refrigerator, and the jellied meat starts shaking. "Don't fear," he says, "I've come for the sour cream!" The whole country today is one boundless mound of trembling jellied meat, and even if you stab it with a knife or a fork, the holes will instantly seal back up again. Sort of like Russia after the Civil War: "We got you good!"—and "We got you good, too! So, let's have a drink, Batya." I hate the word *batya*, which is prison slang for "dad" or "boss" or "the big man" or "the big cheese." It hate it especially, even more than "jellied meat," when it is applied to my fatherly commander-in-chief.

I am generally repulsed by this cult of the feast, with jellied meat and vinaigrette, accompanied by the same old songs from Soviet films, by Soviet jokes, with hugs and fights—with anything and anyone, just so long as you're not left alone with yourself. Jellied meat is congealed hash (with the difference that hash is made purely from beef). It is life congealed, life that once teemed and boiled and bubbled, but has now cooled to the state of eternal jelly. You can't grab it in your hand, and you don't ever throw it out. My great friend Mikhail Uspensky wrote a mini-story titled "Meat Jelly," about how someone put meat jelly out on the balcony, and, when lightning struck it, protean life spontaneously arose in it and the process of evolution began all over again. Something similar happened in Russia: the jellied meat of the entire Russian nation was struck by the lightning of war. But such entities arose in it and emerged from the pan that the inhabitants of that living space did not fare well. That's what happens with intermediate substances that are neither liquid nor solid, but both slippery and sticky.

Who are these millions who support the war? They are jellied meat, and all of Russia is now covered with a blotchy coating of semi-congealed broth. It isn't frozen like ice. It is the slippery surface of the aspic, trembling, choate and indivisible. It doesn't matter whether it's been prepared for a funeral or a victory celebration. Jellied meat is eaten on any occasion, and those who eat it turn into jellied meat themselves. They eat and say: "Give us, Lord, the same thing tomorrow." An eternally congealed jellyfish, the only difference being that this particular jellyfish has long since turned into a mythical Gorgon, and woe to anyone who stares at it directly.

Most of all people fear that at the first instance of heat this jellied meat will melt like a jellyfish in the sun, leaking through their fingers and flowing away forever. Then we won't even have meat jelly, the last slime of our joy, the last thing capable of keeping us glued together. Our national bond, our national glue. Jelly or slug. The fifth state of matter—counting plasma.

In principle, you can escape it and slither toward solid ground. But if you have lived in it for too long, you have become it yourself. And at the first moment of hearing the question—what is loftier, the homeland or the truth?—a gelatinous taste appears in your mouth, and a gelatinous glaze covers your eyes.

PART THREE

A MYSTERY PLAY

I. TWO CAPTAINS. PUTIN AND UKRAINE

1.

In American biographies, they like to insert all sorts of fascinating stories into the narrative to boost the reader's attention.

To that point: This war was predetermined in July 1966, when the editor-in-chief of the conservative and not-especially-popular magazine *Moscow*, Soviet prose writer and essayist Yevgeny Popovkin, asked Konstantin Simonov for advice. Simonov was one of the Soviet literary generals, a favorite of Stalin, and, after a short period of disgrace under Khrushchev (when he exiled himself to work as an ordinary journalist in Tashkent), he quickly regained his former glory and looked, in the words of the poet Naum Korzhavin, to be the chief liberal among the extreme right-wingers. A famous wartime poet, a prolific playwright, the Soviet Hemingway, he was finishing a massive (and rather mediocre) war trilogy at this time.

Popovkin's subscription base was shrinking. Amid the tense Thaw-era polemics between Alexander Tvardovsky's liberal journal *Novy Mir* (New World), and Vsevolod Kochetov's Communist Party-backed *October* journal, Popovkin was unable to choose a clear position, and he needed a sensation. At that time, as always in Russia during periods of thaw, texts that had been hidden away in writers' desks, or prose written by the repressed and banned during the Stalin era were published in large numbers.

"I have a sensation," said Simonov, "but you won't publish it."

"I'll print it!" Popovkin said firmly. And Simonov, who headed the commission on the literary heritage of Mikhail Bulgakov, told Bulgakov's widow Yelena Sergeevna that publishing his "sunset novel" was, of course, going to be difficult, but sometimes opportunity comes from unexpected quarters. Yelena Sergeevna had already managed once, fulfilling her husband's will, to pass the novel to Stalin through her dressmaker (the wife of Stalin's secretary Alexander Poskrebyshev had the same dressmaker), and the novel, addressed not so much to the mass reader as to a very specific reader, produced an effect. Mass arrests of writers stopped. They began arresting only Jewish writers, members of the anti-fascist committee. Anna Akhmatova, Mikhail Zoshchenko, and Boris Pasternak were defamed in the newspapers daily, but were not touched. Yelena Sergeevna now took the novel to Popovkin, and he, before reading it himself, handed it to Yulian Semyonov, a respected member of the editorial board. Semyonov published a lot, was the author of several political chronicles, famous reports from hot spots (Spain, Cuba, Vietnam, Paraguay, and Afghanistan, to which he travelled immediately after graduating as a scholar of Oriental Studies from the Institute of Asian and African Countries). More importantly, he was the son of the prominent Soviet publisher and literary critic Semyon Lyandres, Nikolai Bukharin's right hand. Lyandres survived the 1930s, but in 1952 he was arrested and his spine was broken during interrogation. He was released from prison in 1954, at the very beginning of the mass rehabilitations, and despite his disability, he published many repressed classics, becoming one of the managers of the State Publishing House. He was a member of the Bulgakov inheritance commission together with Simonov.

Semyonov unfolded the thick folder with Bulgakov's novel and did not look up until he had set aside the last page of the typescript. The impression that this book made on this Soviet individual could have no legitimate comparison. He was no ordinary reader, had nothing in common with religion, and was the son of a major publisher and philologist, but imagine that for the first time in your life you go to the cinema, and they show not the Lumière brothers' *The Arrival of a Train*, but *The Exorcist*.

In the morning, Semyonov told Popovkin that it had to be published, but it could not be printed.

Popovkin was intrigued. The fact is that Crimea also figures in this story—truly a crux of Russian history. In Crimea Catherine the Great bestowed the title of Tauride on her lover Potemkin. It is where the reign of Nikolai I ended ingloriously. During the Russian Civil War the White Guard fled from Crimea to Constantinople; it is where the Red Army met disaster in 1942; and Crimea was gifted to Ukraine in 1954, planting one of the biggest bombs in Russian history (at that time it was a purely formal and completely rational act). And, just imagine, after the war Popovkin was the secretary of the Crimean branch of the Writers' Union, and a deputy of the Crimean Regional Council. Dmitry Polyansky, the chairman of the Crimean regional executive committee, later the first secretary of the Crimean regional committee, the de facto boss of Crimea, warmly supported the idea of transferring it to Ukraine, and this act did wonders for his career. He first became the chairman of the Council of Ministers of the Russian Federation, and then a first vice-premier of the USSR. It goes without saying that the main communist of Crimea had respectful, comradely relations with the head of the Crimean writers. Popovkin read the novel, and he not only liked it, it shocked him to the depths of his soul. He was a good man, Popovkin, although an absolutely typical Soviet writer, the author of the novel *The Rubanyuk Family* about the fight against the fascists on the Crimean peninsula which the Germans captured in the summer of 1942 after eight months of heavy battles. Popovkin realized the only way to publish this novel was to go to Polyansky.

And so he went—not with the novel itself, of course, but with a stack of favorable reviews that briefly outlined the plot of the book, including an internal review by Yulian Semyonov. The Deputy Prime Minister of a great country rarely will have time to read a great novel, even one that is most interesting; but, oh, here we have this sharp satire properly orientated, that is, a justification of a cruel but wise state . . . Polyansky took an extract of the novel to Mikhail Suslov, the main ideologist of the Central Committee, a gloomy ascetic, the Soviet version of the tsarist statesman Konstantin Pobedonostsev, who, however, possessed the rudiments of taste (he is the one who told Vasily Grossman after his novel *Life and Fate* was confiscated: "We understand that you are not our enemy, but your book is objectively harmful, and it will be published in three hundred years." It was published abroad twenty years later, and thirty years later in the USSR). Suslov believed Polyansky and okayed the publication of *The Master and Margarita*.

As such, the first part of the novel was published in issue number 11 of the journal *Moscow* in 1966 (with excerpts comprising about a seventh of the book. Lyandres insisted that the full text be used for foreign translations). Part Two, in the interests of subscriptions, was announced for the first issue of 1967.

The journal's circulation increased by one and a half times—from 160,000 to 250,000 copies. On the black market, a bound copy of the novel cost 25 post-reform rubles—the same as a pair of "original jeans."

But Yevgeny Popovkin did not have time to rejoice in this luck. He died suddenly in February 1968, as if he had completed a mission or crossed a certain line—as it seems to some—literally on the eve of his 61st birthday. He was a big man, strong and robust, and nothing foreshadowed such an eventuality. True, he drank, but who didn't?

Then in 1968, Yulian Semyonov wrote the first version of his novel *Seventeen Moments of Spring*, about the Soviet Woland, which became the basis of the Soviet Union's best-known TV series (made in 1972, it premiered August 11, 1973, and I am writing these lines exactly fifty years later). It was the very model from which the myth of Vladimir Putin was created. He released the genie from the bottle, so to speak, and also died suddenly after a third stroke in October 1993, a month before his 62nd birthday. He, too, was a big guy, a boxer, who taught the film director Nikita Mikhalkov to fight (he was married to his sister). Nothing foreshadowed his death either.

In the last two issues of *Moscow* for 1969, exactly three years after *The Master and Margarita*, Semynov published his most famous novel about Stirlitz, a spy and the basis of a popular film and countless anecdotes.

As a rule, Semyonov wrote very quickly.

2.

A personal comparison of Vladimir Putin and Volodymyr Zelenskyy (they both have the same first names for good measure) is a hopeless notion, although telling: Zelenskyy was a KVN captain for ten years, Putin was a KGB captain for three years (1980–1983). Even the abbreviations are similar. Everything else about these captains is strikingly different.

But why so different? Both marked the return of the two countries to a national template. When Zelenskyy won, many noted that the Ukrainian character is based in a deep sense of irony. Only the lazy did not acknowledge that after 2014 Putin signaled a return to the true Russia.

What is most interesting is that they are, by definition, colleagues. Everyone in 1999 characterized Putin as a performer—calculating, mindful, and obsequious.

RUSSIAN PUBLISHER'S RESPONSE: this is bullshit, ramblings for the ignorant. Already in St. Petersburg he was in charge.

AUTHOR: I'm just passing on what members of the Yeltsin administration told me.

He remains a performer now; only his patron, the boss with whom he signs his contract, has changed. Zelenskyy, too, is a professional performer, that is, an actor. The difference between an actor and a manager is that the actor must believe in what he is doing. If he doesn't, he performs badly. As one political scientist has said, an actor in our time is the only professional who believes in his own words. His success directly depends on this.

But no matter how seductive this contrast between a witty artist-producer and an executive KGB officer, black-haired and blond, young and old, Putin and Zelenskyy do not stand in opposition in terms of personality. More precisely, the personality of Zelenskyy, behind whom stands a nation of many millions, stands in opposition to a much more ancient force than any nation. Vladimir Putin has always been internally empty, which is what made him an ideal performer. Of course, this emptiness began to be filled by something that always fills emptiness, just as weeds take over empty lots.

This is best described by Yury Tynyanov in his main novel, *The Death of Vazir-Mukhtar*: "There were places that only disfigured people, eunuchs, could occupy. For fifteen years his wealth grew and the emptiness of his body grew. He was the sacred property of the Shah's state, the personal property of the Shah. His life was prosperous."

3.

For those materialists who have taken it upon themselves to read this book, we must publish something of a disclaimer. One need not take literally everything I have said heretofore. While testing ideas for this future book in various programs and lectures, the author already encountered the remarks of typical engineers, or, speaking in updated terminology, IT specialists—"What Satan can there be in the twenty-first century!?" As we have seen, he is quite possible in the twenty-first century. Furthermore, the ideological inspirer of this book, Leszek Kołakowski, was probably right when he said that the devil's main success in the era of enlightenment was to convince the majority that he did not exist. But if you find a serious conversation about serious things to be unbearable—a true hell—no one is stopping you from regarding all this as a global metaphor, and sticking to your own ideas about history, according to which history's main engine is bribes, telephone calls from oligarchs, or the plans of the Bilderberg Meeting (i.e., conspiracy theory, i.e., religion of the lowest order).

It would be a mistake to think that the universal Author (what if there were to be, as in *Block 95*, a group of authors?) prepared only Zelenskyy for the world battle. It's beautifully imagined, of course, taking an actor from outside the system, and forcing him to confront absolute evil through careful casting. But a certain audition was also held for the role of universal evil, or more precisely, for the role of the gatekeeper who let evil into the world, although Russia's relationship with the choice-making process is not very good. The fact that the radical confrontation between modernity and archaism which forced the whole world to take sides, was played out, on one hand, by a comic actor, and, on the other, a graduate of the KGB school, is symbolism of the highest order.

Putin's path to this confrontation is no less curious and symbolic than Zelenskyy's career, and this is all the more clear since both of them, in essence, are not in full control of themselves. Zelenskyy, who had no exceptional human qualities other than his amicability, his ability to get along with a team, with people of artistic talent, emerged as the number one defender of Europe. Putin—who from birth had no expressed human qualities but for a determination to make a career about which all his biographers bent over backward trying to provide intriguing or touching details—long and purposefully dug out within himself that absolute emptiness that is always filled by the darkest force.

The fact that a representative of the secret services ended up as the head of Russia is one of history's more whimsical acts. It came into being on the second try (after Yury Andropov from 1982 to 1984), but Andropov died quickly, having accomplished nothing except perhaps putting the world on the brink of nuclear war with the incident of the South Korean Boeing. (These rhymes in history are amazing: With the knowledge of the Russian authorities, a Malaysian Boeing was shot down in 2014, and in the same way Russia helplessly denied it. Under Andropov, Russia was either more self-confident or more honest and admitted everything within two weeks.) Secret services always perform one function, they have no other: they stand guard over the archaic, that is, that very homeostasis that creators and scientists violate at all times. Defending the existing state of affairs is their main task at all times; any violation of this order is rightly considered anti-state and extremist activity.

We will now examine the genesis of the myth about the intelligence officer who merged with the countenance of Vladimir Putin and became his mask.

And if someone is more interested in Zelenskyy's secret connections with the oligarchs, no one is stopping such a reader from writing his own book. As Metropolitan Alexander Vvedensky famously told the first Soviet Commissar of Education Anatoly Lunacharsky in 1925, "let's say you are from a monkey, and I am from God."

To which Lunacharsky answered, not without elegance: "Looking at me and the monkey, everyone will say: what progress! They'll look at you and God and say, what regression!"

4.

Our book is not so much a biographical sketch of Volodymyr Zelenskyy (everything we know about him can be retold in an hour), but is an interpretation of his fate, by way of myth among other things. Everything in our lives is realized only insofar as it is based on myth. It is the only mirror in which humanity sees itself, the only evidence of the most typical and stable plot narratives for humans. Let's first consider the myth of Vladimir Putin, for Putin is older—both as an essence and as an earthly incarnation.

This is where the most interesting things begin, for this war has unleashed the secret springs of history. For a long time—perhaps since the late thirties—these secret springs have not presented themselves before our eyes in such a pure form. We now have the right to expect the reader's undivided attention, for this is not at all a matter of facts: we now have a reason to take a closer look at what moves the world. They say there are no atheists in the trenches. Well, the fact is that we all are in the trenches these days, and as long as such an unpleasant period has befallen us, we are bound to use it to peer into the clockwork of history.

One of the first interpreters of the history of the twentieth century in the light of the myth of the Gospel was the great Polish (and later English) thinker Leszek Kołakowski, whose 1988 article "Politics and the Devil" was the first radical attempt to mix religion and political science. Russian literature is accustomed to the notion that issues of history or politics are considered through the prism of religion, but it is one thing when a writer (Fyodor Dostoevsky) or a religious commentator of an extremely conservative persuasion (Konstantin Leontyev) resorts to such methods. It's an entirely different matter when a strict philosopher with a Marxist background speaks about the role of the devil in world politics. For many of Kołakowski's colleagues, his later articles were a serious shock. Having examined the methodology of the devil liberating an enlightened era from the shackles of the church's power, thereby contributing to progress, Kołakowski moves on to the problems of the twentieth century itself (the final convulsions of which we see in the Russo-Ukrainian war): "In our century and before our eyes, the devil decided to return to the old concept of politics, no longer based on agreement or consensus. We see ideological states, that is, states whose principle of legitimacy is based on the fact that they possess the truth. When someone opposes such a state or its system, he is an enemy of the truth. The Father of Lies used the idea of truth as his powerful weapon. Truth by definition is universal, not associated with any one nation or state. A nation trying to defend its interests, defend itself, conquer new territories, and build an empire, etc., is declared the bearer of universal truth, as during the Crusades. The devil, medieval theologians said, is the monkey of God. Ideological states are a caricatured imitation of theocracy.

"This, of course, changed the nature of war. Since the Second World War, wars have been fought in the name of universal truth and therefore have become civil wars. And in a civil war there are no rules. Prisoners are often slaughtered or forced to defect to the enemy under the threat of death. Moreover, whenever a government wants to mobilize its citizens, it appeals not to universal truth, but to national or imperial feelings. They succeed to a certain extent, but their very successes show the grotesque gap between reality and its verbal disguise. [. . .] The devil is trying to rely on democracy. He appropriates the right of the majority, offering the attractive idea that the majority as such is right and has the right to do anything, including abolish the majority principle itself. Can a democratic constitution commit suicide by its own rules? (*It can, boy, can it ever: we saw this in Germany in 1933, and in Russia ninety years later.—D. B.*) Humans are undoubtedly vulnerable to the devil's temptations, but they also feel the need to coexist, to use their own freedom to establish order, to be distrustful of any truth, and to venture into the unknown realms of the spirit.

"No, the struggle between the devil and God in history is not a pleasant sight. The only consolation for us is that we are not observers, but participants, and our fate is decided on the stage on which we play. It sounds trivial, but some truisms are worth repeating."

There would be nothing sensational in Kołakowski's conclusions (although the observation about the totalitarian states of the twentieth century as a parody of theocracy is witty and accurate). What is sensational here is the very appeal to biblical myth to interpret modernity—and, moreover, the return to the medieval practice of historiosophy, which the Enlightenment seriously supplanted. The fact that Kołakowski, in the same article, calls politics "the devil's favorite sphere" (along with sex—let's put a smiley face here) could be perceived as obscurantism, but since we now live inside a genuine religious mystery play that is marked by amazingly visual, fully materialized evil and good—both of which have no alternative but to build themselves up into ideals—this no longer seems like an exaggeration or an escape from reality. We are present at a duel between the devil and a jester.

Of course, a huge number of people would prefer to remain in a cozy gray world—not a black and white one. For example, as British journalist Peter Hitchens wrote in the *Daily Mail*, which the extreme right-wing Tsargrad-Media (belonging to the militant Putin oligarch Konstantin Malofeev whose one time bodyguard was Girkin-Strelkov) joyfully quoted: "Honestly, if this war had not been so widely portrayed in crude storybook terms as a super-simple fight between total good and total evil, which it isn't, we might have reached this stage before. But better late than never." (He is talking about the West's possible refusal to support Ukraine—the wind, as it seems to him, is blowing in that direction.)

Tsargrad translates Hitchens relatively accurately. Hitchens continues: "If our concern is truly for the people of Ukraine, then we would be much better occupied promoting a lasting peace than in fueling and paying to prolong a war in which actual Ukrainians die and suffer, and gain nothing much in return." How exactly he intends to achieve lasting peace is not directly stated, but it is clear that we are talking about the formula, "Peace in exchange for territory," popular among latent Putinists: "It is that the large-scale recapture of the land lost to Russia in 2022 looks less and less likely as the days shorten." Since Hitchens, in the best of Putinesque traditions, nullifies Ukrainian motivations—as if to say, Ukrainians get nothing as a result of their heroism—for him, Ukraine's feelings about the loss of its territories are not fundamental. Like, so what? At least it's peace. (To call it a durable peace, of course, is either shameless speculation or unforgivable naïveté. But many are so frightened by Putin's rhetoric that they're ready to agree to a peaceful hiatus: take yourself a fur coat, as long as you do it quietly!)

The Russian press is very fond of quoting the comments of such so-called ordinary people, ordinary readers, so long as they coincide with its wishes. And they even get to the top of Yandex, Russia's main search engine. The comments of ordinary British readers beneath this column are utterly dis-respectful. Too bad Tsargrad does not quote them, they could have learned that "Peter never fails, he always brings us Putin's wet dreams!" One might want to consider Hitchens's background. He is a peculiar character, not in vain called Dr. Change. He started as the Moscow correspondent for The Mail on Sunday, worked in Washington, was a socialist early on, and a Labor supporter, was mothballed in the '90s, became a well-known fighter against same-sex weddings, and now calls himself a Christian conserva-tive, and a British Gaullist. It goes without saying that he is an ardent anti-vaxxer, although he is offended when people call him that. I go on in some detail about Hitchens because in him we see an extremely clear portrait of Putin's admirers among the notorious Anglo-Saxons. He is a defender of the good old values, who sincerely does not understand "what Britain's interest is in waging a costly and risky war in South-Eastern Eu-rope between two corrupt and poorly managed remnants of the old Soviet empire." This is a normal equation between victim and aggressor, for "in Ukraine you cannot take a breath without encountering corruption." Well, Russia is also a mess. An ordinary dispute between two disorderly Slavs. What is Britain's interest?

Britain's interest, pragmatist that it is, is to maintain its own ideal-ism—the only thing that allowed it to survive and maintain influence after the collapse of the empire, the only thing that allowed it to be among the victors of the Second World War. Hitchens does not understand that Putin has all of Europe and, in the future, the whole world in his sights (in Russian bullying terminology—Gayropa and the Anglo-Saxons). He thinks that since Putin opposes non-traditional marriages, calling himself a Christian and a conservative, that he is one of them. People write to him right there in the comments: "He never fails to spout the required propaganda *de jour*. In his interesting mind it is perfectly acceptable for a Superpower to massacre civilians, especially children and the elderly. His friends have been pinpointing hospitals and schools. They have specialized in targeting shelters and apartment buildings in their cowardly nighttime attacks." But isn't there corruption in Ukraine? And aren't many Ukrainians trying to escape from the war across the Romanian border? How much more comfortable is it to live in a world where everything is not so simple and Ukrainians, too, you know, are imperfect. It doesn't happen that some are sinners and others saints!

Unfortunately, it does happen, although the situation is highly disturbing. But a Christian conservative would have to know that metaphysics periodically invades history, that no one has canceled ethical unambiguity, and that the main Christian source (Matthew 5:37) declares forthright: "Let what you say be simply 'Yes' or 'No'; anything more than this comes from evil." From the evil one comes talk about the mistakes and imperfections of Ukraine, and the Russian leader's nationwide support. From the evil one comes a pragmatic approach like "what needs do we have in South-Eastern Europe where two poorly managed remnants of an empire are at war." Before your eyes, one of the largest countries in the world attacked its neighbor, whose territory and population are incomparably smaller. Before your eyes, it kills its neighbor's civilian population, justifying this murder by the argument that NATO is expanding to the East. Before your eyes, it turns thriving cities into smoking ruins, where shelters are bombed and people are tortured in basements. Before your eyes, it kidnaps Ukrainian children and forces them publicly to thank their kidnappers for saving them. And after all this, you claim that there is no pure good or pure evil in the world, because you really have become very spoiled in your comfortable world. The highest value in this world is order, and a few paragraphs later, having already taken up another topic, Hitchens assures us: "Overthrowing tyrants may be good box office, but if you replace them with anarchy, you have made people's lives far, far worse."

What Hitchens is missing is that the goal of overthrowing tyrants is not box office revenue, but the elementary saving of thousands of lives and good, old-fashioned values. And don't think that he is alone. He has a lot of like-minded people among the establishment of any European country: Why are we talking about this Ukraine again? There is no such thing as pure good and pure evil!

Probably, Volodymyr Zelenskyy's chief historical accomplishment will someday be declared to be precisely what he proved: that these things can happen. That is, he returned us to something that may not be a fairy tale (there is a connotation of disdain in this word), but does exist in the realm of myth. Returned us to unambiguous assessments and purity of criteria. That is, he was not afraid to play the role of pure good when pure evil was useful to him. To the credit of his nation, it supported his choice—maybe even forced him to make it. And if this is subsequently declared to be an accomplishment of Vladimir Putin, and they give him some relief in hell for it, so be it. Under the name of Woland, his current primary patron said in the aforementioned *Master and Margarita*: "You pronounce your words as if you do not recognize shadows, or evil. Would you be so kind as to think about this question: What would your good do if evil did not exist, and what would the earth look like if shadows disappeared from it? After all, shadows come from objects and people. Do you wish to strip the entire globe, sweeping away all trees and all living things because of your fantasy of enjoying naked light?"

"I won't argue with you, old sophist," which, in other words, means: Shadow, know your place.

5.

For many in Russia, the transformation of Vladimir Putin from a banal official into a kleptocrat was natural. But his leap from kleptocrat to Führer was somehow sudden and inexplicable. Liberal thinkers who recited Brodsky's mantra, "But a thief is dearer to me than a bloodsucker," were shocked by the very rapidity of Putin's transition from the first category to the second. When God visits the world, he does not care about the comfort of the host.

We do not think that a reference to Kołakowski guarantees us critical immunity. On the contrary, his very name evokes furious rejection among many. We insist only that the religious interpretation of world politics is legitimate, and that following the end of the Enlightenment we now have the advantage—perhaps the only one—that economic and geographical determinism in the interpretation of history no longer lack an alternative approach, hence, history has ceased to be an arena for the function of exclusively dogmatic relations, which are as boring as a red brick factory building. This brick factory was replaced by a haunted house, which may be frightening, but it's an interesting place to wander about.

Vladimir Putin came to power not because he demonstrated his loyalty to Boris Yeltsin's so-called Family, and not because the then-presidential administration considered him an effective bureaucrat. The contribution of the oligarchs to his appointment, the mistakes of his opponents, and the economic situation played a negligible role in his triumph. Vladimir Putin became president because his personal myth lay on well-fertilized soil. Russia was waiting for Mephistopheles, who comprised the functions of a spy, an avenger, and a patron of the arts. To understand the reasons for this expectation, we must go back about a thousand years.

Throughout human history there have not been many major auto-descriptive myths.

The oldest of them is the myth of the fallen angel, a rebel against God.

A certain power that has fallen away from God due to pride, and was, for that, cast down from heaven, is constantly trying to regain its previous position. To do so, it seeks to curry favor by performing a threefold function: punitive (dealing with those whom the Lord disdains), offering patronage (protecting professionals, artists, or scientists) and intelligence gathering, reporting to heaven about the dynamics of earthly life. At some point, the demands of Satan, aka Lucifer, to be returned to heaven become imperative: Either you return me to your number (the Big Eight, Big Twenty, or whatever it is called), or I destroy the world that you have given to me to control. The resolution of this myth is taking place before our eyes, but it has a crucial point: the Son of God is sent to Earth to correct the situation, so to speak, an improved and good version of Lucifer, a kind of Lucifer 2.0. He frees Satan and reconciles him with the Lord, although we know very little about the details of this process. We only know that the first Titan who rebelled against the supreme deity, a Titan named Prometheus, was freed from punishment by Hercules, the son of Zeus, after which, as the myth vaguely indicates, he reconciled with the gods. In Christianity, the hints of such a development are especially dark, but before our eyes, the Ukrainian conflict is finally shedding light on God's plan for human history.

The Faustian part of the myth is the most famous, since it is the only part that concerns humanity directly. Vladimir Putin became president by exploiting this myth—he always positioned himself as an intelligence officer, and the myth of the intelligence officer was more popular than ever in Russia in the second half of the twentieth century. Let's look at this story in more detail, for the genesis and stability of Putin's fame are of particular interest: No political scientist has even come close to solving this riddle, for they all are looking in the wrong place. The Enlightenment absolved Faust, therefore partly justifying Mephistopheles. Humanity was not worthy of God's direct interaction, so He handed it over to the least nasty of the spirits of hell, namely Lucifer, the bearer of light, the patron of the sciences. Let's not idealize Lucifer and his ancient counterpart Prometheus, also a bearer of light: it is obvious that he brings light (or fire) to people not in order to provide them with hot food. He is going to make them his army and lead their campaign against the gods or the one God. It is no coincidence that Prometheus is a beloved hero of atheists like Marx, who dedicated a youthful drama to him in verse. The most popular hero of Soviet literature—or one who was created in Soviet times, but was never included in the Soviet canon—is Woland, who represents a useful and acceptable evil, for the world does not deserve good and is incapable of handling it (ultimately, it's not so simple!). Woland represents an image of power engaging primordial human depravity, and the slavishness of human nature. The idea of useful, and therefore acceptable, evil in general was the central Russian idea of the twentieth century. The Faustian construction of "a Master under the patronage of Satan" was essential not only in *Doctor Faustus*, Thomas Mann's novel that summed up German history, but also in fundamental Soviet texts such as Pavel Bazhov's *The Stone Flower*, Bulgakov's *Master and Margarita*, and in the sixties in the Strugatsky brothers' novel *Hard to Be a God*, and Yulian Semyonov's cycle of historical chronicles about Stirlitz.

Stirlitz in the Semyonov novels conducts detailed dialogues with a priest and a scientist—with the Pastor and Professor Werner Pleischner, respectively—a lesson learned not only from Woland talking with the Master and the Apostle, but also from Rumata of Estor saving Budakh and Father Kabani in *Hard to be a God*. The trio of Woland, Rumata and Stirlitz all share traits with Ilf and Petrov's trickster Ostap Bender, as Maya Kaganskaya showed in her book *Master Gambs and Margarita*—and they all served as the basis of the future image of Putin, who drew on Stirlitz specifically, also worked in Germany, and actively communicated with priests and patronized the arts.

Lucifer, the chief intelligence officer and patron of intelligence officers, a fallen angel, was perceived by humanity to be the bearer of progress and the father of crafts, while Prometheus also seemed to endow people with technology. The trouble is that it was a technology of self-destruction, not development, and under the guise of progress, Lucifer is the carrier of that very thing that Dostoevsky warned about: complete enslavement under the pretense of total liberation. All of Lucifer's technical progress serves solely to limit freedom. It has nothing to do with the creative spirit, and everything to do with comfort.

In general, attempts to take Lucifer "off the hook" have been made more than once in history. Tomas Venclova summed them up briefly in his fundamental article (alas, often overlooked) "On the Demonology of Russian Symbolism." One could call the piece more broadly, "On the Demonology of the Twentieth Century."

> The doctrine of two different aspects, two different guises of demonism was most thoroughly developed by Vyacheslav Ivanov. In them Ivanov poses questions related to the fate of the Russian and world communities, and furthermore seeks to deepen the theolog-

ical concept of the evil spirit (developed dogmatically, as is known, only in general terms). According to Ivanov, at least two "principles fighting against God in the world" must be distinguished: these are Lucifer and Ahriman, "the spirit of rebellion and the spirit of corruption." According to the teachings of the Church, both of them can only be regarded as two faces of a single devil.

Lucifer is involved in the self-determination of individuals, in self-affirmation, including creative self-affirmation. His energy is the underlying basis of a historically given culture (not one transformed into a collegial work). In this sense, Luciferism is not destructive. But if man and culture freeze into stable forms, if the desire for a constant transition to a higher level disappears, Lucifer turns into Ahriman—the spirit of inertia, despair and malice. Ahriman represents evil in all its pettiness, in all its insignificance; Lucifer is the prince of this world, Ahriman is its executioner.

It is easy to see that Ivanov here describes and criticizes important trends in the civilization that was contemporary to him. Luciferism is related to individualism and traditional democracy. The kingdom of Ahriman turns out to be the nationalist, militaristic, impersonally organized Germany (as per Ivanov's essay, "Legion and Conciliarity"), but, to no less an extent, Russia in its historical reality.

We all, alas, know well this Ahrimanian Rus'—the Rus' of decay, standing in opposition to the Rus' of resurrection—the Rus' of "dead souls," of an autocracy that is not only tolerated, but actually idolized, the violation of the shrine of human countenance and human conscience, the subordination of sacred objects to the dominion of this world; the Rus' of arbitrariness, violence and oppression; the Rus' of brutality, debauchery, drunkenness, rotten vulgarity, moral dullness and savagery. In Rus' we know Ahriman's whips and gallows, his executions and betrayals; We also know the Ahriman of our primordial folk nihilism and frenzy, blindly and maliciously destructive.

It would be no exaggeration to say that Ivanov, in his articles of 1916, correctly anticipated the features of totalitarianism, at least to the extent that they matured in the depths of Russian and German societies: The kingdom of Ahriman in his description is the kingdom of an inert "super order," which devolves into the disintegration of human relationships, chaos, and the triumph of entropy.

By contrasting Lucifer and Ahriman, another point also emerges as significant, although Ivanov does not express it so clearly. Lucifer, assisting man in the construction of culture, is involved in signification, in the creation of forms and systems; Ahriman is undisguised anti-culture, the eradication of signs, the aimless destruction of a living system and form, the one who stains and spoils everything (in this sense he is similar to Julia Kristeva's "unnameable").

Lucifer [aka Dennitsa, or morning star in Slavic mythology] is well known in the Christian tradition; Ahriman is primarily a Zoroastrian mythologem (aka Mana, Angra Mainyu), which penetrated into Manichaeism, and the demonology of Judaism, etc. However, Ivanov's idea of the two faces of world evil, apparently, finds its direct prototype in Byron's demonology (to which Ivanov hints himself). Lucifer, the spirit of pride and knowledge, appears in Byron's *Cain*; Ahriman, the supreme deity of evil, monstrous but essentially powerless, is described in *Manfred*.

6.

I suspect that this opposition, which has fooled many, is in essence no better than the opposition between Lenin and Stalin. Lenin was, of course, smarter, and his goal was the destruction of the empire, but before Stalin, he rebuilt that very same empire. Both reduced the world to superficial, material incentives. Both were characterized by a deep disbelief in humans, and a contempt for mankind. Lenin and Stalin were equally inhuman, although Lenin's inhumanity is more fervent and more vibrant in a human way; both lack not in demonic charm, although their types of charm differ. As it happened, Lenin did not live to old age—otherwise, I think, his older years would have been no better than Stalin's, overshadowed by delusions of grandeur, faulty reasoning, and paranoia.

The devil has fooled many with his Luciferian, creative, progressive face. However, the bearer of light—or the bearer of fire, in the ancient Greek version—comes to a person not in order to make life more comfortable, but in order to recruit an army against God. The essence of every Lucifer, no matter how proud a fighter against God and, in a broad sense, a *progressor* (we will need the word *progressor* many times yet), is Ahrimanic, that is, preservative. Every progressor is a representative of the secret service, the secret police, imposing his idea of the norm on the masses. Every Lucifer is a spy and a patron of the arts.

The image of Woland was deepened and expanded in the 1960s. At this time, two key texts appeared that prepared the Putin myth, determining his triumph in the '90s. The first is *Hard to Be a God*, the novel by Arkady and Boris Strugatsky, where, in a medieval society on the distant planet of Arkanar, there is an intelligence officer from Earth, Anton, aka Don Rumata of Estor, a progressor, an aristocrat, an athlete, a witty and arrogant person, who deeply despises the local authorities, and supports a handful of professionals in whom Earth is interested: specifically, the scientists Father Kabani and Budakh, as well as a few individual thinkers and poets. In his free time, Rumata conducts theological debates with Father Kabani and Budakh, as well as the cutthroat Arata the Hunchback, Arkanar's Prigozhin, if you will, who demands he be given an earthly super-weapon. The second novel that defined the final twenty years of the Soviet state, thanks to its cult TV adaptation, is *Seventeen Moments of Spring* by Yulian Semyonov.

Semyonov himself was an unofficial, non-commissioned member of the secret police who maintained contacts directly with KGB chief Yury Andropov, and often carried out his personal tasks. This gave him the opportunity to use classified archives freely in his work, travel abroad regularly, interview former SS men, in particular Otto Skorzeny, but also to solve problems encountered by his fellow writers, to stand up for them, and sometimes to help them defend themselves against the authorities. Semyonov chose this role of a double agent because he realized that the main—and perhaps only—force in Russia is the secret police, a government service that collects all information and specifically opposes any attempts to change any situation in the country. Intelligence agencies around the world are followers and agents of the past. Let us remember how skeptically Woland evaluates any attempts to change humanity, how ironically Rumata Estor speaks about any attempts at revolution in Arkanar, how little Stirlitz believes in any internal changes in Germany (and after his return to Russia becomes convinced that the Russian revolution has also gone rotten). The destiny of a double agent is to defend the status quo: After all, as long as nothing changes in the country, his ideal status remains. Woland is omnipotent only in a world where people remain slaves: ordinary like the majority, or privileged like Faust. No changes are possible in this world—Rumata Estor says this directly. Consider the parallels in Rumata's dialogues with Budakh, where he talks about his own inability to help people, and Stirlitz's encounters with the pastor. The exceptional capabilities of Woland, Rumata and Stirlitz—as well as their superhuman status—are possible only on Arkanar, where the grays or blacks reign, in Berlin, where the blacks are about to give way to the reds, or in Moscow, where boors and informers rule over everything.

Important parallels include Rumata's conversations with his main antagonist Don Reba (his name was originally to be Rebia, which directly emphasized the analogies with Lavrenty Beria), and Stirlitz's encounters with his main antagonist Müller. Both Reba and Müller realize that Stirlitz is an agent of another, powerful civilization. Both secretly admire him and dream of winning him over to their side. Stirlitz and Rumata differ from them in that they have no selfish motives, and serve a certain ideal, which, nonetheless, has long been forgotten during their work in intelligence. They are infinitely far from their homeland, and in their homeland everything presently has gone wrong. (This is especially emphasized in the film adaptation of the Strugatsky novel by Alexei German, perhaps the greatest late Soviet director.) In post-Soviet Russia, the functions of Reba and Müller would be oligarchs who tried to win Putin over to their side, but ended up being sent to prison, abroad, or into the other world, as happened with Boris Berezovsky. Unlike Stirlitz, they are self-interested, and seek to establish their own order in Russia. Stirlitz, Woland, and Rumata come to the terrible worlds of Berlin, Arkanar, and Moscow as retribution. And in each case Moscow understands that it has much to pay for: first for the deeds of the revolution and the new economic policy, later for the excesses of perestroika and unhinged capitalism. Putin also appeared as the retribution that everyone was waiting for. The authority who sent him is not that important—he comes as retribution from history itself, and the history of Russia is such that there is always something to take revenge on. This is the similarity of Putin, as well as Woland, with another demonic figure—the Inspector General, whom Gogol made a symbolic character. In and of himself, he is an absolute nonentity. But his grandeur is predetermined by the scale of universal guilt. All of Russia lives in apprehension of the Inspector's arrival, for it does not comply with a single law. Then characters like Woland, Stirlitz, or Khlestakov come along—characters inflated by our collective fear, the fetid air of lacking freedom for so many years.

Like Stirlitz, Putin worked in Germany—although not, like Stirlitz, in government circles, but rather in the modest position of director of the House of Friendship in Dresden. He does speak German, however, which is also reflected in several anecdotes ("During a conversation with President Putin, the German Chancellor either raised his hands or presented his documents"—meaning that Putin's knowledge of German was on the standard partisan's level of "Hände hoch" or "Ausweis"). Stirlitz passionately loves his homeland, but prefers to love it from afar. Putin is also an envoy of some ideal Russia, from which he receives signals directly in the Kremlin. In the meantime, he patronizes professionals (whose talents might be useful primarily in the military sphere), and conducts long theological conversations with priests. A standout among those is Tikhon Shevkunov, a graduate of the screenwriting department of the Russian Institute of Film (VGIK), and a very popular figure in Moscow government and church circles.

Why does Mephistopheles so like to talk to members of the clergy? Pilate with Kaifa, Woland with the Apostle Matthew, Rumata with Budakh and Father Kabani, and Stirlitz with Pastor Schlag, who sympathizes with the communists, but does not share their atheism? This is a deep, important, and immutable motif in all three novels. The most outspoken of them, of course, is Woland, who is quite plainly called "the old sophist" in the novel. Evil needs a philosophical justification, a collective recognition of its relevance. Let's call it the moral sanction of God. And God gives this sanction—in Goethe's "Prologue in Heaven," in Woland's conversation with Matthew, in Rumata's conversation with central command—which they cannot do without. You are part of a force that always desires evil, but does good against its will. Stirlitz has no delusions about Soviet power; he himself participated in its establishment and understands everything about it. But nothing can combat fascism except Soviet power. Rumata Estor understands all the shortcomings of the "basic theory," which is understood to be Marxism, and does not believe in progress although he is officially called a progressor. But all the Strugatsky texts that are dedicated to progressivism, above all the first novel on this topic, *Escape Attempt*, demonstrate that the course of history cannot be changed. Desperate romantic attempts at change only do harm. You can act only gradually, slowly, carefully, first of all extricating the geniuses and enlighteners. That is how Stirlitz saved the great physicists and Professor Pleischner. It is why the real Lavrenty Beria created a closed institute for the geniuses of Soviet physics, where they enjoyed relative freedom while serving the Soviet nuclear project. Alas, in a closed society, only the option of the so-called *sharashka* is possible for geniuses—a closed institute, a privileged theater, small enclaves of freedom within a huge concentration camp. Attempts to expand these enclaves only end in the collapse of the entire greenhouse. In a closed system, two variants of society are possible: either 10 percent are engaged in creative work, and ninety dig manure, or all one hundred dig manure; this system does not allow for any other structures.

This system worked well in Germany, where Thomas Mann's hero in *Doctor Faustus*, the composer Adrian Leverkühn, succumbed to the devil's temptation. It also worked in Putin's Russia, where millions unanimously swore allegiance to the devil, because he guaranteed them the preservation of the old, stuffy and cozy structure of society, provided guarantees of comfortable slavery and reliably protected them from change.

Regarding the West, Putin's rhetoric literally repeats the rhetoric of Mephistopheles (or the Demon) regarding Paradise. The Demon, Mephistopheles, and Cain always reproach the Lord for arrogance, for his lack of understanding of human nature, and his totalitarian thinking. Mephistopheles would very much like to be in Paradise, but as its leader or at least its beloved steward. He was cast down from there for his pride. Putin would very much like to be among the leaders of the West, and perhaps even become its sole leader—hence his humiliated and condescending intonations. He would passionately love to live in this consumerist paradise, but he was ejected, for he did not show enough respect. He was summarily tossed out of all the international organizations. Now he twists, grumbles, and curses—although all of his curses are prompted by unrequited love. Vladimir Putin's current state is most accurately described in Mikhail Lermontov's epic poem *The Demon*:

> Outcast long since, he wandered lone,
> Having no place to call his own,
> Through the dull desert of the world
> While age on age about him swirled,
> Minute on minute—all the same.
> Prince of this world—which he held cheap –
> He scattered tares among the wheat . . .
> A joyless task without remission,
> Void of excitement, opposition—
> Evil itself to him seemed tame.

COMMENT BY YULY DUBOV: I believe it is a mistake to imagine Putin as Lucifer. I understand your response—the world must finally face up to the existential threat that it faces. But I have a strong feeling, based on what I read in the English-language press, that the world already understands this very well, so in this sense you are trying to force your way through an open gate. This is the first point. Secondly. He is not Lucifer. He is Gollum, who seized the Ring and realized its power—not Sauron. He cannot pretend to attain Sauron's stature by any stretch of the imagination. I have some personal experience in this area, and I know what I'm talking about. Third. When all is said and done, "Two Captains" is not merely a section from a book, it is a precise shot aimed at the occupant of the Kremlin. This shot might have had maximal effect had you said you were shooting at a pygmy who seized power. Your warhead may be well be suited for Lucifer, but it would be better, it seems to me, if you would define more clearly the nature of your target. You know well that by abasing your enemy, by showing him without pants, with a saggy belly, and saliva dripping from his lips, you employ the most effective, most deadly polemical technique, especially since this is much closer to reality than depicting him in the form of a Defeated Angel, let alone in comparison with Woland, Bulgakov's most attractive character. Yes, we must understand the enemy's strength, we must understand the threat he poses, but raise him up?

AUTHOR'S REPLY. Thank you, Yuly Anatolyevich, I would very much like to think that way. But I read your *The Lesser Evil* and to a certain extent kept it in mind as I wrote all this. There is nothing lesser about it.

7.

The demonic nature of evil in this case is masked, because Bulgakov wrote his novel for a single reader with a single message: We give you complete moral sanction to deal with these little people as you please, they deserve nothing more. But preserve the artist, for he will be remembered, as you will be, son of a shoemaker. Of course, Stalin patronized those arts which, to the extent of his understanding, he considered to be of use, and he supported the sciences that contributed to defense. But this localized patronage should not blind us to Satan's main goal: He wants absolute power or, alternatively, to destroy the world. Yes, sometimes he does good while desiring evil, in full accordance with Goethe's formula; but his main goal is precisely to cause the greatest possible evil. It gives inspiration to the artist, who inevitably disintegrates in the end, as Mann shows on the example of Leverkühn and German art in general. He gives the country prosperity, but only on the path to final destruction and complete ruin. It is enough to remember in what form Rumata leaves Arkanar, which he intended to save; how Woland says goodbye to Moscow; and what Berlin looks like when Stirlitz disappears. Russia after Putin will look about the same, although throughout the 2000s it looked unusually rich and well-fed under him. Even liberals agreed that Russians had never lived so well. In fact, they have never been bought off at such a high price. Selling your soul is generally a profitable business, especially at that moment when you receive the money.

Woland's function as a patron of the arts is revealed to us not only in the history of the Master (the notion of the Master is generally one of the key words of the thirties), but primarily in the history of Beria's *sharashkas*, his elite retreat for the elite. It's no surprise that the thirties and forties were such a Mephistophelian era, the time of the writing of *The Master and Margarita*, the time of Stirlitz's patronage of the pastor and Pleischner, and the time of Oppenheimer's work on defense. (I'll finish writing this chapter and then go watch Christopher Nolan's film: everything has come together!) In that era the work contract was in the hands of the state, specifically the intelligence services. There simply was no other opportunity for creative work. Beria, the patron of the *sharashkas*, played Mephistopheles to Lev Landau, Andrei Sakharov, and Igor Tamm. He was a Mephistopheles not devoid of cynical humor, and they formally served progress (sincerely believing that they would make war impossible by making it self-destructive for humanity). In fact, they put into Russia's hands a means of universal blackmail. Everything that is happening now is forged in those *sharashkas*. Let me go further: The massive support of Putin and his Z-war by workers in the Russian sciences and arts is a consequence of the same Faustian temptation. Artists and craftsmen sincerely believe that Lucifer will give them a source of inspiration and universal protection. He'll give them a whack, and in the end he'll certainly discard them, but the very moment of the fall is traditionally associated with ecstasies, and what ecstasies they are! It's no surprise that the main participants in this war on both sides are writers, mainly science-fiction writers. In my 2014 article "A War of Writers," I analyzed in detail the role of science-fiction writers on the Russian side (allow me to remind you that the initiator of the war in Donbas, Igor Strelkov, published two very bad novels in the fantasy genre). Volodymyr Zelenskyy first played a president in the film *The Servant of the People*, before the film continued on in reality. Finally an old religious plot imposed itself on this same reality with great power: the myth of how the son of God had to descend to Earth to bring order. Undoubtedly, Prometheus already possessed the characteristics of Christ—the scene of him being chained has all the hallmarks of the crucifixion—but Christ's earthly mission is fundamentally different from that of Dennitsa, aka Lucifer, aka Satan. Here is their dialogue as interpreted by Matthew:

> **1** Then Jesus was led up by the Spirit into the wilderness to be tempted by the devil.
>
> **2** And when He had fasted forty days and forty nights, afterward He was hungry.
>
> **3** Now when the tempter came to Him, he said, "If You are the Son of God, command that these stones become bread."
>
> **4** But He answered and said, "It is written, 'Man shall not live by bread alone, but by every word that proceeds from the mouth of God.'"
>
> **5** Then the devil took Him up into the holy city, set Him on the pinnacle of the temple,
>
> **6** and said to Him, "If You are the Son of God, throw Yourself down. For it is written: 'He shall give His angels charge over you,'

and, 'In *their* hands they shall bear you up, Lest you dash your foot against a stone.'"

7 Jesus said to him, "It is written again, 'You shall not tempt the Lord your God.'"

8 Again, the devil took Him up on an exceedingly high mountain, and showed Him all the kingdoms of the world and their glory.

9 And he said to Him, "All these things I will give You if You will fall down and worship me."

10 Then Jesus said to him, "Get behind me, Satan! For it is written, 'You shall worship the Lord your God, and Him only you shall serve.'"

11 Then the devil left Him, and behold, angels came and ministered to Him.

The canonical Church Slavonic translation of 1581 does not say, "Get behind me, Satan," but, "Follow me, Satan," which emphasizes the role of the wandering teacher, the son of God. He comes to try to return Lucifer unto the hand of the Lord. We have not yet seen how he does this (and the myth is silent about how Hercules did it). But it is he who must do this, for there is no one else. He repeats these same words to Peter (Matt. 16:23) when he tries to dissuade him from coming to Jerusalem: "Get behind me, Satan! You are an offense to me."

(In some interpretations, "get behind me" is explained as "follow behind me, don't dally." This seems to me a classic case of over-interpretation, as if to say: follow me, because you are in my power.)

What are the key differences between Dennitsa (Lucifer) and Christ? The three question-temptations record them with the utmost clarity: Lucifer is interested in power in all its manifestations. He understands progress as the possibility of endlessly obtaining new material benefits (Prometheus in Aeschylus is proud of the fact that he gave people science and material civilization). He interprets faith as slavish worship. In all three cases, Christ answers with a decisive "no." His faith is based on different foundations. Here, history follows the myth with almost excessive clarity: It is no secret that today's leader of Russia believes only in material acquisitions and material attributes of power—quantitative ones. He sincerely believes that victory is achieved by force of arms and the size of an army; the greatness of a country is determined by its territory, etc. Napoleon's statement that God is on the side of large battalions confirms precisely the Luciferian nature of Napoleon: God is on the side of high-quality battalions, and magnitude here is of minimal significance.

In other eras, the Luciferian has been able to gain a certain popularity, wherein the enemies of God even resemble humanists. Byron's rebels against God—primarily Cain—appear as biblical revolutionaries, while their uprising looks like an impulse toward freedom, toward the abolition of hierarchies. Alas, the goal of their rebellion is not to re-establish the world, but only to seize property or power. Not a single Luciferian revolution has yet led to a change in the world. Revolutions of the spirit are a different matter, but their examples in history are extremely few. The true conclusion of the Maidan revolution was the rise to power of Zelenskyy, an event, I would venture to say, more revolutionary than the ouster of Yanukovych.

The archetypal plot on which all the world's bestsellers are based is the picaresque novel, the genre in which *The Servant of the People* was also made. The rogue is not a primitive deceiver, but a wandering wizard, a teacher, a magician: in a word, a trickster. The greatest picaresque novel in history is *The Odyssey*, an even more significant book is the Gospel, variations on the same plot are found in *Hamlet*, *Don Quixote*, *The Adventures of Sherlock Holmes*, Ostap Bender in *The Twelve Chairs* and *The Little Golden Calf*, and *Harry Potter*.

This plot (as in *The Servant of the People*) has seven constant features that are widely illuminated in literary criticism. First, this hero always dies and is resurrected, since he appears in dark times and is intended to be a reminder of a wonderful past, and the promise of a bright future. Thus did the Gospel appear between antiquity and the Renaissance in the dark times of the decline of Rome; *Hamlet* and *Don Quixote*—simultaneously between the Renaissance and the Enlightenment, Ostap Bender—between the Russian Silver Age and the 1960s, *Harry Potter*—between two world wars that served to defeat fascism.

Second, a woman cannot stand beside such a hero. She is always waiting for him somewhere in the distance, as Solveig waits for Peer Gynt, Nele waits for Thyl Ulenspiegel, and Guljan waits for Hodja Nasreddin. She cannot share his journey with him, since her business is to preserve the hearth, and his business is to destroy and rebuild the world.

Third, such a hero always has a rather preposterous friend: Lamme Goedzak, Sancho Panza, Ron Weasley, Doctor Watson, or the apostles. This is a space for reader identification; we look at such a hero through the eyes of a naïve and devoted simpleton, without understanding the logic of the hero's actions.

Fourth, this kind of hero always has problems with his relatives; he is an outcast in his own family. Christ's father is God, Hamlet's father is a ghost, Bender's father is a mysterious Turkish subject (Jews received Turkish citizenship for bribes in order to escape the Pale of Settlement), no one in the family wants to know Sherlock Holmes except his brother, and Harry Potter is an orphan. It's understandable: the genesis of a trickster is always a mystery. It is as if he came from nowhere.

Fifth, the enemy of such a hero is always a changeling, a double agent: Judas pretending to be an apostle, a fishmonger pretending to be a friend of Claes in *Till Eulenspiegel*, Professor Moriarty pretending to be a mathematician in the Sherlock Holmes tales, or the death-eater Snape pretending to be Dumbledore's friend (and actually being him) in the *Harry Potter* series. Over the years, this kind of character has become an increasingly positive hero. Humanity, as it were, is absolved for betraying the wandering wizard who did no one no harm.

Sixth, such a work is always written in the genre of high parody. It does not mock the original, but merely moves it into a different semantic range. The Gospel in many ways literally parodies the Old Testament, reinterpreting the words of the prophets. *Don Quixote* is a parody of chivalric romances. *Hamlet* is a very subtle mockery of the chronicles of Saxo Grammaticus; Ostap Bender is a comprehensive parody of the literature of the neo-romantic era; *Harry Potter* is a story about successful orphans from Dickens and the Brontë sisters.

Finally, a role-playing game always arises from such a text: Sherlock Holmes's "house" appears on Baker Street with the address of 221B; a role-playing game based on *Hamlet* is performed on all the stages of the world; all the children of the world play Harry Potter; excursions are conducted along routes taken by Don Quixote; and a role-playing game based on the Gospel continues to unfold in all the churches of the world, especially beautifully on the day of his Nativity and Resurrection. (As for *The Servant of the People*, it culminates in the creation of a political party called Servant of the People. As I say, visualization has become the main feature of our time.)

All seven structural features, seven plot nodes of the christological myth, are present in the biography and political activities of Volodymyr Zelenskyy. His wife does not participate in his activities, but waits somewhere in the distance, like Nele or Solveig, sometimes presenting her book program in Frankfurt or posing with him while visiting Western leaders. He has a Sancho Panza-like squire (for now, his head of administration Yermak is best suited for this role); there is an alleged double agent (of which there are many candidates here); and there is a strong element of parody in his activities, just as in the Gospel there is a clear element of parody of the Old Testament or at least its ironic reinterpretation. Finally, Zelenskyy's activity is a continuation of a role-playing game, a series—just as the action of *Hamlet* is continued in a play called *The Mousetrap*. The last such node is death and resurrection (in the case of Zelenskyy, say he were to have resigned in 2024 only to return five years later), and direct contact with the primary demonic opponent, although the results of this contact are still unpredictable. Zelenskyy loves to speak in parables, his main weapon is irony, and he works miracles regularly—Russia's retreat from Kyiv in April 2022 and the liberation of Kherson in October 2022 have already been called such miracles. Attempts to explain these miracles solely by arms supplies from the North Atlantic bloc are as naïve as attempts to explain the catastrophe of the German army by Russian frost and distances.

We will be able to judge very soon how the dialogue between Christ and Satan is resolved. So far, Zelenskyy's response to all proposals for such a dialogue has been the same: Putin doesn't exist for me, I don't know if Putin is alive, I don't see the point of talking with Russia while it is headed by Putin. Back in August 2021, to my direct question whether he, as an actor, is capable of playing Putin (after he played Napoleon), Zelenskyy replied: "I haven't taken on episodic roles for a long time." This all sounds a lot like the "Get behind me, Satan" response. But our job is to listen to the answers that myth provides. And in the myth, Hercules, the son of Zeus, reconciles Prometheus with the gods. This is the plot of *Prometheus Unbound*. Although the play has not survived, we know it via quotes and paraphrases. "Follow Me, Satan" suggests a very different outcome. This may be a translation error, or perhaps one of the revelations. In the new version of the Gospel, aka the saga of Harry Potter, Voldemort dies, but he is left with a daughter, whose fate we will learn no earlier than 2025, when J. K. Rowling promised a continuation of the saga of the adult Harry Potter. But by this time the Ukrainian war may give us all the answers in reality.

Frankly, I have little faith that Zelenskyy will lead Putin to reconciliation with the West and repentance. Rather, he, like Hercules, will liberate Russia, although no liberation will happen there without the efforts of Russia itself. Will Lucifer be forgiven or will he finally break his teeth in the last act of his drama? Will Christ need to sacrifice himself one more time to save the world and give birth to a new religion? Who will be Judas this time? (For now, Arestovych is being actively promoted for this role.) These are the questions on tap today, and with all the tragedy of what is happening, we at least have had the privilege of being not only spectators, but also participants in the largest event in world history—maybe even the last one.

If we think of *Prometheus Unbound*, how can we fail to see an analogy with the current mass emigration from Russia? Perhaps someone has decided finally to cut Russia loose from its vast territory, on which it is too dependent? The nation would then move into a higher state—the state of dispersion. That is how the Jews entered world history, and how much nobler is identification by means of religion and culture, than by means of blood and soil! Perhaps we create the "Dispersed Russia" party?

If everything said here seems to you a clumsy attempt to involve mythology in the interpretation of a local war, remember that for historians like Josephus, Christ and Christianity were just episodes in the "War of the Jews." And today Josephus Flavius himself is an episodic witness of the Gospel story, whom we remember mainly because he once again confirmed the historical authenticity of the Gospel. Those who refuse to consider an actor from Eastern Europe as the savior of the world are reminiscent of those who asked: Can anything good come from Nazareth?

This is what Nathanael told Philip, according to John. Philip gave a pithy answer: Come and see.

8.

It goes without saying that Mephistopheles is always alone, because he is bored with people, and he is not allowed to see the angels, and God calls on him mainly just to give him some new task, and that only happens about once every century, or even less. This isolation faced by intelligence officers is constantly emphasized in the main texts written about them. We will touch on that now, but let us not forget Vladimir Putin's confession: there is no one to talk to but Mahatma Gandhi. In fact, the spy is bored with all these little people, since a special services agent sees humanity only through arrogance: He either communicates with people while recruiting them, that is, cynically buying them off, or during torture, that is, when breaking them. He has no path to mercy, for loyal subjects are not suitable for communication—he is much too powerful for that. Even exterminating them is a bore, since the victims' behavior is always the same. Mephistopheles' only entertainment remains communication with Faust, who, however, also degenerates over the years.

We could dwell on other characters of the Faustian myth—for example, Faust's woman. It is clear that a professional is always surrounded by women, for, unlike a trickster, he does not destroy, but strengthens everything around him and, as it were, guarantees a certain standard of living. This is important for a woman in troubled times. Unlike the trickster, Faust is almost always surrounded by feminine love, which for a woman is both redeeming and destructive. Redeeming because it frees her, takes her out of prison, as in Ivan Turgenev's story "Faust," although this freedom almost immediately kills her. This is how women die in all the Faustian plots of Russian literature—Aksiniya, Margarita, Lara, Lolita. We will refrain from considering today's analogy of this plot.

Serving the devil is one of the most powerful, albeit short-term, pleasures. The devil never has any goals but to propagate evil: preserving the world as it is to the very end. By preserving it from growth, he ultimately faces the need to destroy it. Death is the only universal cure for development. The world can never be bad enough for the devil, which leads him to attempt to destroy the entire Universe, to destroy all of God's plans. This is how Hitler led Germany into a suicidal war, this is how Rumata of Estor destroys most of Arkanar in *Hard to be a God*, his mission ending with a grandiose massacre. By the same token, Vladimir Putin threw Russia into conflict with the rest of the world, seeking to set the world on fire— whether from one end or the other, following a series of forays into Africa and the Middle East, choosing Ukraine as the place of confrontation. War is an inevitable consequence of the development of such regimes, for the devil knows no other way to stop history. War is a space of total lies and monstrous cruelty, and that is all that the devil desires. As such, anyone who signs a contract with him is doomed to self-destruction. Furthermore, the Lord probably had no other way to demonstrate all this to people than to let them feel it and experience it by way of their own skin. It is impossible theoretically to explain the harm of demonic temptations. The Lord's plan, as we see, was not to hand humanity over to hell, but to expose any arrogant attempts to do without heaven.

This is where we need Kołakowski again—probably his most famous essay, "Can the Devil Be Saved?" written in 1974.

His main idea is that by allowing for the transformation of evil, we can relativize it. And, indeed, we know many examples of this. Kołakowski cites two of the most revealing in his estimation—Hegel's "The Phenomenology of Spirit" and Teilhard de Chardin's "The Phenomenon of Man." In the end, the entire Enlightenment tried to make Mephistopheles, if not an ally of God (a role to which he always strived), then at least his occasionally-employed ally, a secret agent, a clandestine, like-minded individual. He is needed to arouse or awaken a person. This view is expressed by Goethe, and in the USSR at the end of the Stalin era, by Marietta Shaginyan in her book about Goethe (1951), where she specifically wrote that Mephistopheles was an agent of progress. Compared to Marx's Prometheus, this is nothing new. Bulgakov went even further down this path, presenting Woland as an executor of God's will in certain cases: when it is necessary to save the Master or deal with someone like Aloisy Mogarych, no better executor than Woland can be found. And up to a certain point, he truly is a reliable ally—right up until the moment of payback; here he is implacable and, from a boisterous, cheerful student, instantly transforms into a decrepit old man, almost more ancient than the world itself.

The very idea that this predator can serve good is very fruitful for historical and cultural speculation, but all the more dangerous. If the ancient myth assumed the reconciliation of Prometheus with the gods, the Christian myth contains no such assumption. It is the relativization of evil, according to Kołakowski, that serves as the most dangerous hypnosis of our time. In his book *Religion: If There is No God*, Kołakowski arrives at a simple and convincing conclusion: no matter how absurd miracles, sacraments and faith are, a world without them is even more absurd. Continuing this thought, we have the right to say that a world where the devil can be saved is even more absurd and aesthetically unacceptable than a world of atheists where there is neither God nor the devil.

Whatever the intermediate outcome of the war (which may well end in temporary concessions on the part of Ukraine, although that would only delay the inevitable finale), its final outcome will be the victory of the world over the Russian regime, and the liberation of Russia. Of course, Lucifer will not abandon his attempts, but with each new defeat his chances become more elusive. If we try to seek consolation—although the very thought of consolation and compensation is blasphemous—we are left with Kołakowski's courageous words: Let us at least be consoled by the fact that we are not spectators, but participants in this earthly theatrical performance where our destinies are decided.

9.

It remains for us to consider the last paradox of Russian history, on which humanity has expended a great deal of thought in the era of the Russo-Ukrainian war: How does one explain the absolute and unshakable omnipotence of the secret police throughout the last seven centuries.

After all, if you think about it, this is the only unshakable feature in Russia from the sixteenth to twenty-first centuries. Once you shout, "The Sovereign's word and deed!" you are guaranteed everyone's attention and complete impunity. Only work in the secret police guarantees immunity under all regimes. Of course, turnover takes place there, too, and such heads of the secret police as Nikolai Yezhov or Viktor Abakumov faced their own moments of truth. But it is impossible to abolish the institution of the secret police, no matter what you call it: the oprichnina, the secret chancellery, the Third Department, the Okhrana, the Cheka, the KGB, or the FSB. Vladimir Putin merely brought this service to the surface, but from the very beginning it was the prime moving force, rearranging everyone and everything with its own hand. This raises a related question, which every historian inevitably encounters: Why does this special service so persistently torture its victims? Whether during the Great Terror of the 1930s or today, it has never needed the confessions of these victims. The sentences it hands down have nothing to do with guilt, and they can manufacture any testimony that they want. Why do they find it necessary, at any cost, to ensure that the victim incriminates himself?

A prolonged study of Russian history—particularly of specialized sources, such as *The Rack and the Whip*, a book by historian Yevgeny Anisimov—leads to the notion that the main task of the secret police (and, consequently, of the entire Russian government) is not to reveal anti-Russian conspiracies, often cooked up by the secret police themselves or by victims being tortured, but rather the very engagement in the process of sophisticated and painful torture. In other words, Russia has been ruled for five hundred years by a sadomasochistic satanic sect, which has no goals except to torment the nation's population in various creative ways. The entire population participates enthusiastically with the authorities in this, indeed, truly exciting game, for sadomasochism is the state idea of Russia, and no constructive government tasks can interfere with this obsession. That is why every state regime in Russia slides into repression, and these repressions themselves unfold for any reason. It is why the main state staple of Russia is the prison, also known as the GULAG. It is why the first thing Russia does in any occupied territories is to establish a so-called "basement" where they begin to torture suspects without telling them what they are suspected of doing. They have to come up with that on their own.

This was the case in Donetsk and Luhansk, and this was the case in Bucha, Mariupol, and Izium. The first thing the Russian world brings with it is torture. When once speaking about Vladimir Sorokin's novel *The Day of the Oprichnik*, Artemy Troitsky mentioned the sadomasochism of Russian patriotism as something generally recognized. The genesis of this sadomasochism has interested me for a long time and, it seems, has never been described properly by anyone. There is no doubt something erotic and, moreover, painful in being so ardently devoted to one's homeland, and so desirous of it inflicting violence on you. Although this, of course, is not only a Russian phenomenon. But the fact of the matter is that this tendency takes on curious features and a very persistent sadistic coloring in Russia. I remember a newspaper story from 1979, I think, where *Komsomolskaya Pravda* wrote about a basement in which high school students played Gestapo. I emphasize that these were high school students, and not some young pioneer scouts. These "Gestapo agents," having seen their fill of *Seventeen Moments in Spring* and much more, staged sexual orgies, simulated hangings, executions, and interrogations—all with the participation of girls who not only did not object, but who fully bought into the game. All this was described, albeit with an ardent pathos of disgust, but in a very frank way for those times. One sensed that the authors treated what had occurred with a lively interest. Inevitably, the story ended with a civics monologue: these young people had access to cinemas, and libraries, even a stuffed animal club, but they were inexorably drawn to a basement. What is that all about?!

It seems that all our conversations about Russia's paths are somewhat reminiscent of this helpless roundelay. We have at our service all kinds of advantages, national projects, healthcare, education and the establishment of real democracy, but for some reason everyone is inexorably drawn down into the basement of their shared national subconscious, into the parceling up of those who exterminate and those who are exterminated, into a nationwide orgy, which, first some, then others tirelessly seek to provoke. But why? Because it is more interesting. It is clear that sadomasochistic games are much more interesting than a stuffed animal club. We are soft, stuffed animals ourselves, and at the first opportunity we will huddle in clubs— the excuse might be anything, including growing tomatoes. You can toss off the most innocuous botanical slogan in Russia, and the population in response will immediately be divided into Westerners (debauchers) and home-grounders (prohibitors), after which what will flow is not tomato juice. The current stability in Russia is fraught with the dangers of this basement. This amazing mix of Russian eros and Russian power is clearly demonstrated on numerous sadomasochistic internet sites.

This distorted but extremely interesting space first revealed itself to me when I was collecting materials for my novel *Justification* in 2000. It describes a sect of self-torturers who continuously subject each other to sophisticated violence, and, for authenticity, I needed a website dedicated to the history of torture in Russia. Oddly enough, there was not much on torture itself, but the entire prose section of the site was chock-full of stories from countless anonymous authors, whose creations far surpassed the late Pier Paolo Pasolini in ingenuity. Almost all of these stories—some fantastic, some historical—contained representatives of the authorities who inventively raped and executed representatives of the people. The powers represented were different—sometimes they were fascists, sometimes commissars—but it was all equally grim and relentless. Also, in all the stories and fantasies that flooded the site, there were noticeable familiarities with the "Pioneer Heroes" book series, which I clearly remembered from my childhood. These collections were a true delight for a sadomasochist: stories from a series of Men Tormenting Children were offered up in detail and with gusto, while the descriptions of the poor pioneer's heroic exploits took up no more than a third of the story and were written, frankly, with a cold nose. But as soon as the tales came around to torture and massacres, hangings and shootings, interrogations and bullying—the authors generously demonstrated all their available talent. Even in Leonid Brezhnev's *Virgin Soil Upturned* a Komsomol member encourages Cossacks to donate grain by way of a detailed and vicious story about the torture to which a foreign Komsomol member was subjected:

> . . . So, they agitated for the overthrow of capitalism and the establishment of Soviet power in Romania. But they were captured by fierce gendarmes. One was beaten to death and the other was tortured. They gouged out his eyes and pulled out all the hair on his head. Then they heated a thin piece of iron until it was red hot, and began sticking it under his nails. [. . .] The gendarmes then began cutting off his ears with sabers, and they cut off his nose. "Will you talk?" "No," he said, "I'll die by your bloody hand, but I won't tell you a thing! Long live communism!" Then they hung him from the ceiling by his hands and lit a fire beneath him . . .
>
> "Damn, what butchers they are! It's horrible!" Akim the Younger said indignantly.

The fact that many popular online resources dedicated to sadomasochism are created in Russia is telling in and of itself. But even more interesting is the fact that all snuff forums or BDSM sites of foreign origin so highly regard Russian photographs, while Russian visitors make up a good half of the international sadomasochistic contingent. They supply these sites with the lion's share of stories published there about the interrogation and torture of a brave Komsomol member in 1943, or the punishment of a negligent oligarch's secretary half a century later.

> I'm sitting in the office. The workday is nearing its end. A secretary enters. Renata. I never hire secretaries myself; the human resources manager does it. But he knows well the type of girl I like to see in a

secretary. Slender, long legs, an oval face, gray eyes, and long, dark, braided hair. For a second I imagine how I will grab Renata's braid and she will arch backward, looking at me with her big eyes.

It's not difficult to guess what he will do with Renata now—and how. It makes no difference whatsoever whether he is a businessman, an NKVD officer or a commissar. Just as was true in Russia in the twenties or the forties. This is not some long-known connection between eros and Thanatos, described by the Freudians. Thanatos here takes on clearly-defined governmental, authoritative forms. The victim is always a woman who is either beaten, raped, or hung from a nearby tree. The executioner is almost always a man in a position of authority. In this sense, the stories of one anonymous author, who in the Torture and Punishment library specializes in descriptions of repressions acted out in school—strangulation of feckless students, etc.—are quite interesting. It is especially interesting that all these executions take place with the strictest adherence to bureaucratic procedure: The person to be executed must wait for long periods in a reception area and fill out countless forms as cackling women in white coats constantly grumble, complaining about the lethargy of the victims and cursing their own bitter fate. This element of bureaucracy, creeping into the darkest and most secret dreams of BDSM fans, clearly illustrates one of the main features of the Soviet consciousness: In order to endure the unbearable, Russians learned to perceive it erotically. This is the sauce that allows you to eat anything. As a result, sitting in an endless line to see a doctor or a housing official takes on salacious sadomasochistic overtones. After all, it is in Russia, as a rule, that a private person is tortured most cruelly and inventively—with no clear purpose. Here receiving some insignificant certificate may drag out for months, and all without the slightest necessity for the state. All this penetrates the consciousness and is bizarrely transformed into a story about how the execution of an entire family (a story titled, "The Execution of the Chuprinin Family") is accompanied by dozens of senseless, but picturesque additional torments, and is carried out by a rude execution staff. Similar brutishness attends a piece called "The Execution of Olya Vyurkova," although it is pointless to list all these stories, for there are several dozens of them, and they differ only in the author's stylistics. A story called "The Interschool Center" amazes one not so much by its detailed description of the strangulation of a poor student with a garrote vil, but with an equally detailed presentation of the procedure that precedes it.

The phenomenon of Russian taboos is in itself very erotic—although no more meaningful than bureaucracy. I have always been intrigued as to what State Duma deputies and other guardians of spirituality are actually guided by when calling for a ban on one show or another, or taking repressive action against some teen magazine? Of course, this is PR, but PR can be done in different ways, so why is the repressive one so preferable? The answer is simple: Those measures suited to repression are most popular in Russia. There are two ways to fight pornography—or tasteless shows, or liberal ideology—you can either ban them or develop an alternative. But the proposal to develop an alternative looks as naïve as an attempt to send a sadomasochist to a school club. That is why, in turning-point moments for the Fatherland, the State Duma so loves to consider complaints about *The Simpsons* or the Russian reality TV show, *House-2*.

There is probably nothing wrong with all this. Everyone has their own fantasies, and it is better to give reign to them on paper or in an online forum than in daily practice. But another interesting thing is the abundance of Russian themes and Russian authors in this genre. The simplest thing—and the most foolish—would be to say that the Russian character is especially prone to self-torture, and that this is a feature of our sexuality. But that would be an unforgivable oversimplification. In fact, we witness here not the cause, but a consequence of our history. People who have been tortured senselessly and for too long are accustomed to playing with this theme in an erotic way that not only applies tolerance, but even a certain relishing of it. Sex is the lubricant with the help of which traditional Russian state sadomasochism (in the absence of any other practices such as amorous harmony) is somewhat easier to bear. In the end, the stories are written not so much by potential executioners who lack the mental subtlety for such matters, but by potential victims trying at least to spice up their unenviable fate with this sauce.

Someone will object that BDSM art is widespread all over the world, that the author of the most popular sadomasochistic comics, Dolcett, is Canadian and, there is a great and glorious tradition of sadomasochistic cartoons and manga in Japan. So it's probably not worth reproaching Russians for an exclusive love of self-torture. I agree, Russians are not alone in this, and the Japanese, at least, have long made their cravings for self-destruction an object of rapt attention. Hara-kiri is a longtime, deeply considered component of samurai culture, while a genuine cult of suicide dominates among Japanese bureaucrats and managers. (This, alas, is completely alien to their Russian colleagues: Who in Russia would hang himself after being accused of corruption?) The time has probably come for Russians to think about where they get this craving for illicit sex, the desire to indulge in the taboo in any field, this need to identify an enemy, a Russophobe, a seducer, or a poisoner, this eternal conviction that the whole world is raping them, and the passionate desire one day to rape it in return as no one has been raped before. I suspect that articulate psychoanalysis should be able to cope with this complex, because necrophilia is, first of all, an indicator of weakness. The dead need not be persuaded or appeased, things are easy with them. As it was with the stabilized society in which we all lived until February 24, 2022, that is, until the moment when everything went wrong.

The ideology of this sadomasochistic sect which has Russia in its grip, and will not let loose, is quite simple. It is most convincingly laid bare in Pascal Laugier's film *The Martyrs* (*Les Martyrs*, 2008), an avant-garde thriller where the plot centers on a sect led by a mysterious and terrible madam. The sect tortures young girls (the most spirited and resilient of them) so that, under the influence of physical pain, they attain some secret knowledge. When one heroine, whose skin has been almost entirely stripped off, reveals to Madame the secret of the afterlife, Madame immediately shoots herself, taking the revelation with her. Truly, the great sexologist Lev Shcheglov was right: the main goal of every maniac is self-destruction.

Approximately just such a sect rules Russia, practicing its dark rituals from century to century, imposing its obscurantism, sadism, and cult of prohibition on the nation's population. Vladimir Putin has been in power in Russia for almost twenty-four years and is heavily addicted to torment. Without new paroxysms of torment, he begins experiencing withdrawal. To keep the population properly subjugated, he invented a bloody cult of the Motherland that constantly demands sacrifices. From the point of view of this Mother of the Land, a living son is imperfect, and a dead one is ideal for he has already given everything he has. This sect does not promise the state any development other than the expansion of sadism, and any revolution quite soon leads only to new enslavement with even larger-scale and bloodier state violence. In 2023 alone, about 4,000 criminal cases were opened in Russia on charges of spreading fake news about the army, dissemination of extremist materials, working for the Armed Forces of Ukraine, etc. In standing up to Russia, the Ukrainian state stands opposed to priests of a satanic cult with a khaki-colored temple in Moscow's Patriot Park where a cap once belonging to Hitler is displayed as a central relic. This satanic sect long ago subjugated the Russian Orthodox Church, which blesses murder and urges Russian Christians to kill Ukrainians. There is nothing further from Christianity than this godless, sadistic religion with its dark rituals.

The ancient, wise spirit, as Dostoevsky called him, and the wandering teacher who opposes him are playing their drama out to the end. This is most of all reminiscent of Jorge Luis Borges' story "Another Duel," where two knives play out the drama of their masters. Two entities, having penetrated the bodies of our contemporaries, come together in a deadlock and draw the entire world into their confrontation. Meanwhile, there's nothing the whole world can do, for these are inhuman affairs now at work.

II. COLONIALISM

Here we must finally say why this war is not essentially colonial and why Soviet or Russian imperialism has nothing at all to do with it.

Oleksii Arestovych, in a conversation on August 21, 2023, repeated his favorite thesis that Ukraine has never been a colony of Russia, that this term is generally humiliating for it, and that it is still unknown who colonized whom. On this topic, we have a fundamental article by the historian, ethnographer and linguist Nikolai Sergeevich Trubetskoy (1890–1938), "On the Ukrainian Problem," published in "Eurasian Contemporary" in 1927. Trubetskoy was a Eurasianist, an anti-Marxist and an anti-fascist—a wonderful and not so common combination.

> Tsar Peter [the First] set himself the goal of Europeanizing Russian culture. It is clear that only the Western Russian, Ukrainian edition of Russian culture—which had already absorbed some elements of European culture (in the Polish edition of this latter entity) and showed a tendency toward further evolution in the same direction—would be suitable for carrying out this task. On the contrary, the Great Russian edition of Russian culture, thanks to its pronounced Europhobia and tendency toward self-satisfaction, was not only unsuitable for Peter's goals, but even directly interfered with the implementation of these goals. Therefore, Peter tried completely to eradicate and destroy this Great Russian edition of Russian culture, and made the Ukrainian edition the only edition of Russian culture that would serve as a starting point for further development.

Let's say that this is debatable. Why exactly Ukrainian, and not German, not Dutch, etc.? Western Europe's influence on Russia, even on the level of linguistic borrowings, is much more obvious than the Ukrainian. But Trubetskoy shows that the editing of liturgical books consisted precisely in bringing them up to the Kyivan standard, the Kyivan edition of Church Slavonic. The rhetorical tradition of Feofan Prokopovich and Stefan Yavorsky shaped Russian poetry and the Russian literary language.

> This adhesion to Western Russian traditions and the rejection of Moscow traditions is observed not only in the arts, but also in all other aspects of post-Petrine Russian spiritual culture. The attitude

toward religion and the tendencies of development of church and theological thought would naturally have joined precisely the Western Russian tradition, since the Western Russian edition of the Russian faith was recognized as the only correct one even under Nikon, since the Mohylan Academy became a pan-Russian hotbed of higher spiritual enlightenment, and since the majority of Russian bishops for a long time were precisely pupils of this Academy. The tradition of the post-Petrine Russian school, the methods of the spirit, and the composition of teaching were also Western Russian. [. . .] The Western Russian edition of Russian culture developed in the era when Ukraine was a province of Poland, while Poland was culturally a province (and a remote province at that) of Romano-Germanic Europe; but since the time of Peter, this Western Russian edition of Russian culture, having become a unified, pan-Russian one, thereby emerged as a capital for Russia. Russia itself, by that time, began laying claim to being one of the most important parts of "Europe." Thus, Ukrainian culture seemed to transform from a run-down provincial town into a capital. Accordingly, it significantly had to change its hitherto very provincial appearance. It sought to free itself from everything specifically Polish and replaced it all with the corresponding elements of indigenous, Romano-Germanic cultures (German, French, etc.). Thus, Ukrainization turns out to be a bridge to Europeanization.

One can object to much in this—in particular, note that Peter adopted Dutch and German cultures directly from Germany and Holland, without the mediation of Ukraine. But Trubetskoy is not talking about the language of shipbuilding, architecture, and trade, but rather about the language of culture, and here, apparently, the influence of Ukrainian philosophy and theology emerges as decisive.

It is also impossible to deny the absolutely obvious fact that not only in the creation, but also in the development, of this pan-Russian culture, Ukrainians took an active part along with the Great Russians, moreover, precisely as such, without rejecting their belonging to the Ukrainian tribe, but on the contrary, affirming this identity. One cannot throw Gogol out of Russian literature, Kostomarov out of Russian historiography, Potebnya out of Russian philology, etc. In a word, it is impossible to deny that Russian culture of the post-Petrine period is pan-Russian, and that for Ukrainians it is not alien, it is their own.

It is, of course, possible to deny this if you really must but the question remains: Wouldn't this lead to provincialization, to a wounded and provincial worldview? Who and whose colony was this in the time of Brezhnev who brought the Dnipropetrovsk clan to power, or under the KGB head Vladimir Semichastny? Imperialism was long ago made a bogeyman, and the extreme difficulty of talking about it lies in the fact that, in order to respect the trauma of the Ukrainians (trauma is a very mild word), both Europeans and liberal Russians try not to object to them. Being "soft on imperialism" is a universal stigma placed on anyone who is insufficiently enthusiastic about the topic. So, you find serious reasons to worry about Ukraine? Worry about your own problems! Criticizing Ukraine is an imperial act. Will you not paint the entire Soviet Union in a single color, including the highest manifestations of its culture, such as the films and books of the seventies, moreover in all republics? Then you are not repenting sufficiently for the annexation of the Baltic states and the expulsion of certain peoples. Do you call that annexation and not occupation? Such views can cost you your job in those very same Baltic states.

It is extremely difficult to have a meaningful discussion in such circumstances, but we risk failing to understand what is happening between Russia and Ukraine if we continue to consider the issue in light of the imperial paradigm. Only the anthropologist Roman Shamolin has tried to move away from this argument, writing convincingly that Putin's Russia is not an empire at all, and that Tsarist Russia, as Alexander Etkind has showed, colonized mainly itself. Actually, the Russian population suffered no less from the government than foreigners, and this provided some grounds for the friendship among peoples—Islam got along with Orthodoxy mainly due to common oppression. We will not delve into the history of the relations between Ukraine and Russia, into the polemics about the Ukrainian rebel Bohdan Khmelnytskyi or Catherine II—this angle has now become the predominant point of view. Imperialism is mentioned in the titles of the majority of scholarly works and journalistic articles about Russia. Everyone has the right to their own thematic priorities, and we will not argue with these authors. But it is important for us to emphasize that the nature of this war is not colonial, that everything is much worse, that this is not about Russia's attempt to restore its former territorial greatness, and not about territorial claims as such. That is why it is impossible to make peace by ceding territories—that would make a temporary and fragile truce. Russia as such does not need Ukraine at all. As Vladimir Pastukhov wonderfully formulated, Ukraine was in the wrong place at the wrong time. The object of Russia's claims could be anyone, and the territorial claims are trumped up to such an extent (all of Putin's statements about Lenin creating Ukraine, etc.) that even the Kremlin does not bother to establish a minimal reliability for them, while serious historians refuse *a priori* to discuss them. What is important for Russia is to be in a state of war, something that allows it to stimulate the love of the populace, and to maintain power indefinitely, while destroying the opposition in the bud. This is not colonialism—oh, if only it were colonialism! In ideology and practice, this is the most caveman style of nationalism, carried out in the crudest possible Kremlin manner. It is enough to read any Z-ideologist to recognize the barmy, reeking spirit of lurking pogroms. Zelenskyy is hated by this specific group precisely because he is Jewish. It arrogantly despises Ukrainians, considering them wayward brothers, but it hates Jews with deep hatred, jealousy, and envy. By the way, I sometimes suspect that Zelenskyy is unmistakably aware of this narrative regarding his Jewish instinct, and therefore any thought of compromise for him is as unacceptable as it was for Golda Meir: "We intend to remain alive. Our neighbors want to see us dead. This is not a question that leaves much room for compromise." So, with a Jewish president who is harshly intransigent to pogrom tactics, Ukraine was lucky once again—or rather, it made the only precise choice available to it.

Vladimir Putin has three narratives regarding Ukraine: One for the West, one for his own population, and one for himself personally.

The narrative for the West is: NATO promised us it would not expand to the East, they didn't keep their word, we tried to be friends, they didn't want to listen to us, they humiliated us in every possible way, now listen to me. This narrative is in no way imperial—it is pronounced from a position "on all fours," so as not to say it in a cruder way. I.e., the treacherous Anglo-Saxons put us in this position.

The narrative for his own people is: The West is pitting two fraternal peoples against each other. We must free the Ukrainians at any cost, and save them from the hypnosis of Nazi propaganda. We cannot tolerate the transformation of Ukraine into an anti-Russia. We don't need a nest of enemies in our immediate neighborhood. We will ensure the future of our children, and will deliver our Ukrainian brothers from the oppression of the West. This, too, is not an imperial narrative, for the only way to prevent Ukraine from turning into an anti-Russia is by becoming more attractive to Ukraine than the West. An empire is not built using prohibitive methods. The Incas colonized the population of Mesoamerica not by banning the former deities, but by knowing the secrets of architecture and agriculture.

The narrative for Russia is that it has always been a military power. It came together through the wars it fought, and through them formed its elite. We do not know how to live as a bourgeois society, we only know how to die heroically. Our job is to collect our lands (and our lands by default are everything that exists, for Russia's borders never end). The state can only develop by extending itself, that is, by increasing its lands. Intensive development causes the replacement of values, for it brings creativity and ingenuity to the fore, and our main virtues are brutality (aimed at the enemy) and adoration (aimed at the seat of power). We are a tribe of warriors, our ideal is to die for the Father and the Fatherland, and our security officers are at the vanguard of maintaining society in this state of hypnosis. However, if we settle on the military path of forming empires as dominant, we must admit that Russia has not been particularly successful in its battles, while its path to gaining new lands—primarily engineered by the Cossacks—was rather an escape from centralized government: our people fled until we reached the oceans.

These theories are not mutually exclusive. They are, as it were, three sides of a tetrahedron, the basis of which is the notion of Russian exceptionalism, unsupported by anything whatsoever, and most clearly expressed by the Z-poetess Anna Dolgareva: "The main thing is, don't write too much in your report: we are all after all, Russians, after all, children of the Almighty." This is a direct extension of Putin's version of the future: We will go to heaven, and they will just die.

It is time for the word "empire" to be returned to its original meaning. When Joseph Brodsky said, "An empire is a country for fools," he had in mind, as he did in the entire poem, "Post aetatem nostram," nothing other than the late-period USSR, the realities of which are generously sprinkled throughout this poetic pamphlet. Empire is the form of existence of most successful countries that spread their influence in the world either by military force, through economic dominance, or, ultimately, by sharing their culture. If we talk about the Russian Empire, it never fought especially well, was economically unattractive because it relied on resources and slavery, and itself had remained a settlement of the Golden Horde for too long. Russia has spread its influence throughout the world—at least since the nineteenth century—via extensive emigration. As Neil Ferguson showed in his book *Empire*, the best tactic of the mother country is to create intolerable conditions for living and working in it. Then everyone who is capable of anything flees to newly discovered lands—a Newfoundland—gradually populating them, and then achieving independence. This was true of America, Canada, and Australia. As for Russia, it sent out waves of emigrants who covered the rest of the world with regular frequency. This resembles contractions in a huge uterus, most of the inhabitants of which are in an infantile state and get along quite well with the mother's body, but some eventually outgrow it and begin to demand rights, freedoms, and professional opportunities. They are pushed out into the cold world, where they begin to flounder, gradually acquiring clothes, a car, and a house.

Putin's Russia can only be called an empire on this basis. In general, Russia has never been further from an imperial state than under Putin, for its influence in the world is near non-existent, and rests solely on the presence of nuclear weapons—that is, on fear. Its economy is inefficient, life is mostly meager, its lifestyle is unattractive, especially if you travel thirty kilometers from the major cities. The main thing is that Russia is not cosmopolitan. Cosmopolitanism—that is, the desire to attract all flags and be the object of desire of most of your neighbors—is precisely what distinguishes an empire, a place to which the top professionals and most irresistible beauties strive to relocate. There are features of an empire in modern China, and they are undeniable in America. But Russia, which has taken a course toward national isolation, autocracy, and conservation, does not resemble an empire either by Mongolian or British standards. An empire's self-awareness is based on a sense of its own success and triumph, rather than on suffered affronts and overcompensation for that. In its ideological documents and propaganda programs, Putin's Russia constantly calls itself a victim of the insidious West and its own gullibility. We are, so to speak, the kindest and therefore the poorest, and that is why we will now kill all of you. But wars are not undertaken from the position of the victim. Russia cannot in any way confirm its right to rule the world, and, in fact, it does not make claims to such rule, although its ideology today is determined by *The Third Empire*, a book by the unfortunate Mikhail Yuryev (unfortunate, because he died early and was very unsuccessful in literature: his book encourages Russians to take over the world, but says absolutely nothing about what it should do with it next). Deceived by the West, ruined by its own power, uncompetitive because of its own gullibility and kindness, Russia would prefer to curl up like a bear in a den, take stock, to put it in attractive terms, and turn into the "Island of Russia" described in a treatise by Vadim Tsymbursky, who also died early, and also failed to achieve recognition with his geopolitical fantasies. (One generally gets the feeling that all the ideologists of imperial or conservative Russia were losers, so forcefully do they emphasize the idea that they have not been given their due, and that foreigners underestimated them, while they are unhappy with the assessments of their own kind, because they themselves do not respect these people. It seems as though all these haters of the West wish to be coddled by the West, although how they expect to achieve such a thing by way of constantly promising to destroy the West is totally unclear.) An Empire attracts with its splendor, not with its resentments. And even for those who have longed to become part of the Russian world (for example, Abkhazia or Ossetia), Russia prepares them no utopias, aside, perhaps, from high pensions, although even those are always under threat due to the nature of the oil industry. Russia held Donbas and Luhansk high as banners in order to justify its aggression. But once it annexed them, it immediately mobilized them for war, a wartime that began for them in 2014. Other than engender destruction and total lawlessness, Russia has done nothing to attract new citizens, while masochists in search of such situations are always in the minority.

An Empire—that is, a *Successful Country*, as the book of my long-time acquaintance Valerii Primost is called—spreads its values and, above all, its way of life. But what kind of life does Russia offer if it constantly claims that it was born for war and is called to be the terror of the world (the words of the young Alexander II)? If it insists on constant deprivation, self-sacrifice, and asceticism? What kind of imperialism can we talk about in a country that has closed itself off from the rest of the world with a new iron curtain, wrapped itself in a mantle of traditional taboos and hates with all its heart any change, any modernism? If only Russia really were an empire! If only it had something to share, if only it didn't have the desire to colonize the rest of the world! This wouldn't necessarily be a good thing, of course, but it would at least mean a higher status for Russia. In 2022, it launched a war to ensure that its way of life, that is, poverty, backwardness, and lack of rights, became universal. This is strongly reminiscent of Russian Marxism, whose goal was to achieve equality in poverty rather than equality in wealth. This is the traditional Russian practice—to make everyone feel as bad as we do, and preferably worse. But empires are not built like that. This is how mold spreads, not how power spreads. This, of course, is no empire at all, but banal Russian nationalism in the final stages of degeneration, the last edition of that resentful philosophy that was once produced in a relatively cultural form by the Slavophiles of the 1840s. With us this is neither a dead end nor a vicious circle, but rather a special path.

It is not surprising that the answer to this Russian empire is not Western-style cosmopolitanism, and not the construction of an alternative modernist state (which, for example, Arestovych and like-minded people constantly insist on), but a different kind of nationalism, a different narrow-mindedness, a different refuge of mediocrity. We said previously that Ukraine's struggle against the Russian language is understandable and, in a certain sense, natural. The language of the invader cannot be tolerated in a warring country, and no Israel would exist without Hebrew, a language that gradually replaced the language of exile. But nationalism does not boil down to the struggle against language—it is a program of national self-delusion. It is isolation, and fear of influence, combined with the self-indulgence that flares up against the background of any victory, thus exaggerating the victory. The smaller the country, the more aggressive the resentment, and a discourse of occupation gradually emerges, the conviction that Russia has always occupied Ukraine, exploited its resources and destroyed its intelligentsia. Ukraine's attitude toward Russia is beginning to copy Russia's attitude toward the rest of the world: You have always plotted against us! You have always killed or bought up the best representatives of our intelligentsia and culture! From the very beginning you were ontologically hostile to us, because we are spiritual, and you are pragmatic! (In the case of Ukraine: you are slaves, and we are free people!) Ukrainian nationalists do not see how wretched this reflection is, how ridiculous this attempt to imitate Russia, respond to it in a mirror and smear all Russians in a single stroke. Such nationalism is expressed not in the development of one's own culture, but in the eradication of others; in persecuting their directors and writers who took part in the same festival as Russians; in mass campaigns against translators translating from and into Russian. The worst thing is when this mirror image of Russian chauvinism (which falls short of the empire in the same way that modern NATO falls short of being hawks) spreads to the intelligentsia, that is, to an environment that by definition should rise above geographical and national barriers. When the Armenian and Azerbaijani intelligentsia abandoned attempts at reconciliation and became polarized, it became clear that the Karabakh problem would not be resolved in the foreseeable future. When the Ukrainian intelligentsia began howling at their representatives who communicate with Russians and refuse to recognize them all as neo-fascists, it became clear that Ukraine may not be able to maintain its moral victory. In any case, the most radical nationalists are compromising the country, as if they were acting on Putin's orders (and it may very well be that this is so, for he is accustomed to playing on people's worst instincts. For this, intelligence is not needed, cunning is sufficient).

One of the defining features of Nazism—features that allow it to be accurately diagnosed—is its high contagiousness, and infectiousness when contact is too close. Russia spent four years of war (and the previous two years of alliance) in just such contact with German Nazism. As a result, the ideology of late Stalinism, mixed with anti-Semitism and a sense of national exclusivity, no longer differed from fascism. Today, Ukraine is in such close contact with Russia that contamination is almost inevitable. One can only have high hopes for its immune system.

III. NATIONALISM

Peacemaker and Consequences

Peacemaker is a website created in August 2014 that publishes personal data of the enemies of Ukraine. These are, from the point of view of its creators: everyone who supports the Russian aggression; everyone who spreads "Russian propaganda narratives"; everyone who visited Crimea since March 2014. It is clear that any participants in hostilities end up there automatically.

The founder of the site was the then adviser (later deputy, subsequently again adviser) to the Minister of Internal Affairs of Ukraine Anton Gerashchenko, a man at the same time brash and mysterious. When in June 2022 he organized my trip to Ukraine—on my initiative, so I could see with my own eyes the country at war with Russia—he denied his involvement in

Peacemaker. Since 2016, the creator of the site no longer has anything to do with it. Nevertheless, I was listed on Peacemaker for "public dissemination of Russian-fascist propaganda narratives, participation in acts of humanitarian aggression against Ukraine and its citizens, and manipulation of socially significant information during the Russian–Ukrainian war." The pretext was my claim that I consider any nationalists to be fools, that I place Soviet national policy much higher than any post-Soviet policy, and that the role of Russian culture in Odesa seems extremely important to me (having abandoned its myth, the city, in my opinion, will look pitiful. True, I said this in 2020).

Peacemaker is a site whose list included the prominent Russian film director Valery Todorovsky, who, because of this, was forced to make his film *Odessa* in Moldova; writer Viktor Shenderovich, who, quoting the Dozhd TV channel, called the Russian conscripts fighting in Ukraine "our boys"; theater director Yevgenia Berkovich, who adopted two girls from Ukraine, but for two years wrote perhaps the most striking of all contemporary anti-war poems. Arestovych also found his way onto the list for mentioning that a rocket that fell on a house in Dnipro during an attack on January 14, 2023, could have been shot down by Ukrainian air defense—not "was shot down," but "could have been," and that, before an investigation takes place, it is premature to talk about the reasons why it fell.

Peacemaker became famous for publishing the personal data (including address) of Kyiv journalist Oles Buzina, who was shot near his home on April 16, 2015 (the creators of Peacemaker stated that they published Buzina's data after his murder—it's not clear why they did this after the fact). Buzina's alleged killers were found and released, they denied guilt, and the case remains unsolved, although Buzina's supporters are confident that the men released were the killers, since they participated in the war as part of volunteer battalions.

I suspect that sooner or later Zelenskyy will be included in the Peacemaker database. I am obligated to say this because, as Boris Strugatsky noted, any society that establishes a secret police will sooner or later move on to authorizing murders, and secret thought police are no different from any other kinds of secret police. Identifying enemies is great anti-stress therapy, but it has serious side effects. Ukraine is doomed to consider any speaker of the Russian language an enemy, this is a normal consequence of war. But Peacemaker stokes hatred while lending a sympathetic ear to the most unhinged nationalists like Sergei Sternenko, and this is far from the surest path to victory.

In August 2021, I interviewed Oleh Sentsov, one of the most famous Ukrainians in the world. A Crimean political activist, sentenced by Russia in a fabricated case to twenty years in a maximum security penal colony, although thanks to the efforts of the Ukrainian authorities (including Zelenskyy personally) he was included in a prisoner swap, and, after three years of imprisonment, punishment cells, and a 145-day hunger strike (naturally, with maintenance medications) returned to Ukraine. At that time, six months before the full-scale war, he confidently said: if the Ukrainian president does not become a Ukrainian nationalist, sooner or later—hopefully sooner—he will end up in Rostov. This was an unambiguous hint at the fate of former Ukrainian president Viktor Yanukovych, who lives in the southern Russian city of Rostov with the unenviable status of a refugee, although, perhaps, compared to Putin and Lukashenka, he turned out to be not so much a coward as a humanist.

Here we must ask the main question: what will Zelenskyy do when faced with radical nationalism? He cannot avoid clashing with it, since nationalists play, if not a decisive, then a significant role in the war between Ukraine and Russia.

It will be a disaster if a radicalized society—and there can be no other in a tormented country—demands from the president the same radicalization, and perhaps something even more advanced. Zelenskyy came to power as the president of peace, and became—forcedly, but this does not make it any easier—the president of war. Zelenskyy has renounced nationalism many times, but one of the paradoxes of his fate may be precisely the transformation of a Russian-speaking artist from a Russian-speaking city into a principled opponent of everything Russian. The saddest thing is that this will be explainable.

Zelenskyy spoke very carefully about Ukrainian nationalism before the war: "How can I be a Nazi? Tell this to my grandfather, who went through the entire war in the infantry of the Soviet army, and died as a colonel in independent Ukraine. They tell you that we hate Russian culture. How can you hate culture? I love any culture! Neighbors always enrich each other culturally, but this does not make them a single whole." On April 18, 2019, he gave an interview to the RBC–Ukraine publication: "Yes, we protect Ukraine with information, and we say that Russia is an aggressor. And for them, people like [rock musician Andrei] Makarevich and [popular actress Lia] Akhedzhakova, it's even more difficult. After all, they are there, on the territory of Russia, and they say: The Kremlin is the aggressor, Russia is the aggressor. How could we do that? We took Crimea, and what is happening in Donbas is a shame. It's very difficult for them too. Therefore, we must be open to such people. For me today they are great Ukrainians. I consider them as such. Therefore it must be selective, the list must be selective. As you know, everything in life must be approached selectively. And to answer the first part of your question: Should the government interfere with the media? No, not at all. [. . .] There are undeniable heroes. Stepan Bandera is a hero for a certain percentage of Ukrainians, and this is normal and fine. He is one of those people who defended Ukraine's freedom. But I think it's not entirely correct when we name so many streets and bridges for the same person. By the way, this is not about Stepan Bandera. I can say the same about Taras Hryhorovych Shevchenko. I have great respect for his amazing work. But you and I must remember today's heroes, the heroes of art, the heroes of literature, simply the heroes of Ukraine. Why don't we name things after them—the heroes who unite Ukraine today? There is such tension in society that we must do everything possible to unite Ukraine. [. . .] We have a really large number of people who speak Russian. You cannot take away Russian-language television from them. We have people who speak other languages. You see, there is a big issue in regard to these quotas. No one will cancel the quotas, but there is [a way to] regulate . . ."

All this was relevant until 2022. Now it's all gone forever. Neither the Ukrainian people nor Zelenskyy's team would forgive him if he were to say something like that today. Putin achieved this, the war did. But this is the main law of any war: the one who defeats Goliath has an increased chance of becoming the new Goliath, and the one bitten by a werewolf becomes a werewolf. Russia was bitten very badly during World War II. This disease dissolved in the blood, but came to the surface. And this provides not so much a chance to cure it, but a chance to die from it. Ukraine could become the next carrier of the virus. And since the results of the war may be somewhat more modest than we all imagine in our dreams (for example, the issue of Crimea will remain unresolved and delayed), the breeding ground for the same resentment and vengeful feelings on both sides will prevail. I am not equating the aggressor with the victim, I am just speaking about the inevitable similarity of their rhetoric.

Modern warfare is primarily an internal war: It is a means of vertical advancement for young generals and vain courtiers. I don't know how it is in Ukraine—I want to believe it's not entirely like that—but in Russia vertical mobility is very bad. As you know, the son of a colonel cannot become a general, because the general has his own son. In Russia, the war with Ukraine was supported, lobbied, and advertised almost exclusively by second-tier writers—science-fiction writers, authors of combat fantasy, mediocre social realists. Having no chance of winning an audience and international fame, they sought to take revenge by being recruited into the ideological service of the state. On the Russian side, this is generally a war of losers and deadbeats, starting with the fact that Russia itself is a loser on the modern world market. It has nothing but raw materials, no conditions for the development of science, complete censorship in culture, and lack of normal competition skills. But it would be a mistake to think that such phenomena are impossible in Ukraine. It also has problems with its competitive environment, which is a direct legacy of the Soviet experience, and war is a great way to make your mark.

We must, of course, make allowances for the fact that Russia is much larger, has a nearly unlimited population, and the population has a nearly unlimited supply of patience, plus nuclear weapons, plus huge reserves of outdated but still functioning non-nuclear weapons. For Russia, war is a way to maintain power and the pyramidal structure of society. For Ukraine, war is a question of its very existence. But this does not mean that in Ukraine no one will appear (or rather, has not appeared already) who would use war to assert themselves, and to oust Russian culture from Ukraine while finally establishing their own built on the principle of national and linguistic purity. One prominent director predicted back in 2022 that *raguli*—the rude name given to provincials fixated on their small-town culture—will definitely get their golden chance to be freed of Russian competition, as well as of those who seem insufficiently loyal to the Ukrainian authorities. In wartime, alas, the best commanders are always promoted—but the same cannot be said of cultural figures, at least in totalitarian systems. Only the most naïve people believe that the Great Patriotic War gave legal status to the writers Andrei Platonov and Vasily Grossman in the Soviet Union. Grossman got his payback very quickly, while Platonov was essentially erased from literature. On the other hand, Konstantin Simonov (a hybrid of Nikolai Gumilyov and Nikolai Tikhonov, though not devoid of talent), Mikhail Bubennov and Semyon Babaevsky rose to the occasion. It was they, with *White Birch* and *Cavalier of the Golden Star* who set the tone in post-war prose. If for a short time Anna Akhmatova and Boris Pasternak were allowed to publish in *Pravda*, they were not the ones setting the trends. In wartime, the privilege of fighting is available to everyone, but only a select few have the right to take pride in victory—those whom the victors designate as worthy. In this sense, truly difficult times are yet to come for Ukraine.

Zelenskyy must walk an extremely fine line. He has always been victorious thanks to his humanity, but his humanity may yet be insufficient for him (or, on the contrary, it will be excessively complex for the liberated post-war world). He hoped to come to an agreement with Putin on a humane basis, but that's not possible with non-humans. The post-war world may be calmer (although that's unlikely), but the final battle of the archaic with the future has not yet begun. Unfortunately, what awaits us is not peace, but a peaceful respite. Arestovych noted that winning the war would be an intermediate step, but losing the post-war battle against corruption could be final. During the war, there has been a completely understandable and noble moratorium on criticism of Zelenskyy, both in Ukraine and in the West. After the war everyone will remember everything. The saddest thing is that Zelenskyy in these conditions may turn out to be insufficiently radical, and overly civilized, while some will recall the sins he committed by working in Russia for many years, and others—who knows?—will recall that he is Jewish, because radical nationalism has never been lacking in anti-Semitism. It is terrible, but true: we have plenty of evidence.

Zelenskyy may no longer have a place in a victorious—or at least preserved—Ukraine. With his desire to be the president of all Ukrainians, he may be doomed to become a hostage to the inevitable split. That would mean, if not exile, then at least voluntary departure. One thing is certain, although I would be very happy to be wrong: Zelenskyy will not be suitable for post-war Ukraine. It will need a more radical leader, one, who, alas, may well waste all the moral capital accumulated under Zelenskyy.

Nationalism is not an alternative to colonialism, but is its distorting mirror, a painful consequence. The plague is not an alternative to cholera. Cosmopolitanism, whether nationalists like it or not, is the only acceptable future for all humanity; the abolition of borders and globalism, while preserving the uniqueness of all national cultures, is the optimal environment for those who are not afraid of competition. If Ukraine emerges from the war as a nationalist state, it will mean that the virus did infect it, although, fortunately, we see signs of this in only a few cases. The vast majority of Ukrainians demonstrate a clear desire for a modernist project. It is the same thing, not so much impossible as inevitable, about which Alexander Blok wrote to Vladimir Mayakovsky (although he never sent it): "By destroying, we are still the same slaves of the old world: violating traditions is the same old tradition. There is a greater curse upon us: we cannot help but sleep, we cannot help but eat. Some will build, others will destroy, for 'there is a time for everything under the sun,' but everyone will remain slaves until a third path appears, one that is equally different from construction and destruction."

Zelenskyy came to power on a wave of softening nationalist rhetoric. Poroshenko's slogan "Army, Language, Faith" seemed outdated. All the sadder would be the forced turn of Ukraine's most tolerant politician toward intransigence—and toward ideas of national exclusivity, which in today's Ukraine no longer look marginal. It doesn't matter what Zelenskyy actually thinks of them: nationalism as performed by an intelligent Jewish satirist would not be organic at all. What is more important is that the audience—and not its smallest part—demands precisely this kind of rhetoric, while concession to this audience is necessary, for it is the loudest and most active segment of the electorate. It is also the most unpleasant, we might add, for if, from a historical perspective, the current war is to engender anything good, it will be the final discrediting of nationalism in any form.

It would be truly horrible if the war between modernity and archaism, which Vladimir Putin began on February 24, 2022, eventually degenerates into a battle—a massacre, more precisely—between Russian nationalism, represented by the so-called Z-ideologists, and Ukrainian nationalism. It did not come to this in World War II; the degeneration of Stalinism into fascism took shape by the end of the forties. One of the main—albeit distant—results of the Second World War was the realization that communism and fascism were nearly identical, the main difference being the attitude toward the Jewish question (for this idea, which I put forward at the Dilettante Readings in 2018, I was harassed for six months in Putin's Russia, and accused of rehabilitating Nazism—denunciations numbered in the dozens). It would be very good for the planet as a whole if the current war—which may well turn into a world war, and today has far outgrown the Russian-Ukrainian conflict—led finally to the understanding that nationalism and Nazism are one, for there has long been no difference in their aesthetics or practices. Any nationalist will find it difficult to explain why he is not a Nazi. There is a rather hackneyed mantra on this subject (a nationalist is proud of his nation, a Nazi hates strangers), but world practice shows that one cannot do without the other. Where pride in any immanence such as gender, age, or nationality begins, humiliation and oppression of others begins automatically.

Did Soviet Russia have a chance to turn its victory into a utopia? Yes, it did, and this is precisely what the victors were waiting for. Pasternak most frankly expressed these hopes, which is why the publication (and creation) of his epic poem *Glow* was stopped in 1945.

> We won't stop at words,
> But, as if in a prophetic dream,
> We'll build up even more freely
> And shine brighter than before.
>
> . . .
>
> Horizons with long views!
> The novelty of the people's role!
> Victorious, open expanses
> Stretching off into the distance!

They had their open spaces, but then, starting in the autumn of 1945, the country was beaten back into its stall for eight years running. The glimmer of freedom that sparked at the beginning of the war was so utterly shut down that the victors had no illusions left. Some citizens had even believed that collective farms would be dissolved, and that democratic elections would be introduced at the local level. In Ukraine today there is also a strong expectation of such a utopia that the whole of Europe can get behind; but no weaker is the dream of another utopia—parochial, closed, based on narrowness, and the curtailment of any competition. One that will seek out Russian roots and pro-Russian quotes. If this happens, I hope that Zelenskyy will have enough strength to leave the Ukrainian government (but not politics) and decisively stand in the way of the so-called *ragulism*.

Then we will see him on the Peacemaker list, making it a more and more honorable space.

IV. FOREIGN POLICY AGAIN

The main problem of Ukrainian foreign policy in 2023 was NATO: would Ukraine be invited to join, and what would be the outcome of the Vilnius summit.

The reality now is that Ukrainian foreign policy does not exist. That is, its interpretation depends not on facts, but on the *a priori* views of the person speaking. If the speaker likes Zelenskyy and Ukraine in general, the Vilnius summit is considered a great success for Zelenskyy and Foreign Minister Dmytro Kuleba, evidence of international recognition of Ukraine, and global respect for its heroic struggle. If one is tired of the war and considers Zelenskyy ineffective, incapable of doing the routine work, lacking interest in contacts with the East and South (there are many such people among the most ardent nationalists and liberals), then this person will believe that the summit put Ukraine in its more than modest place in the world's rankings. As for the Russian "patriot," whose opinion we could just ignore due to its complete predictability, this individual believes that the world is bored to death with Ukraine and will soon be dumped like a ballast, and, moreover, this will be the end of NATO which is deathly afraid of death, while Russians fear nothing. But let's not analyze the Z-agenda here, because it was already dead back in the time of the reactionary Black Hundreds in the early twentieth century.

It is impossible to objectively assess Ukraine's position in the world today, since the world is passing through a bifurcation point. There are too many unknown and unpredictable quantities in it, and therefore Ukraine can only be assessed from the point of view of its own internal integrity and consistency. It has been represented with dignity at NATO summits. On March 24, 2022, Zelenskyy spoke remotely, and on July 11, 2023, in person. After the first day of the summit, he spoke on Lukiškės Square in Vilnius. He was expected to reproach NATO for indecisiveness; on the contrary, he reservedly thanked NATO, and promised everyone that there would be no more occupations in Europe.

"We are a civilized and normal people. We understand that while there is war, Ukraine cannot become a member of NATO. All this is absolutely understandable, but today very important signals were heard at our bilateral meetings. These were signals that Ukraine would be a member of NATO, and this confidence, it seems to me, was being felt for the first time. We will become a member of NATO when the conditions are right.

I understand that this will happen when it is safe on our land," he said restrainedly before returning to Kyiv.

I would not call this a defeat, much less a fiasco, as *Arguments and Facts*, *Komsomolskaya Pravda*, and other official Russian (read: trash) media wrote. It was not a victory, although the first meeting of the Ukraine–NATO commission had taken place. It was a declaration of confusion. Many in Ukraine rightly wrote that those running NATO were not the brightest, while Thatcher and Reagan in their time . . . But what about Thatcher and Reagan? They boycotted the 1980 Olympics in Moscow? Nothing can be done about a nuclear monster, and if this monster had not fallen apart according to its own design flaws, I'm afraid no Western world would have been able to cope with it.

The uniqueness of Ukraine's current position in the world lies precisely in the fact that it has no choice but to be heroic. It is already fighting, the decisions have been made for it. The rest of the world still hopes to strangle Russia with sanctions, to crush its army with the hands of the Ukrainians, but after all, Putin is not eternal, and the patience of the Russians cannot possibly be elastic . . . Sooner or later, everything will crack or be resolved on its own, and for now we will support Ukraine—just enough so that it won't lose. But no one will let it win, either, because you never know what might happen.

However, there seemed to have been a turning point when Ukraine began sending drones deep into Russia, causing damage to airfields, hitting residential buildings (for some reason the Russians consider this terrorism), and NATO allowed Ukraine to use weapons in Crimea. This is Ukrainian territory, not Russian.

I don't presume to say how this situation will develop further, but I can detect changes in Zelenskyy's intonation. It is the intonation of someone who wields power.

The United States at one time insisted on holding presidential elections in Ukraine in March-April 2024 even though that contradicted the country's constitution which prohibits elections in wartime. The elections ultimately were postponed to an indefinite future, although the issue has not gone away.

Zelenskyy himself understands that he cannot be an eternal president—after all, as we have repeatedly said, Ukraine is at war with Russia so as not to become Russia. But even now it is clear that elections in Ukraine will not take place at least until the spring of 2025 (although the situation remains unpredictable and nothing is guaranteed. One thing is certain: every extra day in office as president undermines Zelenskyy's legitimacy). That's all right, however, Zelenskyy doesn't mind. He will merely invite American observers monitoring the integrity of the elections to go straight to the trenches where the majority of Ukraine's male population will vote. And with absolute, even mocking confidence, he speaks about the fact that he will stand for a second term: "Can I really abandon my beloved country?!"

There is a grotesque, almost mocking harshness in this: You don't give us the weapons we ask for, while at the same time continue to teach us about democracy in time of war? Excellent. Let's debate the degree of our democracy under fire. And, do you know, I feel he has the right to employ such intonation. I even repeat it sometimes myself: That's how to deal with them, they don't understand any other language. The most curious thing is that the West also recognizes his right to such a tone. Today, Zelenskyy-the-actor has two speech masks left. One is of admiration, veneration, and pride—the one he uses for conversations with Ukraine. The other, for the West, is one of restraint and slight arrogance. You no longer need to ask for anything. Everyone understands who they are dealing with. They will come and give everything of their own free will.

Who is stronger here is still a big question.

Finally, one cannot help but touch upon the skeptical position of many pundits (including those who sincerely sympathize with Ukraine) regarding the possibility of Ukraine's military victory. For example, Russian economist Vladislav Inozemtsev believes that Putin's regime will not collapse even if Ukraine returns to its 1991 borders, while transferring the war to Russian territory would ultimately unite the Russian population and make them believe a "holy war" has come. While Russia is the aggressor, there may be discrepancies in opinion, but when the Russian people are being hit, paroxysms of patriotism are guaranteed to arise among those who will be displaced. And, anyway, who believes in this return to the 1991 borders guaranteed by the Budapest Memorandum? There is one such political strategist, Alexei Kungurov, who became a political scientist in his early youth, at the end of the '90s. These people, alas, came of age at the wrong time, when Russia stopped handing out big money for political technology, and began handing out long prison sentences. Kungurov served two and a half years in a colony settlement on a charge of justifying extremism, expressed in his condemnation of the Russian Federation's military operations in Syria. Now he sharply criticizes both Putin and the Ukrainian authorities—a position, as we remember from Peter Hitchens, that is widespread and logical. Here's how he assesses the prospects for the war:

> From a strategic point of view, Ukraine's victory in a war of attrition with a resource-superior enemy is, in principle, impossible. I hope there is no need to explain that the Russian Federation has four times more manpower, twice the army, and its economy is twelve times (!!!) the size of Ukraine's. In such conditions, waging a war of attrition is the height of stupidity. But if the weaker side attacks, that is, actively expends its resources, this is complete madness.
>
> This is not my opinion, it is a basic axiom of strategy. The only chance for Ukraine is to defeat the Russian Federation politically, because it is the internal instability of [Russia's] political system that is the very needle at the end of which waits the death of Koshchei the Deathless. Moreover, this instability exists as a potentiality, and in order to access this potential you must work hard. Instead, Kyiv says: "Let's butt heads with the Muscovites—maybe their skulls will be weaker than ours." There you have the idiotic carnage that we now witness.
>
> Moscow cannot win not just because it is weaker, but because it has no goal in this war. If there was one, it was lost long ago. By definition, Russia will lose no matter what takes place at the fronts. Ukraine, however, despite the fact that its goal is quite obvious, is unable to win straight-on. Not only because it is obviously weaker, but primarily because no operational successes can lead to the stra-

tegic defeat of the Russian Federation. It doesn't matter at all where the front line will lie—along the Dnipro River and Tauride steppes, or along the Syvash, the Sea of Azov and northern Donetsk. The war will go on and on. Putin will not stop, even if the front takes the contours of the borders of 1991. And if the Ukrainian Armed Forces invade the territory of the Russian Federation, this will only give the war a second wind.

It is obvious that today the global confrontation is not between the "forces of good" and the universal evil represented by the Putin regime, as the Ukrainian media presents, but between the United States as the world's supreme leader, and China, which is trying to challenge American hegemony. In this context, the defeat of Russia will cost Washington a lot of resources, but will not strengthen their position in their competition with China. The situation is entirely different if the Russian Federation succeeds, firstly, in giving [Ukraine] a good thrashing, and secondly, in dragging [China] over to its side. In the ideal case, the Russians would become cannon fodder if things led to a hot war with China. If this means sacrificing Ukraine, the States will sacrifice it without blinking an eye. Big politics is like that, there is no place in it for ideals, friendship and other such tinsel; it all comes down to benefits and interests. At present Ukraine acts as a whip, which the trainer uses to force the lion to submit. But when the whip has fulfilled its role, there will be no need for it. Then Russia itself becomes the whip with which China will be punished.

We won't bother to remind Kungurov of a statement he made in March 2022 that the Ukrainian army was defeated and was only putting up local resistance. And let's also forget his book about how the Molotov-Ribbentrop protocols are a fake. And we'll keep silent about his lack of military experience and basic historical education—there are always a lot of self-taught geniuses in Russia. We won't even mention his membership in the January 25 Committee created by Igor Strelkov, although there are few characters in Russia more disgusting than Strelkov. As G. K. Chesterton said, "monstrous wrong and monstrous revenge cancel each other." It is important to show here the main features of the Ukrainophobic discourse which we have already mentioned previously:

1. It is impossible to defeat Russia on the battlefield, it is too big.
2. Ukraine must instigate revolution in Russia, and if it doesn't, it won't win.
3. In big politics there are no principles, but only interests. Simply put, this is not a war between Ukraine and Russia, but rather a global geopolitical clash, in which Ukraine, as such, is of no importance to anyone, and will be abandoned.

The last principle is easy to explain: a black-and-white situation requires everyone to decide and act, while a gray, mundane situation lets one continue to proclaim a plague on both houses, in fact, then, supporting the strongest. Making a decision is always difficult and risky. At the same time, conspiracy theories are fundamentally irrefutable, and America, indeed, just might surrender Ukraine, and all the talk about how there are no friends, only interests, is always passed off for some reason as political realism. There is nothing impossible in the complete defeat of Ukraine; that is, in its destruction with nuclear or conventional weapons. Furthermore, there is nothing fanciful about Ukraine quarreling with America—were Kyiv to refuse to negotiate with Moscow, it would be punished for disobedience. That is, the most pessimistic scenario can come about without any effort on the part of Donald Trump.

All this is true, assuming a certain viewpoint on things (defined as sober or pragmatic), but it all serves to do just one thing—increase the self-esteem of the author of pessimistic forecasts. From the point of view of public opinion, it is always better to be a pessimist—you look smarter. The more Ukraine grows tired of the war, the wider this discourse will spread, both in Moscow and—I don't exclude the possibility—in Kyiv. But all this realpolitik has absolutely no meaning, for victory in modern warfare does not lie in the annexation of territories. Ukraine will not be conquered because it cannot be conquered. The only thing Russia can achieve, and is successfully achieving, is its own complete isolation. Ukraine has moved the war to a level, to those spheres where quantitative indicators mean nothing. Ukraine has shown an example of samurai-like readiness for anything. No deserters or bribe-takers will compromise it. Russia, as always, provided it with a moral pedestal. But the maniac who raped the child did not defeat the child. He earned the torment of hell in this and the other world, nothing more.

People love to be good, we should not forget that. The joy of being bad is a very short-lived disposition, at least for most. Zelenskyy and his nation gave everyone the opportunity to feel good—even if it was by means of comparison with Russia. Even if it was a reverse comparison, the experience was invaluable. For the sake of this emotion, people will donate to the Armed Forces of Ukraine, participate in battle, evacuate loved ones to safe places, write anti-war books, and accept Ukrainian refugees.

This is the complex emotion that Russian poet Olga Bergholz spoke about in 1942 in a poem titled "February Diary": the emotion that in our time unites Ukrainians in bomb shelters and Russians taking political refuge; everyone who has been torn from their place in life, who has lost their job, their loved ones, their prospects, but who are involved in a great enterprise, and who do not disgrace the moment in time.

> In the dirt, in the darkness, in the cold, and in sadness,
> Where death, like a shadow, stepped on our heels –
> We were so happy then,
> We breathed such furious freedom,
> Our grandchildren could only envy us.

And ours will envy us. While the Z-ideologists are already envious.

V. CORRUPTION AGAIN

As promised, we now return to this topic from the military chapters. It would be extremely pleasant to say that corruption in Ukraine fizzled out during the war, that the nation rallied around Zelenskyy and even parted with those vices that had already transformed from vices into national characteristics. But no, nothing like that happened. Even those who sincerely and passionately support Ukraine must admit: War does not improve morals, even when it is a war with a cruel and completely immoral enemy, compared to which any petty thief is squeaky clean. Well, not squeaky clean, for the scale of all evil increases in wartime: In besieged Leningrad, the NKVD continued to function properly, interrogating and killing, while the black market flourished, and cases of cannibalism were recorded. In wartime Ukraine, bribery spread so much that on August 11, 2023, Volodymyr Zelenskyy fired all the country's military commissars, proposing to appoint disabled people and veterans in their place. They, Zelenskyy said, can't be bought. I would not be too optimistic on this score—perhaps we could look at this as just a kind of compensation for those who were disabled by their injuries, for the position is not only risky, it's lucrative. The dismissal of all military commissars in one fell swoop has the feel of a PR campaign, but there is no time to get to the bottom of each individual case in the middle of a war. The number of young Ukrainians in Europe speaks for itself: Europeans claim that there have never been so many, but the male population has been mobilized, and borders are closed! Apparently, borders can be overcome, and a draft card can be bought off, costing, according to various sources, approximately $10,000. (The Guardian calls it $5,000, in Odesa the Ukrainian Security Services uncovered a syndicate that charged $7,000, which included a blank ticket and a border crossing.) According to Russian publications that toss around all kinds of numbers, it costs anywhere between $1,200 to $1,700 to be removed from the military register in the Lviv region. A whole team was discovered that regularly issued blank tickets on false pretenses. This company included doctors and a city council official supervising the entire business and $217,000 was allegedly confiscated from it. That was a trifle compared to what one Odesa military commissar was found to possess: $5 million, plus real estate in Spain. The discovery of an entire syndicate in Odesa helping people evade the army led to the resignation of, and criminal charges against Odesa mayor Hennadii Trukhanov.

One has the option of leaving the country as a volunteer. This was mentioned in *Moskovsky Komsomolets*, a newspaper that long ago went over to the side of the Russian authorities, and even in the '90s had the reputation of "lying for cheap," but my Ukrainian friends confirmed that there is such a loophole. There is the so-called *Shliakh* system, which, pardon the pun, is supervised by Ukrtransbezpeka (roughly: Ukrainian safe transport), and for 1,500 to 2,000 bucks you can leave the country as a volunteer traveling for humanitarian aid, or convoying automobiles back to Ukraine. The well-known *Shliakh* website offers all the services, including information about the pitfalls of such a venture. Maybe this is how they lure deserters, I don't know.

You can leave the country on a business trip, and a company can send no more than 10 percent of its employees abroad. This is done officially by filling out a form on the Internet one week before the trip, and depositing two hundred thousand hryvnia in the Oschadbank account (roughly $5,000).

Friends, who are also prone to emotional exaggeration, although I cannot suspect them of working for Putin's propaganda machine, report with bitter laughter that the level of corruption during the war did not exist when Yanukovych or Poroshenko occupied the office of president. People are stealing as if there is no tomorrow. Zelenskyy is trying to fight this, but he will ultimately be named responsible for this unbridled behavior. A new way of extorting a business has emerged: a representative of the Ukrainian Security Services comes to a victim and says he has found it has Russian connections. Simultaneously, a million rubles show up on the victim's bank account. In a word, blackmail by the authorities has reached new heights—infiltrating a military-political level. It is frightening to imagine what is happening with American and European financial aid.

Yet we are compelled to repeat: corruption in Ukraine is the reverse side of people's independence, initiative and ingenuity. As soon as any ban appears in Ukraine, the next day the Internet will offer ten ways to circumvent it.

In Ukraine they steal, and they will steal because it is a way of protecting the people from the state, because it is a manifestation of a grassroots initiative, and because today's lawbreakers sometimes become tomorrow's economic engines. In general, we must make a national myth out of something that cannot be dealt with. In fact, this is precisely what *Block 95* did. It is a belated, but most accurate definition of its essence: "It may be late, but we've begun."

VI. OPTIONS

In July 2023, I received a letter from Kyiv. The author is a genuine thirty-year-old Ukrainian (I checked by calling him). He, of course, had not read this book, but he had heard several lectures that formed its basis.

> Your book is not about Zelenskyy, but about his media image. In regard to this, I would like to ask you to pay attention to some other facts about Zelenskyy, which I have listed below, and which are not usually talked about for a number of obvious reasons.
>
> 1. Zelenskyy deliberately, by his own admission, suppressed and/or denied the danger of an invasion by Putin's troops in the final weeks before the start of the war. As a result, a huge number of people simply did not have the time or opportunity to evacuate and thereby escape torture, execution and rape;
>
> 2. Under the current system of power in Ukraine, the highest sacred value is the state (the state as a bureaucratic machine operating in certain territories). And in order to save the state, you may sacrifice everything else: lives, well-being, freedom of citizens, and

democracy in general. The population is not a subject, it does not have the right to speak out;

3. Ukraine has actually been turned into a GULAG for the male population. Even having all legal grounds for traveling abroad, border guards do not let people out. [Original syntax is preserved.] People are caught on the street by military registration and enlistment officers who use force doing it. Everyone is always fit for a medical examination.

4. An authoritarian system of power has been established in Ukraine; laws work selectively as the state requires it.

5. The decision to reject an alternative to total victory at any cost as Ukraine's position in this war was made without public discussion, without a referendum. *(It would be interesting to know how the author imagines a referendum on this issue.—D. B.)* The assertion that the majority of citizens support the war to a victorious end at any cost has no basis in reality. Considering that leaving the country is prohibited, we can conclude that there is real support for such a strategy.

6. Total censorship and self-censorship in the informational space.

To summarize: Ukraine was a free country and it became unfree, not because of Putin, as everyone feared, but because of Zelenskyy, which no one expected.

It's clear that all these declarations are not facts, but assessments. Some of them (the belated reaction to American warnings) have already been discussed here, others are expressed regularly. I responded noting that Ukraine is at war with a very large and very cruel neighbor, that mobilization does not prevent the author of the letter from getting his family out, and that wartime involves certain censorship restrictions. But the main thing is clear: The author is not prepared to endure all these restrictions or to make the required sacrifices. Ukraine hasn't just now begun to get tired of the war (it got tired of it much earlier). Ukraine will also get tired of Zelenskyy if he becomes associated with an endless war and endless extensions of power.

Based on this, the future options for Ukraine and Zelenskyy might be absolutely anything. The world is going through such a bifurcation that the number of unknowns increases daily. All versions are equally probable, from a nuclear disaster that will reset the future for everyone, to the prosperity of Ukraine on the path of progress, with Zelenskyy as a national hero.

The most discussed version today (by political scientists, the more outspoken politicians, and Ukrainian pundits) is the Koreanization imposed on Ukraine. It first surfaced in January 2023, when Oleksii Danilov, the Secretary of the National Security and Defense Council of Ukraine said: "We are now being offered the Korean option. The so-called conditional 38th parallel. These are Ukrainians here, but here, not Ukrainians."

The 38th parallel marks the line between North and South Korea. This would mean peace in exchange for territory, the transformation of the four separatist regions in Ukraine into an analogue of North Korea, only with half the size, and the gradual establishment of a bad peace. Of course, South Korea does not feel safe, but the Americans have guaranteed its protection. There are already opinions coming from the NATO apparatus (immediately disavowed by Jens Stoltenberg and other top officials of the alliance) that Ukraine has been offered membership in NATO subject to its territorial integrity, that is, turning over the disputed territories to Russia. Although—what and for whom are they disputed? They were annexed with referendums conducted at gunpoint, followed by the erasure of Mariupol from the face of the earth, a tragedy which eclipsed all the horrors of Vietnam and Syria. Koreanization appeals to some American Republicans. It seemed to be the optimal solution for Henry Kissinger (a longtime Putin lobbyist), and it suits Hungarian Prime Minister Viktor Orbán. Koreanization seems unacceptable to the British and, as one could judge from public rhetoric, to Biden. Ukrainians will never accept Koreanization, although their war fatigue is snowballing quickly. True, they have nowhere to retreat. Regarding the reality of this option, I have spoken with many experts, and to my words that Ukraine will never accept it, they answer almost unanimously: "It will. They'll press it, and it will be accepted."

This sounds convincing, because Ukraine's economy depends to a huge extent on the West, and its military power even more so, although the main military force of Ukraine continues to be the motivation of the Ukranian armed forces and the military art of its generals. That is, pushing through this option may require more months of war and thousands of casualties, plus a change of power in Washington, which Russia is counting heavily on, and also a political crisis in Ukraine. Then an option is possible, which is widely covered in Russian political science spheres: Zelenskyy ends the war on terms of territorial division, and pays for it by immediately resigning. Thus, he will pay for peace with his political career and personal reputation, and an unsteady truce will be established in Ukraine, which will consolidate the status quo either until a change of power in Russia, or until a change of power in the United States.

Do I believe in this option? Having observed Zelenskyy for a long time, and trying to reconstruct his psychology, no, I don't. For him, reputation is more important than life, and therefore he would not end the war with such a political compromise. He understands that Ukraine's main resource is faith, and this option would irreversibly undermine the country's faith in itself. For a country that is ready to disappear rather than humiliate itself, Koreanization will not work, and General Zaluzhnyi is right when he says: if American aid stops, we will fight alone. We will have to die, and we will die.

I think that it will be extremely difficult for Zelenskyy to retain his post after the war. More importantly, he won't be interested in this option at all, since all the problems that the war pushed aside will immediately come tumbling back down on Ukraine. As we have seen, Zelenskyy, with all his accumulated authority, was unable to cope with them in peacetime, although Ukraine has managed to change a great deal. The onset of fatigue may lead to disorganization, compromise—albeit one that is necessary, salvational, and on decent terms—and disappointment, and Zelenskyy will pay for it, as Churchill did in 1945.

This scenario seems optimal to me: Zelenskyy will go on vacation, visit Hollywood, and play the lead role there in a blockbuster called *Zelenskyy*. If David Fincher made a movie about Zuckerberg in 2010, who is stopping the same Fincher (or better yet Oleksii Kiriushchenko who already has experience working with this actor) from making a movie about Zelenskyy? I would consider it an honor not merely to write dialogue for this film or to discuss plot twists, but to perform any technical work on this set. A film like this would win an Oscar, and this Oscar would be the highest award the world audience could offer Zelenskyy—more prestigious, I think, than the Nobel Peace Prize, which they won't give him anyway.

No one could play this role better than Zelenskyy, but the film, naturally, must not be made in Ukraine—not because there is little money there, or because it will be stolen, but because this film, a tribute to Ukraine and its leader, must be produced by the best forces of world cinematography. It should be a film of a complex genre, a combination of all those genres that we tried to collect in our book—a comedy on the verge of farce, a tragedy on the verge of eschatology, with the genre of mystery play synthesizing them all. For Russia this would be an invaluable experience—Russia thought it was filming a project called *The Titan*, but it really was *Titanic*! At least three plots must be intertwined here: the history of the President of Ukraine, the death rattle of the Russian regime, and a complex ordinary character, whom I see ideally as Igor Volobuev, a Russian voluntarily fighting for the Ukrainians. We need to give the Russians a chance to show that they are not all alike.

As you see, no one can forbid our dreams.

I absolutely rule out only one option: the violent death of Zelenskyy in the final stages of the brutalization of the Russian regime. It seems to me that I am not devoid of a stylistic flair, which sometimes turns out to be prescient: history has other plans for Zelenskyy. His evolution was too large-scale to end overnight and by tragic accident. In everything that is happening now in the world, there is a feeling of stuffiness, crampedness, incompleteness—a terrible thirst for novelty, when, after a long period of suffocation, you want to breathe freely with your entire body. Zelenskyy has already demonstrated the ability for radical transformation, and it is he who must make the next breakthrough. Ukraine is doomed to become the center of a new utopia—or to disappear. This challenge is comparable to the one it responded to in '22.

> **COMMENT FROM A RUSSIAN STATE PUBLICITY OFFICER** (on condition of anonymity): Your interpretation is interesting. But with all due respect, life is a much more subtle playwright.

It was not so difficult to be considered a decent person in the seventies. To avoid living by lies was something you could do easily. Even in the eighties, the demands were acceptable, but with the end of the USSR, tectonic shifts became inevitable. This was, to call a spade a spade, a revision of the results of the Second World War, because the main result of the Second World War was the victory of humanism, with which the USSR managed to be associated. It had a very tangential relationship with humanism, but that's what happened.

This revision could not but lead to an era of new barbarism and new simplicity. Not only Russia, but the world as a whole has become greatly simplified. This has affected the United States, Europe, Central Asia, and the post-Soviet space. I can't speak about China, that is a world unto itself, known superficially by most everyone, not only me.

Zelenskyy's victory in Ukraine was a short-term revenge of the intelligentsia, in Zelenskyy's personal case, the Soviet intelligentsia, the middle class that was almost completely destroyed in the '90s. For Ukraine and the world, Zelenskyy's opposition to the new barbarism in the guise of Russia is a unique chance, again speaking in Nabokovian terms, to "dramatically raise life back to its former heights." And today we are all answering the question: are we ready for such a psychological breakthrough?

This means making much greater demands on yourself. It means great amounts of work restoring cultural and intellectual life in society. In this, one no longer confronts the decrepit predator of Soviet power, but the much more ancient and eternally youthful temptation of the devil. This requires of humanity regular and conscious effort. The problem, as in Ukraine, is that there is nowhere to retreat. If this opportunity is missed, there will not be another. There will simply be nowhere for it to come from.

I would have finished this book long ago, but it lacked an ending. The open ending of the troubled sixties with their opportunism and ideological uncertainty has long gone out of fashion. Our times require responsible and consistent statements. I finished this book in the spring of 2023, when the whole world was waiting for the Ukrainian Armed Forces' counteroffensive. Russia in its propaganda had reached the point of complete shamelessness and was sinking lower every day, Zelenskyy complained about the lack of ammunition, Arestovych gave assurances that Ukraine was making unprecedented diplomatic efforts to obtain weapons, but then I remembered the words of my Cornell neighbor (I work at Cornell and live on Cayuga Street; Nabokov rented a house half a mile from me on Seneca).

"'To finish writing something,' whispered Cincinnatus half questioningly but then he frowned, straining his thoughts, and suddenly understood that everything had in fact been written already."

Everything really has been completed, for we are not writing the history of the war between Russia and Ukraine. It is unlikely to end within the next year, and in its cold stage it may not end this century. Furthermore, a complete biography of Zelenskyy, thank God, is impossible, because he is alive and will live for a long time. This man who could have been eliminated so many times clearly has patronage in high places, and he must still fully experience both fame and ingratitude, maybe even exile. We are writing a book about one particular turning point in history: about how a nation, in a stroke of genius, chose a man who, at a fateful moment, did not shy from a great historical role. Everything has already been done—regardless of whether the Ukrainian counteroffensive fizzles out, or whether in fact there will not be a single occupier left on the territory of Ukraine in six months' time. This is important for history, but not important for the future. The war was won that very moment when Zelenskyy did not leave Kyiv, when he did not propose a speedy evacuation, and responded with the phrase: "I need ammunition, not a taxi."

Therefore, Zelenskyy's Easter speech, delivered on April 24, 2022, in Kyiv, can put a worthy period to this book. Let us quote the main thoughts from it.

Great people of great Ukraine!

Today is a great holiday. And I'm in a great place. The Great St. Sophia Cathedral. In the cathedral, which was founded a thousand years ago, on the field of the sacred battle where the army of Kyivan Rus'-Ukraine defeated the Pechenegs. In the cathedral, which was not destroyed by the Golden Horde invasion or the Nazi occupation, which withstood in spite of everything!

Today we all believe in a new victory for Ukraine. And we are all convinced that we will not be destroyed by any horde or evil.

We are enduring dark times. And on this bright day, most of us are not in bright clothes. But we are fighting for a bright idea. On the bright side. And the truth, people, the Lord and the holy heavenly light are on our side. The power of the patron saint of the human race is [the virgin] Oranta. She is above me. She is above us all.

The unshakable pillar of the Church of Christ, the unbreakable wall of the main stronghold—Kyiv, the Unbreakable Wall of the State. As long as there is Oranta, there is Sophia, and Kyiv stands with her, and the whole of Ukraine stands with them!

Above the image of Oranta are the words from the Psalms: "God dwells in that city; it cannot be destroyed. From the very break of day, God will protect it." On this Great Day, we all believe that our dawn is coming soon.

Oranta in Latin means "one who prays." We have all been praying for the last two months. And in the Resurrection of Christ, which symbolizes the great victory of life over death, each of us asks the Lord for one thing. And speaks the same words to heaven. The words of a great and united prayer.

Great and Only God! Save our Ukraine!

Protect those who protect us! Heaven, protect those who defend the native land. Strengthen the will of those who protect us from captivity. Save those who save Ukraine. These are our soldiers, national guards, border guards, our territorial defense, intelligence. These and all our other warriors of light.

Help those who help them, the volunteers and all people who care. From Ukraine and around the world. Give strength to all who give all their strength. May everyone who seeks always find. May everyone who is on the road always overcome it. And may everyone who does everything possible to save Ukraine never lose faith that everything is possible.

Save the lives of those who save the lives of others. These are all our medics. Our firefighters, rescuers, sappers. May the victory of life be a symbol not only of this holiday. May life win the battle against death every day.

Take care of our mothers. Give endurance to those who are waiting for a son or daughter from the war. Give fortitude to those who, unfortunately, have lost their children on the frontline. Help those who have lost their children in peaceful cities and villages, where Russia has brought death, to overcome unbearable pain.

And give good health to all our mothers and all our grandmothers for many more years. So they may see their loved ones. See peace and victory. See justice. And the happy old age that the invaders are trying to steal from them. And instead of knitting scarves and sweaters for their grandchildren, today they weave camouflage nets. So give many years of peaceful life to them.

Take care of all our children. Give every boy and every girl a happy youth, maturity and old age, which will allow at least a little to overcome the memories of their terrible childhood during the war. The scary games, not fit for children, that they were forced to play. Hide and seek, but in the basement, from bombs. Running, but from gunshots. Travel, but because of the loss of home, fleeing the war.

Save all Ukrainians! We did not attack anyone, so give us protection. We have never destroyed other nations, so do not let anyone destroy us. We did not seize other people's lands, so do not let anyone seize ours.

Save Ukraine! Its right and left banks—at a time when we are being beaten viciously on both our right and left cheeks. At the end of winter, spring did not come to us. Severe cold was brought to our home. Dawn brought us opaque darkness.

We believe, God, that in your judgment you will not forget them all. All those who have forgotten all your commandments.

You will not forget about Bucha, Irpin, Borodianka, Hostomel. All those who survived brutal crimes. Give human happiness to them and to all our land.

You will not forget about Chernihiv, Mykolaiv, Kherson, Sumy, Kharkiv, Izium, Kramatorsk and Volnovakha, Popasna. All other towns and villages that hear the terrible explosions. Let them and all of us hear the fireworks of victory.

You will not forget about Mariupol and its heroic defenders. One can destroy walls, but you cannot destroy the foundation on which our spirit stands. The spirit of our warriors. The spirit of the entire country.

Our hearts are full of fierce fury. Our souls are full of fierce hatred for the invaders and all that they have done. Don't let fury destroy us from within. Turn it into our accomplishments from the outside. Turn it into a force of good to defeat the forces of evil.

Save us from strife and division. Don't let us lose unity.

Strengthen our will and our spirit. Don't let us lose ourselves. Don't let us lose our longing for freedom. Therefore, do not let us lose our zeal for a righteous struggle. Do not let us lose hope for victory and self-esteem, and therefore our freedom. And therefore Ukraine. And therefore faith.

Take care of yourselves. Take care of your loved ones. Take care of Ukraine!

Christ is Risen!

He is Risen Indeed.

Many in Ukraine wept while listening to this appeal. The war made everyone affected by it emotionally vulnerable: I noticed in Ukraine that many easily move back and forth from laughter to tears, and no one is embarrassed by their tears. After all, tears are not a sign of weakness, they are an opportunity for relief. Tears wash away pain and hopelessness. The most terrible grief is a tearless one that cannot find a way out.

Easter is a time when the most complete and hopeless darkness gives way to brilliant light. Easter is a time when there is no hope left, when faith has been desecrated, when the best human is subjected to the most shameful execution, and the people, once chosen by God, overwhelmingly approved his execution. It is a time of the greatest fall, a night that did not promise dawn would come. As it is said in the best of all Easter stories, Anton Chekhov's "The Student," "Oh, what a terrible night it was, grandma! An extremely dull, long night!"

This night now hovers over Russia. This night brought darkness to Ukraine when, at the beginning of the winter in 2022, its civil infrastructure was destroyed and one by one Ukrainian cities went out without heat or light.

This war is only the beginning of a long series of conflicts and schisms, as the world experiences turmoil comparable to the first century of Christianity. We, the Author and his sympathetic readers, were lucky to be on the right side of this war—on the side of the future. Ukraine was the first to face the aggression of a rabid, doomed, archaic nation. It survived this confrontation and led the free world. The Russian project has suffered its final defeat, although its convulsions will last a long time, and may yet cost its population countless victims. But the outcome of the confrontation is obvious even now as speakers on Russia's federal channels chew sand in helpless rage.

We leave our hero at an extremely difficult moment. Although, truth to tell, we don't want to part with him, and we will certainly return to his biography when the military stage is over. The opportunities to maneuver among extremes, preserving the nation in the fine form that it reached in the spring of 2022, are very small, and this might easily be called Zelenskyy's second miracle, especially striking against the backdrop of the turmoil into which Russia will almost certainly plunge. This second miracle—or drama, which is by no means excluded either—may yet become the topic of a second volume of this book, one which will still have to be written, for we are all still far from the denouement.

But our task here was to record the unique experience of a nation that intuitively chose an unpredictable, unconventional leader—and proved that in extreme situations, at the loftiest points in history, systemic politicians are powerless, and an exception to all the rules is needed. Zelenskyy showed the way toward politics in the twenty-first century. Art takes the floor when the voices of reason, calculation, and sober analysis fall silent in fear. For only art can make a person rise above himself, leap higher than his head and accomplish the impossible. Regardless of Zelenskyy's future fate, he met his finest hour with dignity.

Zelenskyy can employ this capital in both the best and worst ways, and this will in no way diminish his feat. As is well known, Yury Gagarin, the first man in space, was not always ideal in his everyday life. He drank excessively and even, horror of horrors, cheated on his wife. But the immortality of his name is ensured by the 108 minutes he spent in space.

As such, there is nothing uncommon in the fact that literature, the mother of all arts, would describe this situation. Economists, military historians, and chroniclers will also find work to be done here, but only after literature makes sense of what is most important.

I usually only start writing a book if I have the final line. The easiest thing would be to end it the way Zelenskyy ends his speeches. But I don't have the right to do that, and that is not my goal.

My task, in general, is formulated very simply:

Musa gloriam coronat, gloriaque musam.

P.S.

Many Russian books of the seventies—samizdat and tamizdat—contained a postscript: I would like to thank the author's assistants and consultants, but such gratitude could cost them their freedom, if not their lives. I never thought (I want to write "I didn't dare hope") that I would have to write something like this. But I cannot name the editor of this book, my beloved old friend. The fees for his labor, which was prodigious, believe me, could be excessive.

I cannot thank the first ten Russian readers who pointed out to the author his many omissions. They still must live and work in Russia. I swear, friends, in the very first Russian publication I will . . . But now—and I quote merely to capture the spirit of the times—"The Administration of the President of Russia has demanded that the Kremlin-controlled media stop calling the President of Ukraine Volodymyr Zelenskyy president. This requirement applies to all forms of media: from television channels to on-line media." Call it demons introducing sanctions for mentioning incense in church. In these circumstances we are somehow bound to curb vanity. I myself am very tempted to sign this book, "A WELL-WISHER."

Thank you and deep bows to all.

D. B.

ONE YEAR LATER

An Anti-Epilogue

1.

In the year that followed the publication of this book in Russian, neither Zelenskyy's future nor that of Ukraine, which is closely intertwined with Zelenskyy's, have become any clearer or brighter. The war continues. The United States elected Donald Trump, and the three basic branches of government in the U.S. are under the control of the Republicans. On one of the first days after the election, still a good three months before the inauguration, the newly elected American president called Zelenskyy and, in his guise as a professional charmer, promised him, "You will be fine with me." Elon Musk, who over the final months of 2024 openly supported Trump in myriad ways, took part in the conversation. Trump then called Vladimir Putin and warned against any escalations in Ukraine. He did not coordinate his call with the Ukrainians.

Over the past year, life has confirmed two of this book's assumptions that weren't derived from any inside information, but were simply based on the logic that all plots follow. First, Oleksii Arestovych, one of the main spokesmen for Ukraine, found himself not only in the opposition, but also in exile after several criminal cases were brought against him with the threat of arrest. As I was preparing to write this chapter I invited him to Rochester, where I now live and teach at the local university, and arranged a meeting with him for American students and the Ukrainian diaspora. The room was packed, the commentary was frank, and in this chapter I will quote some of the thoughts that Arestovych authorized me to share. Second, the commander-in-chief of the Armed Forces of Ukraine Valerii Zaluzhnyi was dismissed from his post on February 8, 2024, and awarded the title Hero of Ukraine. He left due to growing disagreements with Zelenskyy, none of which, however, were ever aired officially. Zaluzhnyi was dismissed from military service (retaining the right to wear his uniform), and on May 9 was dispatched as ambassador to Great Britain. Some analysts believe that this contravenes one of the main conditions for his potential participation in future presidential elections in Ukraine: According to Article 103 of the Ukrainian Constitution, a presidential candidate must have lived in the country for the last five years. However, the Constitutional Court of Ukraine noted as early as 2014 that the methods for determining the period of residency in the country had never been sufficiently clarified, and it is possible that the authors of the Constitution did not specifically have the last five years in mind.

Another of my assumptions was also confirmed. Oleksandr Syrskyi, to whom we devoted an entire chapter, was appointed to replace Zaluzhnyi, although he never achieved anything close to Zaluzhnyi's popularity. As of November 2024, Zaluzhnyi remains the most highly trusted of all Ukraine's military leaders, even though technically speaking he is no longer in the military. If presidential elections had been held in Ukraine at the end of 2023, Zaluzhnyi would have polled significantly higher than Zelenskyy—assuming, naturally, that they both had chosen to run. (The difference between the trust and distrust ratings in the case of Zaluzhnyi is 59 percent; in the case of Zelenskyy it is about 5 percent.)

Zaluzhnyi was accused of many things—from fundamental disagreements with the president to various incidents that played a crucial role in the escalating conflict between the two. For example, on November 6, 2023, near Kyiv, Zaluzhnyi's assistant, Major Hennadii Chastiakov, was killed by a live grenade explosion. His comrade-in-arms, Colonel Timchenko, had given him a bottle of whiskey and six live grenades. Chastiakov, thinking the grenades were unique shot glasses, pulled the ring on one of them. As a result he was killed, and his thirteen-year-old son was wounded. There was no malicious intent—it was an ill-fated joke that the recipient did not understand. Against the backdrop of a large-scale power struggle, however, any such random event may be of use to someone. Zaluzhnyi was also criticized for receiving a PhD in December 2023—not exactly the perfect time for something like that! The central bone of contention between the president and the commander-in-chief was that Zaluzhnyi insisted upon a transition to defensive tactics, while Zelenskyy believed that the Armed Forces of Ukraine had not fully exhausted their offensive potential. In public statements Zaluzhnyi assessed the state and condition of the Armed Forces of Ukraine more critically than the president, speaking of the need for additional mobilization (although he explained repeatedly that he had not submitted draft laws on mobilization to the Upper Rada because he did not have such authority under the law).

Following Zaluzhnyi's dismissal, a large-scale shake-up took place among the Ukrainian Armed Forces leadership, primarily as a result of the failure of the 2023 offensive. Zelenskyy stated that "some commanders do not have sufficient training and experience." Dmytro Hereha, the commander of the Ukrainian Armed Forces support forces, was replaced on March 4, 2024, (although he was reinstated on May 9). The commanders of the southern (Andrii Kovalchuk) and western (Serhii Litvinov) fronts were replaced, although they were not dismissed from the Ukrainian Armed Forces. Both were transferred to academic positions—Litvinov to the National Defense University, and Kovalchuk to the Odesa Military Academy. Brigadier General Hennadii Shapovalov took over the command of the southern region, while Volodymyr Shvediuk assumed control of activities in the west. Chief of the General Staff Serhii Shaptala was replaced by Anatolii Barhylevych. It was Barhylevych who was credited with creating a powerful territorial defense throughout Ukraine a year before the full-scale invasion. Zelenskyy, announcing the appointment, called Barhylevych "an experienced general who understands our goals in the war." The deputy commander-in-chief responsible for drones and unmanned aerial vehicles also changed: Vadym Sukharevskyi was appointed to replace Mykhailo Zabrodskyi. At thirty-nine, Sukharevskyi was one of the youngest and most experienced Ukrainian generals (he fought in Iraq, and participated in battles in Donbas in 2014). His call sign is "Badger." In June, he reported that over the first six months of 2024, the Ukrainian Armed Forces had put six times more drones into action than in all of 2023.

Volodymyr Horbatiuk (replacing Oleksandr Kirilenko) became responsible for the work of headquarters, planning and management. He had previously commanded the Ukrainian contingent in Kosovo. According to Ukrainian military observers, he is considered one of the most promising Ukrainian military leaders today. In September 2024, Mykhailo Drapatyi was named to head the Luhansk Operational Strategic Group. In a private conversation with me, Arestovych called him the most promising and talented of all the Ukrainian generals. And then on November 30 insider information was confirmed that Drapatyi had been appointed the new Commander of the Ground Forces of the Armed Forces of Ukraine. There are persistent rumors that he will soon replace Syrskyi as the head of the Armed Forces of Ukraine. However, such rumors have been swirling ever since Syrskyi's appointment, and before that they followed Zaluzhnyi everywhere no matter what he did. But Ukraine lost more than 80 settlements in the Donetsk People's Republic throughout the fall of 2024, and rumors flew fast and heavy that the front was about to collapse. Zelenskyy himself publicly admitted several times that there was insufficient personnel in place, and, as the end of November 2024 approached, he began speaking about the fact that there were not enough forces to restore the Ukrainian borders of 2022. One can imagine what it cost him to utter these words, but he had proven many times that he was not afraid of making painful confessions.

One of the most high-profile and polarizing events of the entire war took place on August 6, 2024. On that day, three brigades of the Ukrainian Armed Forces (approximately 10,000 soldiers) invaded the territory of Russia's Kursk region, and over the next week captured a thousand square kilometers (385 square miles). That was more territory than Russia had seized in Ukraine throughout the entire year of 2023. More than thirty settlements came under the control of the Ukrainian Armed Forces, including the city of Sudzha with its population of five thousand. Russia repeatedly claimed it would drive Ukrainian troops out of its territory before winter; reported many times that it had encircled huge groups of the Ukrainian Armed Forces; and, through declarations of Apti Alaudinov (commander of the Akhmat battalion and deputy head of the military-political department of the Russian Armed Forces), pronounced the complete defeat of the Ukrainian groups. Meanwhile, Alexander Dugin, the chief ideologist and philosopher of modern Russia, howled daily that since the August incursion began, Ukrainians had been raping Russian women and children in the occupied territory, as a result of which he urged people to cancel vacations, avoid night clubs, and use their time constructively by weaving camouflage nets! In fact, at least twenty settlements remained under the control of Ukraine in early December 2024. Many believed that after the rapid raid on Russia's poorly defended territory, where the Akhmat battalion let the Ukrainian Armed Forces through practically without a fight, Ukraine should either have expanded its operations, or quickly withdrawn. Incidentally, stories circulated that many in the Kursk region lived in perfect harmony with the Ukrainians, for many of the residents there had friends on the other side of the border. I even began concocting a novella about Ukrainian troops launching an attack on Moscow accompanied by malcontents from Kursk who join them as cooperation between the two sides deepens. The invading forces acquire many Russian supporters along the way, before finally reaching Moscow itself. However, once they encounter serious resistance, the Russians surrender themselves and the Ukrainians, placing all the blame on the latter. In the end, the people of Kursk once again begin cooperating, although this time it is with the internal security forces of the Russian Federation.

In reality, of course, nothing of the sort happened—including the supposed mass rapes of Russians in the occupied territory. Tsargrad television and other Russian propaganda media reported—with no basis whatsoever—

on dozens of citizens being tortured in the Sudzha district, their eyes being gouged out and fingers cut off. (Back when I was in the first grade, my desk mate told me that the kindergarten guard, a Jew, stole children and gouged out their eyes, sometimes even cutting off their fingers. I don't know what is more suspect here—the eyes-and-fingers thing or the guard being Jewish, but sadistic stories of this kind are immortal in Russia.) Correspondents for the *New York Times* interviewed Russians who said the Ukrainian troops had treated them well. "What won't you say at gunpoint," was the response from Tsargrad. Some residents of the Sudzha district explained to journalists that they were not leaving their homes because, first, the Russian authorities bungled the evacuation, and second, they were afraid that in their absence Russian troops would loot their homes. Many residents of the Kursk region appealed to Putin: "Come save us!" By contrast, residents of the Russian-occupied territories of Ukraine never sent any such appeals to Zelenskyy. They had become quite self-reliant through their experience with territorial defense.

2.

As I was writing this epilogue, the one thousandth day of the war came and went on November 19. On November 21, Russia struck the city of Dnipro with an Oreshnik intercontinental ballistic missile, thereby equating Ukraine with a separate continent. Despite the seriousness of the situation, the strike evoked a rather bemused response from Ukrainian analysts. A heavy, expensive missile designed to deliver a nuclear warhead had arrived with a loud crash. The Ukrainians failed to intercept it, but it did not explode either. Frankly speaking, it all looked like the coquettish posing of a bathing beauty dipping her foot in the cold autumn water, but not daring to swim—say, in a painting by Lemoine or Draper, with the only difference being that the bather was neither young nor beautiful, but gray-haired, like the Russian Motherland, and completely covered with varicose veins. Not a particularly erotic sight, to be honest. Whether it wants to or not, Russia will have to dive into, and swim through the hellish waters of Styx. The question of whether Putin was sufficiently determined to use nuclear weapons is akin to the question of whether a man falling into an abyss has enough determination to reach the bottom. He had nothing to grab onto, nowhere to turn, and the world could only pray that he would die during his descent. But even that would have had no effect on his personal fate: He had already taken the plunge on February 24, 2022. After that moment, he never had any other policy aside from a continuous and increasingly expanding global war. The only thing Putin could sell as victory after that was world domination, which, incidentally, was becoming increasingly plausible as I wrote these words. Russia had entered a stage of its existence—initially programmed into its makeup, I might add—that was incompatible with the existence of the rest of the world. According to this potential narrative, the world would either have to submit to Russia, or perish together with it. There was, however, a third option, in which the remainder of the world would accept the challenge thrown at it, and begin to resist. We will just have to live and see what happens.

One potential image of Russia might look like this: a solitary water lily floats on a black surface, a sick flower in a sick ecosystem. In fact, it is all one big swamp that has accumulated a critical amount of peat, and is doomed either to catch fire and set the entire forest ablaze, or cease to be a swamp, and be reclaimed by nature. Along with the swamp, in all likelihood, many amazing inhabitants will also be destroyed—for example, the intelligentsia, of which there are already almost none left, and the artists who are accustomed to justifying the existence of the swamp because it is so unique. After all, only in this environment could all the amazing creations of the logocentric Russian civilization exist: the gigantic machine of state propaganda, and the structure of civil society opposing it; the state mafia, and anti-state sectarianism. Russia stewed in its own juices for seven centuries, while it invariably positioned itself as an antithesis to the rest of the world. But in the end it occasionally broke through and spilled over into neighboring nations, as it did in Czechoslovakia, Afghanistan, and Georgia. But only in the case of Ukraine did Russia encounter the stubborn resistance and consolidated indignation of the rest of the world. Russia offered humanity an unenviable choice—either the world submits and recognizes the supreme right of Vladimir Putin to decide the fate of the world, or it agrees to a military draw, which is tantamount to mutual destruction. This was just how the dilemma looked a year ago when my book was published in Russian. And that is how it looks now—with two modifications: First, the world gradually grew to understand the utter absurdity of the situation. The world populace reluctantly understood that it found itself in the same position as Ukraine, doomed either to resist or to vanish. Second, the last remaining breeding grounds for internal resistance disappeared in Russia. The vast majority of Russians came to believe that Vladimir Putin was the ultimate guarantor of Russia's existence in its past form, and, what is worse, they were right about that. That is, it was not necessarily true at first, but now there is nothing to be done about it: at this point it is a done deal. Russians are undergoing another attack of Stockholm syndrome. They believe obstinately that the rest of the world is hostile to them, repeating the phrase of the American naval officer Stephen Decatur in 1816: "Our country, right or wrong!" They completely ignore the essential clarification made by Senator Karl Schultz in 1873: "My country, right or wrong; *if right, to be kept right; and if wrong, to be set right.*" And they certainly do not know the aphorism of Edmund Burke (in his 1790 book, *Reflections on the Revolution in France*): "To make us love our country, our country ought to be lovely."

No, for Russia to be lovely at this point in time is an unacceptable compromise for Russia itself: anybody could love them if they were as pure as driven snow. No, true greatness is to love your Fatherland unconditionally when it is wrong—that is the main motto of the Russian world today: "We tried to be good, but you did not appreciate us. Now you'll have to love us for being bad, being worse than you, worse than everyone else, much worse! No Herod exists that we are not capable of out-Herod-ing. We will lead from the back of the line, and we will rush into the abyss in order to amaze the world with miracles of irrationality and suffering— our own and those of others. We will stake our claim to the most desolate desolation—and if we perish, we will take everyone down with us."

It would seem that the world has never faced danger on such a scale, and that Voldemort really did turn out to be worse than Grindelwald, who at least adhered to some principles, and made at least minimal demands on himself. Extreme evil arrived in Russia at precisely the same time that the nation began to reject any and all criteria for quality. This is a suicidal strategy, of course. But will Russia manage to collapse before it deploys nuclear weapons, or will it provoke some kind of response? Or, perhaps, will it intimidate the whole world and achieve a conclusive victory once and for all? You never know what might happen! The very possibility of this question being raised only proves how absolutely serious it is.

It is quite possible that Volodymyr Zelenskyy is building his strategy based on this very fork in the road. He clearly hopes now that Russia will be finished off not by Ukrainian resistance (whose resources are clearly deficient), but by the weight of its own problems. Zelenskyy, a producer and screenwriter, possesses an innate sense of composition. He sees the pace at which Russia is deteriorating, and he has no doubt about what the outcome will be. With each new ban Russia institutes, and each new threat it makes, it looks more and more ridiculous and scary. But we must admit that it clings to one last hope: The Russian population is even less inclined to resist than the Germans were in 1943. Russia doesn't have an Ernst Thälmann, or a Stauffenberg family. Members of the Russian opposition—including conciliatory ones like the Yabloko party which urges both sides to lay down their arms—do not understand how one can wish defeat upon one's own people. No one would vote for a politician who wishes death upon our boys! These people probably still think there are actual politicians in Russia, and most importantly, that power in the country can be changed as a result of elections. Well, take that flag and wave it if you can. Good riddance to them.

3.

At the same time, one cannot help but see that things are getting worse in Ukraine. The protracted war, the absence of full-scale and consistent support from the West, and a clear shortage of its own spectacular victories like the Kursk incursion are causing Ukraine to lose confidence and strength. No nation can be expected to show endless courage and 100 percent readiness to resist to the last man. People are fleeing mobilization wherever and however they can. The words of one young Ukrainian who escaped through the Carpathian Mountains and, unlike Ostap Bender, was received quite hospitably by Romanian border guards, are the source of a lively discussion on the Internet: "I will never return," he said, "to the yellow-blue garbage dump." This is an extreme opinion, and a relatively rare one. And yet hundreds of thousands of young Ukrainians have absolutely no desire to sacrifice their lives for their Motherland. We are not talking here about corruption or some other kind of sinful behavior, but simply stating that at all times a normal person is inclined to yearn for life and comfort, rather than for death in a cold trench; to save oneself alone, not in tandem with the Fatherland. The short-term rush, during which endless lines formed at military registration and enlistment offices, has subsided. As always, fear and fatigue followed shock and pain. Ukraine is not ready to give in, and it has no stomach for compromise. It did not resist desperately for three years in order to throw up its hands and not only relinquish one-fifth of its territory, but agree to full Russian control over its army. But it is also becoming increasingly difficult to endure nightly bombings, electrical blackouts, and heating stoppages, especially when the prospects for that changing are so unclear. Even the long-awaited permission to fire long-range missiles (ATACMS from the U.S., and Storm Shadows from France) is no longer especially inspiring. The Russian Oreshnik missile had nothing to do with this—it was simply the fact that heroism of all kinds is an expendable resource. Zelenskyy was forced to admit publicly (in an interview with Fox News on November 20, 2024) that Ukraine did not have the means at its disposal to return the country's borders to where they were in 1991, and that even the return of Crimea was no longer an urgent task. Ukrainians grumbled in response—for three years he had been saying something entirely different. But they also quite soberly realized that Zelenskyy was being honest.

Zelenskyy was also being asked to perform still another miracle. After the drubbing Ukraine delivered to Putin's original blitzkrieg plan; after the liberation and return of Kherson; and after the successful incursion into Kursk: people wanted still another, even more clear-cut, turning point. But the fact is that such a turning point was most likely impossible, and no amount of Western aid could guarantee it. In a war of attrition, Ukraine had far fewer chances than its northern neighbor which possessed an endless source of people and money (well, not endless, of course—money could run out before people's patience—but for the time being Russia still had enough for the largest military budget in history, for payments to mobilized soldiers, and for compensation to families who lose their breadwinner). More and more voices—and not only in Russia, but in Ukraine itself—supported a compromise plan, freezing the war along the dividing lines, the commencement of negotiations, etc. Putin openly mocked all of this. Here is what he said at the meeting of the Valdai Club in November 2024: "They finally realized that Russia cannot be defeated on the battlefield. I praise them, I praise them." Actually, it is possible. That's the point, it is very possible. But a different degree of determination and solidarity is required, and the world is not yet ready for that. As such, the option with "the most difficult, humiliating peace"—as Lenin once characterized the Treaty of Brest-Litovsk—is considered the most likely. But here a fundamental clarification is required: Zelenskyy is not the one who should have to sign this peace agreement.

A hero is a rare commodity, especially in the contemporary world. A hero needs help to survive, so as not to be turned into a compromiser or a negotiator. Zelenskyy played his exceptional role, he evolved into a non-systemic politician, ready to take action in an extraordinary, non-systemic situation. He himself stood firm, and helped the nation stand firm. He became its leader and its symbol, while managing not to turn into a Supreme Leader. For three years, he found the right intonations, the only possible words, the most convincing narratives. Today, he can and should be replaced by a professional military man, a diplomat or a negotiator, or at least an economist—anyone, as long as this individual, unlike Zelenskyy's situation, does not prohibit negotiations then turn around and lift his own ban. Ukraine cannot compromise its hero—it must retain a symbol of resistance in its past, one who managed to crack jokes in unbearable circumstances, and visit the most dangerous parts of the front to personally reward heroes.

4.

The question of what to expect from Donald Trump's second term as president is an entirely different matter. With him, there are entanglements so complex, and situations so unmanageable, that it is precisely the excess of alarming factors that may lead to a happy ending—call it the subversion of subversion if you will—where menacing harbingers are mutually destroyed, the most delicate balances are violated, and the simplest factors like mercy or war fatigue gain a path to victory. It sometimes happens that several mortal dangers are piled on one another simultaneously, and you end up with something like this moment in Valentin Pikul's old historical novel, *The Unclean Power*: "I am deeply grateful to the revolutionaries. They saved my life! As a consumptive in the final stages of illness, the doctors sentenced me to death in absentia. The Socialist Revolutionaries also sentenced me to death. But one condemned twice will not die . . . When the executioners fired, one of the Socialist Revolutionary bullets entered my chest and forever closed the fatal cavity lesion in my lungs!" Trump is in the position of playing the role of this fatal bullet: He introduces an element of total unpredictability into a world that is already seriously overcomplicated. His showmanly and semi-professional desire to mount spectacular, dramatic stunts constantly leads him to make wild statements that sound less and less credible. In one case, he threatens to create genuine hell for Hezbollah if the Israeli hostages are not released, while demanding that this be done in time to mark the solemn day of his own inauguration. In other cases he reminds Putin that NATO has troops in Europe (of which Putin himself, of course, is well aware); or appoints eighty-year-old Keith Kellogg to be his authorized representative for Ukraine, the same Keith Kellogg who repeatedly stated that the only condition for peace in Ukraine could be the complete withdrawal of Russian troops back to the 1991 borders, but whose April 2024 plan for peace appears to suggest nothing of the sort. I think even Donald Trump's supporters have no doubt that his two main goals are precisely to stage dramatic stunts and secure personal gain—no worldview reinforces his actions. Bob Woodward warned about that in August 2024 in his book *War*, where he truly divined the word of the year and, perhaps, the decade. Trump does what he finds either personally advantageous or socially scandalous. Narcissists are usually populists. After all, how can you admire yourself if millions don't share your admiration? Expecting Trump to have sympathy for the Jews, whom their aggressive neighbors wish to exterminate entirely, or for the Ukrainians, who have the same problem, is extremely naive (for which reason the strong Israeli sympathy for Trump and optimistic expectations for his presidency don't so much irritate me as strike me as evidence of inexhaustible Jewish optimism).

My status as an American professor imposes on me not restrictions as such, but rather obligations: My personal political sympathies must not affect the objectivity of my assessments, or the coherence of the narrative. Ultimately, however, the position of being in opposition to power is quite familiar to me, and I perceive my lack of agreement with the majority as more of an incentive than a threat. The basic premise of one of my novels is the magical ability of Russians in emigration to retain, and re-root their old problems wherever they may be (just as the residents of Harmont in the Strugatsky brothers' *Roadside Picnic* increased the number of calamities by their mere presence at any location on the globe). Perhaps Russians enhance the environment in this way: I, for example, would really find it unnatural to live in a country where I completely agree with the authorities. I think if I were a citizen of Ukraine I would have many more questions about Zelenskyy, which does not nullify my admiration for his courage and wit in many situations. I will not hide it—as the vast majority of American professors do not hide it—I am not delighted with the election of Donald Trump, and I would like to have hope that the American political system will survive his impending four-year one-man show. And by that I mean to say I hope the election which he won will not be America's last. It is quite possible that, in order to demonstrate the risks of populism with the greatest clarity, the Lord chose to convince doubters by means of proof by contradiction. But it cannot be ruled out that Oleksii Arestovych is right again to think that Trump may turn out to be the joker who will bring down an ossified political system, and create fertile chaos wherein the healthiest and freshest forces will win. War in itself is abominable, and revolution is hardly more attractive, but they are catalysts that set the wheels of history in motion. True, there are instances when revolutions (and, less frequently, wars) expedite the destruction of the obsolete, but lead to the triumph of subterranean forces by summoning dark underground currents to the surface, and liberating destructive elements that heretofore even a rusty, outdated political system was capable of restraining. This is what happened in Russia in 1917, and this happened in the late 80s under the cover of so-called perestroika. It is something that happens all the time in deteriorating systems—although America most likely remains on an upward trend, is on a path of refinement, and is unlikely to collapse from four years of indulging the instincts of the masses. Whatever the case may be, Trump is quite capable of playing the role of the erratic actor in a situation where Ukraine appears to be doomed. He might bring about such stormy chaos and unpredictability—such singularity, to put it fashionably—that the devil himself could tumble and break a leg, and I mean that quite literally. Vladimir Putin is convinced that any form of boorish simplicity works to his advantage, but Trump's boorish simplicity just might confound the world situation to such a degree that everyone on all sides will make capricious mistakes. Should that happen, everything will turn out as the Russian absurdist Daniil Kharms put it: "Life again defeated death in a manner unknown to science."

So far, Trump's plan for Ukraine looks like double-barreled blackmail—or, as Nikolai Gogol once said, "figure out who is right and who is wrong, and then punish both." This does not add any optimism to the matter. Trump hopes to force Ukraine into accepting peace by promising to cut off all military aid if it continues to reject negotiations. In its turn, Russia, should it reject the peace plan, is being blackmailed with the reverse option—Trump promises to pump Ukraine full of weapons of all possible kinds. It is not entirely clear what Trump will do (or what Kellogg will advise) if both sides persist in belligerence. Zelenskyy repeatedly rejected the prospect of freezing hostilities along the current front lines, but he reformulated his conditions as winter 2024 approached. Ukraine, he said, is ready to surrender territories seized by Russia—about 20 percent of its land, with the hope of regaining them later through diplomatic means—in exchange for NATO membership. Ukraine's entry into NATO is not included in the Kellogg-Trump plan. It promises vague support, primarily financial, but NATO remains a dream for Ukraine, an eternal utopia. No one doubts that Vladimir Putin will not stop after having annexed a fifth of Ukrainian territory. He will not be satisfied with Ukraine alone. One writer in the Z-community, with whose name I wish not to tarnish these pages, has already reported that the patriotic public will accept only one outcome of the war: the complete destruction of Ukrainian statehood, plus the withdrawal of the Baltic countries, and Finland, from NATO. The message, so to speak, is this: "We will not abide hostile neighbors, for this directly threatens our security. Everyone with whom we share borders is doomed to become an eternal buffer zone." Putin repeatedly called for "conditions on the ground" as the starting point for negotiations, i.e., the transfer to Russia of four Ukrainian regions that had only been partially captured so far (Donetsk, Luhansk, Kherson, and Zaporizhzhia), plus the permanent non-aligned status of Ukraine, plus control of Ukrainian weapons by Russia. We probably should add to this the condition of the complete lifting of sanctions. (Russia insisted on this, but is ready to begin negotiations before it happens.) Furthermore, if you'll allow me to have a little fun with it, Putin would like the Ukrainians to appear at the negotiating table in a kneeling position, their heads sprinkled with ashes, while performing the ritual of kissing the ashes beneath the feet of the Russian negotiators. We see no softening of Russia's position, while, in fact, it repeatedly promises to ratchet up demands in accordance with the successes of its offensive in the Donetsk and, hypothetically, Kharkiv regions. Vladimir Putin makes no secret of his plans to intensify the offensive around Kharkiv and Odesa, since he considers both of these cities to be Russian, without any discussion of historical reality.

When Russian journalist Andrei Kolesnikov asked about the prospects for further use of ballistic missiles, Putin responded with a Soviet joke about forecasting the weather: "In the course of the day, anything might happen." He is not very good at creating his own jokes, but he is passionate about quoting old Soviet jokes—it seems to be the only segment of Soviet culture with which he is thoroughly familiar. Paradoxically, he is right—anything is possible, because regimes like Putin's collapse rapidly, and not necessarily as a result of military defeat. A currency collapse is possible (the dollar threatens to grow to 120 times the ruble before the end of 2024, and this is by no means the outer limit). A rebellion at the front is possible—something like Prigozhin's uprising of 2023 could be repeated at any moment following the ongoing purge of the Ministry of Defense throughout 2024, quite possibly under the leadership of General Ivan Popov, codenamed "Spartak." Spartak has every chance of becoming a new national hero, although his popularity among the troops is somewhat exaggerated. There is no general now capable of inspiring an outpouring of love among the army, since, no matter how much money is thrown at it, the current army is no more motivated than the Russian army was in 1916. If today's Russia had a real hero or even the remote possibility of such a leader, the omnipresent propagandists would not have supported Putin as strongly as they did, and, in fact, they would have been the first to defect. But the decay has reached deep, and Putin's elites are equally incapable either of sincere service or of true rebellion. This is what is most unpleasant—when there is no one around to support you, but no one around to replace you either. Such a crisis can end in an overnight collapse, or it can drag on for years of continued decay (although few doubt that the margin of safety of this regime is small: most likely, Putin and I will go our separate ways in the second half of the twenties). Zelenskyy understands the fragility of Putin's system, despite its apparent invincibility, with its endless resource of patience among the Russian populace, and the inherent opportunism of so many countries in the world. Zelenskyy is counting on the enemy regime to destroy itself.

If that does not happen, Ukraine will have no choice but to accept peace on difficult and humiliating terms—after equally difficult negotiations.

Here we must recall the September 2024 dismissal of Dmytro Kuleba, the Ukrainian Minister of Foreign Affairs, who had held this post since March 2020. Kuleba was nicknamed "Harry Potter" in the ministry because of his round glasses, and his typical Gryffindor courage. He was the youngest Minister of Foreign Affairs in Ukrainian history and one of the most prominent figures in the Shmyhal government. Nonetheless, he was replaced by the very talented diplomat Andrii Sybiha. For quite a while nothing definite was said about the reasons for Kuleba's resignation. Zelenskyy himself declared several times that his ministers were tired, and that rotation was in order. The old fire was lacking. There was even a version stating that Kuleba himself submitted his resignation and was considering the possibility of becoming the ambassador to London (where Zaluzhnyi had been sent). Speaking of Zaluzhnyi, we cannot help but mention another version—that Zelenskyy does not want his ministers to be popular; that he increasingly seeks out the gray but loyal ones so that he has no competition. The real reason for the dismissal was revealed only in November, when Kuleba spoke out—that is, he gave several interviews, including one to the *Financial Times*. This interview, to tell the truth, made a rather comical impression, perhaps due to the particularly detailed description of the breakfast that accompanied it, and Kuleba's confession of his love for blood sausage (he often mentions his passion for simple, traditional food, such as the Poltava lard his aunt sends him—apparently to counteract in some way his image as an intellectual). But perhaps this small talk was intended to deflect attention from the ex-minister's primary and gloomy statement: "If this continues, we will lose."

Indeed. Such words about the possibility of defeat—and not in a nuclear war, but in a conventional conflict with Russia—had never before been spoken so plainly in an interview with a Ukrainian official. The point was this: We can lose, albeit not completely, albeit locally, and it will not be the end of the world. We can give in to pressure from Russia and, let's face it, the rest of the world, which is tired of this war, although that cannot be compared to the fatigue of the Ukrainians themselves. Still, the world is tired, because, let's be honest, there is nothing more tiresome than helplessness. There is no way you can spend three years contemplating your utter inability to deal with a bunch of thugs who, for the fun of it, arm themselves with theses about their own holiness and exceptional spirituality. You cannot listen for three years running (in fact, many more) to nonsense about Russia defending its Russian brethren, traditional values, and the Orthodox family. Russia continues to plunge Ukraine into fire and ice as it incessantly bombs infrastructure, and, who knows, in the future they may yet reach a nuclear power plant. No restraining factors remain in Moscow; that cannot be doubted. Meanwhile—let's call a spade a spade—Russia figuratively spatters the entire world with feces, and it is still unclear which of these situations is more disgusting. The tone of the Russian press, which we have mentioned frequently in this book, became utterly indecent over the past year, although we can assume that no one in the West reads Russian newspapers. It is not even Vladimir Putin's tone that delivers the sense of mockery, for few people listen to him either. But, before our very eyes, a large country is destroying a smaller neighbor—which, incidentally, voluntarily relinquished its nuclear weapons long ago—all because Putin, who increasingly talks about having claim to the Baltics and to Poland, needs an eternal war. All of this is deeply harmful in a moral sense. It's even capable of ruining one's appetite. The situation is such that he can do anything he wants to you, but you can do nothing to him. He has molded his people into an ideal state, where not even the thought of rebellion arises, where the regime itself can collapse only under its own weight, and where any politician who answers to voters with even the most minimal responsibility will cave in to a benighted representative of the secret services who led his country into absolute spiritual and cultural degradation. Ukraine at least resists, and many people now hate it for this. Even if it is with a growing sense of doom, Ukraine at least is attempting to do something, while the rest of the world simply rots, and, out of despair, increasingly votes for right-wing Neo-fascists, further fueling the Kremlin's impudence. The contemporaries of a genius are in an awkward position since, compared to the genius, they are petty, envious people. But the role of a hero's contemporaries is even more unenviable: He will die, and will be fine, while you will demonstrate a whole range of dubious virtues from conformism to stupidity as you grow increasingly disgusted with the image of your face in the mirror. Perhaps these are the precise considerations underlying the universal admiration being showered on Alexei Navalny's book *Patriot*, which is selling well all over the world: Here was a man of principles, talented and brave, and here are the terrible things that happened to him. Are we to blame for not wanting such terrible things to happen to us, our parents, our wives, and our children?

If Zelenskyy had resigned, he could have been forgotten easily—as the world forgets dozens of retired politicians, regardless of their previous merits. Had Zelenskyy been killed, he would readily have been placed in the pantheon and ritually honored with words about how we failed to protect him. But Zelenskyy is alive, and he is a living reproach to the West. He continues to remind everyone that Avdiivka was lost due to a lack of weapons, and that Ukraine is still ready to stand up to Russian aggression in order to protect the rest of the world, but for this the world must muster its courage and, at least one time, oppose Putin in some substantial way. The world matured, thank God, coming to a sober understanding of the fact that there is fascism in Russia. The world grew used to the idea that Putin would not limit himself to Ukraine. But it is one thing to talk, and another to arm: Joe Biden allowed Ukraine to fire ATACMS at Russian territory only when he had nothing left to lose. In this position, two months before leaving power, you can allow yourself to fulfill at least some of your most cherished desires: Let Ukraine strike deep into Russia and pardon your own son Hunter. By the way, I approve of both of these decisions. I don't like it when tsars kill their own sons. Neither Ivan the Terrible nor his son Peter arouse approval in me. Stalin too, who let his son Yakov Dzhugashvili die in a Nazi prison camp, was no paragon of morality when he declared, "We do not exchange soldiers for marshals." But these are just asides.

Kuleba, in all likelihood, hinted to Zelenskyy that, while perseverance is a good thing, it was time to change tactics; and if for some reason it is impossible to change the hero's tactics, it is necessary to change the hero. Someday we will learn everything (I'm not sure about the Russian secrets, but the Ukrainian secrets will be revealed sooner or later). And I suspect that the disagreements between the minister and the president arose precisely in regards to changes in tactics. Kuleba knew the mood of European diplomacy very well; this is what ensured his authority in Ukraine. And he was the first to make Zelenskyy understand that negotiations would be inevitable, and that there would also have to be an admission of defeat—in this exact wording. No one will blame Ukraine for this: it did everything possible and more. For three years, it stood against an infinitely stronger, albeit not particularly smart, enemy. It lost a million people, and that's by the most merciful estimates. A significant part of this number were civilians, including approximately a thousand children and teenagers. We won't even mention the number of destroyed homes and separated families. Refugees will return (about a third already have), and houses will be rebuilt. Ukraine never doubted for a second that it was in the right. Its president never showed weakness, its officials were absolutely loyal to the commander-in-chief—including the eternal trickster Arestovych, who went over to the opposition, spoke a hundred times about the need for peace, but never spoke an insulting word about the president. They simply have different notions of honor, entirely unlike Boris Yeltsin and his renegade bodyguard Alexander Korzhakov. Ukraine has every right to a truce of any formulation. No decent person will cast stones at Zelenskyy for he was obliged to do the impossible, and no responsible politician today would dare give him advice.

5.

Zelenskyy's situation was truly difficult in the extreme. The war could not be stopped, so why, then, did all those people die? The war could not be continued, because how many more would now die? Demanding a new super-human effort from Ukrainians, especially with winter setting in, and especially during renewed power outages, would have been inhumane. Zelenskyy could not remain in his post, because he had forbidden himself to negotiate; he could not leave, because elections during a war are not provided for by the Constitution, and the very feasibility of holding them in wartime is questionable. The best thing to do would be to find opportunities to hold elections, and not participate in them (in the rating of potential candidates, Zelenskyy is second only to Zaluzhnyi, who would have about 32 percent of the vote to Zelenskyy's 23 percent). But there are voices (it would be dishonest to remain silent about this) saying that Zelenskyy's team will simply not let him leave. The allegation is that they have stolen too much. I have heard various figures from various people, including those who are unquestionably familiar with the situation, suggesting that 30 to 40 percent of military aid had been stolen. Even if we assume that Zelenskyy himself is impeccably honest, he did not defeat corruption, and probably could not have. So we have that irreconcilable formulation of "don't stay don't leave." I have heard a version that Zelenskyy is simply not allowed to leave his post—he knows too much. And since Zelenskyy is a man of art, and his biography was built from the very beginning according to the plot of a bestseller, there is a version that he will just be killed. There is no other way for a person in Eastern Europe to remain a hero.

I passionately hope this will not happen. I believe that this book will have a sequel or at least a more optimistic afterword. I have no doubt that Zelenskyy will go down in the history of Ukraine as a hero and nothing else.

But I also must admit that today, as I finally resolve to submit this final chapter to my U.S. publisher in December 2024, Ukrainian President Volodymyr Zelenskyy, the main character of this book, is in an utterly hopeless situation.

I don't know whether he (along with the sympathetic reader) can be consoled by the fact that the entire world finds itself in the same hopeless situation. It's all well and good, of course, to repeat Fyodor Tyutchev's words: "Blessed is he who visited this world in its fateful moments / he was summoned by the angels as a guest to a feast." But this is almost a banality, especially if you consider the riffraff that was invited to the very same feast for entirely unknown reasons. However, the question is not merely one of finding a seat at this feast's banquet table, but also one of how you leave it without disgracing yourself. Visiting the graves of my relatives at the Vostryakovskoye Cemetery in Moscow, which resembles an old Moscow communal apartment, I recognize many of the kinds of people I encountered in my childhood—in both the Russian and the Jewish halves of the cemetery. Many were born after the Second World War and died before the Third (what's the point of being timid—the latter became a full-fledged entity on February 24, 2022). Should I envy them? Should we envy those whose entire lives coincided with the Soviet period of Russian history, those who managed to die without ever stepping over the bounds of Soviet illusions, feeling only a slight, almost cozy anxiety from the great storms raging beyond the walls of the Soviet greenhouse? I don't know, because the future is unknown to me, and I am not at all convinced that I will be able to behave with dignity amidst the new twists and turns of world history (my own homegrown period of history is ended for now, and it is unclear whether it will ever be resumed). It is good to talk about trials when they are behind us, and even then, provided that you have not messed things up. In the case of Zelenskyy, the special difficulty is that it is not enough to prove your mettle once, twice, or three times—you must pass the test every day. One mistake can destroy your entire reputation along with all of its previous achievements. The phrase "I need ammunition, not a taxi" is enough for you to go down in history, but not enough for you to remain a hero in it. As another great actor whose last name rhymes with Zelenskyy, the current artistic director of the Moscow Art Theatre Konstantin Khabensky, told me in an interview that the horror of the profession is that you must prove your worth every day. And if his professional reputation remains unblemished so far—I hear he recently staged a fine production of *The Seagull*—we know that as the head of his theatre he was forced to fire and replace actors who spoke out against the war. And while, at the beginning of the war he refrained from making public pronouncements, over time he had no choice but to pose in photos with veterans of the "special military operation" in Ukraine. We cannot condemn those who are trying to maintain at least a semblance of neutrality in the openly fascist Russia. I personally know Khabensky to be a man of exceptional personal merit. His foundation has saved many lives, and his theatre helps many colleagues and viewers avoid losing their minds. But he made his choice by remaining at the head of the theatre, and now he is paying for that choice. It was far more difficult for Zelenskyy. And he behaved much better. Yet it is far from certain that he will be able to endure much longer.

Far be it from me to fall into a state of panic. I easily recognize that all humanity is now experiencing the inevitable backlash of the archaists, that this backlash is, in all likelihood, the final one, and therefore, the representatives of the "axis of evil" will resist stubbornly to the very end.

Historically, they are doomed, and have nothing to lose. But for the first time in history, the archaists are armed with the most modern of weapons. As such, in the event of Russia's evident defeat (Russian propagandists call this an "existential situation"), Vladimir Putin will be able and willing to use nuclear weapons, no matter what the intercontinental missile will be called—Oreshnik, or "hazel nut," as its post-Soviet developers affectionately called it in their botanical traditions, or Rozgi, or "birch cane," as the head of the *Russia Today* agency Margarita Simonyan suggested. If Russia loses the war against the entire world, something for which it will have no one to blame but itself, it will prefer to continue dragging it out in a stalemate, that is, to destroy both itself and humanity. Judging by the frequent references to such an ending—I mean the genuine nuclear hysteria that engulfed the entire Russian public sphere—Vladimir Putin is internally prepared for this denouement. Osip Mandelstam's optimistic formulation that "only an equal can kill me" has lost its relevance. A virus has proved that it is capable of killing millions, yet it still lags far behind the potential of a single man, no less humanity. It so happens that a pale moth, a Chekist rat, a faceless KGB agent, or whatever else Vladimir Putin's external and internal opponents call him, is quite capable of destroying the world if it succumbs to that ancient, formidable force that has long been ranting at God with ultimatums: Either let me back into heaven, or nothing will remain of your beloved creation. However, as regards this "beloved creation," that may well just be our own self-delusion. What if He has tired of us and has decided to sacrifice us rather than accept the terms of his old enemy?

The situation all over the world reminds me of Vladimir Nabokov's formula in his novel *The Gift*: "a solution was indicated to a problem which had seemed so complex that one could not help wondering if there was not a mistake in its construction." But there was no mistake. Furthermore, we anticipated precisely this scenario, but that at the fateful moment . . .

And in that terrible hour, when from a scoundrel,
Like a rifle shot, the cry of final ends rang out,

And a face crawled out from underneath a face,
And a mask leaped out from underneath a mask, -

A fragile man ran in,
Stood in the middle of the entire globe,
His exhausted face, like snow in spring,
Melted by a nearby fire.

This is from Novella Matveeva's poem "The Dream," written in the year of the Cuban Missile Crisis (1963). But at that time, the people in power in the United States and the USSR still remembered the Second World War. We don't have that advantage today. We are accustomed to the Lord stepping in at decisive moments to work miracles like the one that saved the world in the forties, when Hitler never achieved the nuclear bomb, although he came very close to it. But either the decisive moment has not yet arrived, or humanity will have to take it upon itself to cut through the knot of problems that has arisen. This will be the final test of maturity, without any abatements. And just so no one harbors any doubts about the gravity of the moment, the Lord has so scorched the earth that there is virtually no one left to rely on. There is not a single force left that one would wish to support, or that one would want to rely on. Zelenskyy, it seems, remains the last politician who evoked hope and sympathy among the majority of Earth's population. But he, too, today, is trapped in a situation where he is doomed either to leave, or to betray himself. This reminds us convincingly of various notions of the end of the world, and of the last chance for the world to come to his senses. But we can only come to our senses together, by staring into the true abyss, and turning away from it in horror.

After all, this is far from the first time we have abandoned a hero in a hopeless situation. For many years I have hosted a program called *News in the Classics*, or *Classic News*, where I examine literary analogies for current political news. Why not play this entertaining game here too? Vladislav Krapivin, the classic Soviet writer of tales for children, loved to abandon his heroes in hopeless situations—say, in battle with far superior forces. This is just how his novellas *Riders from Misty Station* and *Lullaby for a Brother* conclude. Both are romantic books that all Soviet teenagers, both Russian and Ukrainian, grew up with. Another romantic, Arkady Gaidar, ended his best and most disturbing novellas, *A Drummer's Fate*, and *Timur and His Team* in just the same way. This also describes the ending of the best, in my opinion, novel by the Strugatsky brothers, *Distant Rainbow*, where a mysterious Wave approaches a tiny colony of scientists from Earth, reducing all their other disagreements to insignificance. (There is still a chance that a rescue starship will reach them in time—or maybe the Wave is not deadly, but only alters people beyond recognition. I wrote just such an ending in a story I titled "Nearby Rainbow," and which I have every intention of publishing if there is no nuclear war, or if nuclear war alters us for the better.) Martin Brest's melancholy comedy *Going in Style* (1979), where three great old Hollywood actors played perhaps their best roles, ended with George Burns's character in prison telling a young visitor that he'd been in much worse situations than this, prison didn't frighten him. In general, half of the world's cultural output seems to be devoted to the matter of defeat, from the quip of the rooster chasing a hen in the old Russian joke, "If I don't catch her, at least I'll warm my bones," to the violinist's phrase to his fellow musicians on the Titanic—"Gentlemen, it has been a privilege playing with you tonight."

Since Zelenskyy and I both belong to the glorious tribe of creative laborers, I will say, first, that we always value the opportunity for a sequel, which, for us, means that cutting away from the narrative at the climax is good form, provides a worthy hook, and inspires one in the preparation for more work to come. Second, if, due to certain circumstances we are not destined to continue both his brilliant career and this no less brilliant description of it, allow me to say: "We've been in much worse situations, this one doesn't frighten me," and, of course, "It's been a privilege for us musicians to play for you tonight."

AFTERWORD, FROM A FRIEND

At the very beginning of September 2023, Dmitry Bykov sent me the manuscript of a book about Volodymyr Zelenskyy with a request to say a few words about it.

I wrote to him about my impressions this morning. I think I can share these observations with you here. After all, we are talking about the philosophical content of a new book, not about personal matters.

Here is the text of my letter to Dmitry (minus a few personal paragraphs):

> First of all, I must say that one reads the book in one sitting. From the very first pages, you manage to capture the reader's attention and hold their attention to the very end of the story. Sometimes the narrative teeters on the edge of a divertissement, but it never crosses the line.
>
> On the other hand, I couldn't shake the feeling that this was some new genre in front of me: a mixture of historiosophy with myth-making, biography (in a solid, non-fictional form), with literary fiction ("fiction" in the noblest sense of the word). Gradually, I began to perceive the text as a kind of theological commentary (more on this at the end of the letter).

I'm not a literary scholar and so hackneyed phrases about an epoch as main character and so on pop into my head. I'll try to paraphrase Hegel: If philosophy is an era captured in concepts, then your story is an era captured in the creative imagination. Moreover, your creative imagination takes the form of documentary prose and creates the complete illusion of reality, its "factual" image. I could not shake the feeling that I was encountering an endless game: Documentary research played at "wonderful personal history," and myth-making was disguised behind the impartial and sober gaze of an insightful historian and chronicler.

The text gives the reader a happy opportunity to reflect with you on the events of recent history. To think moderately seriously, moderately ironically, moderately detached and moderately biased.

When I read your book, [Sergei] Averintsev's phrase kept spinning in my head: "Everything could have been just the opposite." This is me in regards to your image of Zelenskyy. Sometimes, as the description progresses, it is easy to exchange pros for cons, the heroic for the comic (and vice versa). But you, of course, remember who said that a real poet knows how to combine tragedy and comedy. You succeeded quite well.

I'm afraid that by the time the book is published, many of the emphases may have changed radically. By the end of the story, you yourself predict difficult times for Zelenskyy. I myself still cannot answer the question: is it good or bad that a comedian, a KVN performer, a person who was completely unprepared for the role of a political leader, became the president of a large European country? Especially becoming a leader during "hard times."

So far, it seems that Zelenskyy is managing to cope with his role. Some even argue that this is precisely the actor's advantage (even an actor from a light genre): to be in such a place at such a time. In a situation like this, the best choice is to play your role well.

After all, politics was originally associated with theatre, with staging, with rituals, with the tradition of gestures and words (in antiquity, the Middle Ages, early modernity). Only earlier was it done in a "lofty style" with majestic poses (it was not for nothing that ballet flourished at the court of the Sun King), while from the middle of the last century politics began to turn into an easy (sometimes even frivolous) genre of art. Today politics is a mass spectacle.

Most likely the boring Scholz and the faceless Sunak represent the exception to the rule. In Macron, the beauty of gestures and the overall polished profile are not able to compensate for the paucity of personal content. Give us the Clintons, Berlusconis, Trumps, Johnsons (of the Boris ilk) and other showmen. So why not Zelenskyy? And who today can distinguish a game from "reality," a mask from a face? I don't know.

Incidentally, you write about the Block as a kind of political theater in one of the sections of your book (very successfully and vividly in my opinion).

You dream of that blessed time when countries will be ruled by actors, artists and musicians. This is a kind of transformation of charismatic power into artistic power. I would support this idea with reservations. When the citizens of nation-states are so mature, and the role of states itself so small (the "minimum state"), then all state power can be given to actors and artists. Moreover, representatives of the light genre.

Then the silliest things will transpire in parliaments and government institutions (as in *In Praise of Folly*), and the citizens of the world will do without politicians, without borders, and without states.

By the way, such a picture today does not look so utopian. If the prophets of the technological revolution are to be believed, politics and political power may indeed be redundant. Here Occam's razor can do its noble work of ontological and conceptual pruning.

Perhaps today we are experiencing the last convulsions of "serious" politics (with its "geostrategies," "national interests," wars and other museum rubbish). And then we can describe Zelenskyy as a harbinger of new times.

So far, the comedian has performed the role of a political leader better than "real" politicians. But, in my opinion, this is a very convincing illusion. For all my sympathies for Zelenskyy, politicians are judged "by the fruits of their labor." And those fruits may turn out to be bitter . . .

Forgive my verbosity. In short: the book beautifully, intriguingly and thoughtfully builds the Zelenskyy myth in a philosophical way. But since we are still inside the myth, the story is not yet over. And this circumstance is associated with certain risks for the book and its author. It's as if we were performing *The Odyssey* in public before Odysseus returned to Ithaca. The action is not completed. The hero is still on his journey. We don't know what will happen to him at each subsequent turn in the story. Perhaps in the second part of the novel the signs will change and the emphases will be placed differently.

But I understand that you take these risks consciously. And, by the way, this gives the whole book a special appeal.

I will now allow myself a few quotes and brief comments.

The very first sentences of the book draw one in. "Before describing someone else's biography, you must at least briefly touch on your own. That is, you must explain why anyone should listen to what you have to say. Throughout my literary life in Russia I have published approximately ninety books, among them several biographies, mainly of writers. But that is not why you must read what I have to say."

A very unexpected move (further in the text you substantiate this idea very well). But I was intrigued by the word "must." I have never seen things the way you describe them here. This necessary connection between someone else's biography and one's own (the author's and the hero's) has never been the subject of analysis and detailed description. Maybe I'm wrong. But this "necessity" is very catchy at the very beginning of the book.

"This book was written for entirely different reasons. The author sincerely wants to grapple with the primary mystery of the twenty-first century. Over its first two decades plus, this century has offered us nothing more entertaining than Zelenskyy. Not COVID, nor the mass insanity of Russian citizens, nor the subversion of the Big Bang theory by recent observations (apparently the most distant galaxies are not flying off anywhere after all!) are capable of standing alongside the riddle of Volodymyr Zelenskyy."

The reader is given the opportunity to discern a riddle in Zelenskyy. That the Zelenskyy case is a riddle is far from obvious. Actually, the reader must do two things as he reads:

— understand (feel, guess, see) that there is a "Zelenskyy riddle."

— thoroughly rack your brains over it together with the author.

The first task is more difficult than the second. But the book offers an exciting game. Not everyone eventually will cope with the proposed puzzle.

"Paradoxically, he was precisely where he needed to be, but this is not only about him, it is also about the unique place that he occupies. The situation reminds us of some of the greatest twists and turns of history, the consequences of which are not fully evident even to distant descendants."

Is "the uniqueness of place" one of the "greatest twists of history"? Place of action, time of action, mode of action?

I want to believe that we are experiencing the greatest turn of history. But it may well turn out that this is a prelude to something else, more important.

I'll be honest, I don't feel like this is the greatest turning point. But for narrative architecture, it's a very opportune find.

"Right in plain sight, Yevgeny Schwartz's fairy tale about a dragon, read and watched by all of Russia, despite all the Soviet prohibitions, is now in the process of coming true. A great empire is collapsing, trying to trap in its zone of influence its unloved stepdaughter, with whom it has cohabited for 450 years, all the way from the time of the Pereiaslav Rada when Hetman Bohdan Khmelnytskyi led Ukraine into an alliance with the Russians."

Really? Lancelot vs. the dragon? Perhaps "Soviet prohibitions" are no longer about *To Kill the Dragon* (a film made in 1988, the prohibitions were very conditional). It's unusual to read "unloved stepdaughter" (Ukraine here turns a little into Cinderella). Common vocabulary: "brotherly peoples" (then "little brother," of course, in quotation marks) or "sisters" (if churches). But if it's a stepdaughter, then the kingdom of Moscow appears in the form of a stepmother. Bold metaphors.

And the phrase "led Ukraine into an alliance with the Russians" might cause heated debate. Who then was Russian?)))

"There are actually two mysteries here: how Zelenskyy won the presidential race in the wake of the most serious political crisis in Ukrainian history, and how he stood his ground at the head of a nation that entered the most serious war in its history. How did David defeat Goliath once again? And how did this David, who composed psalms in the format of feuilletons, manage to remind the whole world of the inviolability of the great biblical truths—he, who just yesterday was amusing Russian leaders at corporate parties, or portraying a phallus playing the piano on his own show?"

The dynamics of the text are fascinating. One mystery turns into two (and toward the end of the story a third mystery emerges—what will happen "after"?): Lancelot turns into David, and the dragon turns into Goliath.

The conclusion of this fragment is especially successful: the will of circumstances elevates KVN tomfoolery to the level of biblical solemnity.

Again the risky formulas of "How did David defeat Goliath once again" and David "manages to remind the whole world." I really want to believe them. But the story is still in full swing.

"This is one of those divine miracles, about which legends are later composed. And although the miracle was forged by the people of Ukraine with their examples of heroism and self-sacrifice, the miracle bears Zelenskyy's expressive Jewish face, Zelenskyy's quick brown eyes, Zelenskyy's familiar, husky voice. Whatever his fate, he was in the first half of the '20s an instrument of that Absolute One, in whose existence the world, corrupted by its inability to distinguish between good and evil, and by the myth of ubiquitous corruption, hardly believes in anymore.

"Could a writer have a more weighty topic? It is rather like a dinosaur emerging from the forest, and addressing you in a human voice.

"And I would add: think as you will, but don't pass this book by."

After all, a weapon of the Absolute One! This was already evident in the previous paragraph. Then it turns out that God chooses "the little ones"? To humble the pride of the arrogant? To put the wise men to shame?

Here is the first explanation of the "Zelenskyy riddle": a divine miracle, an instrument of the plan. A theme for a legend. The theme for a myth. For a writer, there is no more serious topic than myth-making (in the sublime sense of the word).

I hear a slightly alarming musical line in "regardless of his future fate." But Zelenskyy has already become a tool of the Absolute One. Although the divine plan is still far from clear (if it becomes clear at all in the coming decades). And here is Zelenskyy's fourth riddle: the riddle of the Master Plan.

These are no longer questions in the form of "how?" but questions in the form of "why?" and "for what purpose?"

But then the writer, who sets out to solve these riddles together with the reader, becomes, in part, a theologian, almost a prophet.

By solving the mysteries of Zelenskyy, he, intentionally or not, draws closer to solving the riddle of the divine plan for the world and for history.

It's hard to imagine a more weighty topic . . .

DMITRY BYKOV has published 96 books, including 12 novels, 6 biographies and 25 collections of poetry. He has won The Big Book literary prize three times and Strugatsky Brothers Prize four times. He participated in the Russian opposition movement and was a member of the Oppositional Coordination Council, was poisoned in 2019, but survived. He has taught at Princeton, UCLA, Bard, and currently teaches at the University of Rochester, where he is the inaugural Scholar in Exile. He lives happily with his wife, two sons, and daughter while working on *Fright. The Poetics of the Thriller* and a sci-fi novel, *In Team*.

JOHN FREEDMAN is an American writer and translator who lived in Russia from 1988 to 2018 when he relocated to Greece. His books include: *Silence's Roar: The Life and Drama of Nikolai Erdman* and *Provoking Theater: Kama Ginkas Directs*. He has translated 150 plays, and he translated and edited the award-winning anthology *A Dictionary of Emotions in a Time of War: 20 Short Works by Ukrainian Playwrights*.